DATE DUE

13 DEC 1996		
3		

2519

Sport in
Australian
Drama

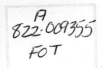

SPORT IN AUSTRALIAN DRAMA

Richard Fotheringham

Department of English
University of Queensland

The right of the
University of Cambridge
to print and sell
all manner of books
was granted by
Henry VIII in 1534.
The University has printed
and published continuously
since 1584.

Cambridge University Press

Cambridge

New York   Port Chester   Melbourne   Sydney

Published by the Press Syndicate of the University of Cambridge
The Pitt Building, Trumpington Street, Cambridge CB2 1RP, UK
40 West 20th Street, New York, NY 10011-4211, USA
10 Stamford Road, Oakleigh, Victoria 3166, Australia

First published 1992

Printed in Hong Kong by Colorcraft

National Library of Australia cataloguing in publication data
Fotheringham, Richard, 1947–
Sport in Australian drama.
Bibliography.
Includes index.
ISBN 0 521 40156 9.
1. Australian drama — History and criticism. 2. Sports in literature.
I. Title.
A822.009355

Library of Congress cataloguing in publication data
Fotheringham, Richard.
Sport in Australian drama/Richard Fotheringham.
Includes bibliographical references and index.
ISBN 0-521-40156-9
1. Australian drama — History and criticism. 2. Sports in
literature. 3. Sports — Australia. I. Title.
PR9611.7.S67F67 1992
822.009′355 — dc20

A catalogue record for this book is available from the British Library.

ISBN 0 521 40156 9 Hardcover

Contents

Acknowledgements

Thanks are due to a number of people who assisted in bringing this project to completion. Veronica Kelly, who discussed the project with me at length and whose breadth of knowledge and enthusiasm were invaluable, must come first. The staff of the Fryer, Mitchell, La Trobe, Dennis Wolanski, Australian National and Alexander Turnbull libraries provided first-class research facilities, as did the Australian and the New Zealand Archives, the Australian War Memorial, and the Australian National Film and Sound Archive. Others who assisted include Thelma Afford, Barry Andrews, Brigadier M. Austin, Genny Blades, Ronald Conway, Ross Cooper, Sue Cullen, Peter Edwards, Ken Goswell, Ian Jobling, Alan Lawson, Harold Love, Jim McKay, Leo Power, Jeremy Ridgman, Clive Sowry, Alrene Sykes, Graeme Turner, and Lisa Whitcher.

Permission to reproduce photographs has been obtained from the above libraries and archives, from the Tate Gallery in London, from John Sexton Productions, and from the Greater Union Organisation. It has not always been possible to establish if copyright still exists in some early films; if copyright in any photograph has been inadvertently breached, the author would be happy to pay an appropriate fee.

Earlier drafts of some sections have appeared in *Australasian Drama Studies* (1, No.1), *Sporting Traditions* (5, No.2), and *Australian Drama 1920–1955* (Armidale, 1986). I would also like to acknowledge the essential financial and technical assistance of the English Department of the University of Queensland, and finally thank Roslyn, Claire and Tom, for putting up with the stress which such a large project imposed on our family life for so long.

Richard Fotheringham

List of illustrations

Sport and Drama:
the Uneasy Playmates

Sport *versus* drama: twentieth-century perspectives

The late twentieth-century reader, faced with phrases such as 'sport and the arts' or 'sport and drama', is likely to interpret them according to a dominant system of codes and oppositions very different from that which obtained in Western society until the First World War. The superior importance of sport in the structure of modern culture has led to a system of preferred values that venerates sport as an activity which is spontaneous, expresses ideas and ideals through action, conceals effort and pain, is structured but unpredictable, and which has unplanned resolutions but with results that can be objectively, empirically measured. In contrast, theatre is supposed to be artificial, verbal rather than active, given to exaggerating effort and suffering, predictable, and with contrived, pre-planned conclusions, and judged by non-empirical (and therefore rather dubious) standards of 'taste' and 'technique'.

Sporting writers and commentators offer endless examples of this dominant ideology. 'There's a bit of acting going on out there' is a favourite phrase for non-essential sporting behaviour designed to waste time, psychologically disadvantage the opponent or otherwise draw attention to behaviour other than that appropriate to 'pure' sporting achievement. The 'mere theatrics' of a 'prima donna' have wide currency in non-sporting discussions, but are particularly savagely attacked on the playing field. 'He's a bloody actor' growled the former Australian cricketer Jeff Thomson of a younger, flamboyant player with a punk hairdo called Greg Matthews, who hopefully would 'grow up' and settle down to playing the game.[1] 'Ice dancing not Olympic' declared a headline in an Australian newspaper after Jayne Torvill and Christopher Dean had become the sensation of the 1984 Winter Olympics, with the commentator going on to declare:

There is no doubt that Torvill and Dean turned on a brilliant piece of theatre . . .
But was it an Olympic sport? If it was, the next step has to be Olympic ballroom

dancing, then ballet, and on to opera . . . 'Gold for Australia! Gold! Gold! Gold!'
Norman May could screech as Joan Sutherland hit high C in the main stadium.
. . . dancing on ice is good to watch, but sport it is not. Theatre it is.[2]

Nevertheless, sports analysts are also inclined to see exciting or memorable
incidents in a sporting event as like theatre (in the most obvious cliche, 'high
drama'), provided there is no question of these moments being artificially
manufactured or 'stage-managed'. (In the late 1970s this was one of the
criticisms levelled at the 'contrived' exciting endings in one-day cricket.) 'I
wanna know who wrote the script for this', the American commentator on
Channel 10 kept demanding as the yacht *Australia II* came from behind on
the second last leg to take the America's cup from the United States for the
first time in 132 years. Journalist, Adrian McGregor, in a long re-creation of
the John Landy/Roger Bannister confrontation in the 'Mile of the Century'
at the 1954 British Empire Games in Vancouver, wrote that the race was
'Beautiful for its drama. And in truth Vancouver became a moving tableau
in which Landy had been cast in a role of Shakespearean complexity, tragic
for the athlete, though not for the man.'[3] 'You might say it was great theatre,
the height of drama' declared another commentator, more mundanely, after
a cricket test match in which a West Indian fast bowler had aimed short-pitched
deliveries at the body of an Australian batsman who, already injured, had
hobbled out to try to avert a seemingly inevitable defeat.[4] In more sober vein
the distressing sight of Gabriela Andersen-Schiess, a Swiss competitor in the
first Olympic women's marathon who limped in agony to the finish line while
officials stood uncertainly nearby, unwilling to intervene, moved one reporter
to write:

'What remains in the mind . . . is an unfading imprint of the distillation of courage,
and the thought that the Greek tragedians of the first Olympic period regarded as
the essence of their task and the heart of tragedy: the creation in the spectator of
catharsis—a purging of the heart and mind by pity and terror.'[5]

This apparently strange mixture of dependence and contempt is reversed
in the value systems of supporters of the performing arts. They tend to see
sport as an obsession which diverts society away from more intellectual,
'cultured', and 'enduring' activities. In Australia this counter-construct stretches
back to the colonial period. In 1892 an amateur versifier, H. C. J. Lingham,
offered a clear expression of what was already a common literary-intellectual
attitude (the Frank Slavin referred to was a prominent heavyweight boxer):

> Australian Natives are too much inclined
> To honour muscle at the expense of mind.
> They hold a Slavin is a greater hero,
> Who with the shoulders, neck, and head of Nero,
> Pounds his opponents to a senseless jelly,
> Than Tadema, Leighton, Keats, or Shelley.[6]

G. A. Wilkes in *The Stockyard and the Croquet Lawn* has chronicled the attitudes to sport of a large number of Australian authors, ranging from the enthusiasm of the early male jockey-poets Adam Lindsay Gordon and 'Banjo' Paterson to the trenchant criticism of many colonial women writers and of most twentieth-century authors of both sexes.[7]

Current discourse assumes an irreconcilable opposition between the two leisure activities. 'Thomas Keneally on Sport versus the Arts' headlined the *Sydney Morning Herald*'s 'Good Weekend' magazine on 5 March 1988, while an earlier, more controversial, example occurred in November 1986 when Donald Horne, the Director of the government arts-funding body, the Australia Council, used the occasion of the then approaching defence of the America's Cup to question the emphasis Australians placed on sport. According to a hostile newspaper report from Perth, Horne had suggested that 'Art was eternal whereas sporting achievements are ephemeral'. The commentator then went on to chronicle the strong rebuttal offered by the Western Australian Governor at a popular celebration held for the unveiling of the cup.[8] Following Horne's lead, the Australia Council's General Manager, Max Bourke, declared (implausibly) in 1989 that while thirty years ago cricketers and tennis players were the role models for young Australians, they had been replaced by creative artists; later he used the name of the former Australian Rules footballer Ron Barassi as an example of sporting philistinism, unaware that Barassi had in fact recently appeared in television advertising for the Victoria State Opera.[9]

Nevertheless just as sporting commentators have freely used the concepts and terminology of theatre for expressive effect, writers on the performing arts have been keen to argue the similarities between sport and the kinds of dramatic entertainments they support. John Cargher, for example, began his book on *Opera and Ballet in Australia* (1977) by pointing out the aesthetic similarities between ballet and football;[10] Roger Covell in *Australia's Music: Themes of a New Society* (1967) described the soprano Joan Sutherland as 'in the first place . . . a vocal athlete':

. . . the tenor's high C or the soprano's stratospheric trill can induce an emotion in a large audience not essentially different from that provided by a perfectly executed football goal or a brilliant clinching shot in tennis . . .[11]

Given this background of extensive cultural interpenetration and awareness between these two leisure industries it is not surprising that two of the twentieth century's most significant dramatic theorists, Bertolt Brecht and Antonin Artaud, both offered essays on the relationship between sport and theatre. Interestingly, both used sport as a model which theatre should look to if it was to revitalise itself as an art form, and both dramatic theories hint at their authors' awareness of the success and social importance of sport, and at their unease at the inability of theatre to compete emotionally and (in Brecht's iconoclastic view) intellectually. In 1926 Brecht wrote 'Emphasis on sport', in which he suggested that sportsgoers were 'the fairest and shrewdest audience in the world', while the professional theatre of his day had lost contact with the public.[12] Brecht's translator, John Willett, has pointed out that in other fragmentary writings at this time Brecht was already exploring the idea of an audience which was detached from the performance and maintained a critical attitude to it. Based on his research for a projected biography of the German middleweight champion (and screen actor) Samson-Köhrner, Brecht's experience of boxing stadiums where spectators sat back and smoked during the events led ultimately to his famous *verfremdungseffekt* or 'alienation' effect, where the techniques of stage presentation were to be manipulated to induce a more analytical and objective attitude in theatre audiences.[13]

Artaud's essay 'An Affective Athleticism', written during the 1930s, argued that actors ought to become 'athletes of the heart', finding in their emotional response to the world a quality which would touch an audience as profoundly as does the athlete's physical response:

An actor is like a physical athlete . . . The actor relies on the same pressure points an athlete relies on to run, in order to hurl a convulsive curse whose course is driven inwards. Similar anatomical bases can be found in all the feints in boxing, all-in-wrestling, the hundred metres, the high jump and the movement of the emotions, since they all have the same physical support points.[14]

Again parallel analyses may be found in the world of sports criticism. In his classic study of cricket in the West Indies, *Beyond a Boundary* (1969), C. L. R. James went to the art historian, Bernhard Berenson, for the concept of 'significant movement'. Like Brecht, James suggested that through the action of the game spectators learn the technique of watching critically and, like Artaud, he saw a link between physical and emotional 'pressure points', with each stroke or ball bowled being 'received in the tactile consciousness of thousands who have themselves for years practised the same motion and know each muscle that is involved in each stroke'.[15]

A detailed analysis of this kind of cross-referencing can be found in Benjamin Lowe's book *The Beauty of Sport: A Cross-Disciplinary Inquiry* (1977), where he surveys attitudes to sport as art and examines the links between sport and various art forms, including drama, although he remains equivocal about the extent to which their similarities should be emphasised over their differences.[16] But from the point of view of the present work the essential difficulty with all these observations and approaches is that they fail to historicise their findings, and so fail to realise that their oxymoronic rhetoric—the 'surprising' juxtaposition of seeming opposites—is itself a product of minority discursive strategies based on the mind/body split of Western intellectual culture. The alternative *mens sana in corpore sano* ('a sound mind in a sound body') of ancient Greek and Roman society, while it is occasionally alluded to in general terms, is considered irrelevant. It is part of the intent of the chapters which follow to suggest that such discourse needs to be historicised, particularly in relation to the study of popular culture where, liberated from the need to defer to 'high' culture with its appropriation of formal intellectuality (and therefore its classification of sport as 'other'), storytellers and story receivers seem to be far less concerned with such assumptions. The historical record suggests not that sport and theatre were different entities with surprising similarities and interpenetrations, but a single concept of leisure behaviour which gradually bifurcated into separate but nevertheless linked and associated forms.

Sport *and* drama: the historical background to 1788

Only in the last twenty years has it been widely recognised that sport and theatre, the two forms of organised leisure activity which share the use of the words 'play' and 'players', have done so since at least Roman times and in the English language since the early Middle Ages. Theatre was then seen as a kind of imitative game. V. A. Kolve, in his influential work on medieval religious drama *The Play Called Corpus Christi*, pointed out in 1966 that as the medieval world struggled to define and locate the emerging proto-dramatic forms of imitative behaviour, the words most frequently used to describe this activity were the Latin *ludus* and the English 'play' and 'game'.[17] By the late-fifteenth century short plays were called 'interludes', indicating both a dramatic 'ludus' between courses of the feast in a great hall, and a 'game' between 'players'. In these plays the vices—those entertaining villains who gave life and colour to the narrative—had two favourite words for their antics: 'sport' and 'game':

Mercy: Hie you forth on foot, brother! in God's name!
Mischief: I say, sir! I am come hither to make you game. . . .
Nought: Shall I break my neck to show you sport?

(Mankind, ll.68-69, 77)

This *bricolage*—the understanding and incorporation of the new through the use of pre-existing terms and concepts—has been retained to the present time. Most people, if asked to gloss 'play' as used in sport and in drama, would presumably distinguish 'taking part in a game' from 'a theatrical performance', but there remains a core of shared meaning within the generic term. Glynne Wickham, while noting that the distinction between gladiatorial games and mimetic ('imitative') games was already important to the ancient Romans and led them to attach specifying adjectives to *ludus*, has argued that there remained a significant common factor:

however different the characteristics of the *ludus* athletic or mimetic, the game or recreational element is paramount. . . . Thus a tournament, to take an extreme case, though it could result in injury or death for one or more of the contestants, was conceived of as a violent game to test skill and endurance, never as war. However nearly it approaches the reality of battle, rules exist to prevent the imitation extending to the actual, just as the tragic heroes of mimetic games, however realistically their deaths may be portrayed, arise to repeat their performances on other occasions. Both are imitations 'in game' and not 'in earnest'.[18]

There was another early link between sport and theatre for which there is fragmentary but growing evidence. During the period from the sixth-century AD onwards when theatre was violently suppressed or officially repressed throughout Europe, the itinerant athletic performer went side by side with the strolling actor and other professional entertainers.[19] The unofficial (and often illegal) world of popular entertainment—mountebanks, jesters, jugglers, animal trainers, fighters, wrestlers, swordsmen, magicians, mimes, minstrels, dancers, rope-walkers, hoop-jumpers—freely used both quasi-sporting behaviour (tests and demonstrations of strength, skill, speed and endurance) and quasi-theatrical practices (characterisation, costumes, masks and story-telling). This combining of the athletic with the histrionic is noticeable in sanctioned entertainments from the fifteenth century onwards, and ranges from the licencing of such itinerant groups and individuals by civic authorities, to the appearance of sporting displays in plays. Mary McElroy has documented the rise of organised professional sporting contests in the Elizabethan period and points out that it was directly attributable to theatrical entrepreneurs. Early 'player-athletes' like the clown Richard Tarleton were trained swordsmen as well as comedians; later the manager Philip Henslowe presented fencing matches at the Rose playhouse, and fencing, bear-baiting and wrestling also kept the Swan and the Red Bull open for many years after actors ceased to play there, a contemporary commentator noting 'these small things were as profitable and as great get pennies to the Actors, as any of our late famed playes'.[20]

It is not surprising therefore that athletic contests found their way into English renaissance theatre—the wrestling match between Orlando and Charles in Shakespeare's *As You Like It* is one—and of course swordfights are endemic in plays of the period. The use of live animals on stage can be found as well: Launce's dog is the essential prop for his stand-up comic routines in Shakespeare's *Two Gentlemen of Verona*, and 'Exit, pursued by a bear' in *The Winter's Tale* (III,iii,57) a later echo of bearpit sports. As David Wiles has convincingly argued in *Shakespeare's Clown* (1987), Elizabethan audiences did not experience the Bard's tragedies as fundamentally different from bear-baiting. Both used the same descriptive language, and audiences read both sign systems according to codes of game, ritual and symbolic action. Rather than polarising sport against theatre from a humanist perspective, 'people used animal combat in order to give meaning to human activities', just as they constructed the meaning of the figure of the Earl of Warwick in *2 Henry VI* from the bear crest on his helmet, metaphoric references to him as a bear, and his 'roaring' when goaded.[21]

References to sport and to sporting characters, behaviour and equipment are widespread in plays written between the fifteenth and nineteenth centuries. These give us a rich picture of the leisure pursuits of young and old across half a milennium, and such emblems and actions have already been transformed into a system of theatrical codes which came to have conventional (and, to some extent, transhistorical and cross-cultural) meaning determined principally by its narrative and rhetorical context. Sport could suggest innocent fun, as in the ball which the third shepherd gives to the Christ child in the fifteenth century *Secunda Pastorum* before suggesting he 'go to the tenys' [tennis] (l.736). Alternatively it could indicate idleness and un-Godly mischief, as in New Guise's cry 'Lend us a football' in *Mankind* (l.737) after Mankind has abandoned his work and righteous living for sloth. In *As You Like It* Orlando's victory over Charles is proof to the Duke that he is 'a gallant youth' (I,ii,219) and makes him sexually and romantically interesting to Rosalind: 'It is young Orlando, that tripped up the wrestler's heels and your heart both in a instant', (III,ii,210-11).

But sport could also be associated with gambling and violent bad-temper as in Cloten's entrance in *Cymbeline* (II,i,1) after he has lost at lawn bowls and split his opponent's head with the ball. Shakespeare's images of hunting, fishing, archery, billiards, bowls, tennis, and football have been shown to be widespread, with one entire play, *The Taming of the Shrew*, arguably constructed around a central image drawn from training and hunting with falcons.[22] For Gloucester in *King Lear* there was 'good sport' at the begetting of his bastard son Edmund (I,i,23), and 'sport' and 'play' had connotations of sexual activity which go back to their earliest usages in English.[23] But at least since Susannah Centlivre's *The Gamester* in 1705 (based on a French original) sport and gambling have also been represented as a woman-rejecting and woman-excluding world: in that play the heroine is obliged to disguise herself as a man in order to enter the 'sporting' (i.e. gambling) world and win her errant lover back from the card table. 'Sport' is also a common term for war (another woman-marginalising activity); Marlowe's Tamburlaine, having first helped Cosroe to become King of Persia and then decided to become King himself, declares 'bid him turn back to war with us/that only made him king to make us sport'. (*Pt 1* II,vi,101). There is 'good sport' on the battlefields outside Troy in *Troilus and Cressida* (I,i,117,119), which, for Hector at least, is conducted according to the rules of 'fair play' (V,iii,43). Financial speculation is also covered by the same terms; when Sir Walter Whorehound in Middleton's *A Chaste Maid in Cheapside* leaves the stage for the last time, his exit line: 'Gamesters, farewell, I have nothing left to play'. (V,i,150) brings together in a single image his financial ruin, his defeat in the game of sexual intrigue, and the ending of the actor's contribution to the theatrical 'game'.

Between his own time and the nineteenth century the centrality of Shakespeare to English literary culture helped to conventionalise this system of sporting indices and symbols, and his influence over subsequent authors led them to appropriate and perpetuate such usages. But the shift of theatre as an art form from low to high culture in the early seventeenth century, when the new monarch James I began to commission theatrical pageants rather than sporting contests for court entertainments and when Shakespeare's company began to prefer the more exclusive indoors Blackfriars to the popular outdoor Globe, ought not to conceal the fact that the world of popular entertainment continued to allow the free interpenetration of professional sport and commercial theatre. The idea of theatre as 'a game' was lost from the increasingly elitist and neo-classical recording and analysis of performance, though not from less well-regarded popular theatrical practices, as the pastimes of the people at the time of the white invasion of the Australian continent shows.

The hippodrama in Australia

It was at this time that the hippodrama appeared in English and French popular theatre. In 1768 the trick-riding artist Philip Astley is supposed to have introduced into his season at Halfpenny Hatch a trained-horse act with a narrative basis 'The Taylor Riding to Brentford'.[24] From that time what subsequently came to be known as the hippodrama began to explore the possibilities of staging stories which combined actors, exhibitions of physical skill, and trained animals, particularly horses. The acting and dialogue were often minimal, as evidenced by the famous comment of the hippodrama star and stage director Andrew Ducrow, after watching a rehearsal of *Hamlet*: 'Cut the dialect and come to the 'osses'.[25] Nevertheless two fundamental ideas were introduced: that of the athlete as actor, and of physical displays and sporting contests having some kind of basic narrative sequencing. Over the next century medieval chivalry (e.g. *The Blood Red Knight*), Eurasia (*The Brave Cossack, Timour the Tartar, Mazeppa*), highwaymen (*Jack Sheppard, Turpin's Ride to York*), war (*The Battle of Waterloo, The Siege of Sebastopol*), and sport, particularly hunting, racing, and boxing (*The High Mettled Racer, The Steeplechase, Tom and Jerry; or, Life in London*), all provided material for 'horse drama'.[26] From 1782 Charles Hughes, Charles Dibdin, Astley and others in London and Paris began to add a peripheral theatre stage to their circus rings, and they transferred to this platform those acts which could benefit from proscenium presentation and stage machinery.[27] In the 1820s Ducrow worked both at Astley's and at the two patent houses—Covent Garden and Drury Lane—as the legitimate theatre began to absorb hippodramatic techniques into its repertoire.[28]

The changes this wrought in English drama were profound, as the character of an English playwright in Edward Geoghegan's 1844 comedy *The Currency Lass* explains in expressing his delight with Sydney:

Positively, the sun of Australia seems to possess wonderful powers in fertilising genius! What a fortunate idea was mine to abandon a country where envy blights merit, where authors sink into insignificance before scene-painters, mechanists, tailors and property men, and actors play second business to goats, monkeys, horses, dogs and elephants![29]

His optimism was misplaced: in the same decade circuses, hippodramas and trained animal acts arrived in Australia. Even earlier Barnett Levey and his successors had staged a number of hippodramatic plays at the Sydney Theatre Royal,[30] although it is unlikely that they were able to make more than a token gesture towards the kind of staging which had been used in London for these works. However, by 1837 in Hobart *Timour the Tartar* was given at the new Theatre Royal with a white pony on the stage,[31] and in 1845 Mrs Coppin rode 'a real live horse' as Joan of Arc.[32] By 1847 a hotel-owner in Launceston, Robert Radford, had established a circus/hippodrama; by 1849 his horses were being acclaimed for their 'astonishing sagacity' in narrative adventures.[33] In the next few years several other touring circuses arrived in the colonies, and hippodramatic plays such as *Mazeppa, The Steeplechase*, and the perennial *Billy Button; or, The Tailor's Ride to Brentford* began appearing regularly at these venues.[34]

Although the hippodrama was an overtly popular form of entertainment, its appearance in Australia coincided with, and was influenced by, the emerging middle-class ideology of sport as a weapon in the struggle against carnal desires, as the Victorian doctor, William Acton, observed in his book *The Functions and Disorders of the Reproductive Organs:*

At a very early age the pastimes of the boy and girl diverge. The boy takes to more boisterous amusements, and affects the society of boys older than himself, simply because they make him rougher, or, in his opinion, manlier playfellows. The girls' quieter games are despised, and their society, to a considerable extent, deserted. This . . . may almost be regarded as a provision of nature against possible dangers. (p.1)[35]

This concern with inhibiting pre-marital sexuality was to be particularly prominent in the school sports and physical fitness curriculum, as Acton's book urges:

it is of the most vital importance that the mind be directed into a different channel, and that every means be taken to check the secretion of semen. Experience has proved that to effect this, there is nothing so good as gymnastic exercises regularly employed . . . A taste should be encouraged for cricket, rowing, walking, swimming, and other athletic amusements. (p.14)

One of Acton's sources for his assertions was the writings of Thomas Arnold, the headmaster of Rugby between 1828 and 1842, and in the same year (1857) that Acton's often reprinted book first appeared, one of Arnold's pupils, Thomas Hughes, published *Tom Brown's Schooldays*, celebrating his Rugby education and starting the movement known as 'muscular Christianity'.[36]

In the eugenics, fitness, and Empire-obsessed nineteenth century this educational pedagogy became linked to the myth that sexual intercourse saps male energy, and became a reason for promoting sexual repression in adult men as well as youths.[37] It was not simply a matter of controlling sexual impulses in the young male, but of establishing a lifetime habit of sexual restraint combined with intense indoctrination in both the moral and physical virtues of sporting activity. Keeping men out of the boudoir and the brothel late at night by getting them on to the playing field early in the morning ensured that they would be fit and ready for the ultimate test of manhood on the playing field of war; it also meant when they did breed that the semen which sired their sons would not be weakened by 'excess' (p.102) or worse, be accompanied by the venereal consequences of immoral dalliance. (In 1864 Acton served on a committee established to 'report on the best means of protecting the army and the navy from the ravages occasioned by venereal disease'.)[38] Both purposes were achieved by arguing that manliness, physical fitness, sporting success, and military prowess were linked to sexual abstinence, and frequent references were made to the supposed practices of ancient gladiators (Acton believed that unused semen was reabsorbed into the circulation 'giving buoyancy to the feelings, and the manly vigour which characterises the male' (p.170). By the 1860s such ideas had triggered a vast popular movement, with speakers throughout the Empire emphasising the need to separate the sexes and insisting on the military value of sport:

should a day unhappily arrive when the youth of this country shall be led to . . . exchange the manly games of the recreation-ground and the healthy and animating field-sports of their forefathers for the refined, the gentle, the delicate amusements of the drawing room and the croquet lawn—then, I can tell you, what will assuredly and rapidly pass away—the freedom—the long cherished freedom, and with it the power, the influence, the prosperity, and the happiness of this great Empire.

This speech, given at a gymnastic festival in London in 1867, was approvingly reprinted in a Hobart magazine which attacked the 'gawky, ill-timed stride' and 'lazy lounge' of Tasmanian youths, who were failing 'to train themselves as soldiers to protect us and all our "gains".'[39] As the modern social historian, Wayland Young, wittily observes in *Eros Denied*:

If every value and every force surrounding an adolescent tells him that his bodily affections must at all costs be transformed and sublimated into physical effort, intellectual prowess, competitive zeal, and manly friendship, how can he not found empires?[40]

In the 1850s hippodromes were built in both Sydney and Melbourne, and part of the rhetoric of their self-presentation was the assertion that their horse-riding and gymnastic displays were practical evidence of this emerging contemporary ideology of sport as rational recreation, moral purifying agent and para-military training; they also promulgated the myth of the singular society, united by a common love of sport and participation in games and pastimes. At the opening in 1854 of Melbourne's Astley's Amphitheatre the builder, Tom Mooney, was able to speak plausibly of 'the necessity of providing rational amusement for the people, in order to content them in this new land, and fasten them to the soil'. ('Content' was a loaded word in Victoria in 1854, the year which ended with the rebel flag raised and bloodily lowered at Eureka.) The Chairman, Mr O'Shanassy MLC, was moved to reply 'that though he seldom attended places of public amusement in Melbourne, he would occasionally come with his family to this new amphitheatre'.[41] This rhetoric, particularly the emphasis on rational recreation, family pastimes, and social control, is borrowed directly from the contemporary arguments about the benefits of sport.[42]

The first lessee of the Melbourne Astley's, George Lewis, advertised his theatre as a place where such benefits were encouraged through watching and participating in sport, as in this major piece of puffery in the *Argus*:

ASTLEY'S AMPHITHEATRE. Mr George Lewis would claim the attention of the inhabitants of this city and colony to a few brief remarks relative to his public enterprise in their midst.
It is admitted by all lawgivers, legislators, and jurists, that amusements form a portion of the philosophy of government. People must be amused as well as fed, clothed and housed, otherwise they will fly like birds to the place of enjoyment.
The Ancient Egyptians invented or adopted various modes of amusement. Traces of their dancing processions are yet discernable on the granite monuments of Thebes.
The Jews had their eleven-stringed harps and their religious dances. The Greeks, more polished, introduced the Olympic Games, which were athletic exercises, whereby the physical development of the body was superinduced, and tended to raise and discipline a race of men like the three hundred who successfully defended the Pass of Thermopylae against ten thousand warriors. The Spartan legislators induced by every means the creation of an athletic, symmetrical and beautiful race of men. Amongst the agencies they adopted was the Riding School, the Shooting ground, and the Manual Race Course. The Athenians, refining upon their predecessors, resorted to the prepared dialogue of the stage as a medium of instructing the multitude; and hence the stage plays which, with more or less success, have continued their spell upon mankind. . . . Athletic sports formed, for several ages, a permanent part of the household education of the people of England and the adjoining countries; but time and change have diverted the minds of the million into other excitements which are less healthful, and which lead to decrepitude and degeneracy.
This marked decay among the present generation of men has not escaped the calculating notice of the great thinkers of the day, and hence they advise a return to the amusements and enjoyments which tended to make a vigorous race of men.
Mr. G. Lewis, feeling with the profound thinkers, has made arrangements for giving

daily lessons in Chivalrous and Calisthenic Exercises, whereby grace in motion
may be combined with a healthy development of the body.
. . . Meantime he has much pleasure in announcing Mr. and Mrs. Melville
from Liverpool, a valuable addition to his troupe of equestrian performers;
also Mr. Devere, the American clown.[43]

Here Lewis, like Arnold and Acton, justifies his ideas about sport with similar
historiographic beliefs, derived presumably from Gibbon's *Decline and Fall
of the Roman Empire* (1776–88). The year 1854 was also the year in which
the Crimean War began, so Lewis's mention of the military value of sport
and drama was a pointed one; hippodramas by implication assisted in encouraging men to keep themselves fit and trained in military skills such as
horse-riding. Lewis's opposition, Rowe's Circus, had already staged on 29
August that year a 'Grand Equestrian Festival' with a 'splendid Military
Evolution' for the 'Benefit of the Widows and Orphans of Soldiers and Sailors
Engaged in the East against the Russian Tyrant'.[44] Lewis replied on 6 October
with a similar Benefit Concert for the relatives of those who had died
'maintaining the Liberty of Europe'.[45] This link between sport, war, and theatre
was to resurface again later in the century in the genre of the 'sporting and
military melodrama' staged at Drury Lane and elsewhere.

Lewis's arguments about the circus and the hippodrama were not unique.
In 1866 the Grand World Circus, in a long advertisement of its season at the

The wicked squire chases the poor but honest girl: giving a narrative basis to circus
acts at Astley's Amphitheatre London *c.*1840 (from *Manners and Customs of Ye
Englyshe, c.*1856).

Haymarket Theatre, announced the show's revival of ancient Greek and Roman customs and the 'brilliant Olympian exploits' which it claimed would inspire youths to develop their bodies as well as their minds. The moral purity of the program was also emphasised: 'So cautious has and will be the selection that the tender father, the affectionate husband, or admiring lover need not fear that the blush of modesty will be affected by any exhibition within the arena.' Although theatre was of dubious moral value, 'Olympian' sports were pure. However this advertisement, directed like Lewis's at the respectable readership of the *Argus*, then went on to advertise the man-monkey (a gorilla) and two learned mules.[46]

The hippodrama was never the major force in Australian theatre that it had been in England. It was in decline in England by the 1860s, by which time the hybrid pit-and-stage arrangement was devolving back to either circus rings or proscenium stages.[47] The various lessees of both the Sydney Royal Circus and the Melbourne Astley's found the limited hippodramatic repertoire and the speciality acts available were insufficient to sustain a full-time amphitheatre; consequently the circus rings in both structures were later replaced by seating. The Royal Circus, refitted 'in a beautiful and costly manner' in 1854[48] retained the capacity to revert to pit-and-stage productions where necessary, as on 26 May 1862 when a number of dramatic and equestrian entertainments were offered, together with 'good old English sports and grand tournaments'.[49] In 1857 the Melbourne Astley's was converted into the first Princess's Theatre; it also retained pit-and-stage capabilities, which were used by Gardiner's American Circus in 1863. This company apparently specialised in displays of 'Sports of Merrie England'; during their Melbourne season these were combined with other equestrian events, jesters, balancing, gymnastics, and a 'mythological, physiological and numerical rural burlesque'.[50] The *Illustrated Melbourne Post* on 28 March commented on the increased patronage at the theatre, and noted that 'equestrian and circus feats and associated drama are very popular'.

Circuses continued to offer narrative acts involving trained horses, with the American Wild West making a major contribution after about 1875. In 1894 Fillis's Great Circus was at Redfern doing both *Mazeppa* (with '200 people and horses') and a play about one of the heroes of the paperback novel, *Deadwood Dick*:

Here with realistic effect was produced such a picture of cowboy and Indian life and of road agents' villainies as would satisfy the most gluttinous devourer of yellowback literature. A special feature was the cleverness of Hassan, an Arab horse, in releasing his master Deadwood Dick.[51]

A late survivor was the E. I. Cole Company, which reintroduced tent theatre in a major way between 1903 and 1930. *Turpin's Ride to York* was one of its earliest and most popular pieces, until 'Black Bess' died in Tasmania in 1912, and horses continued to be displayed in sporting and dramatic feats throughout the life of this company.[52] There was also some continuation of the hippodramatic repertoire and the use of trained animals in early twentieth-century legitimate theatres—both Bland Holt and the provincial actor/manager, Dan Barry, had trained dogs which appeared in comedy-drama sequences, as did Stiffy and Mo (Nat Phillips and Roy Rene) in some of their early revue and pantomime routines in the 1920s.[53]

Another lasting influence of the hippodrama on Australian theatre was in the design of theatre buildings. Most were multi-purpose structures, with provision for hippodramatic acts to be placed on the stage, if not in a pit area as well. This meant that the stage had to be large enough to contain a circus ring (approximately forty-four feet or fourteen metres in diameter) and there had to be some provision for horses and other large animals to be able to get on to the stage. The 1855 Melbourne Theatre Royal was capable of accommodating equestrian acts on the stage, although if needed a forestage could be built out over part of the pit area. Burton's Equestrian Troupe performed there in 1862 with an advertised forty horses and the combined talents of three different circuses. The circle was built on the stage—for the first time, according to one reviewer—and arranged and lit to represent 'a beautiful garden lawn'. The lawn was surrounded by a 'judicious arrangement of scenery', making it appear 'to have been formed in the middle of a grove, the horses making their entrance through a lane of foliage'.[54] For one of their farewell performances in late July, Burton and his company staged a fox hunt as a 'Grand Sporting Night'. According to the advertisements 'J. Henderson kindly lent for this occasion an English fox and his pack of beagles' and the action was described as including 'The meet. The breaking cover. The view halloo. The chase. The death.'[55] 'Gentlemen in pink' were admitted free, and the spectacle 'attracted a large number of the lovers of sport to the house'.[56] In 1866 Foley's Californian Circus was at the Melbourne Haymarket with equestrian acts, gymnasts and a gorilla. For James Cooke's benefit there on 17 September a 'Great Kangaroo Hunt' was advertised, in which kangaroos were reportedly 'introduced for the first time in the arena, chased by mounted horsemen, rending the scene as exciting as in an open plain'.[57]

The possibility that this kind of entertainment would have to be staged in an otherwise legitimate theatre persisted until late in the century; in 1874 the new theatre at Sandhurst (Bendigo) had, according to the *Australasian Sketcher* (11 July), a stage which could also be 'arranged for giving equestrian performances, a large folding door opening into the right of way'. As late as 1887 Wirth's 'Grand Circus and New York Equescurriculum' performed at the Alexandra Theatre in Melbourne with all the acts apparently on the stage.[58] To some extent this was still due to the lack of specialised performance buildings; the net effect was from the 1850s through to the First World War— by which time most of the live theatres used until the 1960s had been built— stage technicians were familiar with the problems of staging sporting spectacles, and were working in theatres designed and equipped for those kinds of performances.

Although the iconography, the ideology, and to some extent the story structures of sport were exploited extensively in the hippodrama, it was not in this area of live entertainment that what might be called a sporting narrative emerged: that is, one in which the progress and resolution of a story was based on preparations for and the representation and outcome of a sporting contest. Animals and sporting spectacles became two major motifs in commercial melodrama from the 1860s to the 1910s, and the major genre to exploit them was sporting drama, which certainly owed a major debt to the ideas and techniques of hippodrama. For its language and extended narrative sequencing sporting drama looked elsewhere.

Imagining a sporting society

The origins of the sporting story, like those of many other genres of modern fiction, probably lie in popular novels and magazines of the early nineteenth century. It seems likely, as we shall see in chapter 3 in discussing Dion Boucicault's *Flying Scud*, that when the first major sporting playwrights and novelists began working in the 1860s, they were aware of a significant tradition of previous writing and used it extensively, as well as borrowing from substantial works in related genres. But the discourse of narrative 'evolution' can only partly explain the remarkable flowering of the sporting story between that time and the present day. Before a story could be written in which the dominant preoccupation of the characters was sport, it was necessary for that social sub-group to exist in a substantial way, or be at least conceivably of importance. If it was not possible to imagine a sporting community as a significant actant in society, then no such world view could be promulgated in plausible narrative.

In this context, the rise of the sporting story in the second half of the nineteenth century must be seen as a product of the remarkable growth in mass leisure activities during the same period. On one hand was the moral pedagogy of sport as urged and practised by Arnold, Acton, Hughes *et. al.* who introduced sport into the educational system and the armed forces and urged the playing of sport as a force for both 'manliness' and social harmony in mid nineteenth century society; on the other was the increasing commercialisation and professionalisation of sport, the increasing visibility of (and opportunities for) gambling on a massive social scale, and the emergence of groups of employers (racehorse owners, sports promoters, bookmakers, entrepreneurs and caterers), employees (trainers, jockeys, clerks, professional athletes), sporting clubs and officials, whose lives centred on sporting activity.

As the century progressed it became increasingly possible to read sport as a sign of sufficient significance within the symbolic order for it to carry strong metonymic and metaphoric associations: to be both an important part of social life, and symbolic of it. In 1800 the word 'sportsman' could refer to someone from the English upper classes who hunted, shot or fished; it could also indicate a middle-class city-based professional gambler of doubtful honesty. The distinction between the two meanings was along lines of class (upper/middle) and geography (country/city). A century later the kinds of sports in which a 'sportsman' might be active had been widened to include most of the activities now generally identified as such; some of sports' class-specific connotations were beginning to be erased; its value in developing character, physique, sexual restraint, military preparedness and community leadership had been generally accepted, and the negative sense of the term had largely disappeared. The sporting story was figured by a diverse group of character types from different classes; gambling became, in certain circumstances, an acceptable means for otherwise 'worthy' or 'manly' individuals to gain or regain a fortune; and the sporting arena—in particular the horse-racing track—had been constructed as an allegorical site of social struggle of good *versus* evil, imagined in terms of community *vs* individual, selflessness *vs* selfishness, conservative *vs* democrat, agrarianism *vs* industrialism, aristocrat *vs* capitalist.

At first the development of the idea of a sporting community in narrative can be seen as a distortion, or dominant motif, in a parent genre constructed from both the *contemptus mundi* of classical and medieval times, the salacious guidebooks to city high and low life with their depiction of the traps for the country bumpkin which emerged in Elizabethan England and became a major area of publishing in eighteenth-century London, and the simultaneous fascination with the picaresque rogue or hero in the novels of Fielding and Smollett.[59] The rejection of the court (or city) in favour of rural isolation is a major theme from Seneca's *Thyestes* through the medieval period to the misanthropy of Shakespeare's Timon and Moliere's Alceste; elsewhere in Shakespeare the distinction between city and island, court and forest (or desert or seacoast of Bohemia) is crucial, with the influence of the 'natural' order of the wilderness either reinvigorating the civilised world or laying bare its hidden barbarity. At the same time Shakespeare's contemporaries, Greene and Dekker were exposing the tricks played by city sharps on country gulls, and beginning to document the London underworld. The structuring of narrative as a journey—possibly deriving from picaresque novels like Fielding's *Tom Jones*—provided a unifying framework for the exploration by a young upperclass rural man (or occasionally woman) of a large number of different citybased experiences. The tension between the supposed ennobling 'honesty' of the country, and the temptations of London—the great metropolis, the new Babylon, the sinful city—became the dramatic frame for literally hundreds of the plays of the English and Australian professional stages from the 1820s to the early twentieth-century. In the second half of that period, many of these major texts were sporting dramas, and no sporting play existed whose plot was not pre-structured by the 'country and city' genre.

The text which indirectly brought together country and city, a picaresque journey, tricksters and simpletons, representations of major sporting events, a choice between sexual excess and restraint, and the staging techniques of the hippodrama, was Pierce Egan's Regency bestseller, *Tom & Jerry: Life in London; or, the Day and Night Scenes of Jerry Hawthorn, Esq., and his elegant friend Corinthian Tom in their Rambles and Sprees through the Metropolis* (first published 1820–21).[60] Egan's novel deliberately juxtaposed London 'high' and 'low' life in a manner which was to set the pattern for many later plays and novels, but it was only occasionally and incidentally concerned with sport in the sense of organised game playing as we understand it today. It was the many dramatisations of Egan's work, particularly W. Barrymore's at Astley's Amphitheatre (17 September 1821), W. T. Moncrieff's at the Adelphi (26 November), and Egan's own version at Sadler's Wells (8 April 1822), which added sporting spectacles to the story.

Moncrieff's script (the most successful and one of only a few versions which have survived)[61] begins in Somersetshire at 'Hawthorn Hall' where stuffed animals, arrows and crossbows on the walls and numerous references to fox hunting indicate 'healthy' country sports, but where the Squire's son Jerry is allowed to go with his cousin Tom to observe 'living in London'. Tom is a 'Corinthian': a true gentleman, not a snob, able to mix easily with all classes in society, and a city 'sportsman' or gambler, though Egan (and Moncrieff) are careful to distinguish him from less reputable members of the same group. In London Tom and Jerry team up with Bob Logic, an ex-classics student at Oxford (a role which Egan later played in his own dramatisation). The three explore the delights of the town but eventually find themselves in the watchhouse and, still later, bankrupt. As Logic observes: 'The paths of pleasure are all very amusing, but not when they lead to the gulf of ruin'. Redemption comes through Jerry's fiancee, Susan Rosebud, who decides to 'follow him to this dangerous London' in disguise, and who teams up with Tom's love Kate. They arrange for Tom and Jerry to be fleeced at cards in a gaming house, to 'cure them of this worst of vices of life in London':

Bob: [Rising] Completely cleaned out! . . .
Jerry: Oh, that ever I should have been so foolish! . . . This would never
        have happened if I had remained at home, with Susan Rosebud,
        innocence, and true love. (p. 23)

In spite of such sentiments, and Egan's argument that 'The obnoxious scenes of life are only shown that they may be avoided', *Tom and Jerry* was a controversial and much condemned play, with Methodists and others arguing (no doubt correctly) that, in fact, audiences interpreted such representations as carnivalesque *celebrations* of the pleasures of London life.[62]

Irrelevant to the plot, but a feature of all the dramatisations, were stagings of major sporting events which Tom and Jerry attend as spectators; the introduction of characters (grooms, jockeys, athletes, etc.) from the world of horse-racing, boxing, and other entertainments which offered opportunities for gambling; and dialogue laced with sporting and low-life 'cant'. (The word 'slum' enters written English through Egan's novel.) Astley's hippodramatic version staged the English Derby,[63] Egan's included a boxing match and ended with Tom and Jerry at the Grand Sweepstakes, where 'six ponies raced three times round the auditorium to the winning post on the stage'.[64] Moncrieff made the most original use of a scene at Tattersall's Bazaar, introducing the character of an upwardly-mobile cockney gull 'Jemmy Green' who buys a worthless horse, and also developing two blackface characters as a performing comic duo. Both ideas were to be widely imitated, as was the 'language lesson' scene in which Tom and Bob attempt to explain 'cant' to Jerry.

Tom and Jerry caused considerable controversy when it finally reached the Australian stage in 1834;[65] some years later it was twice localised, though neither script appears to have been allowed to be performed. *Life in Sydney: or, The Ran Dan Club* was banned by the Colonial Secretary in 1843, and two years later the convict James Tucker wrote *Jemmy Green in Australia.* In both plays Jemmy foolishly bids at an auction.[66] Although censorship prevented such representations of colonial high and low life being performed, sections and motifs from the original play found their way indirectly on to the Australian public stage. Localisations of the 'language lesson' in which currency lads and lasses explain Australian slang to a 'new chum', became a favourite motif in local melodramas for the best part of the following hundred years, and in both England and Australia hippodramas continued to use the idea of the 'guided tour' to link sporting, equestrian and other spectacles.

However, neither *Tom and Jerry* nor any known direct derivative, can be thought of as a sporting *narrative*. Spectacles, character types, story fragments and theatrical 'turns' with a sporting flavour were exploited on the stage, but it was not until the 1860s, forty years after Egan's story became the hit of the London season and after the massive growth of sport in both contemporary industry and ideology, that the outcome of a sporting event was linked in an extended storyline to the fortunes of a story's characters and a specific and highly codified genre of sporting drama began. Between 1867 and 1930 such plays appeared and flourished on the commercial stage; their narratives and their impact on Australian society are discussed in chapters 3, 4, and 5. However, as chapter 2 seeks first to demonstrate, these stories were located within a 'legitimate' drama industry which like the hippodrama was exploring sporting dialogue, images, demonstrations, and contests; using sportsmen-actors; and promoting and promulgating an image of a sporting and fun-loving nation by developing the phrase 'sport and drama' as a rhetorical strategy which implied that both were pleasures enjoyed by all civilised white Australians.

These abundant connections did not imply a simple or consistent relationship between the two major forms of organised leisure but rather a shifting, flexible interpenetration which varied according to the precise area of contact being considered. The practices and ideologies of professional sport and commercial theatre—and the language in which they were constructed, argued, and advertised—clustered around two modular constructs: that of the *production* of sport and drama, and that of its *consumption*. At one extreme was the unity of much sporting and theatrical capital; at the other the tendency of marketing practitioners to identify particular sub-groups within the general Anglo-Australian community which were particularly responsive to offered entertainment, and the tendency of social commentators and other agents of myth formation to reflect and develop those real or perceived differences as oppositions between different leisure forms and different audience tastes and interests. The language of sport and drama as it was then used can only be understood in its economic and social context: in terms of the emerging capital exploitation of leisure as a marketable commodity and an invitation to pleasureable indulgence, in 'civilised' society as an index to class and gender interests, and in educational and political ideology as an expression of the countervailing understanding of sport as a unifying social force and as a mechanism for diverting young men from such pleasures and directing their energies back towards duty, effort, and empire. The tension in sporting narrative lay in working out these paradoxes.

Although they targeted specific groups, early leisure entrepreneurs also aimed to bring within the one cultural product sufficient diversity of material to provide 'something for everyone'. So, as analysed in chapter 4, a play described as a 'sporting' or 'racecourse' drama would be expected to include both scenes of a horse race (sport, action, excitement, gambling on the result, for male audience members), and of the race ball that evening (music, dance, courting and fashionable dress, for female spectators). Both popular appeal and middle-class morality required the socio-centralising by sport of different and possibly contradictory preferences; the term 'sporting drama' covered this diversity. The overwhelming preference amongst sporting plays and films for horse-racing was in part a reflection of the industrial links outlined in chapter 2; a comment on its cross-class appeal in colonial and early Federation society; and evidence of that sport's ability to subsume different interests and different groups into a complex, heterogeneous but harmonious image of society. Consequently an extremely successful formula for popular sporting drama became possible, resulting in dozens of these plays being staged and attracting such large audiences that at least two of the early racing dramas—Dion Boucicault's *Flying Scud; or, A Four-Legged Fortune* (1867) and Paul Meritt's and George Fawcett Rowe's *New Babylon* (1880)—were frequently referred to as the most successful dramas ever staged in nineteenth-century Australia. Later, particularly after the First World War, certain social renegotiations and oppositions—most obviously, those based on militarism, nationalism and intellectuality—came to be seen by sufficiently large numbers of people as important enough to be articulated in spite of their lack of universal appeal.

Different kinds of sporting and anti-sporting drama emerged in response to these demands as the dominant ideologies of Australian society shifted, as the population and cultural milieu became large and diverse enough to support minority cultural preferences, and as the funding bases of the now different industries (sport, theatre, film) also diverged. The language and iconography in which their narratives were written, produced, advertised, and criticised took on new connotations.about the composition and interests of Australian society.

The Sport and Drama Industry 1788-1930

Historians with an insatiable desire to compartmentalise have seen . . .
different forms of entertainment in isolation one from the other—there are
histories of sport, of drama, of pantomime, and of the circus. Yet what is most
striking is the connections between these different forms of entertainment,
connections so strong that one can speak of this world of entertainment as part
of one close-knit popular culture.

Hugh Cunningham, *Leisure in the Industrial*
Revolution c.1780–c.1880[1]

From a modern perspective, where sport and theatre are usually conceived
of as separate and often antithetical forms of leisure activity, it is perhaps
difficult to conceive of 'sport and drama' as a unified concept. Nevertheless
for much of the historical period during which Anglo-Celtic traditions have
dominated Australian cultural history, for sports patrons and theatregoers that
phrase implied a natural affinity; indeed the 'world of sport and drama' was
a cliche, a shorthand description of all organised leisure activities. It was
assumed—by producers and consumers alike—that there would continue to
be links between each in terms of all the areas of commercial exploitation:
organisation, financial backing, personnel, promotional material, and target
spectator/audience groups. In one extreme populist and consensual reading
of the phrase 'sport and drama', both activities were of equal interest to all
white Australians. The emergence of significant levels of oppositional attitudes
(stereotypically, males to theatre, and women and intellectuals to sport) was
suppressed by leisure entrepreneurs as far as possible for as long as possible.
There were good economic and social reasons for this attitude, since the
breaking up of mass leisure activities into specific class, gender, and interest
groups was threatening to the stable social consensus on which entrepreneurial
activities depended, and since they had a relatively small population base on
which to operate. There was also a long tradition in Britain of the joint commercial exploitation of sport and drama; a tradition which was largely trans-
planted to the Australasian colonies during the first years of white invasion.

The sport and drama timetable

The patterns of leisure in Britain in 1788 and through the rest of the eighteenth and nineteenth centuries brought those sporting events and theatrical performances which required capital outlay into a close commercial relationship. In the English provinces in particular an economic link between organised sport and professional drama was well established by the time of the First Fleet. The basis of the provincial theatre industry had been worked out at the beginning of the eighteenth century, and formalised after the disruption caused by the Licencing Act of 1737 had been resolved. It was based on a number of performance circuits. The idea of a theatrical circuit suggests the first factor which the developing Australian colonies and the English provinces would share: scattered towns and cities where lived relatively small populations of potential audiences who could support the commercial provision of entertainment only for short, well-spaced periods in any one year. Since in such conditions it was not only the quality and diversity of a company's repertoire but the spending capacity and willingness of audiences to consume the offered shows which determined the economics of survival, it was logical for travelling companies of actors to arrange their visits to each town to coincide with days when larger-than-usual numbers of people would be likely to be present, and on occasions when that enlarged populace would be in a festive mood and willing to spend well. There was, in short, a sport and drama calendar, and for theatre companies the equation was a simple one: the larger the centre and the more important the carnival, the longer the stay and the more performance nights per week, although there was a greater likelihood that other competing entertainments would be present.[2]

In the provincial towns of Britain, markets, fairs, local holidays and the visits by circuit judges were regular events which fulfilled these criteria; in the countryside, feast days, particularly those where the local aristocrat or squire hosted his community, were similarly predictable and popular occasions.[3] All these events provided a setting for 'old English' games and pastimes: horse races, early forms of cricket and football, and commercial and/or gambling sports: boxing, wrestling, ratting, cock-fighting, and athletic contests of many kinds.[4] Strolling players hurried to these events to take over in the evenings where the daytime sports left off. In a study of the social life of late eighteenth-century actors on the Yorkshire circuit, Arthur W. McDonald traced the touring patterns of one company in particular: that organised by the manager Tate Wilkinson.[5] Between 1769 and 1803 his troupe performed each year in the coastal city of Hull during the winter months when the adult male population was at home because the weather was not suitable for fishing; moved to York for the Spring assizes; and went to Leeds in early summer where the 'rich and numerous' feasts in neighbouring villages ensured a large number of patrons. Then from August to October the company 'followed the horses'; first the 'gala race season in York', then Wakefield in September and Doncaster in October where similar race weeks meant that 'the most glittering array of patrons appeared'.[6] So closely were theatre performances tied to horse races that at Stamford in Lincolnshire the theatre was built at the racecourse,[7] and in Oliver Goldsmith's story 'Adventures of a Strolling Player', published in 1765, the comedian describes to Goldsmith how his company 'left the town, in order to be at a horse-race at some distance from thence' but arrived too late, 'which was no small disappointment to our company'.[8] Provincial theatre was often a parasitic form of entertainment, unable to draw crowds on its own account and reliant upon sporting events, particularly (almost overwhelmingly) horse races, to provide them. It is not surprising then that white Australia's most colourful early rogue, George Barrington, was a strolling player transported in 1790 for stealing a watch on Enfield racecourse.[9]

The 'bespeak' system also reinforced the English provincial theatre's subservient position in society and in many cases its dependence upon the goodwill of sportsmen. A performance—and sometimes a particular play—would be requested and paid for by a Lord or Lady, a group of military officers, a sheriff or grand jury, the racing carnival stewards, or a gentleman's sporting club, particularly a riding, racing or hunting club.[10] Other sporting clubs also requested theatrical performances; the father of the prominent Australian theatre entrepreneur George Coppin, touring in the south of England in the 1830s, provided bespeak performances for cricket and bowling clubs.[11] By the middle of the nineteenth century such special evenings often included a performance of a comic play which had been adapted to include sporting characters and a sporting setting, and sometimes even provided the opportunity for some of the club members to participate on the stage.[12]

This phenomenon of professional theatre following and celebrating sport is discernible in Australia from very early times, and continued undiminished through to the 1930s. In 1844 in Sydney, the actor playing Edward Stanford in Edward Geoghegan's *The Currency Lass; or, My Native Girl* opened that play by outlining the pleasures which he and his fiancee hope to enjoy over a holiday break: This evening she has promised to accept my escort to the theatre—tomorrow to the Homebush Races—the day following a cruise to the Heads—on Sunday to Church . . .[13] In establishing this relationship the English provinces provided a closer model for Australian colonial society to imitate than did the London metropolis. The conditions of performance were similar, and nearly all the early Australian actors and managers who are known to have had prior theatrical experience in Britain before coming to the colonies gained it in the provinces, although many claimed, spuriously in some cases, to have also performed in London.[14]

After the coming of the railways the shift from the stock companies to a system of visiting troupes altered these touring patterns, but the circuits were still fundamental to the exploitation of a region.[15] Most provincial actors continued to travel widely throughout the British Isles both before and after becoming associated with the Theatres Royal of particular provincial cities;

Alfred Dampier, for example, was married in Birmingham in 1866, his first child was born in Newcastle-on-Tyne a year or two later, and he was performing on the channel island of Guernsey near the end of the decade; during this period he was for a substantial part of each year a leading actor at the Manchester Theatre Royal.[16] The colonies of south-eastern Australia became rather more distant English provincial circuits, which these entrepreneurs and others who learnt from them set out to exploit in the same way as any other province.

In Australia, from the 1840s onwards the opening of theatres, the dates of performances (particularly where or when theatres were not open throughout the year), the touring patterns of individual companies, and the kinds of plays offered, all show strong links with sporting carnivals. For example, in Melbourne the first theatre, the Royal Pavilion Saloon, opened with a season of concerts in April 1841 during the week of the then annual races,[17] and in 1845 it was noted with regret that its successor, John Thomas Smith's Theatre Royal, would not be ready to open during the race season that year.[18] The same problem did not prevent George Coppin from prematurely opening his new but unfinished 1872 Theatre Royal in Melbourne Cup week.[19] In 1892, after the financial depression had closed all the Melbourne theatres at different times, the 'Dramatic Notes' column in the October issue of the *Lorgnette* was able to report: 'Once more all the Melbourne theatres are open. It needs not to be said that this happy state of affairs is due to this being the racing carnival season.' Soon after the end of the races all the theatres were again closed, this time simultaneously.[20]

The establishment of an autumn racing carnival in Sydney and a spring carnival in Melbourne, particularly after the Melbourne Cup commenced in 1861, made possible a regular pattern of touring between these two cities by major managements. One of the first to exploit this was the actor/manager George Fawcett [Rowe], an enthusiastic supporter of cricket and racing, and later the author of several sporting plays.[21] He performed in Melbourne with Julia Matthews at the time of that first Melbourne Cup, continued his perform-ance season during the visit of the first English cricket team to Victoria in 1861-62, and arrived in Sydney in time for the autumn races in March.[22] In both cities he donated trophies for the sporting events, which were given at presentation ceremonies between the acts of the evening performances.[23]

All kinds of performing entertainments—from circus and vaudeville through popular melodrama to more refined 'society' drama and opera—crowded into the one city during the racing weeks, indicating that all sections of society were assumed to be either enthusiastic racegoers or at least to be interested in joining in the celebrations associated with racing carnivals. The French writer Edmond Marin La Meslee commented in 1882 that 'There is no extravagance which the Australians of every class do not permit themselves on the great day.' His account of a typical Melbourne Cup, based on those he had witnessed after arriving in Melbourne in 1876, concluded with his observations of its effect upon the theatre: 'After dinner this evening the city will be every bit as lively as the race-course was this afternoon. The theatres will be so crammed that movement, except on the stage, will be impossible.'[24] Popular entertainments such as circuses naturally took advantage of this atmosphere. In 1906 *Table Talk* noted on 8 November that 'Wirth Bros. circus and menagerie is quite a regular feature of Melbourne Cup festivities; it would not be Cup time if we did not have that clever combination with us.' But even theatre companies like that managed by Robert Brough and Dion Boucicault Jnr from 1886 to 1896, which consciously aimed at a more refined bourgeois audience with plays by J. M. Barrie, H. A. Jones and A. W. Pinero, tried to provide fare suited to sporting occasions. When Brough/ Boucicault brought Barrie's first play to Melbourne for the Cup in 1892, the *Criterion's* critic remarked on 27 October: '*Walker, London* is . . . very seasonable, because all the characters are accomplished punters'. Three years later the same company's Melbourne Cup offering was a sporting farce, Ralph Lumley's *The Thoroughbred.* The opera entrepreneur W. S. Lyster organised an 'Opera Night' for the visiting English cricket team in 1862,[25] and interrupted a concert at Maitland in 1867 so that a presentation could be made to an Aboriginal cricket team, who watched the entertainment from a box.[26] This is not to say that differences of taste and specific preferences did not exist; Harold Love in his *The Golden Age of Australian Opera* quotes an opera critic in 1863 who objected vigorously to individuals at the opera talking about the races during the performance.[27] However, horse-racing, which was warmly encouraged and patronised by community leaders and was to some extent a reflection in miniature of the social order itself,[28] was sufficiently popular with a broad cross-section of the Australian community for such complaints to be marginalised until late in the century.

The tendency of many companies to follow the horses caused undesirable competition. Brisbane, where there was a winter racing carnival leading up to the annual August Show, had Bland Holt, Alfred Dampier and the Fitzgerald Brothers' Circus all opening on the same day in July 1896. The *Lorgnette* observed: 'Too much for the northern capital at one time!'[29] By this period of Australian sporting history, however, there were enough major racing carnivals for companies to work to flexible touring patterns; there was, for example, a steeplechasing season of races in Melbourne in winter with the principal event, the Grand National Steeplechase, being second only to the Melbourne Cup in public estimation;[30] Bland Holt revived his racing melodrama *A Million of Money* at the Melbourne Theatre Royal 'to coincide with Grand National Hurdle day' in 1895.[31] But even when Holt was at the peak of his career as an actor/manager (*c.*1895–1907) when his enormous popularity made it possible for him to run much longer seasons of plays in the capital cities, the same concern for the horse-racing season can be discerned behind his timetable. In 1900 he opened a sixteen-month season at the Melbourne Theatre Royal on the Saturday before the Melbourne Cup Tuesday.

He stayed there until February 1902 then opened in Sydney in March at the beginning of the autumn races and lasted thirteen months through to the end of the next annual Sydney racing carnival.[32]

Little research has been done on the organisation of provincial touring in Australia, but by sampling surviving colonial newspapers for two provincial cities, Bendigo in Victoria and Maitland in New South Wales, some indication of the connection between theatre and sport in such centres can be gauged. In Bendigo in 1860 the prosperity of the district allowed two theatres to operate year-round, so no simple pattern emerges. However the annual races on 9–10 May that year coincided with a season at the Haymarket Theatre by a major visiting theatre company, and at the rival Lyceum Theatre the second night of a new play was advertised as being 'Under the Patronage of the Stewards of the Bendigo Races'.[33] By 1880 a stronger focus on the now early December race meeting was evident. The Royal Princess's Theatre, which had been closed for much of the preceding months, had the Austrian Strauss Band followed by a benefit performance of Boucicault's horse-racing drama *Flying Scud*, while Monaghan's Exhibition Band was at the Masonic Hall and the Great Exhibition Circus performed in its tent.[34]

In Maitland, a smaller centre based on the more stable coal-mining district of the Hunter Valley, there was an even stronger dependence on the race week. In 1855, the first year surveyed, it had no theatre, agricultural show or sporting carnivals, and only very occasional short theatrical and circus seasons were given in conjunction with local hotels.[35] Interestingly Noble's Olympic Circus, which was at the Northumberland Hotel in February, appears to have been imitating another English provincial practice by following the District Court circuit, and the attendances were 'pretty numerous'.[36] By 1865 there was an infrequently used Olympic Theatre and a School of Arts, where the West Maitland races on 18–20 October broke a long lull in theatrical activity, with the Olympic Theatre announcing 'For Six Nights Only—Dramatic Season During the Race Week', after which the theatre went dark again.[37] In 1875 the race week was a month earlier and Holloway and McGowan, lessees of the Newcastle Theatre Royal, came across to Maitland for a season which also concluded on the last night of the races.

Later in the century agricultural shows began to replace race meetings as the major event of each year which drew crowds from the surrounding district to the regional centre. In some towns show and race days remained separate; in others they were combined. Bendigo in 1890 had both an agricultural show in October and the races at the end of November, and these weeks both show an unmistakeable peak of theatrical activity. The 'Grand Spring Show and Sporting Carnival' from 13–17 October had the Dampier Company in town for six nights;[38] after this the amusements column in the *Advertiser* had little to offer until the Jockey Club spring meeting on 26 and 27 November, when Harmston & Son's Circus erected its tent in the showgrounds, and the Royal Princess's Theatre under the heading 'RACE NIGHTS—RACE NIGHTS' offered 'The Popular Comedian' Mr Newton Griffiths in a sensational drama.[39]

Again Maitland's relative poverty gives a clearer picture, since its horse-racing clubs seem to have disbanded by the century's end. In 1885 there were only the East Maitland Amateur Races in January, and instead of using this as the basis for a six-night season the Dampier Dramatic Company targeted the Anniversary Day Sports a week earlier.[40] In April the Agricultural Show attracted Hussey's Minstrels and Ashton's Circus, and the local Garrick Amateur Club occupied the Victoria Theatre on the Show nights.[41] By 1905 the major races were at Wallsend and Newcastle; again it was Anniversary Day (called Australia Day after Federation) with its sporting carnival which attracted theatre companies to Maitland.[42] The Show was in April immediately after the nearby Newcastle Cup meeting, and attracted both theatre perform-ances and the Royal Hippodrome 'Grand Circus and Sports Combination'. This entertainment shows something of the interest taken by circuses in sport: it combined wire walking, clowns and monkeys with champion wrestlers, boxers, buckjump riders, weightlifters, 'The Queensland Prince, Champion High Jumper of the World' and even 'Jack Marsh, the famous Fast Bowler . . . Maitland Batsmen are kindly invited to take a bat against him.'[43]

There is therefore an abundance of evidence to show that, from the time of the establishment of professional theatre in Australia, whenever and wherever economic or demographic circumstances dictated the frequency and popularity of performances, theatre companies focused their efforts on local carnivals, particularly Christmas and New Year festivities, Anniversary Days, horse races, and agricultural shows. All such holidays were celebrated by major outdoor sporting occasions, and it was not only the sporting appeal of horse races which travelling theatre troupes sought to exploit. In Bendigo on 2 January 1860 Abbott's Lyceum Theatre celebrated the inaugural Highland Games in that city by offering the Melbourne Theatre Royal production of *Rob Roy*,[44] and Randolph Bedford, briefly travelling with a small troupe in country Victoria in the 1880s, describes an humorous incident in which they noted newspaper advertisements for Hibernian sports in one town and promptly set out for it, rehearsing, rewriting and retitling the play *Peep o'Day* as *The 'Ould Sod* to appeal to the expected local Irish sentiment.[45] By the 1870s, in addition to these appeals to ethnic minorities, sporting narratives were being written for the legitimate stage, and they were particularly favoured during sporting carnivals. The community sporting and commercial dramatic calendars had moved into a close relationship in both small towns and large cities, with sport clearly the major social institution of the two. It had become essential for theatre to cultivate its connections with sport in order to survive.

Celebrating sport in theatre

There were social as well as commercial reasons for the theatre profession to cultivate a relationship with sport and sportsmen. As the nineteenth century progressed the playing of field sports came to be widely applauded as being highly beneficial to society. Cricket, football, athletics, gymnastics, rowing, boxing, and other outdoor activities were considered to be manly pursuits which cultivated both the body and the mind, prepared young men for war, and developed team spirit, moral fibre, sexual restraint, leadership qualities, and a willingness to accept the rules of the game and, implicitly, the rules of society.[46] As 'muscular Christianity' this doctrine was taught in English and Australian schools, promulgated in Australian newspapers and journals,[47] and joked about in plays:

Blinker: Muscular Christianity—it's all the go, now, Mrs F.
Directly a child can move its fists, put the gloves on 'em.[48]

By the 1850s champion Australian sportsmen were also being acclaimed as embodying an emerging spirit of national achievement and excellence. They were used as proof that white Australia's convict origins had not resulted in a degeneration of the race, and that Australians were at least the equal of any race of people in the world. This sporting nationalism was particularly evident after the mid-1870s, when the Sydney sculler Edward Trickett became Australia's first undisputed world sporting champion, and when Australian cricketers and boxers began scoring victories in international competition.[49] The sport of horse-racing, as well as sharing many of the above attributes, was closely connected to the Australian social hierarchy, with many political, business and community leaders occupying positions of importance in the racing clubs.[50]

In comparison to this, the professional actor at the beginning of the nineteenth century was all too often considered a rogue and a vagabond in the eyes of society. The historian Michael Baker, who has documented the social status of the actor in Victorian England, has suggested that the series of Royal Command performances at Windsor Palace from 1847 onwards, and the knighthood first offered to Henry Irving in 1883 and eventually accepted by Irving in 1895, were some of the major steps in the Victorian actor's slow ascent up the social ladder to respectability.[51] The actor in Australia found it harder to achieve the same social esteem,[52] and usually did so—as in George Coppin's case—for public duties additional to his or her theatrical activities. As late as 1880, at Hamilton in Victoria, some members of the Stray Leaves Opera and Theatre Company, including the prominent actress Ella Carrington, were arrested, charged with infanticide, jailed and generally humiliated for apparently no better reason than that they had been performing in that town when a baby's body was discovered.[53]

Not surprisingly, therefore, Australian actors made strenuous efforts to upgrade their image in the eyes of society by prominently advertising the reputation they had acquired and the dramatic successes they had achieved in England; the propriety of their performances and the respectability of their audiences; their associations with clergymen, gentlemen's clubs, vice-royalty, and other pillars of the colonial establishment; and their philanthropic gestures to local clubs and charities through benefit performances. The improved image of professional theatre in return contributed to increased attendances, both in general and specifically through group bookings by sporting clubs.

Sport and sportsmen came to have a special significance in this campaign by actors for social recognition and popular success. A number of different approaches can be identified: associations with amateur and professional sporting clubs; presentation ceremonies at theatres after sporting contests; and attempts to represent theatre as a form of national endeavour which gave to society the same social benefits as sport, and which was therefore deserving of the same acclaim.

By associating themselves with sport, members of the theatre profession were able to integrate themselves into Australian society and to achieve upward mobility through sport rather than, or as well as, through their profession. Community contacts with sporting clubs were encouraged both on and off the stage. In 1857 an early example of a bespeak performance occurred at the Melbourne Theatre Royal:

The performances on Thursday were under the especial patronage of the Melbourne Hunt Club, and the prospects of good sport pointed out in the programme brought one of the largest audiences of the season. The farce of the 'Irish Attorney,' in which Mr. Brooke, of course, played *Pierce O'Hara* , was succeeded by a new local sketch, [*The Melbourne Hunt; or, A Club Night at Cheltenham*] in which the audience are afforded an insight into the manner in which members of the club are wont to enjoy themselves after a day with the hounds. The stage is arranged to represent the interior of the Cheltenham Hotel, the palatial tryst of the 'pinks,' and a number of the most prominent members of the club are discovered . . . a bet is undertaken that no one present will undertake to perform the celebrated feat, said once to have been accomplished by the Marquis of Waterford, namely, of riding his horse over a five-barred gate set up in the room. The bet is accepted by Mr. George Watson; and had it been a *bona fide* wager, would have been won by him, as the gate having been set up on the stage, our Australian Nimrod, mounted upon his hunter Peter, performed the conditions. The horse was ridden at the gate from the P.S. wing, cleared the jump, but on landing, the smoothness of the stage caused the animal's hind legs to slide under him, and he fell without much force, Mr. Watson, however, maintaining his seat. The next attempt was successful, the horse, although striking the top bar with his hind feet, landing firmly on the other side.[54]

It is significant that what brought 'one of the largest audiences of the season' to the theatre was not so much the work of the 'celebrated tragedian' G. V. Brooke, but 'the prospects of good sport'. As in England the bespeak performance was marked by the special production of a short play (in this case simply a series of speeches followed by the horse-jumping) which celebrated and even demonstrated the sporting prowess of the host club, and gave some of its members the chance to appear onstage; the theatre company in return was assured of a large attendance at the theatre. A later example of this kind of interaction occurred in 1889, when the theatrical managers' journal *The Call* reported on 26 December that the Theatre Royal pantomime *Cinderella* had, as well as a hunting scene with dogs, rabbits, and horses on the stage, members of the 'Champion Clubs of Victoria' taking part in a 'Grand Football Tournament'. Sporting teams were key target audiences; in Brisbane in 1908 it was announced that the visiting South Australian Lacrosse team would be attending the Friday performance, and the New South Wales cricketers were similarly announced the following year.[55] Actors could also donate their professional skills *gratis* in return for social status. In 1869 when some members of the Albert Cricket Club in Sydney gave an amateur performance of Tom Robertson's *Caste* under vice-regal patronage at the Prince of Wales Theatre in order to raise money for their club, the female roles were played by professional actresses from the resident theatre company.[56]

Offstage, members of the theatre profession were keen to be seen as good sports. No doubt many of them were, but it was also good publicity. One of the earliest of many social cricket matches involving theatre companies took place in 1863 when a 'Press *vs* Stage' game was held in Richmond Paddock, the stage team being captained by Robert Heir. More selfishly, George Coppin organised a burlesque cricket match to help raise money for the rebuilding of his Melbourne Theatre Royal, destroyed by fire in 1872.[57] At Maitland in 1885 the Dampier Dramatic Company combined sportsmanship, social responsibility and good publicity by playing a 'Novel Cricket Match' against a team called 'The Pickwickians' in aid of the Maitland Hospital. The players were all in character costume, with Pickwick, Sam Weller, and other Dickens' characters represented in the home team.[58] A costumed football match occured on 27 August 1881 at the East Melbourne Cricket Ground as the main event in a benefit afternoon for the family of the late Marcus Clarke;[59] another took place in 1894 at the Melbourne Cricket Ground when a 'Grand Fete' was held in aid of the homes for aged needy actors and actresses. It was reported in *Today* that 'Various lissome fairies from the Princess's [Theatre] will occupy most of the tents' to sell confectionery, smiles and kisses.[60]

In 1904 J. C. Williamson took this idea of charitable theatrical sport to new heights in both Sydney and Melbourne. According to the *Age* advertisements his 'Grand Theatrical Carnival', held at the East Melbourne Cricket Ground on 16 March, had on the programme a 'Ladies Cricket Match' between the 'Hiawathas' and the 'Country Girls' which had earlier played to 20,000 people in Sydney. It was followed by a 'Costume Burlesque Test Match' between the Royal Comic Opera Company and an Old English Eleven, as well as animal races, costume races, and refreshment tents presided over by the leading ladies of the Opera Company. In the same decade the actor/manager, William Hawtrey, went even further than these occasional charity events; he maintained a private cricket team which, when his theatre company was on tour, played against local teams in each and every town. According to Gregan McMahon:

Hawtrey's cricket team was famous. If during a tour he came across a likely player, the man would, if willing, be immediately placed on the pay-list as a dresser or a secretary. Heavens knows how many dressers and secretaries were nominally employed by William but actually attached to the Company to play cricket. I remember that Leonard Monk, now advance agent for Alan Wilkie, was 'captured' in New Zealand by Hawtrey because Leonard was the best bowler in Otago.[61]

In the years after the First World War, the Bert Bailey Company, travelling with Steele Rudd's *On Our Selection*, continued this tradition of challenging local teams (often composed of journalists from the local newspaper) to a game of cricket. The Nellie Bramley Company did the same, and even printed in their theatre programme the team's results during the previous twelve months.

Fetes, cricket, football and support for charities and amateur theatricals were good fun, good publicity and were intended to show Australian society that actors were decent, community-minded ladies and gentlemen. But, as a measure of social standing, participation in the racing world was in a class of its own. Throughout the nineteenth and early twentieth centuries most of the major theatrical entrepreneurs and actor/managers were also breeders and racers of horses. Coppin did both, and donated a Shakespeare Cup annually as the prize for a race at Geelong; there was also a Coppin Cup in Adelaide.[62] Bland Holt maintained a stable of steeplechasers outside Melbourne; it provided him with trained horses for his stage dramas, and on one occasion his mare Sylvia won a jumping event at the Adelaide show in the afternoon and that night appeared as the winning (male) horse 'The Duke' in his steeplechase melodrama *The Prodigal Daughter* at the Theatre Royal.[63]

Sports-loving citizens: the Nellie Bramley Theatre Company cricket team (*Souvenir Anniversary Programme* Theatre Royal, Brisbane, 21 April 1928–20 April 1929).

Charles MacMahon and J. C. Williamson raced horses and exchanged tips,[64] and Williamson's horse Blue Book dead-heated for first prize in the 1909 Caulfield Cup.[65] Four years later, Bland Holt's competitor in popular melodrama, William Anderson, won the Bendigo Cup with his horse The Beggar Maid, named after one of his wife's favourite stage roles.[66] Minor theatrical figures seem to have been as interested in sporting matters if less prominent in them; an obituary in the *Lorgnette* in April 1897 for George Hill, 'proprietor of the Sydney Criterion Theatre and owner of the old Queen's Theatre' mentioned that he was 'always identified with every form of sport'.[67]

Presentation ceremonies were a second part of the theatrical profession's campaign for commercial success and personal popularity. Through the active support of some lessees and actor/managers, theatres came to be the usual venue for speechmaking and celebrations after major sporting events. It was almost obligatory for the jockey who had ridden the winner in a major race (and sometimes the horse as well) to appear 'in his racing colours' at one of the city's theatres that evening to receive an award. This practice was already established in Melbourne by the late 1850s when a presentation was made at the Olympic Theatre to the 'youthful jockey' who had won the first Australian and New Zealand Champion Sweepstakes at Flemington in October 1859.[68] In May 1862 at the Victoria Theatre in Sydney, George Fawcett and Julia Matthews presented the comedy *Everybody's Friend*,

'after which, by the kind permission of John Tait Esq., his celebrated horse TALLYRAND, winner of the three handicaps, will appear on the stage, when Mr Fawcett will present a handsome whip to his rider, Mr James Ashworth, who will appear in his winning colours'.[69]

In 1868 James Ashworth again received an award for his win in the 'Great Metropolitan Handicap', this time at the Prince of Wales Theatre; the horse was absent but Ashworth was 'supported by the presence of all his brother jockeys on the stage'.[70] In Melbourne the *Magpie* reported on 3 November 1865 that 'At ten o'clock last night a little event came off at the Haymarket Theatre which shewed that the Christy's Minstrels were not only good singers but good sportsmen.' These 'melodious blackbirds' commemorated the Melbourne Cup run that afternoon by presenting 'a very handsome mounted racing whip to the jockey who rode Toryboy for the Cup'. Thirty years later such presentations were still common, and a novel variant was introduced at the Alhambra Palace of Varieties (the former Prince of Wales Theatre) in 1893 when the Melbourne Cup winner Tarcoola was ridden on to the stage by the singer Florrie Forde between two acts of an entertainment entitled *At the Races*.[71] This revue company emphasised sport in several of its shows. Earlier the same year the first half of their programme was called 'Football' and was 'designed and arranged in honour of our national game'. The list of events was set out like a football programme, beginning with an overture 'Hurrah for Football' and finishing with a grand finale of the 'Siamese Troupe of Football Jugglers'. Sport as the subject matter for revue and variety sketches became increasingly common after this time, but the practice of putting champion horses and jockeys on the stage seems to have become less frequent. When J. C. Williamson's jockey appeared in a tableau on the stage of Her Majesty's Theatre in 1909 after Blue Book's Caulfield Cup victory, the *Argus* thought this was 'a decidedly novel effect',[72] though the practice remained common through to the 1920s in smaller cities and towns.

Other kinds of sporting heroes also appeared on Australian stages after their triumphs. One period of intense activity was during the years 1861-64, when two English cricketing elevens visited Australia and the Australian champion sculler R. A. W. Green competed in England. It is particularly interesting that the stage links with both the cricketers and the sculler operated on a number of levels. The theatre was used to give formal recognition to sporting activity, was financially connected to it, and exploited it for its publicity value. There was also a clear development of stage imagery which invested the events with meaning additional to that generated by the contests themselves. A closer investigation of these series of events shows some of the complexities of the interaction between sport and theatre on the levels of industry, diplomacy, image-making and myth-formation.

The moral virtues of cricket had been frequently promulgated in sporting writing during the previous decades. The first issue of the *N.S.W. Sporting Magazine* in October 1848 carried a long reprint of an English article which was an appraisal of the 'Healthiness of Cricket'. It included such assertions as 'The author has known many instances where the dissolute have, by being allowed to meet their pastor and the gentlemen of their neighbourhood at cricket, become excellent members of society.'[73] Strong links were also asserted between behaviour on the cricket field and the disciplined manliness supposedly appropriate to the battlefield. After the Intercolonial Cricket Match between New South Wales and Victoria in 1860, the actor Richard Younge made a presentation to the captain of the successful Victorian team at the Pantheon Theatre in Coppin's Cremorne Gardens, and was reported in the *Argus* as expressing the hope that 'should the Australian colonists be called upon to defend their homes, the same determined Anglo-Saxon spirit may be shown in meeting the enemy as that which animated you and your gallant band in this match'.[74] The friendly competitiveness of cricket was also considered to be a unifying factor between the colonies; an earlier Intercolonial Match in 1858 was shown in a drawing in the *Illustrated Melbourne News* with a batsman and a bowler shaking hands, and banners carrying the words 'New South Wales—Advance Australia—Victoria'.[75]

The visit of the first English eleven which arrived in the colonies in December 1861 was seen in particular as a symbol of the unity between England and Australia, and was commemorated by ceremonies in theatres asserting this fact. The tour had financial connections with Australian theatre as well. George Coppin had attempted to form a company to finance the tour, and when he failed to do so, the restaurant owners Spiers and Pond, who were the caterers for Coppin's Theatre Royal, brought the team out at their expense.[76] Both Coppin and the *Argus*'s theatre critic, the journalist James Smith, served on the organising committee which amongst other duties selected the twenty-two Victorian players who met the English eleven on New Year's Day in 1862.[77] (All the matches were played under handi-cap conditions.)

The 1861 Christmas pantomimes in Melbourne anticipated the team's arrival. The Pantheon Theatre, doubtless under strict instructions from Coppin, incorporated some anticipated events of the tour 'turned to humorous account' into *Jack and the Beanstalk; or, Harlequin Heads of Department, Life on the Moon, and the Pranks of the Good Little People*, 'localised by Mr. Mulholland'.[78] Not to be outdone, George Fawcett's version of *Harlequin Mother Hubbard and Puss in Boots* at the Princess's Theatre (the converted Astley's) had a scene of 'the view of the Melbourne Cricket Ground, with the accompaniment of a "grand new bat and ball ballet"'.[79] During the tour there were presentations of trophies and cricket bats at this theatre after the Melbourne combined colonies match in early January[80] and at the Victoria Theatre in Sydney after a game against a New South Wales twenty-two at the end of the month. Fervent Anglophilia and the admission that the colonies were not yet England's sporting equals were particularly evident at this latter presentation:

The curtain rose at a quarter to ten o'clock, and discovered the All-England Eleven on the right hand of the stage, and the Twenty-Two of New South Wales on the left. . . . A voice from the pit, calling for 'three cheers for Old England,' which were given with right good will from all parts of the house.[81]

The commemoration of a high point in England-Australia relationships is clear, as is the implication of cultural unity between England and Australia. The stage image—eleven players on one side balanced by twenty-two on the other—admits the present inability of the colonies to achieve an equal status in team sports, intensifying colonial admiration for the English and inviting still greater efforts in the march of 'civilisation' into Australia. The loyalist cheer 'from all parts of the house' suggests the ability of sport and thoughts of England to overcome class and cultural differences amongst colonial white Australians through a surge of unreasoning admiration for these sporting representatives of the Imperial power. The fact that the English team had lost several matches due allegedly to late-night carousing,[82] and that cricket was at the time a sport characterised by brawls, intense gambling and corrupt result-rigging[83] was irrelevant to the stage image. It was not simply the reality of an important sporting tour that was being celebrated, but the evolution of an ideal, and the theatre was one important public meeting place and forum where ideals rather than realities could be powerfully expressed.

This first visit by an English sporting team initiated a series of further exchanges, in which the stirrings of nationalism through the assertion of superiority in sport can be seen more clearly. The most significant challenge was by the Australian sculler Richard Augustus Willoughby Green, a 'colonial native' born in Sydney in 1836.[84] During the gold-rush of the 1850s a number of England's best scullers had migrated to Australia, and Green beat all of them convincingly.[85] Green travelled to England in 1862, possibly on the same boat on which the English cricketers returned home, since he seems to have become friendly with them,[86] and returned from England in October 1863 with the second English cricket team to tour the colonies. Green's visit to England was widely seen in both countries as being a colonial reply to the first cricket tour and as an ambassadorial visit anticipating the second, and helping to establish sporting links as important cultural events binding the two countries closer together.[87]

Green competed in two sculling events in London, both of which were unofficially claimed to be world championships. Rowing for the Championship of the Thames in June 1863, Green led convincingly for approximately half the race, but suddenly collapsed with violent stomach spasms.[88] It was widely believed, and Green himself thought, that he had been poisoned;[89] when his opponent withdrew from a planned rematch Green was declared the champion by forfeit.[90] A month later Green proved his worth by winning the single sculls (and, with a partner, the double sculls) at the Thames National Regatta, which *Bell's Life in London* described as 'the highest tribunal for the test of merit, and open to all the world'.[91] This victory was prominently recorded in newspapers in both England and Australia.[92]

The social significance of Green's challenges and victories is most clearly seen in the theatre benefit performances he received in London and Sydney. The first, at the Royal Surrey Theatre on 18 August 1863, appears to have been a considerable triumph. Included in a long and varied programme was a farce on a boating theme, *The Jolly Young Waterman*, in which a number of prominent real-life scullers appeared wearing their coats and badges. Twelve English cricketers were present, including the captain of the 1861–62 touring side, H. H. Stephenson, who spoke eloquently of the hospitality his team had received in Australia. When Green rose in reply:

one would have thought the house was coming down, so hard and long continued were the cheers which greeted Green, who, having shaken hands cordially with the watermen and cricketers, advanced to the footlights, and in thanking the audience, said that he should never forget the kindness he had received at the hands of the British public since his arrival in their country, and both that, and the enthusiastic reception he had met with that night, he should treasure up in his mind, so that he might tell his countrymen when he returned that the old country was as mindful as ever of its children.[93]

The language of Green's speech shows that his nationalistic challenge 'Australia versus the World' had been redefined as a diplomatic mission of goodwill and a plea for Imperial protection.

On his return to Sydney Green received another benefit performance, this time at the Royal Victoria Theatre on 16 March 1864.[94] The staging for the presentation ceremony is an interesting reflection and development of that used during the previous cricketing tour. As before, the English cricket eleven appeared on one side of the stage and the colonial twenty-two on the other, but added to the image was Green, sitting downstage centre in a racing scull.[95] The admission of general colonial inferiority was now balanced by the assertion of individual colonial excellence; both were subsumed into a polite exchange of courtesies and a vigorous assertion of friendship between nation and proto-nation. As these examples show, sportsmen did not only appear on the stage as they might at a public ceremony. Often they were made part of a tableau; a theatrical image which reflected and focused one preferred social meaning of the sporting contest.

The public image of both cricket and sculling was of respectable, manly pastimes, free from the taint of blood, violence, and, though this was certainly untrue in the 1860s, gambling.[96] They were therefore particularly suited to cere-monies designed to convince the respectable public of Australia of its own rising standards of civilisation, and that the theatre was part of that civilisation. Athletics and gymnastics were other areas of sport where notions of muscular Christianity were strong, and they too came under the close scrutiny of the professional theatre. An attempt was even made in 1864 at the Victoria Theatre in Sydney to stage an exhibition of pedestrianism, when it was announced that between two plays offered as a 'complimentary testimonial benefit' to the eight-year-old 'Australian native' John Day, he would 'perform his great feat of walking 1 mile in under 10 minutes on a 22 foot [7 metre] diameter circle'.[97] Presumably this was an early form of revolving platform, since the size of the theatre stage would have allowed him to walk in a larger circle than this.

Presentation ceremonies in theatres continued until the turn of the century. In December 1866 an Aboriginal cricket team played a game 'Black and White Natives of Australia *vs* Players from All Parts of the World' on the Melbourne Cricket Ground, after which they attended the Christmas pantomimes, were presented with cricket bats on the stage, and watched burlesques of themselves in the plays.[98] During the next two decades one particular enthusiast was the lessee of the Sydney Theatre Royal, Samuel Lazar, who donated trophies to the world-champion sculler, Edward Trickett, in 1876 during a special theatre programme 'under the patronage of the . . . various Yacht and Rowing Clubs';[99] to the Australian cricketers after they returned from their triumphant overseas tours in 1878 and 1882;[100] and to the next sculling world champion William Beach in 1884.[101] In 1902 Harry Rickards included in his vaudeville show at the Sydney Tivoli an exhibition of rowing by yet another Australian world sculling champion, George Towns:

Naturally the famous oarsman was heartily supported by the sportsmen of the city, and indeed there is no one who has not some curiosity to see the champion scu'.

of the world and the method which carried his 'shell' to victory in the old country. Mr Towns . . . got into his new rowing machine, which, as he moved to and fro on the sliding seat, turned on its axis in such a way that an 'all-round view' was presented of the central figure.[102]

It is perhaps significant that this demonstration took place in a vaudeville rather than a legitimate theatre. By 1902 there are some signs that theatre was reflecting a more stratified view of Australian society generally; there was, for example, no theatrical presentation to Victor Trumper and the other victorious Australian cricket players of that year. Instead the Sydney Town Hall was used as politicians exploited the popularity of sportsmen much as the theatre had done.[103] Audience tastes had diversified and specialised. Whereas in the 1860s it was appropriate for scullers and cricketers to appear at theatre and even opera houses, forty years later the division between working-class nationalism and middle-class provincialism, already evident in the split between vaudeville and 'legitimate' theatre, was also being expressed within theatre. This was less true of small centres where the bifurcation of audiences would have rendered theatre uneconomic, and vaudeville houses everywhere continued to use sporting champions as a drawcard, particular during the First World War when restrictions were placed on where and when sporting contests could take place.[104]

Theatre advertising occasionally used the national appeal of Australian sporting achievements to suggest that the stage, too, was concerned with national endeavour. On 28 August 1880 an advertisement in the *Sydney Morning Herald* stated that:

Encouraged by the success of Australian scullers, cricketers, athletes etc. etc., Miss Ella Carrington has formed a company of purely Australian artistes, and with entertainments written by an Australian author, and illustrated by beautiful paintings from the brush of an Australian artist, purposes visiting England and America.

However, her 'Australian' entertainments were fairly diluted national efforts, since the dramatic sketches and their accompanying backdrops were of scenes set in London and New York.[105] Nevertheless there was a parallel development in sporting and dramatic nationalism in this period. Sport was undoubtedly the more successful form of national culture, but some dramatists and actor/ managers followed its lead.

In such ways commercial self-interest, improved social standing for the theatrical profession, and public acclaim for sporting figures combined to assert an ideology and an historiography uniting sport and theatre in social harmony. Sometimes the sporting fraternity responded by helping theatre personalities in times of need, principally through a system of benefit performances. In 1887 George Darrell was granted a 'Grand Complimentary Benefit' after his 'severe illness' by the East Melbourne Cricket Club and the

Carlton, Essendon, Fitzroy, Prahran, Richmond, South Melbourne and Williamstown Football Clubs,[106] and two years later a number of Melbourne football and cricket clubs helped the actors in the Brough/Boucicault Company to raise over £1,000 to replace the scenery, costumes etc. lost when the Bijou Theatre burnt down on 22 April 1889.[107] The Melbourne 'weekly family paper', *Gossip*, reported on 21 June 1890 that at a benefit performance for the Australian actor Herbert Flemming who was leaving to 'try his luck in England', the Derby scene from Dion Boucicault's horse-racing melodrama *Flying Scud* was given 'with all [Melbourne's] leading local bookmakers and jockeys' on the stage. Though sportsmen had less obvious need to cultivate their theatrical acquaintances than the theatre did sport, many leading sportsmen were involved and genuinely interested in the professional and amateur stages and in the welfare of its leading players. Some sporting clubs staged farcical comedies for fund-raising evenings; and their lack of female club members (and the reluctance in any case of 'respectable' women to appear on stage) meant that professional actresses sometimes appeared in these performances.

The theatre as sports arena and the athlete as actor

Theatres were often used for the kinds of sporting contests and exhibitions which were suited to indoor performance. An early curiosity was ratting, in which dogs competed to see which could kill the most rats in a given time. In November 1859 at the Melbourne Hippodrome a pit was constructed 'entirely of plate glass' to ensure good visibility for a number of rat hunts, a ferret hunt, and a fight between a mongoose and Australian snakes.[108] This was a complimentary benefit to the proprietor of the Melbourne rat pit, who staged several other ratting nights at this theatre and at hotels in Melbourne.[109] This sport drops out of notice soon after.

Boxing was the obvious major example of sport in theatres, although the dubious reputation and doubtful legality of prizefighting (as distinct from amateur boxing demonstrations) inhibited its appearance in pre-advertised venues until late in the nineteenth century, by which time specialised boxing stadiums and athletics halls were beginning to be built. Nevertheless as early as 1860 a 'Grand Fistic Tournament' was held at the Melbourne Prince of Wales Theatre in aid of a testimonial to the English boxing champion, Tom Sayers. On this occasion the local pugilists, Tom Curran and Harry Sellars, 'repeated' an earlier match; the newspaper accounts are probably deliberately vague as to whether this was a true rematch or a boxing demonstration.[110] Occasional advertisements and notes in theatrical columns show regular repetition of this practice. In 1876 James Christie gave 'glove exhibitions' at the Princess's Theatre in Melbourne;[111] in 1883 and 1885 there were major boxing events at the Melbourne Bijou;[112] in the latter year the Lyceum in Newcastle was used for a boxing and wrestling exhibition;[113] and in 1892 the

Alexandra Theatre in Melbourne was host to several nights of wrestling.[114] According to Peter Corris in his history of boxing in Australia, *Lords of the Ring*, other legitimate theatres such as the Brisbane Theatre Royal and the Sydney Gaiety were used regularly for boxing from the 1890s to the First World War.[115] Halls with flat-floored auditoria could be used for such sports as well as for meetings, showing silent films (after 1896), playing table tennis, laying down bowling alleys and also staging vaudeville and theatre.[116]

A number of other sports were also staged theatrically. In Melbourne there were athletic gymnasts at both the Haymarket (the Lenton Company) and the Royal (the Leotards) in 1865;[117] in November 1873 the *Australasian Sketcher* noted that athletics were the principal attraction at both the Royal and the Princess's, and added that 'very steadily . . . all those pursuits to which the common term of "manly" is generally applied have been taking a very firm hold of the people'. It added somewhat unhappily 'For all this, the combination of acrobatism and the drama strikes one as just a little incongruous.'[118]

Incongruous or not, the next step along the continuum from sporting contest to rehearsed performance was for sporting champions to appear in plays *as actors*. Boxers were again prominent, appearing at frequent intervals in plays and later in films. There were three variants of this. Initially pugilists simply provided a display which the actors watched; this had occurred in *Life in London* in the 1820s in London and elsewhere, and was still going strong in Brisbane in 1907: the Fred Patey and Lilian Meyers Company had the 'well-known Queensland boxer', Paddy Regan, fighting a 'formidable opponent from Melbourne' as one of the highlights of *Saturday Night in London*.[119] Boxers might double the roles of the main actors when the hero and villain squared up in the ring, as happened in several 'fighting parson' plays in the same decade. Often the substitution of athlete for actor was openly advertised, particularly if a well-known sportsman was involved, but the most significant phenomenon was boxers themselves acting as the heroes of stage plays.

The first recorded example of this in Australia was by the negro-Irishman John 'Black' Perry, who arrived in Tasmania in 1847, moved to Sydney in 1849, and who, it is claimed, dominated the colonial boxing ring for over a decade. In 1857 while running a hotel at Windsor and unable to find willing opponents, he is supposed to have appeared in a production of *Othello*.[120] It is not clear which production this was, but in that year there was a burlesque version of Shakespeare's play being performed in Sydney and country New South Wales by William Dind's company.[121]

The peak period for stage boxer-actors was between 1890 and 1920. The West Indian-Australian boxer, Peter Jackson, after spending some years in England and America seeking John L. Sullivan's world heavyweight crown, performed as both an actor and a pugilist in 'Parson Davies' Athletic and Specialty Company' appearing at the New York Brooklyn Academy of Music in 1892.[122] The next year he and Parson Davies both appeared in *Uncle Tom's Cabin*, first at the Park Theatre and then at the Third Avenue Theatre in New

York; Jackson played Uncle Tom and 'Between the acts he sparred with Joe Chynski'.[123] Later he toured across America in the same play before returning to Australia.

Both Jackson and another famous Australian heavyweight of the time, Frank Slavin, had left Australia in the late 1880s to arrange a world title fight against John L. Sullivan, who managed to avoid meeting either of them. Consequently the Australian sporting public was not kindly disposed to

---

☞ **The ONLY PROGRAMME Circulated in this Theatre.**

OPERA HOUSE.

Under the Direction of ... Messrs. MacMahon.

Treasurer . .. .. Mr. Jas. Hendy

John L. SULLIVAN & Duncan B. HARRISON'S
FLYING VISIT TO AUSTRALIA.

SATURDAY, AUGUST 15th, 1891, and EVERY EVENING,

Mr. Duncan B. Harrison's Irish Drama, in 5 Acts,

Honest Hearts and Willing Hands

In which will Appear, Supported by a Powerful Company—

Mr. JOHN L. SULLIVAN Mr. DUNCAN B. HARRISON

Mr. JACK BARNITT Mr. JACK ASHTON Mr. Wm. P. SHELDON

CAST OF CHARACTERS ·

General De Lacy Dare (Master of Darewood) ...	Mr. G. R. Ireland
Arthur Dare (his Son)	Mr. Charles Holloway
John Daly ⎫(of Daly's Range) ... James Daly ⎬	{ Mr. Duncan B. Harrison Mr. John L. Sullivan
Teddy Hinton (of Layrock) ...	Mr. Charles Seagrave
Terence McNab (Attorney at Law)	... Mr. Wm. P. Sheldon
Lieutenant Francis	Mr W Richard
James (Butler at Darewood) ...	... Mr. W. G. Gladstone
Paddy Burns (a Smithy) ... , .	... Mr. W. Reid
Tug O'Brien (a Hired Thug)	Mr. Jack Ashton
Silly Mike	Mr. John Davenport
Master of Ceremonies	Mr. Jack Barnitt
Emily Poignsford (Niece and Ward of General Dare)	Miss Emma Bronton
Martha O'Neil	Miss Alice Deolwyn
Mrs. Mary Daly (Mother of John and James) ...	Miss Meta Pelham
Norah Daly (Mrs. Daly's Niece) ...	Miss Madge Seymour

Peasants, Constabulary, &c.

N.B.—There will be no wait between Acts 4 and 5.

The athlete as actor: John L. Sullivan (Melbourne *Lorgnette*, August 1891).

Sullivan when he came to Australia to star in a play written as a vehicle for his boxing and rather less obvious acting skills. The boxer's reputation as a dissolute, high living and unattractive person also preceded him, although the play he appeared in set out to correct that image. It was a homely Irish drama called *Honest Hearts and Willing Hands* and it starred Sullivan as a humble and simple-living village blacksmith.[124] He was supported on the stage by one of his sparring partners, Jack Ashton; his trainer, Jack Barnett; and the actor/ manager who had written the play, Duncan B. Harrison.[125] The play's 'main attraction is intended to be the exhibition of the powers of Mr Sullivan in the art of boxing' claimed the *Lorgnette* in an advance notice in August 1891, noting that it ended with a three-round fight in the village square between 'the hero [Sullivan] and the rough and tumble fighting man [Ashton] which, as may be anticipated, results in the victory of the former'.[126] *Honest Hearts and Willing Hands* had opened in New York at Niblo's Theatre on 27 August 1890 where it played for ten weeks, then toured across the United States ending with three weeks in San Francisco.[127] Sullivan, Ashton, Barnett, Harrison and several other actors then set out on a 'Flying Visit to Australia' on the *Mariposa*, rehearsing the play in Sydney with Australian actors G. R. Ireland, Charles Holloway and others playing the minor roles. *Honest Hearts and Willing Hands* opened in Sydney on 30 June 1891 but was not a success there; later, however, it played for a creditable three weeks in Melbourne and then toured success- fully to Ballarat, Adelaide, Broken Hill and elsewhere.[128]

While in Melbourne Sullivan refused to fight another prominent Australian boxer, Joe Goddard, until Goddard had proved his ability by beating Sullivan's sparring partner and co-star Jack Ashton. This Goddard did, knocking out Ashton in the eighth round.[129] As Peter Jackson came from Sydney, Frank Slavin from Melbourne, and Goddard from Broken Hill, Sullivan had the sporting fans of the whole of south-eastern Australia demanding that he give one of the local fighters a chance at the world championship.[130] The Goddard/ Ashton fight was on Friday 2 October and Sullivan and Ashton's departure for America the following Monday, although planned well in advance of the fight, looked to the partisan Australian boxing supporters suspiciously like a hasty retreat, and a considerable amount of ill-will remained after they left. Sarah Bernhardt was in Australia at the same time, and typical of the critical reaction to Sullivan was the *Lorgnette*'s sneering comment: 'Bernhardt has the satisfaction of knowing that in Australia she hit harder than John L. Sullivan.'[131] A more favourable comment came from the boxing correspondent for the Sydney *Referee*, who noted that Sullivan had done nothing in Australia to justify the bad reputation which had preceded him and that, while the boxer was clearly out of condition, he still showed sufficient class to be a formidable champion if he would only give up the good life and settle back into hard training.[132] Consequently, this commentator's explanation of the Australian public's indifferent response to the tour ignored Sullivan's lack of acting ability and blamed the lack of real boxing contests instead: 'They had longed to see him in action, for of all the boxing people alive, none are so enthusiastic as the populace of Australia, and when they saw John as an actor they felt bad about it.'[133]

In America in 1892 Sullivan lost his title to another American, James J. Corbett, who also exploited his fame by becoming an actor. He seems to have been rather more successful at this than Sullivan and appeared in a number of plays beginning with *Gentleman Jack* in 1892 and including *The Naval Cadet* in 1895.[134] Corbett's manager and part-author of some of his plays was the major New York theatrical producer William A. Brady. In 1895 Brady began a correspondence with Bland Holt, who had been recommended to him (correctly) as an expert in Australian popular theatrical tastes. Some of Brady's letters, but unfortunately not Holt's replies, are held in the Holt papers in the National Library in Canberra. On 16 August Brady wrote:

I am thinking very seriously of taking James J.Corbett to your country next Summer, commencing about June 1st or 15th to give a series of sparring exhibitions only (not to attempt to produce a play,) but to become a portion of some local entertainments. Do you think this would be a good scheme?[135]

Holt presumably mentioned in his reply the unfavourable impression Sullivan had left behind him, because a later letter from Brady (28 December) was more cautious:

after he had made his appearance and the people had seen him, I might arrange for him to appear as a number in the Music Hall or between the acts in some theatre. You can rest assured that the impression that Corbett would make in Australia would be entirely different from that made by John L. Sullivan. The former is a very gentlemanly fellow. . . . He is also a very good actor.[136]

This tour does not seem to have taken place, either because Brady was discouraged by Holt's reaction to the idea or because he was unable to organise the tour before Corbett retired in 1896. Corbett did, however, tour Australia as an actor during the First World War.

Shortly after Corbett's retirement early in 1896, another boxer claimed as an Australian because he had trained and come to prominence in Sydney, Robert Fitzsimmons, won the world heavyweight crown.[137] Corbett came out of retirement to meet the new champion. Fitzsimmons was also what was disparagingly referred to by another boxer as a 'hippodromer', and his match with Corbett was long delayed, because, as the same commentator observed: 'They don't want to fight, because one will have to be licked, and the one who loses the battle loses all his theatrical engagements.'[138] When the two boxers eventually met early in 1897 William Brady, who was a member of the American Veriscope film company, arranged for the fight in Carson City Nevada to be recorded by several cameras. Fitzsimmons won and Brady, hoping to capitalise on the feats of the 'Australian' world champion (he was in fact born in Cornwall and fought first in New Zealand), instructed one of his employees, George Welty, to contact Bland Holt and to make plans to tour Australia exhibiting the film.[139] Welty arrived in Sydney with the film and a Veriscope projector in the second half of 1897. The film ran for an hour and a half, 'during which the 160,000 pictures that go to make up the general whole flashes before one's eyes, but so quickly that hundreds of them, so far as the organs of vision can detect, appear as one.'[140] The *Referee* quoted the veteran boxer Larry Foley as saying that 'nothing had ever interested him so much' and that 'the Sydney public should not miss seeing this latest development of the present century's science—even if some of them did not care for actual fighting'.[141] However, Brady wrote to Holt on 17 December: 'Am sorry to hear that Welty is not doing well with the Veriscope. I suppose your people are not very much interested in boxing and that is the reason.'[142] Brady's assessment and explanation are puzzling; the film had good reviews and reports of large attendances in both Sydney and Brisbane.[143] Films of boxing contests were frequent in the following decade, and included the famous Tommy Burns–Jack Johnson fight in 1908. Both Burns and Johnson appeared in vaudeville theatres before and after the contest itself.

Sporting actors served the interests of both public entertainments. Many sports were amateur, or at best poorly paid; sporting champions often had to rely on gambling on their own prowess in order to survive. Theatrical appearances gave them an opportunity to convert their reputations into cash. Most sporting appearances were infrequent, for the participants if not for the promoters. Boxers could not fight every week or even every month, and, as the above discussion of Corbett and Fitzsimmons shows, an occasional large crowd at a fight could not equal the regular receipts from a successful stage play performed six nights a week, or a sparring exhibition repeated nightly during a vaudeville show. There were also social benefits for sport and sportsmen: stage and film narratives gave sporting champions the chance to associate their athletic prowess with a heroic narrative. For a sport like prizefighting, which had a dubious official image even if enormously popular with sections of the public, this opportunity to redefine pugilism as noble and manly was particularly welcome. For theatre and film producers it was an opportunity to capitalise on celebrities who were more popular—particularly with working-class male audiences—than stage actors. Since the income to be gained from exploiting sport came from both contests and theatrical appearances, it was predictable that the two entertainment forms at times merged into a single conglomerate of financial interests.

The sport and drama entrepreneurs

There were other sound commercial reasons for capital-enterprise sports and theatre to be closely connected in Australian colonial society. The first of these was the association of both activities with the sale of food and, more importantly, liquor. This did not particularly concern those actor/managers of theatre companies who were only the sub-lessees of buildings, but was central to the financial resources of the permanent lessees and hotel owners on whose land most of the early theatres were built. From the start almost all the theatrical speculators were publicans: Robert Sidaway was a hotelier as well as the force behind Sydney's first theatre in 1796–1800;[144] Barnett Levey's three theatres between 1829 and 1835 were all built on the premises of his Royal Hotel, and at least one of the members of the syndicate which succeeded him, William Knight, was a publican.[145] In Hobart in the 1830s amateurs performed at the Freemason's Tavern and dancers at the White Swan Hotel, and there was a music hall at the Waterman's Arms and an amphitheatre behind Tattersall's Hotel.[146] As leisure entrepreneurs accumulated capital and erected theatre buildings independently of pre-existing hotels, they invariably included a hotel on the premises where audiences could drink during the intervals. This practice has been documented and analysed by the architectural theatre historian, Ross Thorne, who has also listed the legislation passed in the 1880s and later to prevent theatres and hotels being combined.[147] These restrictions do not seem to have been particularly effective until thirty years later when further legislation and then wartime restrictions diminished this close economic link.[148] Even so, advertising in theatre programmes could overcome the separation of theatre and bar; the programme for the opening night of the new King's Theatre in Melbourne in 1908 carried prominent notices for Farthing's Austral Hotel, with invitations to 'Come Next Door' and a reassurance 'Bell Rung Before Raising of Curtain'.[149]

The same connections can be made between sport and hotels. From the earliest years of colonial history sporting publicans were associated with many of the earliest races, athletic competitions, combat sports, hunts, ratting, cock-fighting, and cricket matches, and particularly with individual sports such as quoits, archery and billiards. As the sports historian, Trevor Arnold, has noted: 'Publicans were quick to see that these activities would make their hotel popular with the active sportsmen, the ardent spectator, and the prosperous gambler.'[150] In the 1880s and 1890s some hotels explicitly associated themselves with both sport and drama; a typical advertisement for F. S. Catherwood's Portland Hotel in Melbourne in 1891, described it as 'The Meeting House of the Multitude: Theatricals, Sportsmen &c.'[151] Fred Gunther, the business manager for the Dampier Theatrical Company in Sydney from 1885–87, married in the latter year and took up the licence of the Wheatsheaf Hotel near the Gaiety Theatre where the theatre company was based.[152] In 1904 he was still prospering in the same area, advertising his Surrey Hotel (possibly the same premises under a new name) as 'The Favourite Sporting and Theatrical Rendezvous . . . The Home of the Professional and the Sportsman.'[153] In order to be able to assert this connection, publicans such as Catherwood and Gunther must have been actively involved in supporting sporting clubs, donating trophies for competitions, catering for theatre audiences, advertising in theatre programmes, advising their patrons when performances and sports events were about to start, providing free refreshments for actors and sportsmen, and turning a blind eye to the organised gambling and prostitution which inevitably accompanied professional sport and professional drama, if they were not actively involved in those less-publicised aspects of commercialised leisure themselves.

By this time, however, the balance of support between hotels and the sport and drama industries had changed. Whereas earlier in the century the sale of alcohol was the base industry which supported sporting and theatrical ventures, by the century's end hotels were dependent on nearby theatres and sports stadiums for their clientele. In 1898 George Ramaciotti of the Sydney Theatre Royal wrote to Bland Holt complaining of poor theatrical business and adding 'I believe all the hotel keepers in the area are on their knees praying for Easter and Holt.'[154] Bland Holt had established himself by this time as the most reliable crowd-puller in Australian theatre, and Easter was racing carnival time.

From the 1860s, if not before, it was sometimes the same entrepreneur financing both sport and theatre—and often providing the catering as well. The major example is the ubiquitous George Coppin, who had roller-skating investments[155] in addition to his involvement with cricket and horses, his theatres and theatre companies, and who from his earliest years owned various hotels in Sydney and Adelaide.[156] Although now primarily remembered as a theatre manager, Coppin also speculated extensively in professional sport; in 1870 he financed the visit of an Irish sprinter, Frank Hewitt, who claimed to be the world champion, and promoted a series of match-races between Hewitt and the colonial champion John Harris at the Melbourne Cricket Ground and at the Friendly Society Gardens. Twenty-thousand people turned up for the first of these contests.[157]

There were many other good reasons for entrepreneurs to support both sport and drama; indeed, until 1930 it is possible to think of there being a single mass-entertainment industry, embracing sporting, theatrical (later film), and catering interests and investments, rather than seeing each as separate but occasionally overlapping ventures. Professional sport and professional theatre were characterised by a similar entrepreneurial instinct as to what would draw a crowd, and the same commercial *modus operandi*: advertising and organising publicity stunts to attract the audience; owning, building or leasing a theatre or arena to which admission could be controlled by ticket-selling attendants; providing the crowd with alcohol, food, and peripheral entertainments; contracting, accommodating and touring artists/sportsmen, their assistants and their equipment; discreetly providing for gambling and prostitution while maintaining good relationships with the police; and cultivating journalists and in some cases even controlling sections of the popular press to keep their artists' names continually in the public mind. Between 1890 and 1940 a number of promoters, like Coppin before them, moved easily through both the sporting, theatrical, and later film sections of this leisure industry. By the beginning of the twentieth century many were seen as sporting entrepreneurs also speculating in theatre rather than the other way round; an indication both of the growing financial resources available for sporting investments and the increased importance of commercial sport compared to commercial theatre. The sport and drama entrepreneurs included Frank Smith, a Sydney theatrical promoter who built a professional athletics track at Botany,[158] W. J. Howe, a football star, early film maker, boxing promoter and manager of Fox films in Australia;[159] James Brennan, a racehorse owner and bookmaker, who in 1906 converted the athletic hall in his National Sporting Club in Sydney into a variety theatre and set up the vaudeville circuit later taken over by the Fuller Brothers;[160] Snowy Baker, who was an Olympic athlete and boxing promoter, and who was also a film star and producer of films and vaudeville shows;[161] E. J. Carroll, who began with skating rinks in Townsville before moving into theatre and film exhibition;[162] William Anderson, who did the same, beginning in Bendigo;[163] Harry Keesing, first a theatre owner and then ·a boxing promoter;[164] George Adams, famous for his long-term control of Tattersall's Sweeps in Australia and lessee of the Sydney Palace Theatre,[165] and Rufe Naylor, a bookmaker and major sports promoter both before and after the First World War, who led a syndicate of sportsmen in the building of Sydney's Empire Theatre in the 1920s.[166] Small wonder then that Nat Gould, in his book written shortly after his return to England in 1895 after ten years in Australia, was able to inform his British readers that 'Most artists in the Colonies appear to be fond of racing.'[167] Nor was it only managers who diversified their interests: the New Zealand singer Frances Adler (later Frances Alda), is supposed to have financed her training in Paris, her subsequent stage career and her rather less successful theatrical management ventures by racing horses in New Zealand in association with her husband.[168]

Most prominent of the leisure entrepreneurs in Australia was Hugh D. McIntosh, who was a self-professed admirer of the British drama and sport entrepreneur Charles B. Cochran.[169] According to two flattering and not entirely reliable accounts,[170] McIntosh's first experience of theatre was in 1892 as a chorus boy in one of the spectacular pantomimes staged jointly by George Coppin and Bland Holt at the Melbourne Theatre Royal. McIntosh began his commercial rise to fame selling hot pies at theatres, racecourses, and prize-fight venues in Sydney; promoting professional cycling contests; and building the Rushcutters' Bay stadium where he staged boxing matches including the 1908 world heavyweight title fight between Tommy Burns and Jack Johnson. He also made a reputed £80,000 from the film rights to this fight, and both he and the fighters supplemented this with appearances at vaudeville theatres in Sydney and Melbourne.[171] McIntosh returned to the theatre more seriously in 1912 when he purchased the Tivoli vaudeville circuit after the death of Harry Rickards, and he also staged spectacular musical shows in legitimate theatres several years later. In 1916 he bought the sport and drama newspaper the *Referee*.

Even the ballet and concert hall became part of McIntosh's same commercial nexus. When the minor entrepreneur Claude Kingston wanted to bring the musician, Mischa Levitski, to Australia in 1921, he had to put up a £1,500 guarantee for the tour. He cabled McIntosh, whom he had never met and who had no previous experience in the 'high' arts, but who readily agreed to finance the tour.[172] McIntosh later became a major backer for the Anna Pavlova, Fritz Kreisler and Benno Moisewitch tours.[173] He seems to have been particularly conscious of class and colonial differences and craved both to rise in Australian society and to succeed in England; he saw his rise from sporting pie-vendor to ballet and opera entrepreneur as an upwardly mobile personal odyssey and discarded his lower-class interests such as boxing in order to finance his move into more prestigious management. At the peak of his success in the 1920s he leased and lived at Lord Kitchener's former estate in Kent, where his conspicuous consumption included a private cricket ground with a pitch laid with imported Australian soil so that he could entertain visiting Australian cricket teams and give them the chance to play on their own 'ground'.[174] During the depression he returned less successfully to sports promotion, while maintaining some contact with the upper-class world of the performing arts.[175] Peter Corris has described McIntosh as a 'promotional dilettante and a social climber'[176] and his career does show an acceptance of the orthodox division of sports and the performing arts into lower- and higher-class categories: from sport to theatre, from boxing to cricket, from vaudeville to ballet and classical music. By selling off his lower-class, highly profitable sporting ventures to enable him to speculate in more prestigious theatrical enterprises, McIntosh failed to protect himself against a ruinous bankruptcy during the 1930s.[177] Leisure capital was moving inexorably away from activities associated with social aspirations towards those entertainment forms which had mass popular appeal.

Displacements and divisions: gender, class and work

Divisions within the broad area of leisure entertainments were seldom openly acknowledged by the industry itself. The rhetoric of the production process proposed a simple model of the relationship between sport and drama and between individual sports and particular theatrical forms, since promoters did not wish to limit their potential total audience by advertising that their entertainments were unsuitable for, or unlikely to appeal to, any section of the community. Nevertheless, different entertainments were targeted principally at identifiable social groups within white Australian society— particularly those defined by gender and class.

A useful guide to gender and class divisions, as well as to a more complex model of the relationship between sport and theatre and the audiences at which each was aimed, is provided by the many sport and drama magazines which flourished during the second half of the nineteenth century and through to the 1930s. Most were modelled after the English *Illustrated Sporting and Dramatic News* (1874-1945), a major publication which seems to have been primarily responsible for popularising the phrase 'sport and drama', although earlier magazines such as *Bell's Life in London and Sporting Chronicle* (1822-86) and its several Australian imitations had a similar emphasis on sporting and dramatic reviews and notices. Many later Australian magazines also used sport and drama or a similar phrase to define their area of interest, which was usually a more general coverage of all pastimes and entertainments. Some of these magazines have been lost; there are for example no known copies of the *Sport and Playgoer,* which ran prominent advertisements in Melbourne daily newspapers in 1909.[178] Others survive in incomplete holdings in public libraries; those that specifically mentioned sport and theatre in their titles include *Melbourne Cupper and Racing and Theatrical Record* (Melbourne, 1876-77); *Australian Sporting News and Dramatic and Music Critic* (Adelaide, 1892-1909); *Weekly News, Sporting and Dramatic Budget* (Sydney, 1895); *Sporting and Dramatic Bulletin* (Melbourne; 1898- ?); *Sporting and Dramatic News* (Melbourne, 1904- ?); and *Australian Sporting and Dramatic News* (Sydney, 1928-30).[179] Others, particularly the two major magazines *Dead Bird: A Journal Devoted to Sport and the Drama* (Sydney, 1889-1916 under this and other titles), and *Hawklet: Sport and Stage* (Melbourne, 1895-1931), defined the field in their subtitles. Many other magazines featured sport and drama in more general coverage of 'Society' matters. The *Flag*, a Melbourne-based 'Australian Sporting and Dramatic Weekly Paper', began on 6 July 1895 with a particularly explicit statement:

There seems ever to be such an affinity between Sport and the Stage that it has now become a recognised union in all sporting papers; following the general custom of the universe the proprietors of THE FLAG have determined to devote a certain portion of the space to the details of the Drama and the Concert Hall.[180]

Even the *Bulletin* asked its correspondents in 1880 to provide information on 'matters connected with sport, the drama, and fashion',[181] and devoted space to sporting coverage, although it later emphasised political, literary and satirical subjects. The antithesis of the *Bulletin* was the Sydney *Referee* (1886-1939) which advertised itself in another theatre magazine as 'Australia's Premier Sporting and Dramatic Paper',[182] though elsewhere the 'and Dramatic' was often omitted. Amongst the *Referee*'s early employees was the major sporting novelist Nathaniel Gould ('Verax'), and its approach eschewed satire and politics in favour of 'elevating and recording the people's pastimes'.[183] Gould wrote sporting stories in serial form, several of which appeared also as plays and films. Both professional and amateur sports were covered, and the paper carried substantial theatre reviews which, however, betrayed its tendency to advertise rather than criticise, often verging on promotional hyperbole over the worst of productions. The *Referee* carried for many years the subtitle 'A Journal of Sport, Pastimes, and the Stage',[184] but directed its attention primarily to sport. Only the last page of each twelve page issue was used for theatre advertisements and reviews.

In 1916, when Hugh D. McIntosh bought the *Referee*, it and another magazine with an even more emphatic male emphasis were amalgamated. This other paper had begun as the *Dead Bird: A Journal Devoted to Sport and the Drama* in 1889, changed its title to *Bird O' Freedom* in 1891 and later the same decade became the *Arrow: Sport, Politics and the Drama*, though its political content was never significant. Throughout its existence under these three titles, the *Arrow* heavily emphasised sport, particularly racing and cricket.[185] The low profile given to football indicated its up-market aspirations, although like the *Referee* it had only one page devoted to 'Theatricals', and this was often cut down to allow for advertisements and gossip columns.[186]

This magazine's dominant tone was of the preoccupations and slightly *risqué* humour of a gentleman's club. The gossip column was for many years titled 'Between Drinks'; its serious columns were predominantly about sporting matters; it offered endless jokes about marriage and the trivial interests, irrationality, and vanity of women; and the theatre column, while it reprinted factual reports cut from other papers, put them in the context of the stage as a place where men could watch women (both on stage and in the audience) as sexual objects, and where women went to be so observed. In its second issue (as *Dead Bird*) it placed in one corner of the theatre page a sketch of a well-dressed young woman in a box at the theatre, with an anecdote underneath it which made it clear that she was there not to see but to be seen. In the opposite corner of the page another sketch showed a scantily clad dancer on the stage, with the caption 'What sort? Lend me your opera glass. Gad, I'll sit in the front seat tomorrow night.'[187] These sketches were re-used frequently in later issues without comment, though their iconography remained clear.[188] In other illustrations there was a strong emphasis on the female figure at play. A series of sketches of bosomy and leggy females covered a full page of each of several issues late in 1889: dancing on the stage, playing mock cricket, swimming and lying in the surf with their legs kicked up.[189]

The later *Arrow* aimed at offering as pornographic an image of women as the mores of the time permitted. In 1911 it put a series of 'strange-but-true' illustrated stories on the front cover under the title 'The Ways of the World'. In one, ostensibly dealing with the treatment of prisoners in Czarist Russia, the cover picture showed a pretty but bedraggled young woman in a tight-fitting and torn dress, handcuffed, bending over and about to be whipped on her back and buttocks by a cruel-looking Russian officer on horseback.[190] Women were also portrayed as mysterious and opportunistic gold-diggers. One story was titled 'Fascinating as Cleopatra. An American Girl's Remarkable Career. Her Influence over Men's Hearts Secures

Women and sport: playthings (*Dead Bird*, 30 November 1889)

Fortunes.'[191] In a later issue a cover story on 'Gaby Deslys' 'of Paris' suggested that her name had been added to 'The list of fair women who have caused the downfall of kings.'[192]

The other major approach was that taken by the 'Society' magazines; these usually aimed at a different market in their coverage of sport and theatre, and instead of sex emphasised fashionable behaviour and what they perceived as matter interesting to middle-class readers both male and female. Such magazines often had more comprehensive subtitles which included other categories as well as sport and theatre, such as 'Politics'; 'Satire' and 'Society'. This last always implied the capital-S meaning of society, and often indicated a more expensive format and a supposedly more refined readership. Many sport and drama journals came into this category; the Melbourne *Criterion*, 'A Weekly Journal of Society, the Drama and Sport, and General Review' announced its short-lived existence on 15 September 1892 with the words 'What! *Another* Society Paper!'. This kind of magazine sought a more equal balance between sporting and cultural reports and reviews than did the political and literary *Bulletin* or the predominantly male and sporting *Referee* and *Arrow*. A major reason for this was that their editors (and their backers) identified the sporting market as a predominantly male domain, and the theatrical world as being of particular interest to women, and the middle classes generally as a significant market with excess spending capacity and a particular fascination with overseas fashions and trends. Both class and gender divisions were particularly evident in these papers. The *Criterion* made explicit its male and female, 'equal but different' bourgeois approach with column titles like 'Club and Boudoir';[193] in a later period the *Australian Sporting and Dramatic News* (Sydney 1928-30) carried parallel columns for male and female readers such as 'The Owner Driver and His Car' balanced by 'The Goddess in the Machine—A Weekly Page of Motoring for Women'.[194]

Class differences and distortions were also explicit; to some extent these were between mass market newspapers which sold for a penny and which were directed at working-class male audiences, and threepenny 'Society' magazines which aimed at both sexes in the bourgeois family. Price however was not always a reliable guide to contents or approaches. The *Flag* sold for threepence and made claims to respectability by quoting Shakespeare (Cleopatra's 'Here's sport indeed') and describing itself as the first 'artistically illustrated' sporting paper offered for the 'delectation of the sports-loving public of Australia';[195] but it was unashamedly plebeian in its reviews of the racing melodrama *A Million of Money* and the farce *The Thoroughbred*.[196] Conversely *Today: Society, Drama, Sports, and Politics* (Melbourne, 1894) was a penny paper but took a condescending attitude to such popular plays. On 2 August 1894 it ran an editorial on 'Realism in Art' which suggested that *A Midsummer Night's Dream* was to some people 'far more "realistic" . . . than *Sweeney Todd* or even *A Million of Money* with its real water, real racecourse, real horses, and real nonsense'.[197]

In other respects *Today* was a typical sport-and-drama society journal of its time. For women it carried advertisements for French corsets and 'Fenton's Great Crockery Sale' and for men advertisements for hotels, boxing and 'lessons in the manly arts'. Typical too in articles was its strong focus on what were considered 'women's affairs'. Even the former radical feminist and later Theosophical Society lecturer, Mrs Besant, could be translated into a consensual gush of enthusiasm. *Today* commented on 5 July 1894 that 'Mrs Annie Besant will shortly be in Victoria. She is a remarkable woman in many respects, intellectual, eloquent in speech, with force of character and daring' but added: 'In spite of her brain, she is, or once was, very beautiful.' *Today* ran columns on 'The Modern Girl' ('she *will* speak when she's not spoken to . . . and has the presumption to hold views of her own, one of which is that a modest, unaffected young woman is almost the equal of any man'), attacked coarse male behaviour ('Every popular sport has its curse—and the barracker is the curse of football'), commented approvingly in articles like 'Gowns and Gaieties' on the fashionable costumes in Williamson & Musgrove's musical comedy *Ma Mie Rosette* and ran satirical sketches such as 'A Toorak Tragedy' which began 'Who would have thought that I, Beatrice Plantagenet de Courcey Hamilton . . . ' and concerned the heroine's debate as to whether she dared let out her corset 'at least an inch'. Like many other similar papers, *Today* managed to be both mildly satirical of the *haute bourgeoisie* and utterly committed to their lifestyle. This posture targeted middle-class and lower-middleclass women by presenting them with a possibly attainable ideal; they were presumed to be primarily interested in fashions, high society, gentlemanly behaviour in sporting men, and a construction of female independence of spirit which implied that no effort or sacrifice was necessary to achieve it. *Today*'s comment on 'The Modern Girl' concluded: 'She marries occasionally, and does not always elope with the butcher. Now and then she bestows some slight attention on her household, and instances have been known where she has displayed tenderness, heroism, and devotion under all circumstances.'[198]

The *Australian Sporting and Dramatic News* (1928–30) was one of the last magazines to use such a title, ceasing publication during the depression. Its approach was a logical development of that taken by *Today*, with pictures of Hollywood film stars and gossip about them replacing the earlier emphasis on Australian stage musicals. *Australian Sporting and Dramatic News* was a handsomely formatted and copiously illustrated magazine of light journalism. Its emphasis was strongly female, and it promoted self-indulgence, languid elegance, smoking and fashions. The cover was always of a horse-racing event or sporting personality, but the inside title page often featured a ballet, opera or theatrical star. Both male and female sporting pursuits were covered, but in a highly selective class-based way. 'Evils of the Rugby League Season' was one of its few comments on that working-class interest; indeed, the only football of any kind which it regularly reported was 'Varsity Rugby Union'. Women golfers were given extensive coverage, and substantial film criticism

The Australian Sporting and Dramatic News: a) horses on the cover and b) women on the inside title page (11 August 1928).

included approving mention of the Australian films of the McDonagh sisters, which were themselves 'society' dramas rather than the more energetic adventure melodramas of other Australian filmmakers. Feminism was again encouraged, as long as it was non-threatening and glamorous: an article on early women pilots was headlined 'Why Not a Women's Air Derby? A Cross Country Race Would Appeal to Almost Every Aviatrix.'[199]

The dominant discourses of the sport and drama magazines tell us a great deal about the ways in which writers and editors, and by implication sporting promoters and theatrical managements, saw Australian society. The pursuit of leisure displaced work from the centre of life, and trivialised social differences based around questions of class, power, influence and social control, by representing them as matters of taste and breeding. The editor of the *Theatre of Australasia* declared that he wanted to establish a journal free of 'the ordinary topics of the day'[200] and the 1886 *Referee* omitted the political and satirical sections of its 1880 predecessor. This enabled journalists and editors to identify particular class and sex-specific groups of consumers and to write accordingly, without being seen to be inciting sex or class hostility; and helped them to create limited and limiting (and therefore predictable) patterns of behaviour for individuals within those groups. Surviving images of such paradigms can also be found in early 'documentary' films, which had a strong sport and theatre/film content. An issue of *Australasian Gazette* in 1929 decided that among the most important events in Australia that week were shots of crowds queuing to see films at two Melbourne theatres, the marriage of a 'popular actress' Lorna Helms, and the casts of the plays *Rio Rita* and *The Flying Squad* engaging in a social game of cricket, with the handsome heroes playing and the actresses and the comedy males watching.[201] Actresses were still expected to be glamorous leaders of fashion and passive admirers of heroic sporting men, and taking an interest in sport was still proof that the theatre professional was a good citizen. The political events of the day were ignored and the realities of the 1930s depression—including the drop in attendances at live theatre performances—were by implication denied. The sport, theatre, and film industries could displace labour, politics and economics, when they so chose, from their paradigm of concerns.

In the selectivity of the sports, pastimes and kinds of theatre reviewed, the sport and drama journals reflected the gender divisions in Australian society more strongly than those of class. Both the mass-market magazines and the middle-class male journals emphasised the major spectator sports, popular theatre and vaudeville, and focused on action and adventure. The middle-class society magazines reviewed some of those sports, particularly racing and cricket, with a different emphasis; and gave more extensive coverage to opera, ballet, and musical comedy, noting in particular the costuming in plays and the fashionable dress of sporting men and women. They also covered minority female interests such as women golfers. Implicit in this selectivity was the assumption that men were interested in public affairs, adventure, gambling

The superior attractions of cricket: Freudians might make much of bat, ball, and neglected hoop (*Australasian Sketcher*, 15 October 1881).

Women and sport: Annette Kellerman (*Theatre*, 1 December 1910).

and physical action; women in the home, fashions, the emotions, courting and less physically demanding games with social appeal and a reduced competitive element. While some society magazines offered columns of particular interest to professional men (*Today* ran a legal 'missing word' competition)[202] most were obviously aimed mainly at the middle-class woman consumer. The working-class woman was excluded from this distorted image of society; she could either aspire to middle-class values or read a popular male-oriented sporting paper. In 1907 the *Arrow* published a cartoon 'Heard Last Saturday Morning' which showed a Salvation Army woman conversing with a broom-wielding female servant:

Salvation Lassie: Working hard to get to heaven?
Cissy: No; working hard to get to the football match.[203]

When acknowledged at all, the working-class woman was allowed to exist only as a spectator with the same interests as men.

National achievement: sports men and stage women

Within this deformed image of society as a whole, a strong emphasis existed on sport as an activity where Australian men excelled, and the stage as a place where Australian women had achieved national and international renown. Competitive sports were almost exclusively a male domain. While many women participated in sports such as golf, archery, cycling, croquet, tennis, swimming and steeplechasing, most did so non-competitively and, it was assumed, because they were pleasurable pastimes and because many of these games were associated with courting, rather than ones in which their individual excellence could be acclaimed. The sports historian, Helen King, has described this bias and the emphasis in early women's sports on posture, decorum and grace,[204] rather than on effort or achievement. The first female Australian national and international sporting champion, Annette Kellerman, did not come into prominence until the first years of the twentieth century. In 1902 she was also possibly the first woman to star in a sporting demonstration on the Australian stage;[205] but even Kellerman's remarkable athletic ability was exploited principally through gendered images, since her subsequent stage and film career was based on displays of her body in (for the time) revealing swimming costumes. Her early publicity photographs bear a marked similarity to the contemporary 'Poses Plastiques', a form of mild pornography in which actresses posed 'artistically' in body stockings.[206] In any case it had long been common to use sport as a form of dance to represent the female body in physically uninhibited movement; a pertinent example was a 'Lawn Tennis Vocal Ballet', staged at the Melbourne Theatre Royal in 1892 in association with the play *Bridget O'Brien Esq*; here traditional female qualities such as

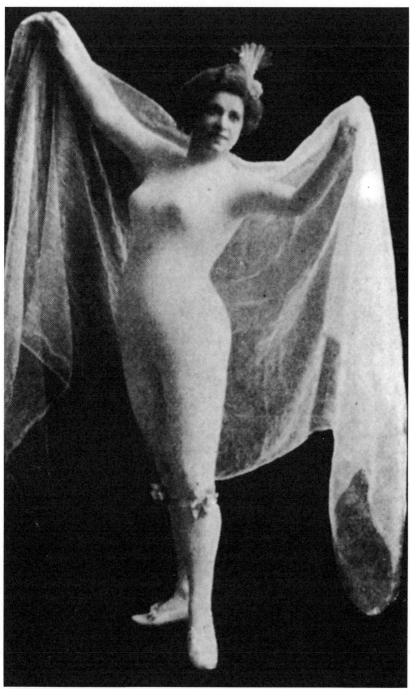

Women and theatre: Juliette Lotty's 'Poses Plastiques' in 1902 (CRS A1723 item 107, Australian Archives).

singing, dancing and display were turned to a sporting subject associated with courtship and middle-class leisure.[207] Putting a woman athlete like Annette Kellerman on a stage (or a film screen) invited a very different interpretation from that assumed for a male boxer or rower.

Playing or performance spaces imposed on any event occurring within them specific but quite different paradigms of possible meaning. The sporting field was considered a place where men could achieve excellence and where women were encouraged to watch;[208] the stage was a place where women could excel and be admired by men. The celebration of theatrical 'stars' was heavily weighted in favour of women. In 1905 the *Australasian Stage Annual* published an illustrated booklet of 'Favourites of the Footlights' which included twenty-two actresses and two men.[209] While male actors (particularly visiting stars) were, of course, prominently publicised, most were acclaimed as theatrical managers as well as performers.[210] More importantly, a number of Australian actresses and singers had achieved success in London, whereas few expatriate Australian male actors had gained more than minor roles on the English stage. This made the stage a place associated with international female achievement, just as the sporting field was associated with male Australian nationalism. In 1891 the journalist Pat Finn published his *Australian Theatrical, Football, Cricketers and General Sporting Songbook*; it contained lyrics he had written and claimed had been widely sung in 'theatres, music halls, hotels, etc.' in Melbourne.[211] In the first of these, 'The Daughters of Australia', Finn celebrated Australian actresses without mentioning any male actors:

> AUSTRALIA has something to boast in her girls,
>   Who've shown us their genius and worth,
> For we've some of the purest and sweetest and best
>   That e'er graced the fair face of earth.
> Yes, the girls of Australia all over the world
>   Have earned reputations widespread,
> And while praising the living—we must not forget
>   That Australia owes much to her dead.
>
> CHORUS: And while praising the living—we must not forget
>   That Australia owes much to her dead.

The song then went on to acclaim Julia Matthews ('She was known . . . all over the world'), Nellie Melba ('in London at present the rage'), Nellie Stewart ('search the world through you'll find few to surpass') amongst others.

In a second song, entitled 'Australian Sport' and possibly sung to the same tune, Finn paralleled the actress's achievements by praising Australian sportsmen:

> AUSTRALIA has cause to be proud of her sons
>   Who boast of the land of their birth,
> Which even the stranger is forced to confess

> The dearest of spots upon earth.
> Then forward Australia, you're still to the fore,
>   And long may your praises resound,
> For I ask ye again, though I ask ye in vain,
>   Oh! where can her equal be found?
>
> CHORUS: For I ask ye again, though I ask ye in vain,
>   Oh! where can her equal be found?

Later verses celebrated the international successes of Australian scullers, cricketers, and boxers.

Although deliberately similar in rhythm, rhyme and overall purpose, Finn's two songs differ in tone. The first is gentle, with elegaic chorus repetitions; the second assertive, with an argumentative, boasting chorus. This attitude to male sportsmen and female actors was also expressed in another piece of popular chauvinism, a song 'Australians for Sport' sung by Frank Corkling at the Brisbane Theatre Royal in 1905.[212] In four verses and a chorus this song concentrated on the achievements of sportsmen, with one verse including the two lines:

> On Opera and stage,
> Her daughters [are] the rage
> They're Queens of the Song and the Hall;
> They're Queens of the Song and the Hall.

Here the inclusion of women and theatre was a token addition to an overwhelming emphasis on men ('her sons hold the fort . . . The sons of Australia stand first on the roll . . . Her sons are in front of the ruck . . .') and on their national and international sporting successes; specifically mentioned were athletics, cricket, football, swimming, rowing, racing, shooting, cycling, boxing and billiards. Australian society was seen by such chauvinist writers as gender-divided, but providing opportunities for both men and women to achieve personal fame and to bring honour to their country. However, for Finn stage achievements were associated with traditional 'female' virtues: grace, beauty, the emotions; sport with 'masculine' traits: strength, determination, the will to win. For Corkling there was also a strong bias towards sporting success which he assumed society at large would see as more important than dramatic fame. Here again gender divisions—seen as natural and inevitable—were more strongly emphasised than class divisions, which were potentially divisive and which were therefore subsumed into a deliberately undifferentiated group of sports in which Australian men had achieved fame. It may not be going too far to suggest that the increasing allocation of theatre (both economically and culturally) into the category of 'women's activities' was a factor in its marginalisation and decline in the early twentieth century, and its re-emergence through paternalistic government subsidy in the 1950s.

The commercial live theatre industry in Australia collapsed suddenly in 1930–31 under the triple pressures of the financial depression, a double tax in some states on entertainment, and the mass introduction of talking pictures. The economic link between 'sport and drama' was consequently broken and seems never to have been reconnected. The Australian feature film industry in the same post-depression period did experiment with putting roller-skating rinks and bowling alleys in empty cinemas, but was never strong enough to significantly rebuild conglomerate interests. The amateur theatres had neither the financial resources nor the desire to include sport in their activities, and the few surviving professional theatre companies (particularly the J. C. Williamson organisation) had few sporting links—though this was less true of the vaudeville circuits, and it is interesting to note that the contemporary circus entrepreneur Michael Edgley has significant sporting investments. The subsidised drama industries after the Second World War (the theatre from the mid-1950s, film from c.1970) were established in social and economic conditions very different from those which had prevailed before 1930. In examining the celebratory and interrogative traditions of Australian sporting drama therefore, we have to take into account the specifics of the sources of capital and the marketing practices which contributed to their production, and the complexities of the social environment in which they were consumed, as well as considering their own intrinsic qualities of character, narrative and spectacle. Equally, we have to consider the far more critical view of sport often expressed in recent Australian drama, and the contempt reserved for theatre by many sporting enthusiasts, in the context of the changing financial and cultural environment in which they operate.

The First
Sporting Dramas
1866–80

Dion Boucicault's *Flying Scud* (1866)

It was the opinion of both contemporary and later critics that the sporting story entered the 'legitimate' drama (as distinct from the hippodrama) not by degrees but suddenly, in October 1866. The place was the Holborn Theatre Royal, the first brand-new theatre built in London since 1840,[1] and the play commissioned to open it was Dion Boucicault's horse-racing melodrama *Flying Scud; or, A Four-Legged Fortune*. 'The Greatest Hit of Modern Times' as it was soon to be advertised[2] opened on 6 October and ran for 207 performances, was taken off while still 'at the zenith of its attraction', and after a 'triumphant progress through the provinces' was brought back to London six months later for another long season.[3]

Although its debt to the various stage versions of Pierce Egan's *Tom and Jerry* forty-five years earlier is evident, reviewers without exception found *Flying Scud*'s subject matter to be strikingly original and, although Boucicault was notorious for his unacknowledged plagiarising of French and American plays, no subsequent commentator has pinpointed a contemporary source. For the subsequent history of the sporting story in English this is in any case unimportant; later writers invariably looked back to it as the primogenetic text both for plays and novels.[4] It codified many of the images and incidents which are still central to the paradigm from which sporting narratives are constructed, with the modern popular author, Dick Francis, being the latest in a long line of successful novelists, including (in Australia) Marcus Clarke, Nat Gould and Arthur Wright, who have exploited the genre. *Flying Scud* preceded by three years the work of the first known major sporting novelist in English, Hawley Smart, and had in the interim been made into a novel itself.[5]

Flying Scud was performed in Melbourne less than six months after its London opening and a month before its New York premiere. In all three countries it was a huge popular success and after the major city seasons was taken on tour to many other provincial centres. In Australia its impact was both immediate and enduring; *Flying Scud* continued for the next forty years to be the best known and loved of all sporting plays. It was revived at major theatres in either Sydney or Melbourne in 1868, 1880, 1887, 1889, 1890, 1892, 1894 and 1898; localised versions appeared in 1867-68 and 1878; and as late as January 1906 it was still vivid enough in popular memory for Max Goldberg's *The Rogues of the Turf*, staged at Sydney's Criterion Theatre, to be advertised as the greatest sporting play 'since the memorable production of *The Flying Scud*'.[6] Successful Australian plays such as George Darrell's *The Sunny South* (1883)[7] and Bert Bailey's and Edmund Duggan's *The Squatter's Daughter* (1907)[8] included substantial rewritten sequences from it, and part of its plot appears thinly disguised in three chapters (XLI-XLIII) of Rolf Boldrewood's novel *Robbery Under Arms* (1882-83).[9] Not surprisingly it also appears in Alfred Dampier's and Garnet Walch's 1890 stage version of that work.[10] These were just some of the more specific and major borrowings from a play which, a few brief scholarly references aside,[11] has been a forgotten event in Victorian popular culture.

The scene in *Flying Scud* most often praised by reviewers was the staging of a scene on Epsom Downs during the running of the Derby Stakes, a mile and a half flat race for three-year-old horses, run on the second day (always a Wednesday) of the summer meeting at Epsom. Since it was instituted in 1780 the Derby has been the most important event in the English racing calendar; from 1848 to 1891 both British Houses of Parliament adjourned from Tuesday to Thursday, and by then the event had become a popular festival holiday on a vast scale.[12] *Flying Scud* brought this sporting spectacle inside the theatres of central London, although the staging was nowhere near as 'realistic' as it had been in the hippodramatic presentations of *Tom and Jerry* forty-six years earlier.

In the first part of his Derby scene Boucicault re-created as a front scene a vast three-dimensional realisation of the artist William Powell Frith's

The sporting society: W. P. Frith's *The Derby Day* 1856-58 (Tate Gallery).

famous panoramic painting 'Derby Day' (1858) in as exaggerated and vivid a form as could be achieved by canvas, paint, props—including tents and a carriage—and a large number of variety artists and extras. This spectacle must have been impressive but it was not the play's only novelty. What Boucicault asked for in his writing, and what the theatre's stage manager and crew were able to achieve in production, was a continuation of this scene using the full stage area and silhouette model horses 'in the distance' to represent as a visual sensation the Epsom Derby race itself. Although it is difficult to imagine that we would find this staging credible today, it was by all accounts a believable and extraordinary sensation for contemporary audiences and a thrilling finale to the Act.

However, the play's extraordinary success cannot be explained by reference to the sensation scene alone. The hippodrama theatres were still exploiting the possibilities of combining horses and other animals with narrative adventures; indeed, Astley's had staged the most celebrated and controversial of all horse dramas—*Mazeppa*, starring the American actress Adah Isaacs Menken—only two years earlier.[13] What has been obscured by Boucicault's own opinions and the bias of subsequent critics—who have focused on the spectacular and sensational aspects if they mentioned the play at all—is the fact that a number of contemporary critics in both England and Australia considered the play to be an original and extremely well-crafted piece of writing about the sporting world. The reviewer for the leading theatrical newspaper the *Era* considered that it was:

Breaking entirely fresh ground . . . the 'Turf' has never been so characteristically illustrated on the stage as in this piece, and the strong dramatic interest which pervades it will not fail to secure the sympathies of the lovers of English sport, and, at the same time, highly gratify those who care nothing for the incidents which excite the attention of the 'Sporting World.' We are hurried on through this justly-named 'racing' drama without the least slackening of the reins of imagination . . . (7 October 1866)

It foregrounded a highly attractive view of the life, work and language of the racing community, and provided its audiences with an engrossing (and, in 1866, original) story about a young hero who wagers his wealth and happiness on the outcome of a horse race. The critic for the London *Times* went as far as to suggest that *Flying Scud's* storyline had contributed far more to the play's success than the sensational race scene:

As a specimen of stage realism, the Derby-day, considered simply as a picture, cannot be compared for a moment with the view of Charing-cross and the fire in the *Streets of London*, or the Telegraph-office in the *Long Strike* . . . But of the skill [of the dramatist] shown in enlisting the sympathies of the audience on the side of the old jockey as the side of right and in giving the most amiable regard to his affectionate pride in the horse, there can be no doubt. (8 October 1866)

When the play appeared in Melbourne, *The Australasian's* James Neild, a literary aficionado who was often condescending towards Boucicault's work, described the dramatic climax to the second Act (the Derby scene) as a moment when 'you can hardly help feeling some of that electric kind of emotion which only now and then is possible in the theatre'.[14]

The storyline, staging, ideology and influence of *Flying Scud* are seminal to an understanding of the paradigm of sporting drama as it subsequently evolved, as well as being an outstanding example of mid-century popular dramatic craftsmanship. It was the first successful attempt to combine the spectacle representation of a sporting event with a dramatic sports-based story and, as Boucicault's first biographer Townsend Walsh noted, it spawned dozens of blatant imitations during the next fifty years.[15] *Flying Scud* itself has survived in a number of different versions; the two examined here are the Lord Chamberlain's copy of the original 1866 play (the basis of all the subsequent Australian productions), and an extensively restructured and expanded American version dating from a significantly later but unknown year.[16] In both, Act I culminates in a will-reading scene which restores a country estate to the son of the original landowners, but at this point the plots diverge. In Act II of the original play the horse Flying Scud survives nobbling attempts to win the Epsom Derby and Act III develops a new plot: the villain attempts to cheat the hero in a game of cards, is exposed by the hero's friend, and a duel is fought on Calais Sands by moonlight. It appears that Boucicault at first closely followed the structure of Moncrieff's *Tom and Jerry* (where cheating in a game of cards leads to the final resolution), and failed to realise the dramatic impact the sporting section of his story would have. By placing the Derby scene at the end of Act II he effectively split his play in half. *The Times* noted with evident puzzlement in its review of 8 October that only the second of the four Acts was concerned with horse racing, and that Acts III and IV were so loosely connected to the sporting plot as to be 'almost distinct' from it. Revisions to the American and several other versions bring the duel forward to the end of Act II and place the Derby Day at the end of Act III, delaying the great sensation scene and giving a better shape to the play overall. Audience and critical response to the early performances, it would appear, helped reconstruct the play to allow for an imagined world entirely dominated by horse-racing.

Although it is only necessary here to consider in detail the narrative structure of the second 'sporting' act of the play, the frame provided by the opening scenes is an essential key to the play's location in the social mythology of the 'country and city' genre. *Flying Scud* begins in 'Love Lane, near Doncaster' with a cottage shown 'embowered in shrubbery' and a water pump.[17] It is a dream of a lost rural simplicity; a pastoral for city dwellers. The south Yorkshire setting also takes the audience directly to the centre of the horse-breeding industry and to that part of the country where the cult of the horse was most intense, as the sporting journalist Henry Hall Dixon ('The Druid') noted in 1856:

A blood horse . . . has always been the idol of Yorkshiremen, who were the first
to chronicle his deeds; and attendance on his race-course levees is an honest, broad
bottomed custom which they will never resign.[18]

Most of the major characters are rural Yorkshire men and women, and the
villains are London-based men. The horse Flying Scud's journey from
Yorkshire's Doncaster to London's Epsom Downs, and his master's
journey from the farm stable to the city gambling club, expresses even more
clearly than *Tom and Jerry* the 'country and city' genre; it is also a pattern
which Australian audiences would recognise later in locally generated
narratives as being the symbolic opposition of bush and city: honesty,
decency, and noble productive toil versus deceit, immorality, and unproduct-
ive financial speculation.

Each of the Acts of the play deals with a struggle—for control of the country
estate, for victory in the Derby, at a gambling club, and, throughout the play,
for the love of the heroine—between the hero, Tom Meredith, and the principal
villain, Captain Grindley Goodge. Tom is, in fact, the Jerry character—the
country son of a squire—from Egan's narrative, and from this time forward
a large number of sporting plays gave the name of Tom to the character of
a country-bred young man discovering the pleasures and corruptions of city
life. This association possibly came originally from Henry Fielding's novel *Tom
Jones* (1749), and similar 'Tom' characters appear in many stories during the
next two centuries from Jane Austen's *Mansfield Park* (1814) to Somerset
Maugham's short story 'The Ant and the Grasshopper' (1921).

Goodge is a 'thoroughbred, heartless, sporting character' (p.3); a middle-
class city gambler indifferent to the traditions and responsibilities of the country
squire. The opposition is both between country and city and between new
money and old: we are informed through retrospective dialogue in the first
scenes that years earlier Tom's father gambled away the estate through his
passion for racehorses, and was replaced as squire of 'Nobbly Hall' by his
own groom, Goodge's uncle. Tom is merely a poor tenant farmer, and when
the play begins the new squire has just died, and Goodge, expecting to inherit
the property, has assumed control and ordered Tom off the estate. Both men
want to marry Katey Rideout, the orphan granddaughter of the play's greatest
character, an old retired jockey called Nat Gosling. In the first Act Goodge
manages to compromise Katey (according to the moral logic of Victorian
narratives) by locking her in a stable with him; the subsequent misunderstanding between her and Tom is not resolved until the end of the play.

Flying Scud gets a major comic dimension, and complicates its narrative
line, with a number of vivid but unnecessary characters and a sub-plot. There
are three other villains or 'legs' (leg: a swindler; *OED*); together, as Nat Gosling
observes, they make a 'quadruped . . . and the heap o' money they've run away
with!' (p.5) They consist of an Irishman (Colonel Mulligan), a Frenchman
(Choisir), and a Jew ('Mo' Davis). The shift in capital from the aristocracy
to the middle classes is the subject of the sub-plot: Mulligan and Davis are

parasites on the fortune of a young Lord, Cecil Woodbie, who is in love with Mulligan's niece, Julia Latimer. Julia is an 'adventuress' used by Mulligan to snare rich young men's hearts while he fleeces their pockets. Lord Woodbie is an immature gull at the mercy of swindlers and the excesses of passion; the role's comic dimension was emphasised by the usual casting of a woman actor to play it. The sporting world is represented by Nat Gosling and other jockeys including the comically overweight Bob Buckskin. The jockey roles (excepting Nat) were also usually played by women, although in the first New York production (1867) Bob Buckskin was played by a young American male called J. C. Williamson, then undergoing his stage apprenticeship at Wallack's Theatre.[19]

The play's two memorable roles were the comic hero, Nat Gosling, who manipulates the action, and the comically inept and cowardly villain, 'Mo' Davis. *The Times*, the *Illustrated London News* and *Bell's Life in London* all commented on the brilliance of Nat's character: 'compounded of intrinsic goodness and of as much honesty as is compatible with a strong infusion of low cunning' as *The Times* put it.[20] The role was one of the great acting challenges of the nineteenth-century stage, and gave central importance to an eccentric working class character rather than to more orthodox romantic heroes and heroines.

'Mo' Davis, who is owed a great deal of money by Goodge, finds out early in the play that Goodge is not to inherit the estate after all. His reaction to the news is typical of this unusual stage Jew: 'Oo - oo, jumpin' Moses! I'm in a hole! . . . There's no trustin' nobody; even ven a fellow's dead and buried, he's down on you in his will.' (p.8) Davis's exclamation 'jumpin' Moses!' became the character's signature wherever the play was performed; in Australia the *Bulletin* noted in 1886 that Henry R. Harwood (who had played the role in Melbourne nearly twenty years earlier) had made the phrase 'a bye word throughout Australia'.[21]

Three other incidents in this first Act need mention. The first concerns the Julia Latimer/Cecil Woodbie sub-plot. Julia, who in spite of her temptress role genuinely loves and 'mothers' Woodbie (her redemption at the end of the play is repeatedly anticipated), manages to draw him away from the billiards table where his money is rapidly disappearing into her uncle's pockets. However, knowing her own 'unworthiness', she rejects his proposal of marriage, and Mulligan enters, billiard cue in hand, to hear news that astonishes him:

Julia: . . . I cannot cheat him in love as you do in play. I will not enter his family like a thief. (*Exit*)

Mulligan: Once in, who cares how you got there? Refuse £27,000 a year! There's no counting on a woman. When you've won the game, she'll revoke and play the divil wid the finest combination. (*Exit.*) (p.11)

Here the conventional idea of love as a game is beginning to be developed into the extravagant conceit based on sporting terms which became a regular set-piece in many later plays.

The second motif which was codified and often copied does not appear in the 1866 script but found its way into both American and Australian productions at some point. In a scene in the stables Nat Gosling offers advice to the young jockeys by describing in a long moral speech how he once lost a race by being foolishly tempted to drink champagne beforehand, and vividly recreates the excitement of the race itself. The 'race-call' speech was a stock solo turn in plays well before *Flying Scud* was written; Boucicault had penned one of the best of its kind for Lady Gay Spanker in his earlier *London Assurance* (1841).[22] But sometime after the opening season Boucicault added a second race-call speech (by the corpulent Bob Buckskin) of how he too once lost a race; the point of the story is comic, not moral:

On we went, foot to foot, muscle to muscle, head to head, neck to neck, nose to nose; and then Vixen gave such a look as never came out of a horse's eyes before, and put out her tongue and won. Won by a tongue. (p.171, American script)

In later years the stable scene was sometimes performed as a variety turn at matinee benefits, and concluded with the jockeys dancing a hornpipe—a sequence in the second Act of the original play.[23] In the revised script this scene adds little to the narrative, but contributes in a major way to the play's colour, atmosphere and characterisation. It celebrates horse racing as a noble pursuit; all the major male characters are obsessed with equine matters and the audience is assumed to share that obsession sufficiently for Boucicault to hold up the narrative development for over ten minutes. The sequence builds to Flying Scud's entrance (p.174, American script); Boucicault crafted his play to give the horse a first entrance worthy of star billing. The animal used on stage had to stand up to the expert gaze of the many who were both racegoers and play-goers and was invariably a real racehorse, often hired from a prominent stable and advertised as such.[24]

The final matter of interest from this first Act is the way in which the will-reading scene invokes both cross-class sporting camaraderie and fulfils a reactionary fantasy in which the social dislocations and financial shifts of the industrial revolution are reversed. The squire in his will acknowledges his humble origins by referring to Nat as his 'friend' and leaving him £300 (p.16); the later version of the play added to this £500 for a school for 'children of old jockeys', £300 for a hospital, and £50 for the members of the Jockey Club to spend on 'a good dinner' (p.182, American script). The 'new-money' squire also acknowledges that his usurpation was a mistake:

Quail [the lawyer]:	'To Thomas Meredith, the son of my old master, I wish to restore the property I made out of his father, and therefore I give and bequeath to him my estate at Nobbley [sic] Hall, together with all my property of every kind therein and thereon, especially the horse I call Flying Scud, with all his engagements, which I enjoin the said Thomas Meredith to fulfill.'
Goodge:	Then what is left to me?
Quail:	Nothing; your name is not mentioned in the document. (p.16)

Aristocratic breeding and tradition triumph over blood; history is wound back several generations to a mythic age of harmony, stability and benevolent patronage where education, health care and good fellowship are all wisely and generously provided for by the good squire.

The second Act takes place about six months later; Flying Scud has in the meantime won the Criterion Stakes and is now favourite for the Derby. Tom, fashionably dressed but unhappily estranged from his fiancee, is seen in London in Hyde Park; the location, as in many country and city plays, indicated the country boy gone astray and succumbing to the corrupt pleasures of the town: high-class prostitution and gambling in the nearby clubs. Two episodes constitute the Act: firstly the villains' attempts to bribe Bob Buckskin and later Nat Gosling; both jockeys accept the bribe money but then outwit the villains' attempts to drug Flying Scud. Nat does so in a pre-dawn scene in which he swaps Flying Scud to another stable so that Goodge and Davis dope the wrong horse. All the dramatic elements of that most obligatory of sporting story episodes, the nobbling scene, are brought together, possibly for the first time: the stealth and suspense of various groups of plotters moving around in the dark avoiding one another; the eerie striking of a village clock in the distance,[25] whistles and other spine-tingling sound effects; the movement of horses and whispered words and commands; and the attempted nobbling itself. One atypical element is a long speech which links the first half of the scene (the substitution of one horse for the other) to the second (the nobbling). It is another race-call speech and became the most famous 'claptrap' in the play. As Nat waits for the nobblers to arrive he strokes and grooms Flying Scud's head while the horse peers out over the stable door, and whispers to him how he wants him to run the race for the Derby: 'Four lengths ahead; time—quickest on record. There's your programme; if ye fall short on it, never put your nose in my face again' (p.30). The wrong horse is then brought on stage and drugged in full view of the audience. (The horse used would have been trained, as many animals in hippodramas and circuses had been, to 'collapse' on cue.)

The Derby Day scene on Epsom Downs concludes the sporting section of the plot. It begins with a Front scene which must have used a backcloth considerably further upstage than the curtain line or first grooves, because the stage space available had to contain:

Crowds of persons, such as frequent races. Thimble Riggers, Negro Minstrels, Vendors of Race Cards and Dolls, Vans, Tents, Drags, Costermongers' carts, &c. WOODBIE and JULIA in a Phaeton. Negro Minstrel song is going on. Enter Gipsey who tells JULIA's fortune, while two Cockneys are taken in by the Thimble Riggers. Enter Policemen. The Thimble Riggers decamp. This scene should maintain several natural episodes in pantomime during the dialogue. (p.31)

The scene is a spectacular indulgence. In this unscripted opening and again after a short dialogue section, the story is held up while variety acts are performed. The major English race meetings of the mid-nineteenth century were closer in spirit to fairs and carnivals than to today's weekly races; variety and sideshow entertainments were common and numerous. The painter W. P. Frith noted in his autobiography: 'Gambling tents and thimble-rigging, prick in the garter and the three-card trick had not then [1858—the year of his painting] been stopped by the police.'[26] Boucicault's stage directions duplicate the major elements of Frith's 'Derby Day': in the painting a tent and thimble-rigger's stand are on the left, while on the right a gipsy woman offers to tell the fortunes of a lady in a carriage. Elsewhere in less prominent parts of the painting are many details mentioned in the stage directions, but the acrobats in the centre of the painting are initially replaced on the stage by a negro minstrel troupe (in the American expansion of this scene the acrobats appear later) and a stage policeman—the play's most famous cameo role[27]—attempts to impose order on the scene. Groups of supernumeraries repeatedly charge across the stage, starting bells ring, and the dialogue for the major characters is written in short staccato sections consistent with shouting over what must have been a scene dangerously close to being out of control:

Mo [Davis]:   Yes, but Flying Scud is—is—
Goodge: What, man? Speak! [*A cheer outside*]
Mo: You hear! He is as clean as I am—cleaner—nothin' the matter wid him. We're done! (p.32)

Goodge and Davis leave in desperation to try to repair their error. Nat and Tom enter excitedly, with Nat observing that: 'the old blood begins to tell inside me; my werry back gets lithesome, and I feel the jockey amovin' in me strong'. This is prophetic, for Bob comes running in with distressing news—Flying Scud's jockey is ill. Goodge, having failed to nobble the horse, has managed to drug the jockey: 'I just took a small drain of brandy as a gent offered me— werry kind he was—and a moment arter I couldn't keep my saddle' (p.33). It is at this point that the critic James Neild began to feel 'that electric kind of emotion'; indeed most critics singled it out as the play's dramatic climax:

Nat: Oh, dear—oh, mussy me! The warmints—they've ruined ye, Tom; and my beauty can't run.
All: Shame! Shame!
Nat: [*Suddenly*] Yes, he shall, by jinks! I'll double on 'em all yet. Peel the colours off that boy; gi' me his cap. [*Throws off his overcoat*] I ain't done it in five and twenty years.
        [*Enter KATEY*]
Katey: Oh, grandfather, what are you going to do?
Nat: Do, girl? I'm going to ride Flying Scud for the Derby. (p.33)

After this intense hiatus the scene bubbles on to its triumphant conclusion. The crowd cheers repeatedly, and to cover the scene change from the front

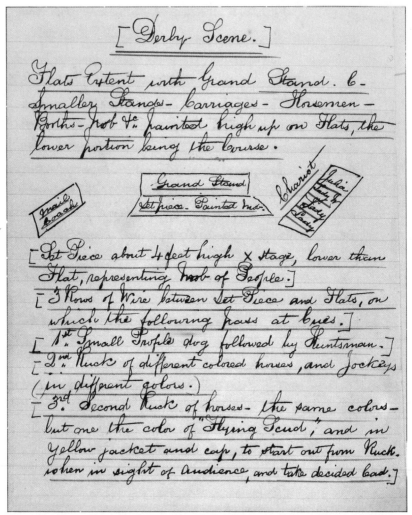

Stage plan for a *Flying Scud* production (J. C. Williamson Papers, National Library of Australia).

scene to the full stage setting a fight breaks out: *'during which a tent is knocked down on one side and the carriages, &c. are moved off at the other so that the whole course and spectators, grandstand, &c. become visible. The police enter. Order is re-established. Bell rings'* (p.218). In the distance the race is seen, with the crowd and individual characters shouting their comments, till near the finishing post 'The cloud of horses and jockeys appear' with 'Rasper' in white and 'Flying Scud' in yellow fighting out the finish:

Crowd: Rasper—Flying Scud—Yalla wins—Rasper wins—Flying Scud—White—
Flying Scud—Yalla—Yalla—Hurray! Hurray! [*Immense tumult. The Grand
Stand is seen to flutter with hats and handkerchiefs. The crowd surge and
sway in the distance; A number is seen to go up in the distance on the post.
Renewed cheers. The course is flooded with the crowd.*]
Tom: No.9! Flying Scud! [*Frantic cheers . . .*]

In all known stagings the scene ended with the real racehorse representing
Flying Scud being led on stage with Nat, exhausted but triumphant, still riding
him, while the villains retired to the corners of the stage, 'stamping with
vexation'. (p.35)

The opening nights of *Flying Scud* in London, Melbourne and Sydney were,
if the many reviews are an indication, occasions for extraordinary scenes of
public enthusiasm. On 6 October 1866 the new Holborn Theatre Royal, which
was closer to the working-class East End than the other city theatres, opened
to 'an enormous crowd . . . had the theatre been twice as capacious as the
largest structure existing there would have been a very great number of persons
. . . doomed to disappointment'.[28] *Flying Scud* began at 8 o'clock, and the
progress of the narrative was carried by the 'great character actor'[29] George
Belmore as Nat Gosling, whose 'quaint figure and countenance, and his general
get up', were 'very striking, and . . . he is never happier than in the little
bits of Yorkshire talk and his knowing allusions to racy subjects'. When the
Epsom Derby scene was reached *Bell's Life in London and Sporting Chronicle*
stated that the 'genuine sensation of the action took the house by storm and
secured the approval of the densely-packed audience;'[30] *The Times* went
further, observing:

To describe the excitement of the audience during this scene would be impossible.
Carried on by the course of events, they had so completely identified their own
feelings with those of Nat Gosling that they watched the progress of the mimic race
with an anxiety that could scarcely have been surpassed if every one of them had
actually put his money on Flying Scud. The shout from pit, boxes and gallery that
greeted the old jockey when he came forward as the victor expressed not only
violent approbation, but a strong sense of relief.[31]

One preoccupation which recurs in discussions of *Flying Scud* was the play's
ability to cause all classes of society ('pit, boxes and gallery') to identify closely
with the play's ideology as channelled through Nat Gosling's character.
Although the audience was not deluded into thinking that an actual race with
real racehorses was taking place, the technical means by which this illusion
was achieved were sufficiently convincing for disbelief to be suspended and
for audiences to believe passionately in the race as the apotheosis of their
identification with the struggle of good against evil. Achieving the illusion of
reality by technical means was not simply a matter of providing a thrilling
scene; it was transforming reality into a just and moral world.

The play's Australian premieres were anticipated by a combination of luck and good planning. The first fortunate and coincidental piece of publicity was Frith's 'Derby Day' painting itself which had been exhibited in Melbourne, Sydney and elsewhere during 1864 and 1865. The crush of people queuing to see it in Melbourne was claimed to have equalled that at the Royal Academy in London, where an iron railing had to be erected to protect the work.[32] A more carefully planned programming decision was that by J. C. Lambert, the lessee of Coppin's Melbourne Theatre Royal, to open the first production on St Patrick's Eve (16 March); a sensible date for appealing to the pockets of the Australian working class of the time. The London production was then approaching its 100th performance, and the advertisements claimed 'This piece has had an unprecedented run in London, and it is confidently expected will enjoy the same popularity here, where everybody takes such a warm interest in sporting affairs.'[33] A major racing carnival—the Victoria Racing Club's autumn meeting—had just begun, ensuring that many country people (squatters, selectors and hands) would be in town with money to spend on evening entertainments. The *Argus* said after the play opened that 'It was like continuing an excellent day's sport through the hours that had to elapse between the winning of the Hack race and bedtime.'[34] The Derby Day spectacle inspired the *Age* reviewer to pen several column-inches of copy, including:

The excitement in the theatre when the scene opened and disclosed the Downs was so intense and the applause so loud and protracted as each fresh figure in the motley crowd appeared, that the acting during the scene was nearly all dumb show. . . . The act drop descended on the tableau, in the midst of most enthusiastic applause, which was renewed again and again. (19 March 1867, p.6.)

A local addition was a dog loose on the track who was chased by the clerk of the course before the race started; another was the idea of bringing members of the audience on to the stage to swell the crowd for the race scene. Advertisements stated that 'Any visitor to the Dress Circle will be permitted on the stage to partake in the sports' and later that 'Gentlemen admitted to the stage during the Derby Scene from the dress circle and stalls'.[35]

While the Melbourne run of forty-seven performances may seem small compared with the London production's 207, it was an astonishing success for an Australian theatre of the day, equalled only by the Christmas panto- mimes. A much longer run could have been achieved, for the management seems to have underestimated the play's drawing power and had already booked other entertainments in April and May; *Flying Scud* returned to the stage on 25 May for a further three-week run. A fortnight before it closed, the *Argus* advertisement claimed that 66,000 people had already seen it;[36] Melbourne's population at the time did not exceed 200,000 of a total Victorian population of about 600,000.[37] The play was still a crowd-puller later in the year when it was revived once more for Melbourne Cup week and the visit to Australia of the Duke of Edinburgh in HMS *Galatea*.[38]

Within a year of these triumphs *Flying Scud* had become a legend; a topic of conversation for Australian society at large, with productions in most other major towns and cities. Consequently a number of writers and theatre companies capitalised on its popularity by borrowing, localising or parodying its highlights. The first was an anonymous Christmas holiday burlesque staged at the end of 1867 at the Melbourne Varieties. Called *Jupiter's Frolic; or, Racing Mad*, it was presented by Mrs Annie Bramley and forty-seven singers, dancers and acrobats. The advertisements in the *Argus* show the inventiveness of which variety artists in a sporting setting were capable:

> Incidents on the Flemington Racecourse
> Japanese Jugglers, Top Balancers, &c
> Bilboquet, the Mountebank
> Aunt Sally
> Punch and Judy and Serenaders
> Long Odds and Short Sweeps, our mutual friends
> Runge—Impair et Manque, or the winning colour
> Black legs, long legs, and other legs
> Races Races Races
> The Original Monster's Sweep and Betting Books
> Australian Lightweight v the World
> Presentation and Triumphant Ovation of the Winning Horse
> Great Flourish of Trumpets, and
> Local Song—'All Round My Hat'[39]

Two colonial melodramas were written based on *Flying Scud*, although there was little to suggest that any genuine attempt was being made to localise the story. The first was by the journalist and actor, Robert Percy Whitworth, who had theatrical interests in both Australia and New Zealand. In 1868 he moved across the Tasman to Auckland. Noting that *Flying Scud* had not yet been seen there, he quickly wrote his own version of the story and staged it at the Prince of Wales Theatre commencing on Tuesday 28 July 1868. He was capitalising also on a lucky coincidence: the New Zealand newspapers had just published the fact that Sir Joshua Hawley, an English Lord with New Zealand connections, had won the 1868 Derby with his horse Blue Gown.[40] Whitworth's play was called *Flying Jib; or, The Derby Day*. He claimed to have based it on various novels, but the plot described in the *New Zealand Herald* on 28 July 1868 is at least fifty per cent that of *Flying Scud*. Whitworth himself played Dick Brittan, an old jockey; the principal villains were a Captain Steel and his comical Jewish friend Solomon; there was a hungry stable boy reminiscent of Bob Buckskin; and the action of the play included an attempt to nobble the horse Flying Jib, the swapping of the horses, the drugging of the jockey, old Dick's decision to ride the horse in the Derby, and his inevitable victory. Flying Jib was a well-known Australian racehorse of the late 1850s,[41] but this was the only localised element in the story which was otherwise English in setting and subject. However, in staging the drama Whitworth cleverly arranged to use a genuine and very successful New Zealand racehorse

Dainty Ariel, and the season was a huge success.[42] He then took the play to Sydney, timing his season to coincide with Derby Day at Randwick, and between the Acts on opening night he arranged for the famous advertising doctor and racehorse owner, Dr L. L. Smith, to 'present the winning jockey of the Australian Derby with a handsome mounted riding whip, the jockey appearing in his Randwick colours'.[43] Whitworth's play, although it never became as famous as Boucicault's, was still being discussed (and presumably performed, although no record has been found of this) twenty-five years later.[44]

The second token localisation was *Flying Buck*, staged by a Mrs Reynolds at the old and run-down Princess's Theatre in Melbourne during Melbourne Cup month in 1878. The horse of that name, like Flying Jib, was an Australian racehorse of the 1850s; they (and several others) were named after the reputed greatest English racehorse of the age, Flying Dutchman. Flying Buck was associated in popular memory with a renowned sporting event which took place in Melbourne in 1859, when the Victoria Racing Club announced an 'Australian and New Zealand Champion Sweepstakes' to which horses from other colonies were invited as representatives. It was the first intercolonial test of horse-stamina and breeding, and the pride of all the participating colonies was at stake. The overland telegraph wires from Sydney and Adelaide (which had only been completed the previous year) were extended to Flemington racecourse so that the result could be instantly transmitted to those centres; 40,000 people watched as an unknown Victorian colt romped away with the event and, according to the Victorian newspapers, saved the 'national' reputation.[45] *Bell's Life in Sydney and Sporting Reviewer* received the result on the wire service and published a special late-afternoon edition with FLYING BUCK in 4cm-high letters printed across the front page.[46] The event and the horse were later eclipsed by the more enduring Melbourne Cup, instituted two years later, but would still have been well-enough known to be a crowd-puller in 1878. However, the *Flying Buck* play was simply Boucicault's drama under another name. It was well-staged and well-attended, but was in violation of Coppin's performing right and he attempted to have the unauthorised performances stopped.[47]

Flying Scud itself was revived for a third time in Melbourne in September 1868 where it again proved extremely popular and ran for three weeks; this was the original Sydney production which had been on tour to Adelaide.[48] Apart from Mrs Reynolds' pirate performances in 1878, there were no other seasons in either Sydney or Melbourne between 1869 and 1880. Australian theatrical managers, like their counterparts in England, seem to have been slow to realise that public interest in racing and other sports, unlike their interest in fire engines, railway derailments or ships colliding in mid-ocean, was an enduring obsession rather than an occasional thrill. Scenes from *Flying Scud* were occasionally staged as set pieces in their own right, thereby helping to keep the play in the public memory. Richard Stewart included the jockey hornpipe in a Benefit night he took at the Melbourne Theatre Royal on

11 December 1868[49] and in 1871 the stable scene with Nat Gosling's famous claptrap description of the Derby and the doping of the wrong horse was presented in Sydney at the Theatre Royal. This particular season is interesting in that the rest of the evening consisted of performances of *Mazeppa*, thus combining on the one programme parts of the most memorable and famous horse-dramas of the legitimate and hippodrama theatres. Clara Stephenson was the antipodean Adah Menken, advertised as performing a 'great feat of horsemanship hitherto unrivalled in the Equestrian hemisphere, on the bare-backed thoroughbred racing steed Clearpine, valued at £5,000'.[50]

The later revivals of Boucicault's play began in what can justly be called the Golden Age of Sporting Melodrama, beginning in 1879-80 and continuing until the First World War. In the latter year Coppin decided to restage *Flying Scud*; this was part of an aggressive (but unsuccessful) attempt to prevent Bland Holt, who had gone into management with the racing drama *New Babylon*, from becoming a serious rival to his empire. (This is discussed fully in the next chapter.) Although Holt's season had captured most of the market for racing drama, the *Flying Scud* season which opened on 24 July was received with the usual reports of glowing success and packed houses.[51] One of Coppin's business partners at this time was John Hennings, the stage artist. Hennings had designed the settings for the original 1867 Melbourne season of *Flying Scud*, and continued to do so for all authorised performances of the play until after 1890. Coppin also engineered a masterstroke of publicity by purchasing a number of the horses supposedly used by the Kelly Gang and recaptured after the siege at the Glenrowan Hotel only weeks earlier. Since there was no evidence that Ned Kelly or his companions had any horses with them at Glenrowan, Coppin was compelled to publish lengthy extracts from letters he had purportedly received in order to 'prove' that the horses were those stolen by the gang and used in earlier adventures.[52] The letters also testified to the horses' outstanding racing and cross-country abilities, echoing the association of outlaws with fast and hardy horses which was as least as old as Dick Turpin and Black Bess.

In 1887 the visiting Vivian Dramatic Company gave ten performances of *Flying Scud* at the Nuggett Theatre in Melbourne's Bourke Street East as part of a season of Boucicault dramas; not surprisingly their actor/manager Arthur Vivian played Nat Gosling.[53] In 1890 George Darrell, working briefly for the J. C. Williamson management, staged the play at the Melbourne Theatre Royal. John Hennings continued to supervise the visual representations which, as always, were warmly commended. The principal novelty in the production was the staging of the race, which was done with real thoroughbred horses in imitation of the race sensation introduced by Sir Augustus Harris at Drury Lane in the mid-1880s. However, the production was not a particular success, principally it seems because the actors playing Nat Gosling and Mo Davis were considered ineffective in their roles.[54] Other productions in Melbourne were by the Alfred Boothman company at the Alexandra Theatre in July

1892[55] and by Bateman & Maurice's company at the Theatre Royal in October 1898, opening on Caulfield Cup night. This last was the first Australian production to substantially restructure the play; it divided the scenes into five Acts with the Derby at the end of the play.[56]

Although it could be inferred from the above record of shorter seasons and minor managements that some of *Flying Scud's* appeal had dissipated with the years, this was not the case in Sydney. In 1889 the actor/manager George Rignold staged the play at Her Majesty's, with the visiting English star Frank Ayrton choosing the role of Nat Gosling for his Australian debut. This was undoubtedly the most successful revival, if the *Referee's* 'Footlight Flashes' column can be believed:

it opened to a perfect pack, the galleries looking like beehives, and the circles being filled till standing room was in request, and the stalls flowing over into the circles and back passages. It is many a year since we heard so enthusiastic a house, the telling points of the play being received with frantic cheers.[57]

The *Town and Country Journal*, which like the *Argus* in Melbourne considered itself upmarket from such popular utterance, grudgingly allowed: 'Of course, it was never considered as one which was likely to last very long. But . . . after the lapse of more than twenty years it retained no little portion of the attraction which originally recommended it.'[58] Interestingly, Rignold timed his season not to coincide with a major Sydney racing carnival but with Derby Day in Melbourne.[59] He staged it again in June 1894; John Brunton, Bland Holt's brilliant scenic artist, did the sets and the production again attracted 'an immense audience'.[60]

Flying Scud was still being performed in New Zealand and in provincial Australia by William Anderson's company in the first decade of the twentieth century, forty years after its premiere seasons.[61] Some critics attempted to explain the play's extraordinary longevity purely in terms of its staging of the Derby Day; a writer in the Melbourne *Lorgnette*, for example, observed that it 'may be said to have inaugurated, and been the predecessor of, a special class of pieces more or less dependent on outside accessories than on the intrinsic merits of the plays themselves',[62] thereby blaming it for the whole tradition of sensation melodrama which Boucicault had helped to popularise much earlier with plays like *The Poor of New York*.[63] This argument cannot be sustained; in any case *Flying Scud's* representation of the race had been rendered obsolete from 1885 onwards by the use of real horses in the Drury Lane melodramas staged (from 1887) in Australia by Bland Holt. As *The Times* noted in 1892 in comparing the Drury Lane play *The Prodigal Daughter* to *Flying Scud*, 'reality' had replaced 'realism'.[64]

In assessing the impact of *Flying Scud* on Australian society in general over a forty year period, and on the subsequent development of the Australian sporting drama, we are therefore compelled to look beyond the impact of its sensation scene, and consider instead its narrative as a complex ideological construction; one which different groups in Australian society were able to experience in different ways, yet with each group finding in its storyline the confirmation of social myths to which they were passionately attached. For the play's 'telling points' to have been received with 'frantic cheers' from 'pit, circle and gallery' for some forty years—from the immediately post-gold-rush, urban-growth decades to the years of Federation—its ideological framework must have been both resilient and adaptable, moulding and reflecting Australians' views about their deeper preoccupation with consensual social relationships in times of great social change. It must have tapped deeply felt beliefs which audiences held about society and the part sport played in that society; about audiences' conscious and unconscious concerns over past events and their understanding of them; about their hopes and apprehensions for the future; and about their belief that the sporting contest and the sportsman (and, in later plays, the sportswoman) offered instructive and adequate images of desirable social goals and social behaviour. As an ideological construct the play, its characters and storyline must have summoned up existing personal and public beliefs and moulded them into coherent and believable social myths. The staging of a horse race, with the ultimate triumph of the animal on which the hero's and heroine's fortunes and happiness depend, was only the moment of exultation, the wish-fulfilling finale to a complex and deeply felt set of circumstances in which audiences found themselves.[65]

Using sport as the subject matter for drama, at a time when field sports and games and the carnivals associated with them were undergoing an enormous explosion in popularity,[66] was Boucicault's point of departure in his quest for a text suitable to the new London playhouse; no doubt this was also prompted by his shrewd recognition of the theatrical possibilities of staging Frith's picture. There are echoes in the text (made much more explicit in the American version) of real-life sporting personalities and events. Several of Nat Gosling's traits are taken from the great mid-century jockey Nat Flatman, who sometimes rode Flying Dutchman, the greatest horse of his era whose career is also mined for details of Flying Scud's.[67] All the evidence suggests that Boucicault had researched his scenario carefully. The most likely source for his sporting story, characters and colour would have been 'The Druid', at this time the most famous sporting writer in England.[68] The Druid's real name was Henry Hall Dixon and his books included *The Post and the Paddock* (1856), *Silk and Scarlet* (1859) and *Scott and Sebright* (1862), all of which were rich in character sketches and anecdotes about this and other great moments in turf history. 'The Druid' was also fond of quoting the racing slang and provincial dialect of his subjects, who sometimes sound very like Nat Gosling in *Flying Scud*.[69]

Boucicault's borrowings were not just details of fact, legend, and verisimilitude. 'The Druid' and other English sporting journalists and novelists provided the ideological framework for Boucicault's storyline, and contributed directly and through the play to two major myths of both British and Australian society: the supposed superiority and moral purity of country over city life, and the consensus which these authors claimed was fostered between the classes by the interest and participation of all social groups in the games and pastimes of the village green. Charles Apperley ('Nimrod'), John Mills, K. W. Horlock and R. S. Surtees had pioneered an earlier kind of 'sporting' narrative in the 1830s and 1840s with novels which were mostly concerned with fox-hunting and country life. Surtees' *Jorrocks's Jaunts and Jollities* (1838), *Handley Cross* (1843) and *Mr. Sponge's Sporting Tour* (1853); Mills's *The Old English Gentleman* (1841); Apperley's *The Life of a Sportsman* (1842); and Horlock's *The Squire of Beechwood* (1857) were some of the major achievements of the form, although more representative of the genre perhaps were the serial versions of these novels and many other sporting anecdotes and semi-fictional stories published in the *Sporting Magazine*, the *New Sporting Magazine* and the *Sporting Review*.[70] According to a recent analyst, Virginia Blain, Surtees maintained an anti-romantic distance from his sporting characters, but the other writers saw one of their chief purposes as being 'flattery of the landed classes'.[71] Fox-hunting became a moral testing ground for masculine 'qualities': manliness, nobility, hospitality and good fellowship; those virtues which 'Nimrod' described as pertaining to 'the gentleman and the Christian'.[72]

The historian, E. W. Bovill, has pointed out that 'Nimrod' and Surtees accepted and proselytised a reactionary interpretation of the Industrial Revolution.[73] They rejected the evidence of neglect and exploitation which William Cobbett had presented in his famous 'Rural Rides' articles (published in the *Political Register* between 1820 and 1830) as selectively biased and for failing to distinguish between rural England *as it had been* and *as it was becoming*. In their view the traditional landowners had a 'keen sense of responsibility' towards their dependents and neighbours, governed the counties wisely and fairly, responded generously to genuine distress and were 'loved and admired' by the ordinary people:

The simple social structure of the countryside was held together by the sharing of common interests: love of the land, of field sports, and of the pastimes of the village green in all of which every class could play a part.[74]

This interpretation argued that it was the new-money, middle-class 'uncouth and vulgar industrialists' for whom 'money was the only yardstick' who were destroying class harmony and the old order by acquiring estates, packs of hounds and racehorses, abusing the privileges of high office (in particular their rights under the notorious game laws), joining exclusive clubs, and buying commissions in the Army for themselves and their sons (hence 'Captain' Goodge, 'Colonel' Mulligan).[75]

As the Industrial Revolution progressed the sporting novelists were able to blame all the abuses of the ruling class and all the resentment and resistance of the rural poor on the changes that were occurring. Their stories described how the traditional country values of a benevolent, leisured gentry and contented tenant farmers were being increasingly threatened by the new wealth of the merchants and speculators. They represented this threat in narratives which described as tragic this loss by the 'old money' class of its wealth, property and place in society; and they showed as ridiculous the efforts of the new owners to buy respectability and to legitimise their usurpation. Surtees directed his scorn particularly at the behaviour of the newly rich[76] and by the time of K. W. Horlock's *The Country Gentleman* (1862) the middleclasses have completed their conquest and the result is presented as a horrifying spectre:

country gentlemen are robbed and plundered of their old family estates, and consigned almost to beggary; and the money-made man, with his ill-gotten pelf, stalks through the halls of many an old ancestral home . . .[77]

Boucicault's most important ideological debt is to this group of writers; indeed *Flying Scud* begins by reproducing exactly the dilemma in which Horlock's country gentleman found himself in a novel published only four years earlier: Captain Grindley Goodge is stalking through the ancestral corridors of Nobbly Hall, and the old squire's son, Tom Meredith, is reduced to being a tenant farmer on Goodge's estate. Tom's restoration from 'almost . . . beggary' to his former place in society is a reactionary fantasy; a paean to the lost values of Merrie England. One of the most famous lines of dialogue in all melodrama apparently[78] was first used in the American version of *Flying Scud*; it serves to illustrate how powerful a representation of conservative utterance Boucicault's play was. When Tom surprisingly inherits the estate and the racehorses at the end of Act 1, he tells Goodge: 'quit the house and never darken the threshold of its doors again'. This phrase, later used to turn the erring daughter and her love-child from her father's house, had its origins instead in the context of a successful counter-revolution by a dispossessed country gentleman against a 'money-made man with his ill-gotten pelf'.

The Druid's books, like Horlock's novel written in the years immediately before Boucicault wrote *Flying Scud*, dealt separately but equally with racing and hunting subjects (*The Post and the Paddock*) and linked the aristocratic rural values of fox-hunting to horse racing—a pursuit which the urban masses were also able to enjoy, as spectators if not as participants. The sporting novelists directed the reader's attention to the behaviour and values of a rural Tory workingclass—the jockeys and trainers—who are represented as eccentric, wise, at one with the world and content with their place in society. The sporting writers identified the racing industry, its owners and its employees with the anti-democratic rural world of the eighteenth century where the annual picnic races brought all classes together under the benevolent patronage of the landowner-host; and consequently gave to the sport the moral superiority and communal harmony which they claimed for the social fabric of the countryside. In order to sustain these myths, however, it was necessary to offer a satisfactory explanation for the less savoury side of racing, about which both country and city sports lovers were well aware. Horse-racing, the major focus for the betting industry for most of the century,[79] was often seen as a low calling, tainted by blacklegging and all the sharp practices associated with the temptations of easy wealth. Life on the turf, as the *Illustrated London News* observed in its review of the first Holborn season of *Flying Scud*, had 'its immoralities and its compensations'.[80]

By applying the melodramatic opposition of virtue and vice to the mythology of country versus city and to the pleasures of horse racing versus the immoralities of unscrupulous gambling, Boucicault was able to associate all such criticisms with his four villains and their dissolute, self-interested and egalitarian urban behaviour, while retaining as fundamental dogma the essential aristocratic nature of country life and country sports. In the ultimately just and moral world of sporting melodrama it is only unsophisticated gulls like Lord Woodbie who fall victim to the turf's villains; such innocents must be protected by equally decent but more worldly characters. Julia Latimer is the most extreme example of this character type in the play, for she is the fallen woman redeemed by love; wise in the ways of the world yet essentially uncorrupted by it. She is both mother and lover to Lord Woodbie, distracting him from evil, guiding and admonishing him: 'Don't bet, you lose your money! Don't drink, you can't stand it! Don't smoke, you don't like it . . . do not affect vices for which you have no taste, nor mimic manners of which you are really ashamed'(p.9). Woodbie denounces Goodge for cheating in the gambling club; even he, in a crisis, shows his adherence to the ideals which they all share. The survival of decency and honesty in sporting behaviour—a model for social behaviour in general—is allied to the fortunes of the play's heroes.

In Australian society belief in this social model was if possible even more complete, for horse-racing was closely tied to the emergence of a colonial social hierarchy itself, as the sports historian William F. Mandle has pointed out:

The place of the major racing clubs of the capital cities in the formation of colonial elites, their feuds and recruitment, has been noticed from the early days . . . The combination of the raffish and the respectable that forms so intriguing a feature of horse-racing everywhere is of particular interest in an emerging society, with society being used in both senses of the word.[81]

Mandle also notes that Nat Gould, who wrote a number of Australian racing novels from 1891 onwards and whose role and status in colonial society was similar to that which 'The Druid' had occupied in England thirty years earlier, found horse racing in the colonies to be still characterised by 'the relationship between the landed class and the murkier world of the gambler'.[82] *Flying Scud*, which influenced later racing novels like Gould's just as surely as it did racing drama, makes the curious relationship between Tom and Goodge the linking element between each episode. It is inappropriate to ask why Tom, having banished Goodge from his house in Act I, continues to seek his company. Boucicault is examining a well-documented social phenomenon—the links between the gentry and the gambler—rather than presenting the experiences of individual people.

Another ideological link the play shared with Australian popular myth was the idea that the English ruling class needed to experience lower-class (and later, colonial) life before assuming high office. Tom Meredith's assumption of power is not simply a matter of lineage; his essential 'goodness' springs from his country origins and his years as an unpretentious tenant farmer and stable groom. Interestingly, little is made of the difference in social standing between Tom and the lower-class orphan Katey Rideout; it is not a bar to their marriage. The play's essential and successful ambiguity in an age which was negotiating a consensual path between aristocratic conservatism and democratic reform is that it can be read either as a reactionary fantasy or as a democratic triumph. Tom was born to rule but apparently has accepted his low station in life; both his breeding and his experience of humble toil contribute to the unstated assumption in the play that he will rule well. (In later years the young upper-class Englishman sent out for colonial experience—a stock figure in many Australian dramas —was undergoing a similar if more consciously short-term fitness trial.)

In its attitude to gambling *Flying Scud* stands half-way between middle-class moral attitudes which condemned it as the ruination of rich and poor alike, and later popular sporting plays where the hero's happiness depends exclusively upon the successful outcome of a race on which he has gambled all his assets. In *Flying Scud* gambling is an accepted part of the sporting world, subject to the same morality (and abuses) as anything else, and for Tom Meredith gambling on Flying Scud's success in the Epsom Derby is initially perceived as the only way in which he might recover the fortune his father lost. However, it is a more traditional plot motif—the will of the late usurping squire—which achieves this end. (Again, we can note the extent to which Boucicault seems to have found almost by chance the sporting narrative paradigm.) It is only when Tom foolishly gambles with Goodge later in the play and finds himself in the position of possibly losing his wealth and his estate, as his father did before him, that the outcome of the race becomes essential to the plot. But the play does not mention the fact that the happiness of all those employed by Tom, including Nat Gosling and Katey Rideout, is endangered by Tom's dissolute behaviour; nor does it exult over (or even mention) the considerable wealth the working-class Nat also must have gained through his gambling investments on Flying Scud. The sign of success in *Flying Scud* is good breeding; gambling is not used to promote social mobility but rather to prevent it. Luck always favours the well-bred.

Breeding in the context of all the major dramas of the turf is based on eugenic assumptions about both horses and humans.[83] Selective breeding determines

both who should win on the racetrack and who should live in the manor. Both
Goodge and Tom seek Katey Rideout as a wife; not because of her wealth
or nobility—she has neither—but because both appreciate her as they might
a good filly; as a beautiful ornament to their stable and as a potential breeder
of their fine young stallions. The impulse is eugenic rather than any
commitment to social mobility. As we might expect in a play bound
conventionally by Victorian respectability, Katey's status as a potential breeder
is not referred to directly but is obliquely suggested by the analogy between
horse and woman. It is not by chance that she is locked in Flying Scud's stable,
for throughout the play she is described, particularly by Nat Gosling, in
language appropriate to a blood mare. Comments on a misunderstanding
between Tom and Katey such as 'The girl is scratched, she don't suit your
book no more'(p.16) is one of many metaphors of this type, and Nat considers
that life would be a good deal easier if women *were* horses: 'you can give
a warranty'(p.19). Katey's surname Rideout is sexual innuendo but also
suggests her own horse-riding ability with its connotations of liveliness, pluck
and directness; qualities which the later horse-riding heroines of the Australian
stage were to exploit.

The play's narrative centres on the struggle between Tom and Goodge for
country estate, title, wealth and woman; but its style and part of its uniqueness
is determined by the play's two memorable characters: the comic hero Nat
Gosling and the comic villain 'Mo' Davis. Nat speaks on behalf of those who
found themselves in a contradictory and less favourable position during the
Industrial Revolution. This group most obviously includes the dependent rural
poor, but Nat Gosling's behaviour could be seen as dignified and appropriate
for any member of the working classes. It is here that the play, in spite of
its dominant conservative ideology, can easily be read as a radical reminder
to the Captains and Lords that they rule only with the consent of the ruled.
Flying Scud takes up as a major theme the dilemma of such employees—loyal
to old consensual, class-based ideals of social harmony but now forced to serve
unprincipled new masters. This is discussed early in the play, and Nat's 'honest
cunning'—evidenced later by his willingness to accept a £2000 bribe and then
trick the bribers—is presented as the only reasonable solution:

Nat: . . . when Goodge finds he has got a flier in his stable—a Derby crack—he'll
     give you the lease, or whatever you ask him, for fear you should blow the
     secret and spoil the odds.
Tom: But I would not betray my employer.
Nat: I know it, lad. But he don't believe in honesty, except what's paid for
     ad walorum! And that's where these sharp 'uns get licked. Leave it to
     me, boy.(p.6)

Later Bob Buckskin, like Nat, is bribed by the 'legs'; he too accepts the bribe
while thwarting their intentions. For these workers, respect and honest dealing
are not given freely; the master earns their allegiance by his behaviour. In sport,

as in other communal enterprises, there is an ideal to be aspired to and codes of behaviour which are only adhered to if they are mutually respected.

By making his new-money men exclusively villains, and by suppressing all criticism of the traditional ruling class and of Tom Meredith in particular, Boucicault is able to avoid admitting the worker's right to double-deal with any exploitative or neglectful employer. Instead, the play's overt ideology is based on a reactionary assertion of faith. Tricking Goodge and his companions is justified not only by their unscrupulousness but by their lack of noble blood or rural upbringing. If they had been of the county manor born and bred, we are asked to accept, they could not behave as they do. There is no particular reason to think that all working-class audience members accepted this reassurance, but every reason to see the enormous attraction which Nat Gosling's character had for them as being worthy of emulation in his approach to all forms of authority. Nat does not seek high office himself, but selects the squire to whom he gives his allegiance. In terms of theatre history he stands mid-way between the cunning but loyal slave of Roman comedy and the cunningly anarchic Good Soldier Schweik; in terms of nineteenth century experiments with democracy he represents a non-threatening argument for extending the electoral franchise.

Mo Davis, the cowardly and childish comic villain, is perhaps the play's clearest indication of the way in which sporting melodrama lightened the tone of melodrama generally. In an article on Victorian domestic melodrama from 1820 to 1870, Martha Vicinus has suggested that:

Domestic melodrama was the working out in popular culture of the conflict between the family and its values and the economic and social assault of industrialisation . . . a cultural response to the growing split under capitalism between production and personal life.[84]

It provided temporary resolution of conflict, for the villain seeks 'to destroy the family' and is rebuffed; traditional values are reasserted.[85] Sporting melodrama, beginning with *Flying Scud*, emerges just as the domestic melodrama began to decline, and takes up a new theme: it is not the family which is under threat but the wider social consensus; the key setting is not the symbol of the individual family (the domestic interior) but the symbol of general social harmony—the annual festival; the 'Olympic Games of the Island Kingdom' as the *Argus* once called the Derby.[86] When compared to the world of domestic melodrama it is evident that the weather has fined up and the symbolic values of indoors and outdoors have been reversed. The open field has lost its menace and its anonymity, and flowers grow around the door of the rural cottage which is seen from the outside, not from within. Most important is the change in the stature and function of the villain. In domestic melodrama the villain usually acts alone and is a serious and frightening figure; in *Flying Scud* Goodge begins in this mould but is quickly upstaged by his eccentric and more colourful companions, Mulligan and Davis, who specify and diminish his and their collective villainy. Sporting villains challenge the social fabric not as political radicals or as captains of industry but as those who prevent the pursuit of innocent pleasures; the 'love of the land, of field sports, and of the pastimes of the village green in all of which every class could play a part'. As in domestic melodrama the villains are rebuffed even though the solutions are conservative, consensual, temporary and based on chance; they fail to address fundamental questions about the control and abuse of power. Nevertheless in Nat Gosling's and Bob Buckskin's isolated acts of 'honest cunning' the possibilities of popular resistance are obliquely suggested. The balance of power has shifted back towards the masses.

We can only speculate on the precise reading by Australian audiences of this peculiarly English conglomerate of reactionary, consensual, agrarian, aristocratic and anarchic mythologies of society. Obviously there were major differences between the two societies; the Australian colonies did not experience an industrial revolution, although the memories of that experience would have been strong for many migrants. Nor were the bitter memories which most workers from the English provinces must have had of the clearances and the gaming laws likely to be as deep, as divisive, or as subversive to the notion of a lost age of rural innocence, in a country where neither injustice was attempted. Nevertheless, the play's implicit message—the social benefits of re-establishing a leisured, benevolent, hereditary aristocracy—clashes oddly with the widely-held historical belief that the pseudo-aristocratic Australian squatters were a widely disliked section of society, resisting as they were from the 1840s onwards the efforts by colonial governments to break up their vast runs for the benefit of the small selectors. Nevertheless, as we shall see in later chapters, class-based and eugenic ideologies appear unquestioned in many of the most successful of Australian localised and locally written sporting plays. Symbols of old authority—members of the Royal family, officers of the British Navy, visiting Lords and men of letters—were all enthusiastically welcomed in the colonies; evidence in plenty for many colonists that the decent, stable and noble England they wished to believe in actually existed. Australian audiences may, of course, have identified the squatters (many of whom were former army officers) with Goodge and his *nouveau riche* followers, and chosen to see the play's heroes nostalgically as 'true' aristocrats. Then, as now, horse racing, although enormously popular, was associated with the strong conservative and Royalist traditions in Australian society; given the play's successful ambiguity about its class allegiances it was perfectly possible for the squatting interest in turn to see themselves as the old order being challenged by (and repulsing) the attacks of the selectors.

Colonial horse-racing was not only conservative, Royalist, and an expression of the colonial social order; it was also one area of Australian society where an institution most obviously copied the British model and where colonial modifications were stoutly resisted. Aspects of *Flying Scud*, which reminded Australian playgoers of the colonial, imitative nature of their social institutions and which invited admiration for the English originals, contributed to those traditions. Yet Boucicault's play also invited Australians to indulge in the democratic advantages on which the sunny south prided itself: enjoying the discomfiture of those who falsely aspired to wealth and position, and applauding the tricks of ordinary workers in their endless struggle against the predations of the wealthy and the unscrupulousness of the powerful.

Ultimately, perhaps *Flying Scud* succeeded because it tapped its audiences' need for a simpler, more comprehensible social world; one in which the forces for social unity triumph over those creating divisions. Such a world required a field of common interest (sport), a consensus between rulers and ruled (sporting ethics/ 'playing the game'), and mechanisms for ensuring that fair play would be upheld (the rules of the game, the judge or umpire, the determination of all decent participants to see the game played fairly). While Boucicault only tentatively explored some of these areas as he altered the traditional boundaries of earlier domestic melodrama, he nevertheless stumbled on to a symbol of society which audiences embraced with a passion, and articulated two social myths which were to prove equally popular: the myth of the countryside (the bush), and the myth of the sportsman as the national hero.

Other early sporting plays

Not until the 1880s is it possible to speak of sporting drama as a major genre, but the success of *Flying Scud* obviously invited immediate appropriation and exploitation. In the period (1866-78 England, 1867-80 Australia) between *Flying Scud* and the next key text in the series, *New Babylon*, a number of sporting dramas were performed, but most had only local impact and none provided a clear model for further development. *Flying Scud* was followed into the Holborn Royal in June 1867 by *The Antipodes; or, The Ups and Downs of Life*, a Tom Taylor drama in three Acts suggestive of Charles Reade's novel *It's Never Too Late To Mend*. Like its predecessor it had some 'horse hocussing', although according to the *Era* there was 'no scene to be compared for its excitement with that of the Epsom "Downs" '.[87] There was however 'The very mild dissipation of croquet on the lawn' before the action moved to Australia for scenes of bushranging and gold-mining in Acts II and III. It would be unwise to make too much of a review of a play for which no text has been sighted, but it is perhaps significant that both the sporting incidents mentioned took place in the first Act; that is, in 'civilisation'. The period is that of the first gold-rushes of the early 1850s, but the play was constructed geographically rather than historically, with the movement from civilisation to wilderness reflected by a pattern of sport *versus* lack of sport. The play had a currency-

lass character, played by a newcomer to the Holborn Theatre 'Mrs Watts, *nee* Miss Ellen Terry' who 'sighs for the wildness and freedom of Australia'.[88] For English writers and audiences the displacement in place from England to the colonies was from one where society operated by the rules of sport to one where wildness and freedom (or alternatively opportunism and violent force) prevailed. The presence of sport indicated civilised, ordered values and behaviour.

Dion Boucicault's 'Drama of London Life in 1868', *After Dark*, written and performed in that year, was sometimes mentioned as if it were a sporting drama,[89] but its only direct generic reference was in the first scene of the play which was set at Victoria Railway Station on the evening of the Derby, with crowds of punters and revellers returning to town after the event. As in the Derby Day scene in *Flying Scud*, this was a visually rich crowd scene in which representatives of different social classes and groups were shown enjoying the many pleasures of a great sporting occasion; in this case the 1868 Epsom Derby.

Another major race that year, the St Leger, had been won by a horse called Formosa; however, Boucicault's 1869 sporting drama *Formosa 'The Most Beautiful'; or, The Railroad to Ruin* was not a horse-racing play but a story of the Oxford-Cambridge boat race. It opened at Drury Lane on 5 August 1869 and like the Augustus Harris dramas of the 1880s and 1890s at the same

The boat race scene from *Formosa* (S. Appelbaum, *Scenes from the Nineteenth Century Stage*).

theatre, was the play for the holiday season. As students would have formed a significant proportion of audiences at that time, its use of a storyline about undergraduates down from the universities to enjoy the many pleasures of London life was particularly appropriate. *Formosa* had a minor Australian connection in the character of a returned convict who, after unsuccessful attempts to make a living as a pantomime policeman and as a beggar and seller of pet dogs, sets up as a bookmaker at the Derby and is beaten up by a mob when he is unable to cover his losses (p.25).[90]

Formosa repeated the opposition of country virtue and city vice. Jenny Boker, the daughter of a retired prizefighter and his wife who run a hotel by the Thames, has a secret double life as the notorious courtesan Formosa, 'the most celebrated among the tawny sirens of Hyde Park'(p.12). Although it was the first 'courtesan' drama in English by a living author (excluding the various plagiarisations of *La Dame aux Camelias*), *The Times* thought Formosa's character had been 'most inoffensively treated'.[91] Boucicault portrays Jenny/Formosa as a very remorseful siren who spends most of her time bewailing her lost virtue, is eventually confronted by her parents, and who abandons both her profligate ways and her hopes of marrying the hero Tom Burroughs. Nevertheless, later attacks on the play by the *Illustrated London News* and in the British Parliament made the play notorious throughout the English-speaking world.[92]

Like both *Flying Scud* and *After Dark*, the plot of *Formosa* follows the 'tour of London' pattern of *Tom and Jerry*; indeed it is once specifically referred to as 'Tom's Life in London'(p.20) as the Oxford undergraduate and stroke of the rowing eight gradually falls under the influence of his dissolute companions and relatives. Tom is introduced to London life by his cousin Compton Kerr and Kerr's companion Major Jorum, and induced to gamble heavily on the Chester and Goodwood Cups, at the card table, and on the result of the boat race. Kerr, played in the first production by Henry Irving, fraudulently assists Tom to fall heavily into debt, and plans to have him arrested on the eve of the boat race so that the Cambridge crew, rank outsiders on whom Kerr has himself bet heavily, can win.

In structuring this story Boucicault was able to learn from the experience of *Flying Scud* and rearranged the elements to maximise the impact of the sporting sensation scene. Tom is arrested as predicted at the end of the third Act, and the attention of the play in the fourth and final Act is on getting him out of jail before the time set down for the race. This plot motif, which a modern writer would refer to as a 'time-lock', was to become ubiquitous in sporting drama. The event is set down for a certain time and place, and the struggle of the heroes to be present and ready for the race, and of the villains to prevent them reaching the starting line by the appointed moment, is given increasing urgency by the sense of rapidly passing time.

Fair play is the ideal which all the genuine sportsmen seek. The opposing Cambridge crew 'knocked up the under sheriff at two in the morning and offered their personal securities to any amount'(p.39), even though they are more likely to be defeated if Tom takes his place in the opposing boat. Bureaucratic police procedures threaten to delay his release until after the time at which the race is due to start, and consequently mob-rule prevails. The Oxford and Cambridge crews, assisted by the ex-prizefighter and his 'men of the milling'(p.32) storm the prison and release Tom, sweeping away the illegality of their actions under the simple declaration 'The Money has been paid, the Man should be Free'(p.44). Tom declares 'Thanks, my noble opponents'(p.42) and the teams hurry to the starting position. The play ends with a crowd scene on the banks of the Thames at Barnes Bridge near the finishing position, and acrobats and negro minstrel acts similar to those used in *Flying Scud* entertain the onlookers until the Oxford crew emerge from underneath the bridge arch and row triumphantly across the stage, pursued by the Cambridge team and the following steamboats. The published script contains details for the staging of the race, which was done with the boats, the rowers and the distant onlookers all constructed in 'profile' (silhouettes padded to give a third dimension), including 'groups of profile figures, men and women, miniature' placed on top of Barnes Bridge 'to work, to jump up and down as if to see the end of the race'(p.5).

Formosa's other major development over its predecessor was Boucicault's codified use of a wide range of sporting references to connote different class and gender interests and behaviour. Boxing is at the bottom of the social hierarchy, with Mrs Boker observing 'My Sam was only a prize fighter and such, but I broke him from that'(p.10) as she endeavours to make him more respectable. However, boxing can also be noble, with Tom rescuing Bob Saunders the ex-convict from the Derby mob through his pugilistic skills, and Sam Boker giving a young Lord a comic lesson in the noble art of self-defence. At the refined end of the spectrum is croquet, an upper-class courting game. Jenny Boker first realises that her hold on Tom's affections is not secure when she sees him 'playing croquet on the lawn' with two ladies(p.9). Racing and card games are tainted by corruption and the dangers of gambling addiction, but the Oxford-Cambridge boat race is known by 'the public whose money is put on' to be conducted by gentlemen who are above such practices: 'They know ours is the only race which runs to win, and where the first is the best!'(p.29). The rowers are riotous young men, but gentlemen nevertheless, and fair play requires that their actions, legal and illegal, be seen as correct behaviour in a truly moral world; one which the working-class pugilists are eager to support. The aristocracy and the working class unite in their opposition to middle-class opportunism (one of the villains is again an army officer), and to the agents of bourgeois order: the police.

In Australia *Formosa* was only a moderate success, with three seasons in Melbourne in 1870, 1884 and 1890 running for three, one, and two weeks respectively, though with reports of crowded houses on each opening night.[93] Its premiere night, the Saturday before the 1870 Melbourne Cup, competed successfully with both the Duke of Edinburgh's attendance at the re-opening of the rival Haymarket Theatre, and the popular Gregory's Variety Company, which during the race week introduced into its circus acts at the Princess's Theatre ponies and dogs representing the horses in the Melbourne Cup, monkeys as the jockeys, an 'Exciting Race for the CUP', and a 'Presentation to the Winner Under the Patronage of the Stewards'.[94] In spite of such formidable competition, *Formosa* filled the Theatre Royal 'in all parts'.[95] The distinguished Shakespearean actor, William Hoskins, played the military villain Major Jorum, and his regular partner (later his wife) Florence Colville played Formosa; John Hennings designed the settings. The play's dubious reputation had preceded it, and its controversial depiction of 'the *demi-monde* and the *quartier-monde*' caused sections of the press including, predictably, the *Argus*, to object strongly. While admitting that it had been extremely well staged, that paper declared on 31 October: 'It is a piece which all decent persons should carefully refrain from taking their wives and daughters to see' and added that it would undoubtedly have a 'pernicious effect' on the 'actresses engaged in its representation'.

This extreme reaction blurred the response to the play as a sporting drama, but a number of critics also attacked the play's suggestion that the running of the Oxford-Cambridge boat race was not always above suspicion. In 1870 one critic thought that the idea of a stroke-oar 'revelling in dissipation' within a few hours of the time appointed for the contest was 'absurd', and in 1884 another noted scornfully that 'On the stage, at any rate, even the University boat-race may be prevented from being fairly won'.[96] In 1890 the *Argus* continued its tirade against the play by complaining on 28 July: 'It is difficult to understand why the drama should not have been allowed to die a natural death.' While other papers were less extreme in their reactions,[97] *Formosa* was not often staged, and both the later Melbourne seasons were motivated by considerations other than the play's worth. The 1884 production was rushed on to the stage nine days after the Australian rower, William Beach, won back the world sculling championship from Edward Hanlan, a flamboyant and arrogant Canadian. Hanlan had toured the world triumphantly for four years after defeating the first Australian world champion, Edward Trickett, in 1880, and his defeat by Beach was unexpected and marked by public celebrations of many kinds. Beach was in Melbourne the day the play opened and rowed down the Yarra that same evening.[98]

The 1890 season was part of an entrepreneurial struggle between rival theatrical managements as to which could offer the most entertaining sporting play. At the Opera House the visiting star, William Rignold, was appearing for the MacMahon Brothers in one of his London successes, the racing drama *Now-A-Days*, and Bland Holt was staging a season of Drury Lane dramas at the Alexandra Theatre. Against such competition Williamson and Garner had only been able to offer George Darrell's indifferent production of *Flying Scud*, and *Formosa* was quickly introduced with 'dioramic effects' in the boat-race scene to try to win lost audiences back to the Theatre Royal.[99] Rather more successful was the next production, Darrell's own play *The Lucky Lot*. Though not a sporting drama, this included a new scene which Darrell added to it, 'an episode analogous to the Ride for Life in "Young Lochinvar" ', in which the hero and heroine escape on horseback, leaping over a five-barred gate while pursued by four mounted policemen.[100]

Although there were no Australian productions, and therefore presumably no direct influence on Australian sporting drama, a curious event at the Holborn Theatre Royal in 1870 needs brief mention. This was a dramatisation of the Australian writer Marcus Clarke's first novel *Long Odds*. After the failure of a later lessee, the Holborn Royal was again taken over by the man who had built the theatre and who was also the lessee for the *Flying Scud* and *Antipodes* seasons, Sefton Parry. He re-opened the theatre with a racing play which he claimed as his own and which was entitled *The Odds; or, What They Were, Who Won, and Who Lost Them*.[101] It opened on 1 October in the week of the races at Newmarket, and ran for a very successful eight weeks. In it Parry combined, possibly for the first time in drama, the worlds of sport and of the military, and also managed to include both a scene of a steeplechase race between several army officers, and a scene in which a 'real' railway train killed a man lying on the track. *The Times* sarcastically observed:

If a race drew crowds to his own theatre four years ago, and a railway horror [*After Dark*] proved equally attractive at the Princess's, what will be the effect of a race and a railway horror, fixed as a brace of gems within one setting?[102]

There is little doubt that Marcus Clarke was correct in claiming in 1872 that Parry's play was based on *Long Odds*, though Parry had devised a slightly different group of characters and the later part of the play was taken from *After Dark*.[103] *Long Odds* had been serialised in 1868–69 in Clarke's *Colonial Monthly* and was subsequently published in a single revised volume in 1869 shortly after the last episode appeared.[104] Noteworthy here is the steeplechase scene, which occurs in both novel and play as the result of a bet laid amongst a group of cavalry officers as to which of them can win a cross-country race, each riding his own horse.[105] Parry simplified and conventionalised Clarke's scene, which had ended not with the triumph of the hero's horse but in the death of the main character's elder brother, crushed when his horse falls at the last jump. The brother is an army lieutenant stationed at Kirkminster, and Parry's hero is also a cavalry officer, though the setting is changed to Canterbury. Judging from the plot description in *Bell's Life in London*,[106] the play also took from Clarke his attitude to the army, which is depicted as an attractive and natural career for young men from the aristocracy and gentry, and a socially-progressive link between England past and present:

Kirkminster was a cathedral and a garrison town, and, therefore, aristocratic; but it was also a 'pottery' town, and, therefore, democratic . . . The 'military' was the bond between the Old and the New Town.[107]

In a decade of peace the supposed military value of encouraging young soldiers to gallop around the countryside on horseback is only implied, but even so Clarke's young women of Kirkminster flutter with admiration for the officers. In novel and play the glorification of the cavalry commander is offered as an alternative to the image of the middle-class swindler bearing the title of 'Colonel' or 'Major'.

Sefton Parry also developed in a comic manner an element not in the novel: the connection between women and horses. The heroine, Tilly Price, is loved by both Lieutenant Tom Shuttle, whom she prefers, and by a comic hero, Augustus Jessamy, played by a woman actor. When the predictably named Tom is arrested for debt and prevented from riding in the race, Jessamy takes his place and wins the steeplechase, and Tom's gambling winnings deliver him from custody. The consequent problem of one heroine and two heroes is solved by 'the heroism of Jessamy, who resigns Tilly to Tom, contenting himself with the acquisition of the steed who has so gallantly borne him to the goal as the victor of the race'.[108]

The Odds is a good example of the way in which genres evolve in the commercial entertainment industry: an eclectic pattern of borrowings from earlier narratives, reworked with major and minor variations and modifications determined both by changing social conditions and by the commercial desire to offer 'newer' and more exciting entertainment than any previous drama. Anachronisms are displaced, familiar motifs are revised and repeated in a superficially new guise, proven successful elements are combined and compressed into a more marketable unit. It is difficult to imagine that *The Odds* was not known to the authors of the next key text, *New Babylon*, which developed several plot motifs in a very similar manner. Unfortunately Parry's adaptation was without Clarke's knowledge or permission.[109] The Dramatic Copyright Act of 1833 failed to cover authors' rights over dramatisations of their novels,[110] and so Clarke was neither able to benefit from the Holborn season nor offer the script to other managements, and there do not appear to have been any Australian productions.

These plays demonstrate that from *Flying Scud* onwards sporting drama moved towards a generic existence (in the sense of an ongoing, evolving body of texts drawing elements from a common paradigm). However, during the 1870s only a small number of new plays have been noted. In England there was one more successful racing drama at the Holborn Theatre Royal; this was *Newmarket; or, A Legend of the Turf*, presented in 1874.[111] In Australia George Darrell introduced racing scenes into two of his early plays, *Man and Wife* (1871) and *The Forlorn Hope* (1879); and Garnet Walch had his cricketing pantomime *Australia Felix* produced in Melbourne in 1873.[112] In the United States, tracing the appearances of the actor-manager who was to dominate the Australian popular stage for thirty years shows that there too racing plays were becoming regular occurrences. *The Race; or, The Mysteries of the Turf* was given at the Theatre Comique in 1873, and in the next production a young comedian, Bland Holt, 'from the London theatre' made his New York debut.

Two years later Holt had risen to the status of leading comedian, stage director and inventor of pantomimes at the neighbouring Olympic Theatre, where shortly before his departure for Australia he presented *Jerome Park; or, Scenes at the Races*.[113] Holt's first productions of sporting drama in Australia were characterised by a number of developments in staging techniques, and it seems likely that he brought at least some of these ideas with him when he arrived in Australia from America in 1876. Four years later he was to go into management with the Australian premiere production of a play which his father had staged in London and which can be seen as having inspired the 'Golden Age of Sporting Melodrama': Meritt's and Rowe's *New Babylon*. Holt not only staged this play with great success; he followed it with the Australian premieres of almost all the other major plays in the genre.

The Golden Age
of Sporting Melodrama
1880–1910

Constructing the paradigm

The sensation drama, what shall we say of that? A tissue of absurdities, of startling incidents following hard upon each other without rhyme or reason . . . A farrago of hansom cabs, bursting locomotives, racehorses, fire-engines, collapsed balloons, hanging matches, dynamite bombs, lime-light, real water, and what not else, so long as it be something outrageous and bizarre.
    Editorial, 'The Future of the Stage' in *Lorgnette* (Melbourne), 24 August 1889.

Between *Flying Scud* in 1866 and the last major Drury Lane racecourse drama *The Whip* in 1909 (1867 to 1910 in Australia), the sporting melodrama was perhaps the most successful and sensational genre to appear on the popular stage. If Thomas Dibdin's one-act burletta *What's A Stage Without Horses?* can be said to encapsulate in its title something of the popular theatre's dominant recurring motif earlier in the century,[1] then the question, 'What's a stage without horses racing?' might serve for the later period. When popular stage plays were attacked, as in the 1889 editorial quoted above, the horse-racing sensation was always one of the prime targets and was often seen as the quintessential feature to be singled out for abuse. Another writer in the *Lorgnette* a year later, after a similar tirade about 'real horses, real fire-engines, real hansom cabs, real stage coaches, real water and the like', demanded: 'What human being in his senses would turn his head, much less pay money to look at a real horse . . . while only let one such be announced to be seen on the stage, and the multitude will rush . . . to witness the wonderful sight.'[2] More favourable was the same newspaper's 'Gallery Boy', whose dialect review on 20 April 1889 of Bland Holt's revival of *A Run of Luck* at the Melbourne Theatre Royal began: 'Oh! don't the boys like 'em 'orsey pieces; and don't the people below do the same?' His comment reveals also the unconscious selected appeal of sporting drama: to the male working class and the bourgeois family.

Describing in detail the several dozen major sporting plays which were successfully presented between the early 1880s and the First World War would be a repetitive and extremely protracted exercise, and is not necessary here. The essential structure of nearly all of these plays suggests selections and minor variations from within a fixed register of possibilities, with little progression in narrative preoccupations, but with a continual searching for new and more vivid technical means to stage sporting sensations. Looking only at plays produced by three major managements, those of Bland Holt, J. C. Williamson, and William Anderson, and leaving aside the five key texts to be examined in detail shortly, we find that over a dozen sporting dramas began in the English countryside before moving to London (or in a few cases Paris); most of the others began in the city but with the fortunes of rural gentry or aristocrats prominently plotted. Most obviously representative of the formula (with dates of the first Australian productions) were *A Million of Money* (1893), commencing at a village parsonage; *The Prodigal Daughter* (1894) which began in the 'Hills and Dales of Old England'; *The Derby Winner* (1896) which was set in Yorkshire; *For England* (1898), located in 'England's Hunting Country'; *Woman and Wine* (1899) in 'Malvern's Sunny Hills'; and *Going The Pace* (1903) in Hertfordshire.[3] Three of these emphasised aristocratic pleasure pursuits by showing fox-hunting scenes, and *With Flying Colours* (1900) had pheasant shooting on the moors, with birds 'shot in full view of the audience, and retrieved . . . by . . . well-trained sporting dogs'.[4] Horse races were staged in *A Million of Money, The Prodigal Daughter, The Derby Winner, Sporting Life* (1898), *Woman and Wine, The Favourite* (1901), *The Flood Tide* (1904) and *The Betting Book* (1905); another genre, that of biblical epics, borrowed the sporting plot for a chariot race between hero and villain in *Ben Hur* (1902).[5] Two late examples, Raleigh and Hamilton's *The Whip* and Nat Gould's *The Chance of A Lifetime*, both 1910, show the genre essentially unchanged. The first began with a fox hunt at Lord Brancaster's residence at Falcolnhurst and ended with the Whip's victory in the 2000 Guineas at Newmarket; the second started and ended at Netherby Hall in Oxfordshire and represented the Woodcot Gold Cup.[6]

Novelty sporting exhibitions were introduced into these and other plays. *Sporting Life* had a scene supposedly set at the National Sporting Club in London, although the 'Exciting Scientific Boxing Display' was by J. McGowan, 9st 4lb Champion of Victoria, and Ed Tweedie, the Featherweight Champion of NSW.[7] *Going the Pace, The Betting Book* and *The Village Blacksmith* (1907) also had 'pugilistic encounters'.[8] *The Great Ruby* had a scene set at an England *vs* Australia Test Match at Lord's, and showed an Indian potentate, clearly based on the Indian-born Cambridge graduate Ranjitsinhji, playing for England, and a 'brilliant catch in the long field'.[9] *Hearts Are Trumps* (1901) included a horticultural gymkhana, with decorated pony, dog and goat carts, go-carts and bicycles, though it is not clear which if any of these were actually shown racing.[10] *The Breaking of the Drought* (1902) had a diving and swimming exhibition; *The Betting Book* a football match; *The Great Millionaire* deer hunting and a car chase; *The Price of Peace* (1903) skating; and *The Great Rescue* (1907) a race between a car and a train.[11]

However, it would be wrong to imply that the popular sporting drama in this period can be treated as a genre uncontaminated by other genres or other popular or controversial subjects. Sporting stories were often interwoven with other elements which contributed as much if not more to a play's success; indeed the framing structure of a 'tour of London' used by many sensation dramas invited generic shifts between each Act or scene. Boucicault's *Formosa* was chiefly remembered for the scandal caused by the representation of the *demi-monde* world of its eponymous character;[12] Meritt's and Rowe's *New Babylon; or, Life in the Great City* (1878) contained a shipping collision as well as a representation of the races at Goodwood and other spectacles, and the collision was considered the play's chief novelty.[13] Nevertheless both plays also contributed strongly to the genre of sporting drama. Indeed Clarance Holt, who staged *New Babylon* in London in 1879, claimed with some justification that it gave the great Drury Lane entrepreneur Augustus Harris the inspiration for the series of sensational sporting melodramas which he and his successors presented at 'The Lane' during the next thirty years.[14]

It is useful at this point to compare the paradigm of sporting drama with the classification which an American scholar, Roger Allan Hall, has attempted of another genre of nineteenth-century popular drama: the many plays about the American Wild West staged in the United States after about 1850.[15] Frontier drama can be seen in many respects as a phenomenon parallel to and closely aligned with sporting drama, though sporting drama was essentially an English genre reflecting English social myths, and the Wild West was of course an American construct. But both genres became popular in the same period; were a grouping of plays by subject matter which could involve the use of experts in frontier/sporting skills as well as, or even instead of, professional actors; sometimes included demonstrations of those skills (in frontier drama these included trick-riding, sharp-shooting, knife-throwing and rope tricks); and the narrative usually culminated in a sensational or spectacular scene which emphasised that genre's contribution to an understanding of life as a struggle or competition against forces like those marshalled against the hero.

Three of Hall's categories are common to all genres: key texts (major popular plays and plays by major authors), stock narratives, and parody dramas. In frontier drama there is a major division between plays which were primarily 'star vehicles' for stage actors, and those which starred performers famous for their frontier skills rather than their acting ability. There are also divisions between plays written to provide opportunities for demonstrations of frontier skills within a narrative context, and those which were essentially exhibitions of those skills independent of a storyline or only superficially linked to it. One particular category, plays claiming to be re-enactments of famous events in frontier history, is of particular interest when compared to sporting drama.

Many of the plays starring sporting champions have already been discussed in chapter 1, as have a number of non-narrative exhibitions of sporting skills.

The difficulty of staging sporting contests meant that in sporting drama featuring non-actors there was a selective bias towards those sports most easily staged: boxing, as we have seen, was the major example. Overall, sporting drama was more closely tied to formal narration and stage actors' skills than frontier drama; until the coming of film relatively few sporting champions apart from boxers trod the boards. However, it is star vehicles and historical re-enactments which, by their relative *absence* from sporting drama, point to some of the unique features of the form.

Unlike late twentieth-century sporting plays and films, where biographical representations of past sporting heroes such as Les Darcy, Don Bradman, Dawn Fraser and Phar Lap are common, nineteenth-century sporting plays were almost always set in contemporary society. While they might refer obliquely to past real-life sporting events, as *Flying Scud* had done, the achievements of former champions were unsuited to the narrative strategies then employed. Whereas plays of pioneering (outlaws/bushrangers, the West/ the Bush) were historical, individualistic and agoraphilic, sporting plays were contemporary, communal and claustrophilic. Sport represented society not as it had been but as it wished to be. The opposition of country and city made it possible for complex historical circumstances to be represented by geographical differences in lifestyle rather than by a retreat into a golden age of a mythic past. This dominant form of sporting drama preferred to suggest that the myth of the stable, harmonious countryside was a reality which still existed.

There were also very few vehicles for starring actors in sporting drama, and the form adapted poorly to such distortion. Although sporting plays were often rich in character types, and though major actors eagerly sought such roles as Nat Gosling in *Flying Scud* or Flotsam the Detective in *New Babylon*, the emphasis in sporting drama was almost always on a cross-section of contemporary society, with multiple heroes and villains and a balance of characters representing different geographic worlds and class and gender types all participating in a struggle of good and evil.

The difficulty of adding a starring role to this balance is well illustrated by Boucicault's 1885 drama *The Jilt*, performed during his Australian tour that year. The character Boucicault wrote for himself, Myles O'Hara, is an Irishman in Yorkshire, the 'great steeplechase rider' who sleeps in the stable with his horse Ballinahinch. But Myles is peripheral to a storyline which relegates him and his Irish horse to second place in the Yorkshire Cup behind Thunderbolt, the fastest horse in the stable of the aristocratic Yorkshire family that represents social stability, decency and good fellowship in the play.[16] Unlike frontier dramas with their sharp-shooting, trick-riding *individual* defenders of right, the image of sporting society *collectively* working out its destiny was greater than any individual contribution to it could be. Unlike the cowboy or bush-ranger whose natural environment was the wide empty spaces, the sportsman sought the heady excitement of the great metropolis.

In Australia, nearly all the major performed sporting dramas between 1867 and 1910 were prior London successes; nearly all were written by English dramatists including Boucicault, Paul Meritt, Henry Pettitt, Arthur Shirley, Sutton Vane, Cecil Raleigh and Henry Hamilton, all of whom worked for Drury Lane, the Adelphi, the Holborn Royal and other leading English popular playhouses. Only three plays (*The County Fair, Ben Hur,* and *The Great Rescue*) originated in New York. There were some Australian sporting plays, but it is not just because of their different world-views that they are grouped separately in the next chapter. Of the locally written plays only some of Bland Holt's localisations, and perhaps the several stage adaptations of Nat Gould's *The Double Event,* could be said to have fulfilled the criteria of proven popularity and longevity which the major imported plays could claim. Of the other significant Australian sporting plays, Garnet Walch's 1873 pantomime *Australia Felix* was neither particularly successful nor ever revived, and works such as Darrell's *The Sunny South,* Alfred Dampier's and John Wrangham's *Marvellous Melbourne,* Dampier's and Walch's *Robbery Under Arms,* and Bert Bailey's and Edmund Duggan's *The Squatter's Daughter* were all essentially non-sporting plays with either a single sporting scene or a token sporting-plot motif.

Nearly all the imported sporting plays were staged in Australia with only minor changes to the original text and production plan. An Australian producer who purchased the rights to one of these plays received a complete prompt script with all the revisions and alterations which a London or New York season had adopted, and often was forwarded working models of each scene, a fully orchestrated musical score, notes on costuming and role typing, photographs of key moments in the narrative, and printed posters for use in advertising.[17] Furthermore, Australian entrepreneurs could select, from a large number of proven successes, only those plays which suited their company's resources and house-style, and which they thought would appeal to their Australian audiences.

Consequently, sporting drama in Australia was dominated by a relatively small number of major overseas plays, which established and developed the genre in directions determined by overseas trends, but which were selected by Australian managers on the basis of their knowledge of Australian conditions. Indigenous sporting drama struggled against this hegemony in its attempt to establish a uniqueness, an individuality within this context, but was marginalised for most of the period. Bland Holt's limited and reluctant step towards 'Australianness', which involved localising some of his overseas plays after 1899, was the only significant shift which reflected changing social attitudes in Australia. While Australian audiences read English sporting plays differently from English audiences, and while they must have endorsed the messages they received for the genre to continue, there was nevertheless a sluggishness in the relationship between text and society. The imported sporting play shaped Australian audiences' attitudes to drama, but was only slowly and indirectly shaped by them. Holt, who was responsible for most of the sporting plays of the period, never did stage a play of any kind by an Australian author, in spite of urging from Henry Lawson, Ambrose Pratt, Edward Dyson and Henry Fletcher, though the last two of these did extensive work localising scripts between 1899 and 1907.[18]

Amongst this 'stupendous mass of horse', to use the *Bulletin*'s description of the genre,[19] four plays: *New Babylon* (1880), *The Jilt* (1885), *A Run of Luck* (1887), and *The County Fair* (1891), are key texts in terms of either narrative or staging (or both), and a fifth, *The Great Millionaire* (1902), demands consideration as a significant variation in the pattern.[20]

Bland Holt and *New Babylon* (1880)

The production of *New Babylon; or, Life in the Great City* was marked from the outset by a number of connections with the Australian stage. It was written jointly by the English dramatist, Paul Meritt, and by George Fawcett Rowe, who was the Australian-born George Fawcett mentioned in chapter 1 as a sporting supporter, donator of trophies and author of a pantomime with a sporting scene performed in Melbourne in 1861–62. After a season at the Queen's Theatre in Manchester in 1878, the rights to *New Babylon* were purchased by Clarance Holt and Charles Wilmot for production in London. Like Rowe, Wilmot was an Australian expatriate, and Clarance Holt had spent the years 1854–56 and 1859–64 in Australia and New Zealand. Clarance Holt was probably the most important provincial theatrical manager in Britain in the 1880s, and his unpublished autobiography 'Twice Round the World; or, Fifty-Five Years of an Actor's Life', edited by Charles Osborn, is a major source for both the English and Australian stages in that period.[21]

In September 1878 Holt and Wilmot leased the Holborn Royal, re-named it the Duke's Theatre, and played with limited success for five months in a series of old-fashioned melodramas including *Black Eye'd Susan*. According to Erroll Sherson, the Holborn Theatre Royal was an unlucky venue noted (*Flying Scud* excepted) for the lack of success of each manager who leased it.[22] This makes the achievement of *New Babylon* even more marked. It was essentially a story of gambling: in financial stock, in the betting room, and on the racetrack, and involved the usual tour of London by night: 'London is, of course, the "New Babylon", and the life represented is that which the word in its slang sense indicates . . . the whole round run by the man of pleasure.'[23] The sporting young man in need of redemption (at last called Vincent instead of Tom) gambles all his money on his filly Dahlia's expected success in the Goodwood Gold Cup, but is tricked by his ex-mistress, who bribes the jockey and for once is successful in influencing the outcome of the race. A real filly is led on at the end of the race, which was staged as in

Flying Scud with hurdles added, but Vincent is in despair rather than the usual triumph; his jockey has thrown the race. Vincent's salvation and the moral retribution required for this devastating spread of corruption is deferred until later in the play, when, in an unusually open example of Victorian hypocrisy, Vincent solves his debt problems by marrying his rich young fiancee. She plans to reform him; his mistress is sent to the countryside to begin a new life in the care of her father; and the jockey dies 'in misery'.[24]

The play begins with its greatest sensation: a prologue set in the Grand Salon of an ocean liner bringing a financier named Maltby back from America. As the New York detective, Flotsam, is about to arrest a Spanish-American swindler who is after Maltby's wealth and so render the rest of the drama unnecessary, the ship is accidentally rammed in mid-ocean by another steamer. After this vivid sensation a second scene shows one vessel sinking, and the passengers swimming for their lives. Then follows a scene at Tattersall's Horse Bazaar, with a sale of real horses (as in *Tom and Jerry*); the Cremorne Gardens by night; and Goodwood Races on the Gold Cup day amongst other spectacles.

Clarance Holt, who felt with some justification that his production of *New Babylon* had determined the course of British popular drama for the next thirty years, noted in his memoirs:

How many of these [same sensations] we have since witnessed, in *new* dramas, it is not worthwhile to consider. The characters were also very varied and marked; there had been no melodrama in my time abounding in such a diversity of personages. There was a Spaniard, a Jew, an Irishman [the three villains], an American, a Chinaman, a jockey, a merchant, a young squire and a nobleman. The leading lady had to impersonate two sisters, whose characters were sharply contrasted, and there was the bold drawing of Aunt Crazy, a drunken outcast.[25]

Since most of this international cast of characters had a habit of turning up wherever the scene was set, including the racehorse sale and the steeplechase track, the ability of sport in the theatre to suggest the nation (and a national obsession) had, in the high Victorian years of Imperial expansion, grown to global proportions. Gambling at the racetrack had become a metaphor for international financial manipulations.

New Babylon opened in London on 13 February 1879 and ran for eleven months and 330 performances. It then went on tour, and returned for another 90 performances in 1880. According to Clarance Holt the profit during this period was £21,000. However, its full drawing power was never to be known, as early on the morning of Sunday 4 July 1880, after performance number 440 at the Duke's Theatre and number 518 in all, the playhouse burnt to the ground.[26] A contemporary playgoer, Erroll Sherson, remembered *New Babylon* as 'a good story, exciting and well acted . . . a wonderful show', and independently supported Holt's claim that the Drury Lane Autumn dramas which began in 1880 with Meritt's and Pettitt's *The World* had been largely inspired by its success.[27]

The World opened just four weeks after the Duke's Theatre had burnt down, and Holt, who suddenly found himself without a London theatre, obtained from Augustus Harris the provincial rights to each annual Drury Lane sensation drama. The first eight of these were written by varying combinations of Paul Meritt, George Fawcett Rowe, Harris himself, and another dramatist given his first opportunity for major success by Clarance Holt, Henry Pettitt.[28] Holt and Rowe also wrote other plays in a similar style for performance in the minor London houses and the country, and for most of the 1880s Clarance Holt was the principal organiser and promoter of the many provincial tours of all these extremely successful productions. *New Babylon* itself supported two companies for five years playing weekly seasons throughout Britain, and at least one of those troupes continued playing it until 1893; Holt rejoined it in 1891 to play the detective Flotsam at the suburban and transpontine London theatres. At the peak of his managerial career between 1881 and 1887 Holt boasted that 'One hundred and sixty professionals, minus Supers and Ballet, and twenty-four trucks of Scenery, Dresses and Effects, were moved weekly from town to town throughout the United Kingdom.'[29]

Clarance Holt's successes in the 1880s had direct benefits for his son Bland Holt in Australia. Firstly, Bland Holt was able to secure the Australasian rights for *New Babylon*, which nine years later the theatrical managers' journal *The Call* could still describe as 'perhaps the most successful drama ever produced in Melbourne'.[30] Secondly, Bland Holt was able to negotiate through his father and from a position of strength for the Australasian rights to the plays presented at Drury Lane, the Adelphi and the other popular London houses, and for any of the other plays of the successful dramatists Meritt, Pettitt, Rowe, Arthur Shirley, Sutton Vane, Cecil Raleigh, Henry Hamilton and others who dominated the English popular stage until the First World War.[31] This enabled Bland Holt to prevent other Australian managers from competing equally for the best English plays written for the lucrative mass-audience market. Always a meticulous and dynamic stage director, Holt openly promulgated the fact that, with the scenery designs and set models sent to him by his father, his production would 'assimilate to the London original'.[32] In fact he often improved on the original, as is shown by an extract from a copy of a letter he wrote to his father after *New Babylon* opened:

We have mounted the piece magnificently . . . Our wreck scene has made the greatest hit of any scene ever produced in Sydney—I went away a little from the sketch and introduced two or three novelties that made a wonderful improvement— real steam from the side of the big ship—which is on the roll throughout the scene— smoke and fire etc from the sinking ship—and altogether it makes a startling scene. . . . Another of my introduced effects that goes splendidly—in the race scene—the miniature horses do a false start, turn around (in view of the audience) and start afresh, then the finish of the race is seen—by working life-size horses; with boys on their backs crossing the stage—then the live horse led on etc. This works the audience well up and is a great improvement.[33]

There is considerable evidence that for most of the next twenty-nine years, Bland Holt's production processes were as he describes them here—careful imitations of the London originals, with improvements. Not being the original producer, he was able to wait until the technical problems had been solved and the scripts revised and refined, and then reproduce the polished product, adding his own flamboyant touches. The English playwright, Arthur Shirley, commented admiringly in 1901 on the number of supernumaries and horses Holt used;[34] five years later Shirley wrote to Holt that he had recently met two Australians in London, the swimmer Annette Kellerman and the actor Frank Wetherby, and that they and everyone else who had had the opportunity to witness both the London and Australian productions claimed that 'Bland Holt excels Drury Lane'.[35]

Although Holt thought the shipwreck scene was *New Babylon*'s biggest sensation, the illustrated playbill for its first season set out to generically locate the play as a racing drama by featuring a racecourse in its design.[36] The iconography of the sketch used on the poster emphasised the racetrack's unifying appeal. Aunt Crazy in her concealing shawl of shame stands isolated in the lower left-hand corner, but all the other figures in the crowd are intent on watching the race, and their clothing suggests the military, society ladies, working men, and children. There is also a minstrel in blackface, indicating to potential audiences that they should expect a genre piece similar to the two Boucicault sporting dramas of a decade earlier, and with a spectacular race scene like that in *Flying Scud*. Most prominent in the sketch are a beer bottle and a full champagne glass, lifted in exultation high into the air in the uncluttered mid-line of the picture by, respectively, a disreputable man on the left and an elegant lady in the centre, who stand higher than the other figures. Only working-class females are unrepresented, and only the fallen woman excluded from the picture of society in harmony. This selected representation of genders and classes, and of women according to their sexual behaviour, operated as a distorted image of society to present an image of the 'good' bourgeois woman as the only role-model for women in general. The penniless orphan girl was a regular character in these plays but was usually of middle-class origins and left destitute by misfortune; she was almost always in the care of relatives rather than working for her living, and did not differ from her benefactors in her behaviour.

New Babylon's opening night was marked by the same kind of mass enthusiasm which *Flying Scud* had achieved. The *Bulletin* observed:

Only on Boxing Night, and scarcely ever since, has such a crowd been seen in a theatre as thronged the Victoria on Saturday . . . Long before the performance commenced there was no standing room, all the avenues being filled, and the border of the stage itself having occupants.

Singled out for acclaim was the 'excellence of the piece', 'the superiority of the mounting' and the fact that Holt had drilled his team thoroughly, the usual first-night hitches being completely eliminated.[37]

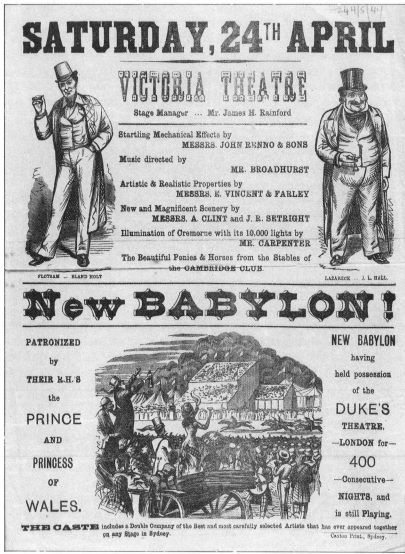

Poster for the 1880 Sydney season of *New Babylon* (Bland Holt Papers, National Library of Australia).

Dion Boucicault's *The Jilt* (1885)

After the death of his first wife in 1883 Bland Holt returned to England for nearly four years, where his father's contacts and his own outstanding talents assisted him in establishing a promising career. During his absence from the Australian stage the only new sporting play of major significance was

Boucicault's final offering to the genre, *The Jilt*, which he wrote in America in 1885 and brought with him to Australia only weeks after its San Francisco world premiere.[38] Incorrectly dismissed by Boucicault's recent biographer Richard Fawkes as a rewritten version of *Flying Scud*,[39] *The Jilt* was in fact an original work, though contemporaries noted borrowings from Sardou's *The Scrap of Paper*, Hawley Smart's sporting novel *From Post to Finish*, and both Boucicault's previous sporting plays.[40]

Like *Formosa* the title role is that of a woman with a scandalous secret, but the tone of *The Jilt* is light romantic comedy. Lady Millicent Woodstock's dubious past is indicated by the existence of some passionately intimate letters she wrote to a former fiance which are used to blackmail her. There is a revelation scene at the end of the play where she resolves to admit her indiscretions to her husband, Sir Budleigh Woodstock, but he, a good-hearted country gentleman, knows both of her former affections and that she now genuinely loves him, and throws the letters unopened into the fire. The implication remains that she may have had a sexual relationship with the man she jilted, an army officer who was thought to have died from unrequited love but who it turns out is now stationed in India and happily married to someone else. Given the mores and the oblique references to sexual behaviour of the time, *The Jilt* can be read as a slight chink in the wall of Victorian sexual morality, and is consistent with the growing tendency of plays in later decades to offer the 'fallen woman' a chance to redeem herself, and to forgive her for her 'mistake'.[41]

However, according to the reviewer in the *Age* after its Australian premiere at the Melbourne Theatre Royal on 25 July 1885, 'There is not a great deal heard about the Jilt, but the horse is discussed from the table up to the drawing room.'[42] Set in country Yorkshire, the play introduced new attitudes to female behaviour in sport more forcefully than it did in relation to their sexuality, particularly in two remarkable female roles: the widow, Mrs Welter, who since the death of her horse-trainer husband has run the stables at Budleigh Hall, and her daughter, Phyllis, who is similar to the many horse-riding Australian heroines of the same and later decades. Phyllis Welter is the only rider capable of mastering the vicious and unpredictable Thunderbolt, a horse whose chances in the Yorkshire Cup Steeplechase have been underestimated because no jockey has been able to ride him effectively. The play's most original moment occurs at the end of the fourth of the five Acts. Phyllis has been teaching the aristocratic young Geoffrey Tudor to be Thunderbolt's jockey, although his father, Colonel Tudor, has forbidden him to ride such a dangerous animal, and only discovers who the jockey is after the race has started. Boucicault added a further twist; during the race there is a sudden hiatus:

Enter Geoffrey. His cap and jacket off and with muddy breeches
Col. T: Geoff!
Geo: I've been in such a mess.
Col. T: What has happened?

Geo: I don't know. It was a false start. When I tried to turn him, the brute reared, fell backwards, and I went a mucker. When I recovered my legs, they had shifted the side-saddle from Phyllis' mare, and she was up—in my place.

Mrs. W: What! my girl!

Geo: Yes! She grabbed my cap and jacket and now she's riding Thunderbolt. (*Cheers outside*) [p.57]

With stones in her saddlebag to make the weight Phyllis rides the steeplechaser to victory and, like Nat Gosling two decades earlier, staggers exhausted, mud-spattered but triumphant on to the stage with her horse. The Melbourne *Leader* did not like this variation,[43] but most other critics did, and, after it had been staged in London in the following year, Townsend Walsh thought 'the old wit flashed out again in "The Jilt" for the last time'.[44]

After the end of the Australian tour Boucicault's son left the company and remained in Australia; in 1890 *The Jilt* became part of the repertoire of the company he formed with Robert Brough.[45] *The Jilt* was still a relatively minor work if we judge its social influence in terms of the number of performances and the extent of subsequent comment, but it is the only sporting play from the 1880s for which a text is readily available, and which therefore can be more closely analysed.[46] As a major playwright, Boucicault's works also had an indirect impact on later scriptwriters.

The Jilt illustrates well one particular characteristic of popular dramatic genres: their ability to adjust to changing social mores while retaining certain fundamental structural patterns. The sporting genre required that, at the last minute, a seemingly insurmountable catastrophe would prevent the race from being won by the deserving characters, and be resolved by help from an unexpected quarter. While this psychologically satisfying pattern of stress and sudden relief had to remain constant, and the fundamental unity of sporting society had to be affirmed, the constituent elements making up the pattern could be varied to reflect different social conditions. That being the case, it is significant that in 1885 the unexpected helper is a woman. The 'woman question' certainly pre-dated the 1880s, but the Married Women's Property Act of 1882, the 1884 Electoral Reform Bill (which William Gladstone 'threatened to drop . . . if the women's amendment were not taken out')[47], and the first stirrings of interest in Ibsen's *A Doll's House* through the staging in London of the emasculated English version *Breaking a Butterfly*, were all events which thrust the question to the forefront of debate in 1885. *The Jilt* is a consensual response to these radical proposals for change in gender power, behaviour and the relationship between the sexes. It acknowledges women's rights and abilities, while directing their energies towards creating social harmony. Mrs Welter, the play's greatest character, is a female Nat Gosling, described on one occasion as 'Yorkshire in petticoats'(p.14). Phyllis is the new woman, attempting and succeeding in an area previously restricted to men, but the play deals equivocally with her. She is both a brash, direct horsewoman and, after the race, an exhausted and tearful young girl. If we add these two characters to the Jilt herself—the sexually experienced city woman who comes to value the simple honesty of her husband and the simple pleasures of the countryside, and who in turn is accepted by her husband as a worthy bride—then the play can be seen as a clever and effective attempt to acknowledge new standards for female behaviour but introduce them into a world where, ultimately, they can be contained, appropriated, and directed towards the maintenance of an ordered, stable, non-democratic society. The values of sport and the countryside are unquestioned and of greater importance than any other.

The woman/horse analogy is also given a new dimension. Lady Millicent (the Jilt) attracts the usual somewhat belittling comments, typical of which are 'he brought her up to the altar and put her nose on the rails, she shied and landed him with a broken life'(p.10) and her own description of her marriage to Sir Budleigh Woodstock: 'A racehorse never fetched a higher price'(p.11). But the image is reversed by Kitty Woodstock, another of the play's bold young women, who objects to leaving Yorkshire for London, where she will be obliged to 'figure in a horse show in the Row—where the prize animal on parade is the girl'(p.17). Also worthy of note is the explicit analogy, as in *New Babylon*, between sport, gambling and capitalism. When Kitty demands to know 'Where in the world are [villains] tolerated?', she is promptly told 'Upon the racecourse and the stock exchange'(pp.30-31).

'A stupendous mass of horse'

Late in 1886 Bland Holt decided to return to Australia, apparently at the request of J. C. Williamson who wanted him to direct and star in the first Drury Lane horse-racing play, Pettitt's and Harris's *A Run of Luck*.[48] Holt worked for Williamson during 1887 and 1888, and they again joined forces during the worst years of the financial depression in the early 1890s. This gave Williamson the performing rights in both *A Run of Luck* and the next Pettitt/ Harris sporting play, *A Million of Money* (1890 London, 1893 Sydney and Melbourne), and meant that Holt was unable to incorporate them into his permanent repertoire. However, during the time he worked for Williamson, Holt began to build up his old repertoire, including *New Babylon*, and he gathered together a company with a primary allegiance to him rather than to the triumvirate. The company performed throughout Australia, New Zealand, and in India until 1907, when illness forced both Holt and his wife to begin to wind down their stage careers.[49] Their regular scene designer, John Brunton, died two years later, further prompting the Holts to disband their company at the end of 1909.[50] Mass audiences were already being lured away from the theatre by the cinema, and although the stage companies of J. C. Williamson, William Anderson, Fullers' and others subsequently staged sporting plays, by the time the Holts retired the genre was reaching the end of the long period during which it was one of the most common genres in popular live theatre in Australia.

The dominance which Bland Holt established over the genre of sporting drama is shown by a comparative tally of the number of such plays he performed between 1887 and 1909. A listing of the first seasons in Sydney or Melbourne of all known sporting pieces performed between *Flying Scud* and the First World War shows that whereas no other manager produced more than three or four such plays, Holt staged at least seventeen. Furthermore the length of his seasons, the regular reports of capacity houses in the largest theatres available, the attitudes of his contemporaries, and the remarkable longevity in light journalism of stories about his productions, all suggest that he dominated the popular stage in a manner unequalled by any manager before or since. As late as 1949, forty years after his last stage appearance, Bland Holt was the subject of nine full-page instalments, published in the Melbourne weekly newspaper *Sporting Globe*, which celebrated the great days of sporting melodrama.[51]

The 'Great Drury-lane Sporting Drama'[52] which brought Holt back to Australia, *A Run of Luck*, has often been credited with being the first racing play to use real horses in staging the contest; however, Michael Booth has pointed out that the Derby was staged with real horses in the 1884 play *Daybreak* at the Standard Theatre in London's East End, two years before Drury Lane.[53] *Daybreak* relates to *A Run of Luck* as *New Babylon* did to *The World*; in each case the play making the innovation was staged principally for working-class East End audiences, and was then used by Augustus Harris as a model for his more prestigious and respectable West End productions.

A Run of Luck's view of history was even more anachronistic than *Flying Scud*'s had been twenty years earlier, since it deals with events similar to those which Boucicault describes as having occurred before the action of his play began. *A Run of Luck* begins with 'country scenery with glowing flowers in the foreground' and features a pack of fox-hounds as well as 'half-a-dozen' racehorses; it represents an idealised Merrie England initially untainted by nineteenth-century problems. Old Squire Copsley gets into financial difficulties and his stable of racehorses is sold off. A young sporting man who is a suitor to the squire's daughter, Daisy, purchases a prize filly, also called Daisy, which the squire had hoped to enter in the Steward's Cup at the Goodwood Races. In the last Act, as the Melbourne *Punch* (14 April 1887) humorously described it:

Daisy the girl sinks into insignificance, and Daisy the filly becomes the star of the act, and upon the plotting and counter-plotting as to whether she may or may not run for the Steward's Cup, at Goodwood, the finale turns. The filly is spirited this way and that, hauled from stables and in and out of railway stations in a most bewildering fashion. . . . Then the fashionable ladies—with doubtful character—get to the lawn at Goodwood, of which Mr Brunton has painted a pretty set, and everybody else in the play, the just and the unjust alike, come here too. The jockeys are weighed whilst the gallery boys recognising the colours call the names of the local carriers thereof.

"Hallo, Ringmaster?"

"Brayvo, Leporello!"

"Tommy Corrigan, how are you?"

There is fierce excitement as the racers sweep across the stage and Daisy, the filly, wins the Stewards' Cup; Daisy, the girl, wins her own true . . . lover . . . [the squire] smiles majestically on all, every man is used according to his deserts, and the now helpless playgoer is led from the circle . . . and has his head held under the tap until his scattered senses are persuaded to return to his cooled brain. . . . Magnificently mounted, superbly dressed, and, as we have already said, as full of sensation as the most hungry of excitement lovers could desire, it will, no doubt, run for many weeks to come.

The play's only original narrative variation was that, instead of a young country-bred male member of the gentry going to London and being almost irretrievably corrupted, it is the daughter Daisy who, after her father's ruin, is obliged to take a 'situation' in London and is lucky to escape from several morally compromising situations, including one where she is drugged and nearly raped. She is assisted in her escapes by the 'sporting' man (in both old senses of the word), who retains an innate decency in spite of his familiarity with 'fast life'.[54]

In Australia *A Run of Luck* was the first play to use real horses in its race, and it established a new benchmark for all future racing sensations. Later anecdotal sources claimed that the race in this and other Holt productions was run with up to fifteen horses galloping out of the theatre, down Bourke Street and back again, but this is exaggerated.[55] Reviews suggest about six racehorses were regularly used. The horses ran out of a side door of the Theatre Royal where they were pulled up, led down the lane into Little Bourke Street and back into the theatre through the main stage door, where they repeated their crossing of the stage. Hurdles, 'miniature' waterfalls and other obstacles were used as appropriate for different kinds of races and fox hunting scenes.[56] The *Argus* on 11 April was amused by 'several equestrians in scarlet trotting across the wings to an imaginary hunting field in Little Bourke-street' with the race following the same general arrangement. For once this paper was kinder to the popular drama than the rival *Age*, which on the same day professed itself appalled by the new depths to which the drama had sunk. The *Argus* critic only remarked mildly 'we begin to think that the future of the British stage may belong to our "poor relations" the quadrupeds. They certainly carry the lion's share of the honours in *A Run of Luck*'.

Holt's production script for the next Drury Lane turf drama *A Million of Money* (1890 England, 1893 Australia), preserved in the J. C. Williamson Collection in the National Library, contains a pencil sketch plan of the stage during its race scene.[57] The sketch was done by Holt's London agent, Arthur Shirley, and indicated the Drury Lane rather than the Australian staging, but was almost certainly copied faithfully by Holt. The general design of the stage is not significantly different from the setting for *Flying Scud*, although the perspective scale must have been altered to allow for full-sized animals rather than smaller profile models. The course was marked by a paling fence on each side and ran from downstage left to upstage right. The horses began in the left wings, crossed the stage going slightly away from the audience, veered right when in the far wings so that if necessary they could use the added pathway through the stage door and into the street at the rear to pull up in, then re-entered the theatre unobserved by the same door and crossed behind the backdrop to the left wings again. The variety acts and games were played on the forestage; an 'Aunt Sally set piece and props' are specifically indicated on the plan, with blackface minstrels and thimble-rigging suggested in the scene heading. Real drags, wagonettes, and the cast were placed downstage of the course and bunched into two groups, one on each side of the stage; this gave the audience an unimpeded view of the horses while they were centre stage, and partly concealed the jockeys' efforts to spur them to a gallop as they entered and to pull them up on the other side. Upstage of the track were freestanding set pieces representing groups of figures, coaches, and small grandstands, with a large grandstand painted on the backcloth. A later sketch plan, for William Anderson's staging of *The Chance of A Lifetime* in 1910, shows a different spatial arrangement with the horses running on the opposite diagonal, but also combined real crowds and set pieces with painted background images, suggesting that audience expectations of stage realism were still low enough for such a *tableau vivant* style of presentation to be effective.[58]

A Run of Luck's other visual innovation, one that was to be an equally important element in all future sporting dramas, was the introduction of a scene, the principal purpose of which was to provide an opportunity for a fashion parade. From this time onwards the major sporting plays were a reflection of what was sometimes explicitly acknowledged as the world of 'sport and fashion'.[59] The form now assumed that male and female interests in sport were in different though complementary areas and so required two obligatory scenes: one containing thoroughbred racehorses, gambling, and the action and excitement of the race (primarily for male audience members); the other decorative and formal, containing beautiful costumes (for female theatregoers). These fashion displays were set usually on the lawn at Goodwood, Epsom or Aintree before the race, or at a sporting or military ball after the race, or preferably both, providing opportunities for a change from race frocks to ball gowns. Leading fashion houses, particularly Worth's of Paris, supplied gowns for both English and Australian productions of these plays. *A Run of Luck*'s Melbourne advertisements claimed:

The Millinery for the Goodwood Lawn and race scenes from the celebrated establishments of Mesdames Elise, Brandon, and Marguerite, London.

The Costumes for the ball, lawn and race scenes from the establishments of Mesdames Derrant and Martin and Madame Bell, Court costumiers, London; and Messrs. Worth and Auguste, Paris.[60]

These scenes were as necessary, and as often commented on, as the race scenes, and were considered essential whether or not they contributed to the plot, as Arthur Shirley observed in a letter to Holt concerning the 1895 Drury Lane drama *Cheer, Boys, Cheer*.

The big scenes are Hurlingham (polo match) . . . Rotten Row with scores of ladies on stage all dressed in Worth's latest fashions—a magnificent picture but not dramatic in the least . . . Last scene a double staircase set with reception of innumerable guests in latest Paris fashions (the *play* was all over in previous act) a truly splendid picture.[61]

George Musgrove, writing from London to J. C. Williamson at about the same time, commented on the costumes of the 150 women in the chorus of this same production, 'They are not the fashions of to-day but what will be the fashions next year. So you can imagine the interest the ladies will take in the show.'[62]

This gender stereotyping seems to have reflected contemporary beliefs about male and female interests in racing in Australian high society as well. The major Australian racing carnivals in the late-nineteenth century were already characterised by extravagant fashion displays by bourgeois women on certain selected days, as the 'Turf Topics' column of the sport and drama weekly paper the *Flag* observed in 1895:

I always notice that on Grand National Steeplechase day there is a larger attendance of the fair sex than on any other occasion, excepting of course, the "toilet day," as the Melbourne Cup is spoken of by them.[63]

The winter fashions were paraded during the July steeplechasing season, and the spring and summer hats and dresses were displayed in November. This provided yet another reason for sporting plays to be co-ordinated with major racing carnivals, since the costumes on stage could display future fashion trends at a time when female racegoers were assumed to be both eager and anxious to be seen to be keeping up with overseas developments. It was a factor too which militated against the localisation of London dramas or the production of those written locally, since fashionable costuming was an important ingredient in the successful theatrical formula, and one where the need to imitate European styles was particularly intense. Fashion ensured that a significant number of scenes in nearly all sporting plays were set in contemporary London or Paris high society.

The major obsession of the popular stage at this time was the pursuit of 'reality', with elements drawn from the real world combining with stage illusions to create a spectacular 'realistic' effect.[64] If a formula became hackneyed, then attempts to reinvigorate it most commonly involved a new visual combination of the real and the illusory which, it was asserted, created an effect which was 'more real'. This was particularly true of racing drama in an age when the level of general knowledge about horses and horse-racing was relatively high, and where horse breeding and pedigrees were widely discussed. Realistic staging began with the need for the horses used in sporting image-making to be visibly of excellent stock; i.e. real thoroughbred racehorses. Audiences accepted elements of artifice in creating theatrical images, but they also expected displays of what they regarded as genuine beauty in horses, clothing, women and men. Avoidable deficiencies were satirised; the *Bulletin*, for example, scornfully asserted that one of Holt's champion fillies in *A Run of Luck* was in fact a gelding, and noted with satisfaction a week later that its observations had been correct and that a 'genuine filly' had replaced it.[65]

If the horses used had to look like genuine champions, from *A Run of Luck* onwards they sometimes had to demonstrate this ability. One of the horses used for the Drury Lane staging of the Grand National in *The Prodigal Daughter* in 1892 had actually won that race some years earlier,[66] and in Australia Holt's mare, Sylvia, was also a genuine prizewinning steeplechaser.[67] Only one or two trained horses would travel with a theatre company such as Holt's, and the remainder were often not used to the glare of stage lighting and the strange conditions under which they had to perform; consequently they were sometimes unreliable. Holt's Melbourne staging of Shirley's and Landeck's *Woman and Wine* represented a steeplechase at the Longchamps Course near Paris, but with a significant and unfortunate variation:

Genuine horses were raced at genuine hurdles, not across the stage, as is customary, but from back to front, in such a way as to enable spectators to calculate on the chances of one or more of the animals tumbling into the orchestra. The first batch of horses took the hurdles hesitatingly, and got safely into the wings, but a couple of outsiders, with diabolical perverseness, resisted the most desperate attempts of their riders to get them on the other side. They were still prancing about, to the discomfiture of the dramatis personae, when the other starters came up the straight for home. It was an exciting finish. The favourite baulked at the last hurdle and threw its rider, as it was apparently intended it should do. But the others, bouncing over the obstacle, charged into what was supposed to be the hillside and brought the whole "landscape" tumbling about their ears. The audience cheered wildly as the curtain fell on horses and riders extricating themselves from the debris.[68]

This appears to have been a particularly spectacular occurrence of a long-standing problem with using horses in drama. In 1871 some horses in the opera *Nabucco* in Sydney had upstaged the singers with their 'restiveness',[69] and when Dan Barry presented a short equestrian drama ' "A Harvest Home" . . . with the most exciting realistic steeplechase seen on any stage' at the Melbourne Alexandra Theatre in 1894, the horses and jockeys and their racing colours were announced as on a racing programme, but the audience were 'requested to keep their seats during the steeplechase, to avoid accidents'.[70] Sometimes, in spite of the efforts of all the jockeys, the hero's horse came in last; this occurred on the opening night of *The Derby Winner* at Drury Lane, causing Arthur Shirley to comment: 'I presume [the hero] lost everything that was at stake on the event, honour, girl, fortunes & etc and the villain—for that night only—triumphed!'[71]

Treadmills, bicycles, and moving pictures

Many of the major developments in staging spectacular theatre were provided by new technology. In racing drama the first problem had been the slippery stage floors which limited what real horses could do; this was solved first by placing coconut matting under the floorcloth[72] and later by the use of sheets of cork or, to give the effect of sand, cork sawdust.[73] The introduction of electrical systems for lighting and stage machinery during the 1880s led to considerable changes in the presentation of spectacular stage effects. Large revolving stages were introduced and powered by electrical motors; the Melbourne Theatre Royal had one by 1887 which Holt used in the *Run of Luck* production. This considerably simplified the presentation of a succession of spectacular scenes requiring elaborate stage carpentry. In *The Prodigal Daughter* and subsequent steeplechasing plays, the scene was changed, possibly by means of a revolve, so that on each successive crossing of the stage the horses encountered a different hurdling obstacle.[74] Nevertheless, the spectacle of the race itself was still limited by the width of the proscenium arch, which only allowed the horses to be seen for a few seconds each time they crossed the stage. By 1895 in London Augustus Harris had moved his stagings of the Derby out to the Olympia, which had a stage 'about 8 or 10 times as wide as Drury Lane',[75] and it was presumably the great depth of the Melbourne Theatre Royal stage[76] which suggested to Holt the idea of running the race in *Woman and Wine* towards the audience, with the unfortunate results described above.

The technological breakthrough made by the American inventor/actor James William Knell (whose stage name was Neil Burgess) in 1888-89 was the use of a combination of treadmills (contained in large cradles) and a moving backscene which together created an illusion of movement on the stage.[77] While some crude forms of treadmills and moving panoramas seem to have been used as early as the 1840s,[78] Burgess's combination of devices was unique, and he established patents over a wide range of similar and complementary machinery, including that used for the Marc Klaw staging of the chariot race in *Ben Hur* in New York in 1899 and reproduced at Drury Lane and in Australia in 1902.[79] Burgess patented his invention in Sydney on 3 July 1890 and his rights did not lapse until 1905;[80] this inhibited imitations of his staging system until then, and, apart from the authorised staging of *Ben Hur,* only Holt's *Riding to Win* in 1901 attempted a similar race scene. Holt used a different combination of devices; it is not clear whether he was violating Knell's patent, but his usage was not challenged.[81]

The effect achieved by Burgess's machinery, which he first used in a bucolic farce *The County Fair* in 1888,[82] can best be described in modern terms as comparable to that achieved by a tracking shot in film, and in fact from *c*.1901 long tracking film shots were sometimes back-projected on to a screen instead of using a moving panorama.[83] The galloping horses on the stage in the foreground of the picture were restrained by concealed wires, and remained in the same place in the centre of the total image, each horse on its own treadmill, throughout the scene. Near the end of the race the entire cradle containing one treadmill and the favoured horse was moved forward while the horses were still galloping, to give the impression that it was winning.

The illusion of movement was achieved by two additional effects. The background consisted of a panoramic scene painted on a long roll of canvas mounted behind the horses. In the American version of the scene this was an endless rotating loop; in a slightly later French version it was a scroll of canvas with a substantial but finite length.[84] By rolling the scenery in the opposite direction to that in which the horses were galloping, an illusion was created that the horses were moving, and that the audience was moving parallel to the horses at the same speed. This explains why reviews sometimes referred to the theatre itself appearing to move.[85] The effect was supplemented by a

Treadmills and moving panoramas: the machinery as first developed in France and America *c*.1889 (Albert H. Hopkins, *Magic*, 1895).

picket fence (in fact made of canvas), which was placed between the horse and the audience and which moved across the stage in the same direction as the background and was synchronised with it. The effect was partly dependent on being seated in the centre of the audience, and when King Edward VII went to see *Ben Hur* at Drury Lane on 14 April 1902, he had a box built in the middle of the pit in order to see the spectacle properly.[86] In *The Great Millionaire* revolving wing pieces were added to give the sense of movement from more divergent angles of view.[87]

The first production of *The County Fair* used three horses, the version which reached Australia in 1891 had four, and later New York seasons expanded this to nine.[88] *Ben Hur* had (at different times) three or four chariots each pulled

Treadmills and moving panoramas: the machinery as improved for *The Whip* 1909 (*Scientific American*, 25 January 1913).

by between one and four horses.[89] However, the conceptual idea behind Burgess's system seems for a time to have been better than the actual effect achieved. When *The County Fair* finally reached London in 1897 Arthur Shirley wrote to Holt that ' "The County Fair" has made no stir at all—the great race scene . . . is not for a moment to be compared with Harris's race scenes'.[90] In 1902 the *Manchester Guardian* made the same complaint about *Ben Hur.*

The effect which it is sought to produce by this sensation scene has been more than once attempted in England, but never on so elaborate a scale. Undoubtedly the three teams of four horses each do attain a considerable speed on their rotating platforms, yet the effect is wholly unillusive.[91]

At least one Australian comment, made some years after *The County Fair* played in Sydney and Melbourne in 1891, also described the effect as disappointing,[92] but Drury Lane refined and adapted Burgess's method of staging, and was finally rewarded with the highly successful racing scene in *The Whip* in 1909.

According to the American theatre historian, Donald F. Recklies, *The County Fair* was a 'simple melodrama', elevated to success by the race scene and by the main character, a comic old spinster Abigail Price, which was played in New York as a cross-dressing role by Neil Burgess himself.[93] In Australia, however, a Miss Sadie Stringham took the part.[94] Abigail is in danger of losing her farm when Solen Hammerhead, a 'Deacon with Mean Principles' threatens to foreclose on her mortgage, but is saved when Tim the Tanner, 'a young vagabond she has befriended . . . trains her carriage horse, Cold Molasses, and successfully rides him for a substantial purse at the local fair'.[95] The deliberately unpretentious setting, the modesty of the prize, and the relatively classless rural community all mark *The County Fair* as a product of a society with different dominant social myths from those being promulgated in England and Australia at this time. The relationship between country and city was also handled differently, since the hero Tim is 'From the Streets of New York; somewhat of a Jockey'[96] and his initiative and ingenuity are a product of street-smart city life, seen as essential to solving the problems of rural people paralysed by economic change. In some respects the play's subject matter and bucolic-farce style anticipate the developments in Australian theatre which occurred after the 1912 staging of Steele Rudd's *On Our Selection*, but *The County Fair*'s narrative had little contemporary impact.

The Australian entrepreneur, James MacMahon, saw *The County Fair* during an American visit. There were two touring companies on the road at the same time as Burgess was playing in New York, and it was presumably one of these which MacMahon contracted for performances in Australia.[97] It was staged in Sydney from 6 June and in Melbourne from 11 July 1891.[98] The scenery and machinery had to be carried in large crates on wagons or railway carriages, and took about a week to set up on the stage; the Sydney opening was originally announced for 30 June but was delayed a week due to difficulties in getting the equipment to work and the horses to co-operate.[99] The seasons were relatively short and the financial slump had begun, so it is unlikely that the tour was a profitable one. For about a decade, therefore, *The County Fair* was remembered as an interesting but unsuccessful experiment; Drury Lane remained the primary influence.

In three plays staged in the first years of the new century, *Riding to Win*, *The Breaking of the Drought*, and *The Great Millionaire*, Bland Holt began to move away from the *tableau vivant* method of staging races and, again copying Drury Lane, came to rely increasingly on complicated stage machinery. The first of these technical sensations, a bicycle race in *Riding to Win*, adopted a system similar to that used in *The County Fair*. The *Australian Cyclist and Motor Car World* on 12 September 1901 published a long description of the race mechanism:

The panorama of the Exhibition Buildings and grounds, which by revolving in an opposite direction to which the cyclists are moving, produces the deceptive effect as though the riders were travelling at top speed. The huge columns, one at each side of the stage around which the scene moves, are fitted with roller bearings top and bottom, and to facilitate the rotary movement, castors are fitted underneath on which the columns revolve. The fence between the audience and the riders also moves in the opposite direction to the riders. The fence is actually composed of rope top and bottom, with canvas to represent the pickets. The fence is endless, and on similar lines to a tram cable, as it runs back to the rear of the panorama after passing before the audience, and the movement is imparted to it by a geared capstan, worked by half a dozen men.

The home trainers, upon which the bicycles are fixed and supported by piano wire, are drawn along by a hidden rope. The back wheel of the bicycle rests on two rollers, one of which is connected by a belt to the roller which supports the front wheel, and when the cyclists pedal the front wheel also revolves as fast as the rear wheel.

At the first production the gallery boys as usual took the opportunity to reply to the bookmakers calling the odds on the stage, and 'cyclists turned up in galore' to witness the spectacle.[100] The mechanism was designed and built by Holt's chief stage carpenter, W. H. Osborne, who claimed to have earlier worked on a *County Fair* production, presumably the 1891 Australian tour.[101] A trick-cycling act preceded the race and two prominent Melbourne cyclists assumed the hero's and villain's roles in the actual event where they were joined by four other local champions. The mechanism, of course, ensured that the victor in the race was pre-determined and that the result had nothing to do with riding ability, but the credibility of the sensation within the context of the plot demanded that the appearance of a genuine and evenly matched contest be simulated. The use of real sportsmen also had marketing advantages; during the season the Inter-Club Cycling Association held a theatre night, and for that performance the 'world-famous speed king "Plugger Bill" Martin' was prevailed upon 'to assume the role of the hero for that night's race'.[102] Martin was an American professional cyclist whose aggressive riding, pugilistic skills and general flamboyance had made him famous throughout Australia; he had settled in Melbourne and ran a Bourke Street hotel. His appearance was widely advertised, and the cycling club preceded the performance with a one-hour amateur variety concert of their own.[103]

Having successfully incorporated Melbourne sporting champions into a play, when next in Sydney Holt contracted the Cavill family to give a diving exhibition at the end of Act III of *The Breaking of the Drought*, with the stage arranged to represent the baths at Little Coogee beach in Sydney.[104] Unlike the bicycle race this seems to have been a variety act, as the trick cyclists had been, rather than being connected to the plot. Its main distinction is that in the subsequent Melbourne season in 1903 the diving champion was Annette Kellerman.[105] Trained in Sydney by Fred Cavill and Snowy Baker, at the age of sixteen Kellerman was giving exhibition swimming and diving displays with the other star pupil of Cavill's baths, Freddy Lane.[106] According to her sister, Marcelle Wooster, Annette Kellerman was not in the original Sydney production but instead met Holt while she was in Melbourne training in the Yarra for a proposed attempt on the English Channel.[107] Wooster's unpublished biography claims that in the play the 'tank was built into the stage, the water pumped in and out of large pumps' and that Kellerman was nearly killed when she foolishly stayed in the pool while it was being emptied.[108] After the season Kellerman went to London, where through Holt's letters of introduction she met Arthur Shirley and other English playwrights and theatrical producers.[109] By 1905 she had expanded the act first seen in *The Breaking of the Drought* into a solo diving and swimming act at the London hippodrome; later she went beyond the staging techniques she had learnt from Holt, and had a glass-fronted tank built on top of rather than under the stage, which she used for underwater swimming routines at the New York Hippodrome and the London Coliseum.[110]

It was inevitable, given the spectacular drama's eagerness to exploit new technology, that film projections should be incorporated into both the narratives and stagings of these plays. In 1900 *Hearts Are Trumps* at Drury Lane introduced a biograph into the storyline,[111] and in 1901 the same theatre experimented with using a filmed backscene instead of a moving panorama for the car chase in *The Great Millionaire*. In both England and Australia documentary footage was also being used in dramatic situations: in 1903 a play staged in Christchurch incorporated a film of that year's Melbourne Cup,[112] and Holt used film of Russo-Japanese war scenes in his 1905 play *Beseiged in Port Arthur; or, Allies and Enemies*.[113]

However the first attempt at creating a *County Fair*-type illusion using film was that for a chase scene in *The Great Millionaire*. At Drury Lane the villain's car faced and was imagined to be moving *towards* the audience (rather than across the stage), with a pursuing car and 'flying trees, posts, gates, &c' seen on the backscreen, but the result did not create an illusion of movement and also weakened the end of the chase where the real car went over a cliff.[114] Consequently, the projections were cut out and a more sensational accident scene devised with the car seen starting off with real people driving, then going over the edge (with dummies inside) and finally the scene revolving to show the wreck on the beach below.[115] Contemporary reviews do not indicate how Holt staged his production, given first at the Melbourne Theatre Royal on 31 October 1903, but a later play, *A Path of Thorns*, gives some indication of how a chase could be staged successfully. The car was shown facing across the stage, as the bicycles and horses had been, in front of a four-minute filmed tracking shot of George Street in Sydney, taken by Sidney Cook 'commencing at the Town Hall, and continuing to the Argyle Cut'.[116] The *Sydney Mail* thought 'the mechanical illusion of a motor car chase is capitally done'.[117] In his last race spectacular, *The Great Rescue*, Holt appears to have used a real car on the forestage, a profile train further upstage, and a filmed background.[118] This chase was from Charters Towers to Townsville, as hero and villain both attempt to be the first to reach a stockbroker's office after the hero's mine has struck gold.

From race to chase: capitalism unmasked

Of these later texts, the one which most clearly recognised the dominant ideology of the sporting drama, and which consciously set out to challenge it, was the 1901 Drury Lane autumn drama *The Great Millionaire*. Its author, Cecil Raleigh, was contemptuously referred to by Arthur Shirley as a 'socialist'. Whatever the truth of this assertion, *The Great Millionaire* was recognised as 'a distinct departure in plot construction from the usual type of melodrama'.[119] In the play Raleigh tried to put the pursuit of wealth and power into a less favourable light by taking as his central character a financial speculator who attempts to corner the world's wheat supplies. As noted earlier, the link between sporting and other forms of gambling was always implicit and often explicit; a character in *A Million of Money* had referred ironically to having 'given up racing and betting, and settled down to business in the city'.[120] In *The Great Millionaire* gambling in sport, which had always been represented as hurting only the gambler and his family, is replaced entirely by stockmarket speculation with its wider social implications. Sport is displaced from the paradigm in order to throw into sharper relief 'the nerve straining and petrifying effect of gambling and the greed for gold'.[121] The play still begins in the countryside at 'Deerwood Park, Devonshire', but the millionaire has already supplanted the traditional owners and his behaviour is the antithesis of aristocratic benevolence; he 'makes himself a terror to trespassers by under-mining his precious park with fireworks and things which "go off" suddenly when walked upon or sat upon by poachers and picnickers'.[122] The play's point of view is still aristocratic, since the millionaire takes as a retainer the former owner, the young Lord Deerwood, who acts as the voice of conscience as he follows his employer about commenting on his actions.

Two events disrupt the millionaire's life. The first is his long and fruitless search for his sole heir, a daughter he has never seen. The second is a sudden reversal of his social standing which occurs in a scene at the Guildhall where, awaiting the arrival of the King and Queen, he is denounced as a company promoter who has engaged in sharp practices and is 'shooed off the premises'.[123] Lonely and bitter at his rejection by 'respectable' society, he takes his revenge by forcing up the price of bread and causing widespread rioting and misery amongst the poor. Eventually the millionaire finds his own daughter amongst those starving in the streets and, at last realising the consequences of his actions, releases his hold on the market. The young woman is more a stock symbol of the spirit of the nation than an individual, and as she is slowly nursed back to health it is announced that she will marry Lord Deerwood, thus reuniting wealth and lineage in a new humane order.[124] The narrative, though not the usual reactionary fantasy, was still anti-democratic and liberal rather than socialist; it offered an allegory of society as a family divided and needing to be reunified through humanitarian impulses.

Raleigh's decision to replace sport as an image of society with that of the family returned the play's allegorical structure, in part, to earlier domestic forms of melodrama; however, capitalist excesses now threaten the family-as-society from within rather than being an external disruptive force. Omitting sport and sportsmen also made gambling a less attractive phenomenon. But *The Great Millionaire* still had to conform to the house-style of Drury Lane spectacular melodramas and, in searching for an alternative to a sporting race, Raleigh devised a new form of sensation—one that seems to have been unique and which, although attempted only a few times in live drama, later became the most easily recognised motif of popular film: the chase. The play ends with the scene in which the millionaire's unscrupulous secretary escapes by car with a cipher book that a rival financier intends to use to renew the socially chaotic capitalist market war and to ruin the now 'remorseful parent'. The young Lord pursues him in another car and the villain's car goes over a cliff, taking him to his death.

While sporting plays had concealed their financial transactions behind a facade of leisure, pleasure and good sportsmanship, later plays like *The Great Millionaire, A Path of Thorns* and *The Great Rescue* which had non-sporting chases were much more nakedly capitalism in action. If aristocratic and rural origins had offered hope that the race would be run in the interests of society as a whole, now the only hope was that in the chase of life the principled capitalists could drive faster.

The extent and the nature of the influence on Australian society of this extraordinary age of sporting melodrama is difficult to estimate, but it cannot have been slight. For both British and Australian theatregoers the 'guided tour of London' was a voyeuristic journey to an imagined world where sexual, financial, and lifestyle mores were very different from those they endured. As 'country and city' plays these texts worked to reinforce and develop reactionary, high-Tory English social myths: the purity, stability and tranquility of traditional, hierarchical country life as opposed to the dangerous and corrupting excitement of the egalitarian city; the belief that society could best be run by those born to rule; the idea of historical change as something to be resisted; of society being shaped by individual decisions based on personal character traits rather than by financial decisions based on the economic system; of personal fortunes being determined by luck and good behaviour rather than by effort, opportunism and unscrupulous behaviour; and of military valour and Imperial expansion as the ultimate glories of British society around the globe. The imported sporting plays did not relate directly to any of the major issues which confronted Australians at the time: the different attitudes to the bush engendered by fear, loneliness, Aboriginal people, droughts, floods, fires and hardship; the different position in society of the squatter as against the British gentry. Nor did they exploit the popular enthusiasm for Australian sporting champions and colonial sporting events. Closely linked to Australian sport through the industrial practices discussed earlier, the sporting drama nevertheless directed attention back to those aspects of Australian sport and society which were imitations of England. The storylines were structured to comment on a society undergoing a change from agrarian aristocratic or gentry control to urban middle-class industrialism, yet were successfully narrated in a pioneering society with allegedly democratic ideals and less rigid class divisions. If the sporting plays were for English society a reactionary fantasy of a lost age of social harmony, they were for most white Australians a dream of a remote utopian 'home' where life expectations were very different from those being experienced in the colonies.

Yet these plays were enormously popular in Australia. The argument has been loaded somewhat here by isolating for separate consideration in the next chapter the Australian sporting plays of the same decades, but it is nevertheless difficult to see the relatively few and only occasionally successful local and localised plays as more than borrowings from, comments on, or (rarely) reactions against the Imperial sporting drama. No doubt Australian audiences selectively read the imported drama, and reconciled its messages to their own experiences and perceptions of life. Nevertheless, it is an almost inescapable conclusion that, at a time when sport was one of the most powerful nationalistic forces in Australian society, sporting drama was working as an anti-nationalist, colonial tool binding Australia to England during the years of political separation.

For the Australian bourgeoisie the emphasis on horse-racing and fashion had a particular appeal in confirming their own advantaged place in society; a perceived superiority which depended on aping European fashions and displaying them in the most class-conscious sporting settings, the major racecourses, and on the most English-imitative sporting occasions, the major racing days. Watching from the dress circle a play about the English aristocracy and the Derby after having attended Derby Day at Randwick or Flemington was to assert that an Australian aristocracy of taste, breeding and *noblesse oblige* did exist. All the plays constructed country and city, rich and poor, fashionable self-indulgence and social deprivation, as inevitable oppositions rather than unwelcome departures from a democratic ideal, to be softened by upper-class benevolence rather than social justice.

In addition to sporting representations *per se*, this Anglophilia was made popular and plausible by stage stories about the Imperial military expeditions in which Australia engaged in support of the mother country at this time. These were another popular ingredient in the spectacular drama, and often followed sporting scenes. In particular the plays Bland Holt selected offered an interpretation of English (and Australian) military history which was used to support British Imperialism throughout the world. From 1893 when he staged *A Million of Money* for Williamson, to the 'melo-farce' *The Flood Tide* in 1904, all his sporting plays had as a major character a young army officer; during the action of many of these plays this character left to fight for his country in a distant land. This motif was particularly marked during the years of the South African campaigns. The four Acts of his 1898 Boer War 'sporting and military' success *For England* were titled 'For Sport', 'For Love', 'For Honor' and 'For England',[125] and another similar drama he staged in 1900, Arthur Shirley's *The Absent-Minded Beggar*, though not a sporting play, liberally sprinkled its military action with sporting analogies similar to those later used by Sir Henry Newbold in poems such as 'Vitai Lampada' ('Play up, play up, and play the game').[126] The worlds of sport and war were inextricably linked in nearly all Holt's productions, and were used for Imperial jingoism wherever possible. His localised 1901 success *Riding to Win* had both a young Australian leaving to fight in China during the Boxer rebellion and Holt himself as an Australian Boer-War veteran who comically barbecued meat using his bayonet as a skillet.[127] Popular attitudes to these wars must have been influenced by the repeated representation on Australian stages of what George Musgrove referred to in private correspondence to J. C. Williamson as 'melodramatic claptrap about the British soldier against the world and a regiment of soldiers about to die giving cheers for the Queen'.[128] Although sport itself was widely used for Imperial and militaristic propaganda and, although some particular sports, particularly horse-racing, were also committed to establishing non-democratic Anglocentric traditions, sport and the live drama as social institutions were by the First World War coming to stand for diverging and sometimes conflicting views on what Australian society was, what it had been, and what it ought to become.

Even after the First World War sporting drama, which perhaps had done more than any other genre to perpetuate admiration for the aristocratic social model, proved remarkably resilient. There was, in fact, one further major

Drury Lane horse-racing melodrama *The Hope* in 1911, but it does not appear to have been performed in Australia and it was never as successful as *The Whip*, which J. C. Williamson's revived in the 1920s[129] and which was still running in London in the early 1950s.[130] Minor racing plays continued to be written and performed; one was Max Goldberg's *Won by a Neck*, staged by the Fuller Bros. in Sydney in 1921.[131] In Adelaide in the same year the *Bulletin* noted wearily:

At the Royal is *Checkers*, which seems to be a well-known racing drama of the U.S.A. It works up to a climax in which the villain disables the hero's jockey, on which—guess it in one—the heroine gets into the saddle and rides to victory.[132]

More significantly the genre was taken up by the narrative cinema, where it is still popular today, although further paradigmatic shifts have occurred to accommodate changing social mythologies. Constructed differently for different audiences, the sporting film has continued to be one of the major genres of popular drama.

The Australian
Sporting Play
on the Commercial Stage

Nationalising the signs of sporting drama

Several previous studies of the nineteenth-century Australian stage have
shown, predictably enough, a particular interest in plays by Australians about
Australia.[1] However, this reductionist approach implies an historical
assumption that is not supported by an examination of the single genre of
sporting drama, which includes both English and Australian plays: the
assumption that a tradition of indigenous stage utterance was successfully if
slowly established; that local authors built primarily on the efforts and
experience of their predecessors; and that Australian audiences by the first
decade of the twentieth century had begun to demand the Australian play
as a regular part of their theatrical experience rather than as an occasional
novelty.[2]

Eric Irvin qualifies his approach in *Australian Melodrama* by pointing out
that the Australian plays he documents were not representative of the industry
as a whole. He suggests that:

In the period 1901–1914 there were two kinds of live theatre, one represented by J.
C. Williamson's sausage-chain, reserved almost exclusively for the London and New
York product, and the other conducted by such independents as William Anderson,
Meynell and Gunn, Philip Lytton and J. Clarence Lee, Edward I. Cole, Bert Bailey,
and a few others. These last rarely refused to take a gamble on an Australian play,
and just as rarely had reason to regret that gamble.[3]

However, the evidence drawn from the genre of sporting drama suggests that
even this careful statement is too nationalistic an assessment of the theatre
of the period, and in any case needs further qualification. Some of these
managers (Lytton, Lee) were minor entrepreneurs who performed solely or
principally in country towns. Cole was a more significant and enduring
manager, but he based his repertoire on American Wild West plays with a
few Australian bushranging stories added to these. The William Anderson
company, later taken over by Bailey, did appear extensively in the capital cities

and presented a creditable number of Australian plays, but the backbone of its repertoire was still British and American dramas. The same is true of Meynell and Gunn, the MacMahon Bros, the Taits, Edwin Geach, and other companies as well as J. C. Williamson's and Bland Holt.

The question of tradition and influence and of whether the Australian play was a mirror of Australian society or of thinly disguised English society is complicated by the different elements which made up this multiple art form. In broad terms Australian playwrights and producers at this time had the opportunity to manipulate seven elements of the theatrical sign: three visual elements (stage pictures and 'spectacles', visual sensations, and costuming); two aural elements (music, speech dialect); and two narrative elements (characterisation and story construction). The present study is concerned primarily with narratives, but it seems appropriate to consider briefly the visual and aural aspects of Australian dramatic craft.

The work of stage designers probably represented the closest approach achieved by Australian theatre in this period to a genuine and significant indigenous tradition in the stage arts. The techniques of scene painting were passed down from European-trained artists such as Alfred Clint, Phillip Goatcher, George Gordon, A. C. Habbe, John Hennings, and W. J. Wilson (some of whom portrayed Australian scenes for plays by Cooper, Darrell and Walch in the 1870s and 1880s)[4] to a younger generation of scene painters. This can most clearly be seen in the work of Bland Holt's designer, John Brunton, who began working alongside George Gordon designing productions for the triumvirate in the 1880s and 1890s before moving to Holt's company.[5] His settings depicting Sydney, Melbourne, and bush landscapes for Holt's localised dramas between 1899 and 1907 involved making extensive photographic and sketch records of chosen locations, and the 'stage pictures' of Australian scenes that he and others painted—principally on the backcloth canvases but also on wing, border and set pieces—were almost invariably the most unequivocally approved feature of local and localised plays. It is only the total disappearance of these huge landscapes (which were painted out when the canvas was required for the next production or discarded when they had deteriorated from use and travel) that prevents them from being seen as at least as important a contribution to Australian art and Australian nationalism in their time as the work of the Heidelberg school of landscape artists. Certainly the stage pictures were far more widely and popularly viewed, and when Tom Roberts returned from London in 1885 with his 'heightened concern for landscape painting *en plein air*',[6] and his determination to represent the scenery and quality of light unique to his native land, Australian stage designers were also making significant steps in the same direction.

If we relate the history of the pictorial stage representation of Australian sporting venues to the pattern found in English sporting drama, then rather fewer examples and some differences in subject and approach can be noted. The first tentative representation was of the Melbourne Cricket Ground in

George Fawcett's 1861 pantomime *Harlequin Mother Hubbard*,[7] and the first full-scale sporting spectacle was A. C. Habbe's design, also of the Melbourne Cricket Ground, in Walch's 1873 *Australia Felix*, a scene (I,iv) almost certainly inspired by the Derby scene in *Flying Scud*, although the cricket match itself is offstage.[8] Oddly, cricket and the MCG disappear from Australian plays after these two early examples, before the era of test matches and the 'Ashes'. It may be that they were occasionally shown in the sequence of panoramic scenes usually included in annual Christmas pantomimes, but neither is known to have appeared in a narrative context after *Australia Felix*.

Local racetracks were also slow to be portrayed, and were never as omnipresent as they were in English sporting drama. Flemington Racecourse was first painted in one of these panoramic sequences for the 1873 Melbourne Theatre Royal pantomime *Twinkle Twinkle Little Star*,[9] but does not appear as the setting for a dramatic scene until John Brunton portrayed it in 1893 for George Darrell's dramatisation of Nat Gould's *The Double Event: A Tale of the Melbourne Cup*.[10] Earlier, Darrell had included a description of the same race in his 1879 play *The Forlorn Hope*,[11] and Dampier and Wrangham's *Marvellous Melbourne* (1889) was a play in part about a heroine and her Melbourne Cup-winning horse, but neither play showed the racecourse itself.[12] *The Double Event* was widely performed by Darrell and another version by Andrew Hodge and Harry Craig[13] was playing in provincial Victoria in 1906 and in Brisbane in 1909.[14] Craig's company also had in its repertoire another racing drama, *Running It Off*, in which Act III was set at Randwick.[15]

This was a rare, but not the first, representation of Sydney's major race-course. The previous year E. W. O'Sullivan's dramatisation of Arthur Wright's *Keane of Kalgoorlie* was staged at the Haymarket Hippodrome by E. I. 'Bohemian' Cole with a Sydney Cup scene.[16] Both were followed by a far-better-known Melbourne Cup play: William Anderson's production of his and Temple Harrison's *The Winning Ticket* in 1910, with scenery and spectacular effects by Rege Robins including two scenes on different parts of the Flemington course.[17] Acclaimed as this season was, it nevertheless also illustrates the relatively limited appeal of the imitative Australian sporting play compared to the imported original. *The Winning Ticket* opened in Melbourne one week before J. C. Williamson's production of the previous year's Drury Lane racing drama *The Whip*,[18] and was evidently an attempt to undercut the expected success of this latest London sporting play with its imported cast. The sensation scenes of the local play were obviously plagiarised from *The Whip*: both used the *County Fair* method of staging a horserace for the first time since that production, and both had as a new sensation a railway accident (in *The Winning Ticket* a near-accident) in which the hero's horse is almost killed while being transported to the racecourse.[19] Both plays were being given their Australian premieres in Melbourne in the weeks leading up to the 1910 Melbourne Cup, and both were only withdrawn and replaced with other plays by the same companies when their drawing power had been exhausted.

The Winning Ticket ran for a creditable thirty-six performances but had to be withdrawn for lack of audiences just as the spring racing carnival was starting (the week the Caulfield Cup was run); *The Whip* continued on through Derby Day and Melbourne Cup week and for three more weeks—seventy performances in all.[20]

Bush race meetings appeared with no greater regularity. Darrell's 1886 *The New Rush* was a mining and quasi-sporting story which had racing characters and a bush setting,[21] but the bush racecourse as a stage spectacle began most obviously with Dampier and Walch's staging of *Robbery Under Arms* in 1890, where they showed in one scene (III,iii), closely modelled on *Flying Scud*'s Derby Day, as much as possible of the diverse scenery and character types associated with the (by then) mythical era of the great gold-rushes, all brought together for the annual picnic races.[22] E. I. Cole's Ben Hall story *The King of the Road* imitated this scene from 1900 onwards, as did several Ned Kelly plays,[23] followed by Philip Lytton's *The Girl from Outback*, a story of the Wagga Wagga Cup, in 1912.[24] As visual spectacles all these made contributions to a distinctive Australian national self-awareness; but as occasional local variants on a genre of English popular dramatic storytelling they emphasised instead a mythical unity between English and Australian social behaviour.

It seems probable that similar claims could be made for another aspect of the theatrical image, stage costuming.[25] There were some distinctive Australian types of clothing, worn by some characters in some Australian plays; there was also a long tradition of locally based costume designers stretching back to Thomas Simes in 1836.[26] But the emphasis in nearly all plays on having at least some 'society' characters fashionably and expensively dressed made local attire a bush or lower-class eccentricity in even an Australian setting. Again sporting drama, with its strong emphasis on high fashion, veered towards the conservative, European-oriented end of the spectrum. Local and localised 'sport and fashion' plays sometimes advertised that clothing and hats had been supplied by leading city fashion houses: *The Breaking of the Drought* featured costumes by Mark Foy's Sydney store and 'Millinery by Grace Bros. of the Broadway, Glebe'.[27] But the world of high society aped French and English fashions, and no mention is made of there being anything distinctively Australian about these designs.

Sporting sensations, the third of the primarily visual elements, were also rather less innovative than they appear at first glance. The staging of Australian horse races imitated the Drury Lane use of real horses (*The Double Event*), used the *County Fair* mechanism (*The Winning Ticket*), or went back to earlier hippodramatic methods (*The King of the Road, Keane of Kalgoorlie*). Even apparently authentic Australian pioneering spectacles, such as the large flock of sheep which crossed the stage at the beginning of *The Squatter's Daughter* in 1907, in fact derived from English originals, in this particular case the 1905 Drury Lane drama by Hall Caine, *The Prodigal Son*, which had begun in exactly the same way.[28] *The Squatter's Daughter* was embellished in various seasons with shearing and/or woodchopping contests and a boxing match between a man and a kangaroo;[29] E. W. O'Sullivan's *Cooee; or, Wild Days in the Bush* (1906) had a wild brumby hunt;[30] even earlier Charlie Taylor's *Unjustly Sentenced* (1894) had a scene set in 'The Home Paddock' during which 'a well-known Melbourne horse' was 'introduced upon the stage in order that an EXHIBITION of AUSTRALIAN ROUGH RIDING may be given'.[31] Wilton Welch's 'Great Australian Drama of Station & Bush Life' *The Wool King*, first performed at the Sydney Adelphi on 31 July 1911, also had a 'Great Buckjumping Scene', the format for which was borrowed from the horse-auction scene in *New Babylon*, thirty years old but still in Bland Holt's repertoire only a few years earlier. Both *The Wool King*'s and *Unjustly Sentenced*'s actual buckjumping sequences went back even further to the earliest trick-riding hippodramatic stories.[32]

One staging innovation which seems to have derived from American provincial practices rather than from Drury Lane was touring tent theatre. Introduced by Edward Irham 'Bohemian' Cole in the last years of the nineteenth century as an extension of his touring medicine show and the hippodrome he ran jointly with 'Texas Jack',[33] tent theatre was also adopted by Philip Lytton in 1907. Both Cole and Lytton had a number of sporting stories in their repertoires, and Lytton's season in Brisbane in 1907 shows something of the staging methods employed. 'His Majesty's Moving Theatre' (supposedly modelled on 'Sarah Bernhardt's American Touring Playhouse') was set up on a vacant block of land opposite the Theatre Royal in Elizabeth Street. It had folding chairs for the audience, an acetylene lighting plant, a proscenium arch over a raised stage, an orchestra, and was according to the *Brisbane Courier* 'a snug little place of entertainment'. For *The Cup Winner* 'under the footlights a straight was railed off, and the finish of the cup was shown in realistic fashion, a large group of competitors galloping home at full tilt', presumably into the tent through a raised section of the canvas wall and out the other side.[34]

There is no known research for this period on the aural elements of Australian theatre—music and the various aspects of spoken language—and the apparent lack of primary research materials will doubtless hamper future investigation. There are, for example, no known surviving scores for the many Australian songs, overtures and incidental music which the conductor Herbert Percy Kehoe composed for Australian plays between 1885 and 1909.[35] These included a 'Race Galop . . . Descriptive of the Melbourne Cup Race' for *The Double Event*.[36] Appropriately nationalistic music and lyrics would have strongly influenced the extent to which audiences accepted a play as 'racy of the soil', but the music was almost never commented on in reviews, and pit conductors for popular melodrama, such as Kehoe, rarely gained even a credit in the advertising.

The linguistic analysis of Australian stage speech and dialect as it is indicated in playscripts of the time lies beyond the scope of this study, but, like music, is obviously of major importance as an aural index by which audiences recognised and appreciated Australian characters. Some reviews of sporting plays suggested that a specialised sporting vocabulary was being extensively used, but extant scripts suggest that this was limited to a few flamboyant phrases. Australian stage dialogue, like most other aspects of theatrical communication, worked within the boundaries defined by English stage conventions; as late as 1910 it was possible for the English actress Daisy Scudamore to play an 'Australian' character less than two weeks after she arrived in the country.[37] Another example is Philip Lytton's and William Edward Vincent's 'Real Australian Drama' *The Girl from Outback* (1912), which was in some respects a more thoroughly local story than its contemporaries; it ended with the drought breaking just as the squatting family's horse Petronella wins the Wagga Cup and saves the family property Eerindi. Set throughout in Western New South Wales with no city scenes, and performed mostly to country audiences who presumably would have been quick to detect inaccuracies, *The Girl from Outback* nevertheless contains working-class Australian characters who freely mix Australian phrases such as 'Right mate' and 'Git yer head read!', English ejaculations such as 'Blimey' and 'Lumme', and servile working-class utterances such as 'You know, though the boss [is] the whitest man on earth, he hasn't got the experience, and even when things are good it's hard for him to manage'(I,i,p.1-2).[38] The sporting dialogue of the upper-class squatter boss: 'Petronella is racing for your sake and for the sake of Eerindi'(IV,iii,p.15) and the reactions of the villainous overseer: 'Curse my luck. After I had made a corner of the jockeys and practically killed Petronella's chance, that damn Drabb turns up as the rider'(IV,iii,p.14) are indistinguishable from their English equivalents. Such analysis must remain speculative—actors could, of course, take their vocal performance style a long way from the written text—but the Australian play as written had to wait for Steele Rudd before it captured more of the nuances of the Australian language than the occasional phrase or short burst of verbal pyrotechnics for the benefit and discomfort of the new chum.

Localisations: the nation as mirror

The comment was made by many critics in the 1880s, 1890s and 1900s that the most successful Australian plays were so because they were virtually indistinguishable from English models, and freely plagiarised their most attractive scenes, characters, and sensations. We can go further here and note that almost every major Australian stage play between the 1870s and 1912 was heavily indebted to the English sporting drama. The Melbourne society magazine *Bohemia* noted in 1891 that Dampier's and Walch's *This Great City*—supposedly an original celebration of Melbourne high and low life— closely imitated *The Great City*, an old play about London.[39] It also borrowed at least two of its sensational and spectacular scenes—a near-collision between two boats, and a scene in the Fitzroy Gardens—from Meritt's and Rowe's *New Babylon*. In 1907 the *Bulletin* went further, describing the William Anderson Company's production of Bailey and Duggan's 'Australian Play for Australian Audiences' *The Squatter's Daughter; or, The Land of the Wattle* as 'a typical modern English bellowdrama Australianised for the Andersonian public'.[40] Another critic pointed out that the same play had borrowed spectacles, sensations and situations from earlier productions of *A Midsummer Night's Dream, Uncle Tom's Cabin* and *Under the Gaslight*;[41] he might have added to these *Flying Scud*, as the heroine Violet Enderby's first entrance was a rewritten version of a sequence from Boucicault's play which had been in Anderson's repertoire some years earlier and in which Bailey's wife, Ivy Gorrick, had played Julia Latimer.[42]

For such critics the difference between a localised and a locally written play was a fine point. Both kinds of Australian plays were heavily dependent on a known paradigm of narrative elements and stage sensations determined by imported plays which were the stock-in-trade and featured productions of all companies. Actors too were trained principally in English theatrical speech and stage performance conventions and, although publicity interviews made much of the pleasure Australian actors took in playing Australian characters,[43] it was often the case, as the *Argus* critic noted in reviewing the Melbourne Cup play *The Winning Ticket* in 1910, that actors had 'not thrown off the manacles of tradition in interpretation as entirely as the authors have in the setting':

There is, perhaps, not a complete recognition that the drama is an attempt to depart from stereotyped conditions and characters in order to present something with which present-day audiences are familiar in real life.[44]

The central narrative problem which Australian sporting dramas faced was the strong structural imprint which English aristocratic/agrarian myths had made in the plotting and characterisation of the genre. As early as 1853 Daniel Deniehy had responded to W. C. Wentworth's suggestion that a colonial peerage be established by labelling the idea the 'bunyip aristocracy',[45] and in the next year, only weeks after the Eureka Stockade on 3 December, F. M. Soutten in his Christmas pantomime *An Argus Extraordinary; or, The Latest from Ballaarat* portrayed Australia allegorically as a delicate youth carrying a millstone on his back, which 'represents the squatting interest'.[46] Yet sixty years later Australian sporting plays like *The Winning Ticket* and *The Girl from Outback* were still content to copy the reactionary social structure of their English predecessors by showing an inexperienced, sometimes dissolute but essentially good-hearted squattocracy being given unquestioning allegiance by the Australian working class, who join with their bosses to defeat the machinations of evil middle-men: station managers, bookmakers, and professional gamblers and speculators. The romantic myth of aristocratic rural

England was localised as an equally romantic myth of the great squatting families and their supposed lifestyle in the Australian bush, where like their English antecedents they were shown ruling humanely and with the unquestioning assistance of their skilful workers.

The first noted example of the cultural transposition of sport within the English class system is Alfred Dampier's and J. H. Wrangham's *Marvellous Melbourne* (1889). In what purports to be a celebration of late-nineteenth-century Australian lifestyles, experiences and values, it is surprising to find that the following two 'life is a race' speeches are both intended to be interpreted *ironically*. They are spoken not by a wronged convict or a democrat, but by the play's villain, Robert Copeland:

Society strove to make me obey the command 'Fall in with the ruck, never think of winning the race, never dare to start for the Gold cup or enter yourself for the Aristocratic stakes, plod on between the cart shafts, toil over the beaten track. Let them whip and gall you and tear your mouth with the curb . . . '. (IV,i,p.1)

I am a rank outsider—nobody knows my stable or my training, my sire or my dam. No-one would bet a tenner on my chances, and yet I may win . . . An outsider has before now carried off the Cup from the Favourite. (IV,i,p.3)

In this period of popular drama outsiders were never allowed to win, in life or on the racetrack, in English or Australian narratives. In the moral and allegorical construction of sporting drama the best-bred person must naturally rule, and the best-bred horse must naturally win, if the races are run on their merits. (The fact that, unlike the English Derby, many Australian horseraces including the Melbourne Cup were run under handicap conditions was ignored.) *Marvellous Melbourne's* heroine, Dorothy Deane, is a vigorous young Australian, a horsewoman and a swimmer capable of diving into the Yarra to rescue a less agile friend, but she is also an 'heiress' who says to her horse Flashlight after the usual nobbling attempt has failed: 'nothing can stand against Australian blood and breeding' (IV,iii,p.16).

Not surprisingly, given his domination of the genre, it is the localised plays staged by Bland Holt which offer the clearest and most significant examples of the difficulties of culturally transposing texts. To understand his approach we have to first consider Holt's attitudes to Australia and Australian audiences, and the climate of historical and artistic change in which he operated in the last decade (1899–1909) of his career.

Holt's marketing strategy, like that of J. C. Williamson, was based primarily around the idea of Australia as a distant English province, to which he was bringing the best London plays. Unlike Williamson, Holt was fully committed to Australian actors, designers and technicians, but, like his rival, Holt's advertising emphasised such details as the London theatre where each play had first appeared ('The Popular Adelphi Military Drama'; 'the magnificent Drury Lane melodramatic production'); the patronage of the elite ('witnessed at various times by the leaders of the English Royalty and Aristocracy'); and the importation of fashionable clothing designs ('Uniforms imported from London').[47] The sporting plays in particular made an explicit appeal to the colonial mentality. They most commonly represented the Derby, the Grand National Steeplechase and other major English races, and were often premiered in Melbourne on Derby Day, the Saturday before the Melbourne Cup. Australian audiences were consequently reminded that their sporting celebrations were imitations of English originals.

An exchange of letters between Holt and the Sydney lawyer, author and dramatist Ambrose Pratt, shows something of Holt's thinking about the selection and marketing of sporting drama. Pressed by Pratt simply to take the time to read a 'perfectly original . . . racing drama' Pratt had written, Holt replied:

You have placed me in an awkward position—Reading plays I don't altogether like when the work submitted is a local one—It cribs and cabins one in case a similar situation [or] dramatic sentiment arises in a Home purchase. The English and American dramas bearing the hall-mark of public and press approval, cost one only a certain amount of purchase money for rights of playing and one knows exactly the position he holds.[48]

In his next letter Pratt mentioned that 'the play is not local in any sense. The mise en scene is in Monte Carlo and England'.[49] Holt replied that in that case he definitely would *not* read the script, as he 'would only produce a local author's work on account of it being *local*—that would be the great charm . . .'[50] Two years later, after William Anderson had produced a dramatisation of Pratt's novel *Thunderbolt* at the Sydney Theatre Royal, Pratt tried once more to interest Holt in his racing drama by offering 'if you wanted the locale to be Australian I could easily manage the change, for the race meeting could be made the Melbourne Cup'.[51] Holt rejected this idea also. He never did stage a Melbourne Cup play, although the popular appeal of such a piece must surely have occurred to him after his localised plays began to become his biggest successes. Holt remained to the end a deeply conservative Anglo-Australian Imperialist, bringing the best plays of the London stage to Australian audiences and deliberately avoiding any real test as to whether or not those plays were what Australian audiences most wanted to see. He suppressed the burgeoning desire of Australians to see their sporting champions and institutions as evidence of national rather than colonial achievement, and offered instead pictures and stories of greater achievements at 'Home'. Perhaps the advertising phrase which most accurately sums up Holt's conception of the relationship between his work and its English antecedents is that which appeared in the *Argus* on 24 June 1899 over a description of his production of Shirley's and Vane's *Straight from the Heart*: 'A STORY OF THE NORTH TINGED WITH THE GOLDEN BEAMS OF THE SOUTH'.

Despite his Anglocentricity Holt counted amongst his acquaintances Lawson, 'Banjo' Paterson, Victor Daley and J. F. Archibald, and some years later he did begin to employ Australian authors, particularly the major short-story writer Edward Dyson and the popular novelist Henry Fletcher. But he only gave them work localising and topicalising English scripts, and, as he had with Pratt, resisted their attempts to sell him their own plays.[52] Holt was well aware of the growing popularity of Australian literature and drama; of George Darrell's successful Australian plays including in 1893 *The Double Event*, a drama of the Melbourne Cup; and of the bushranging stories which Alfred Dampier, Dan Barry, Arnold Denham and others had dramatised with great success. Holt's response to these inroads into his major market was to begin to localise some of his English plays, but to strictly reject any suggestion that they kept such disreputable company. His first localisation, Sutton Vane's *The War of Wealth*, was announced in the *Argus* advertisement of 19 August 1899 as 'proof that [the] sanguinary bushranger and his incarnadine shirt are NOT NECESSARY to a RATTLING AUSTRALIAN DRAMA'. The economics of mass popular appeal involved making some allowance to working-class enthusiasms, while retaining the allegiance of the bourgeoisie who bought tickets in the dress circle and family circle at higher prices.

One of Holt's fundamental assumptions in his marketing strategy was that the interest audiences took in his spectacular stage settings was based on their pictorial appeal to those who were not familiar with the places being portrayed.[53] It is significant that when *The War of Wealth* became Holt's first localisation in 1899, it was staged in Melbourne but set in Sydney, with views of the Harbour, George Street, and the city by night.[54] It appears that during his subsequent Sydney season in 1900 Holt did not intend to offer audiences views of their own locality, and only did so after the then twenty-year-old *New Babylon* failed to draw sufficiently well to carry through until the end of his season at the Theatre Royal. Presented at the end of his five-month lease 'for six nights only', *The War of Wealth* surprised Holt by becoming, as the *Sydney Morning Herald* put it, 'the most vivacious production of the season', drawing 'densely crowded and enthusiastic' houses.[55] In another notice the same reviewer commented: 'There is a general consensus of opinion, largely expressed in the testimony of crowded houses, that Mr. Bland Holt ought to have produced "The War of Wealth" earlier in his season.'[56] It was only after this unexpected and unequivocal evidence that Australian audiences enjoyed pictorial celebrations of the local and familiar as well as the distant and romantically exotic, that Holt began to regularly employ Dyson and Fletcher as localisers of *Riding to Win* (1901), *The Breaking of the Drought* (1902, from Arthur Shirley's *The Sinful City*), *A Desperate Game* (1903), *The Betting Book* (1905), *A Path of Thorns* (1905), and *The Great Rescue* (1907, from Lincoln J. Carter's *Bedford's Hope*). Even after he belatedly acknowledged that white Australian audiences were interested in their geographical surroundings as well as their historical origins, Holt only staged on average one localised script for each four or five English plays he produced. The localised plays were advertised over the names of the authors of the English originals; Dyson and Fletcher got no credit for their work even when a play like *Bedford's Hope*, as Holt and Fletcher both agreed, had required 'practically rewriting'.[57]

Holt's first sporting adaptation, *Riding to Win*, was from the outset an oddity, since it came to Australia without the fanfare of a previous West End production. It was brought to Holt's attention by Arthur Shirley who, as well as being the most prolific of the popular English dramatists of the time, operated as a theatrical agent and who wrote at least weekly to Holt between 1894 and 1907 describing new plays, new trends in drama and the fortunes of different playhouses and managers. Shirley had travelled to the Broadway Theatre in the (then) outer London suburb of New Cross to see *Riding to Win*, which he described to Holt as 'one of the best of the provincial plays. Not violent or gory.'[58] Shirley may have been attracted to the piece by the review in the London *Era* on 28 July 1900, which he forwarded to Holt and which stated:

The racehorse has often formed the pivot on which has turned the interest of famous histrionic narratives . . . and now at last it has been sought to elevate the humble 'bike' to the ranks of an important factor in a modern play.[59]

Shirley's accompanying letter was written on 8 August and would have reached Holt at about the time he was experiencing the unexpected success in Sydney of the localised *War of Wealth*. Holt's business correspondence at this time was extensive, but there does not seem to be anything to indicate who localised *The War of Wealth*. It may have been done in part by Henry Lawson who certainly contributed lists of Australian slang phrases which were to be inserted into the English dialogue of one of the early localisations,[60] and both 'Banjo' Paterson and Victor Daley were writing verse advertisements and plot descriptions for Holt at about this time.[61] But *The War of Wealth* appeared over Sutton Vane's name alone, and *Riding to Win* was even more duplicitously described on the playbills as 'By special arrangement with Arthur Shirley Esq', in order to associate it with a well-known English dramatist's name.[62]

The question of the authorship of *Riding to Win*, and particularly of its localised version, is an important one since Bland Holt's own role of Sam Flutter, a larrikin Australian returned from the Boer War, has been described by Hal Porter as 'a clear indication that the hard-doer Digger type was already, fifteen years before Gallipoli, a well-developed stage type',[63] and has also been referred to by Margaret Williams as 'the first real digger on the Australian stage'.[64] Both quote approvingly examples of Flutter's 'Australianism', and Williams, who has had the opportunity to consult the Lord Chamberlain's copy of the original English script, further states that Flutter's role—originally that of an English servant—had been extensively rewritten and expanded for the Australian production, and argues that 'the Australianizing of one of the minor characters . . . is the great attraction of the piece'.[65] The original London play was by two provincial dramatists, Frank Herbert and Walter Howard,[66] but there is no reason to suspect that either had anything to do with the antipodean revisions. The newspaper advertisements for the Melbourne premiere season were more honest than the playbills, and stated that the play was by Herbert and Howard 'with Revisions by ARTHUR SHIRLEY, Esq.'[67] In Shirley and Holt's exchange of letters about *Riding to Win* they had expressed their mutual dissatisfaction with the lack of good comic roles in contemporary popular drama, particularly in the Drury Lane pieces which were coming to rely increasingly on spectacle alone.[68] On the evidence of this correspondence and the billing he was given in the advertising, Shirley must be credited as the person who revised and expanded Flutter's role, though he did not localise the play.[69]

Most of the localising of *Riding to Win* to a Melbourne setting was done by the major Australian short-story writer Edward Dyson.[70] Norman Lindsay described Dyson in the last of his *Bohemians of the Bulletin* biographical sketches as a 'great humourist' and as a prolific author who successfully supported a large extended family and minor real-estate investments with his writing.[71] During the same period he was working for Holt, Dyson was writing his 'Benno' stories for the *Bulletin*, later collected and published by the NSW Bookstall Company as *Fact'ry 'Ands*.[72] However, a comparison between the Melbourne slum vernacular in those stories and the speeches written for Sam Flutter in the play shows that Dyson was not the author of the play's widely celebrated and supposedly characteristic Australian character. Benno and his mates invariably pronounce 'is' as 'ez', 'of' as 'iv', 'and' as ' 'n' ' and 'you' as 'y' or 'youse'; they also randomly add or omit initial aspirates ('h'). Sam Flutter's speeches have none of these characteristics. His dialect reads and sounds instead like what it almost certainly is: comic cockney written by Arthur Shirley in London, and tinkered with by Dyson and perhaps Holt himself only to the extent of replacing occasional words and phrases with Australian slang equivalents:

Der yer tike me fer a bloomin' mug? When them parliament coves promises er thing fer sure, it's good enough fer me ter know I don't get it.[73]

Er brace o' coupons! How Handy! It will only tike 998 more ter get er glass butter dish, an' fer 2000 I can get er set o' tea spoons! Oh, me luck's chokin' me![74]

Edward Dyson had been a miner and a factory worker in Melbourne; his stories are full of accurately overheard Australian working-class language ('Right-o, then'; ' In arf a tick'; 'Y'orter seen 'er'; 'Knock it off'), similar to that which C. J. Dennis was later to imitate and exaggerate in *The Songs of a Sentimental Bloke*, but they are quite unlike the cockney dialect with occasional Australian references spoken by Sam Flutter. This is not to say that the character wasn't enormously entertaining; the evidence from reviews is that it was one of Holt's most outrageously successful comic roles.[75] However, it cannot be seen as a significant reflection of Australian speech, manners, or social attitudes of the time. The speech patterns and style of humour relate to the English stage tradition of low comedy with which Arthur Shirley was familiar and for which he wrote.

Dyson's letters to Holt, which presumably accompanied manuscript revisions to the playtexts, are neat, concise and usually end with a request for between £5 and £10 for the work done. This was a very modest additional expenditure; Dyson charged Holt £10-10s-0 for his work on Shirley's *The Sinful City* (*The Breaking of the Drought*)[76] at about the time Holt was offering Arthur Collins at Drury Lane £600 for the rights to one of the Drury Lane dramas.[77] Unlike Henry Lawson, Dyson was willing and able to fill the role of a quick, reliable, undemanding and co-operative hack. Substantial script changes were not required; simply the substitution of local place names for the English ones, the excision of obviously foreign references and the insertion of a few topical local jokes. In *Riding to Win* a reference to the bicycling hero 'going for it— like a mad Highlander for a fat Boer' was replaced by comment on Australia's first Prime Minister: 'like Barton to a banquet'.

In *Riding to Win* the English rural gentry family is changed to an Australian squatting family, but the play begins at their holiday home at Queenscliff overlooking Port Phillip Heads rather than on the property itself. The young English aristocrat/soldier going abroad with his regiment becomes the squatter's son, departing 'with the Australian squadron for China'.[78] The high-society sport-and-fashion setting is indicated in the first scene by a garden party attended by two dozen men and women dressed in fashionable tennis costumes, and the tour of London becomes a tour of Melbourne, moving the action to the banks of the Yarra, to Alexandra Avenue, the Botanical Gardens, the Exhibition cycling track, and elsewhere. The hero, Frank Fielding, is a young doctor, though the story offers no evidence of this—the characters central to the storyline were often reduced by adversity to humble working-class lifestyles, but were not shown as being of or coming from the proletariat. Frank's addiction to gambling has placed him in the usual predicament, and the villain's machinations have resulted in Frank and his wife living below the poverty line in a Richmond cottage. But Frank is a champion cyclist. Near starvation and about to have his mortgage foreclosed, he is restored to health and vigour by Bland Holt as Sam Flutter, who improvises an onstage barbecue and 'cooks about two pounds of steak in the view of the audience' just before the bicycle race which Frank hopes to win.[79] The bike rather than the horse is nobbled by having its tyres punctured, but Frank simply borrows another and sprints to victory. Cycling is not presented as a big-money sport in which either the prize (£200) or the associated gambling are passports to prosperity, but is simply a last-ditch stand against life's cruelties which the impoverished sportsman can make:

1st man: It was a thousand to one against him!
2nd man: Was it? He was riding for his wife and home. (IV,iii,n.p.)

Unfortunately for the historical record, Dyson and Holt were both in Melbourne and were able to meet personally to discuss the changes to the script, so there is no surviving correspondence to indicate more fully the extent of their revisions or the thinking behind it. However, by 1902 when Dyson next localised a play, Holt was performing at the Sydney Lyceum; consequently they were obliged to discuss the changes by letter. For *The Breaking of the Drought*, a title which Dyson suggested as better than 'Sydney's Seamy Side', Dyson wrote:

You'll find I've made the old man look upon his troubles as a protracted drought and speak of the dawning of better times as the passing of the dry spell. This will help to carry the new title along if it pleases you.[80]

The extended drought of 1895–1903 was at its peak between September 1901 and November 1902; Dyson worked over the script in June of the latter year. Holt staged it at the Lyceum in December after the first good rains had fallen, including in his advertising a verse description of the events of the last act as:

> The Drought is Broken, peace has come again,
> And hearts are cleansed as by the fruitful rain.[81]

However, the storyline was not changed from the English original. While John Brunton's pictorial renditions of Sydney and the Bush represented Australian scenery with photographic accuracy, the plot had a merely allegorical relationship to the Australian climate, and, as in *Riding to Win*, Australian society was evoked not through accurate observation and description but only to the extent that it could be represented as an exact imitation of British society. The English baronial hall became a squatter's 'station outback' and this time the tour of London's seamy side became a tour of Sydney, including Woolloomooloo, Little Coogee beach, Paddy's Market and Mosman's Bay. Even to some contemporary critics the English symbolic geography and class categories appeared to be awkwardly applied to Australia; high- and loose-living young men and women were shown meeting at 'A Fashionable Flat in Sydney' and the *Bulletin* observed:

The audience is thrilled by allusions to Sydney as a city of terrible and beautiful temptations and much romance. The average Sydneyite has usually regarded it as a place where he is liable to be run over by tram-cars at any moment, and its really high-class sins are not so well known as might be expected.[82]

While in Sydney Holt found a second writer, Henry Fletcher, who was the author of a bestselling comic bush novel *The Waybacks in Town and at Home*.[83] For Holt he localised an American play *A Desperate Game; or, Jim of the Sage Brush* (*. . . of the Salt Bush* in the Australian version).[84] After that time Holt seems to have sent scripts to both Dyson and Fletcher and to have conflated the best ideas of each into a final performance script. It is not possible, therefore, to state with certainty which if either contributor was responsible for the revisions, although of the later localisations *The Betting Book* and *A Path of Thorns* seem from the surviving correspondence to be mainly Dyson's work, and *The Great Rescue* and *The Great Millionaire* mainly Fletcher's.[85] *The Great Millionaire* was not localised, but one character—'Bill Balwyn from Australia'—was rewritten by Fletcher as a 'Wayback', and inserted into the London script.[86]

Dyson's localisation of *The Betting Book* shows the difficulties writers experienced in attempting to modify the dominant values implicit in the construction of the popular paradigm. Sutton Vane had written *The Betting Book* in 1901 during which time, as he reported to Holt, 'They are preparing a big crusade against betting. There is to be a Royal Commission on the subject'.[87] The racing plays had always adopted an easy, cynical attitude to the suggestion that gambling was either evil or avoidable, but *The Betting Book*, after indulging in the usual sport and gambling situations in the first two Acts, showed in a final two Acts of domestic drama the effects on an unsuccessful punter.[88] This had pertinence to the Australian society of 1905 which had picked up the mood of pro- and anti-gambling hysteria. On the Sunday after *The Betting Book* opened, the Reverend John Gray preached on 'The Gambling Mania' at the Cairns Memorial Church in East Melbourne. During the week someone had pinned to the church door in comic imitation of Luther a placard 'The Law of Luck. A Representative of Tattersall's will give an address, and Mr. J. Wren will sing a solo entitled Do Not Murmur.' The outraged Reverend Gray complained that the 'result of the evil was that true sport was spoiled, the mind was unsettled, and intellectual growth was warped' and recommended sweeping new anti-betting laws, outlawing bookmaking and the publication of betting odds, and demanded 'the election to Parliament of men who did not gamble'.[89]

The Betting Book was, according to the *Age*'s critic, 'a theatrical variant of Frith's Road to Ruin'; another of that artist's moral depictions of contemporary English society at leisure.[90] In the localisation the play began with a 'picturesque Australian homestead, a sunlit stream in the middle distance and a range of blue, tree clad hills forming a far off background', and depicted a country football match and a steeplechase at a bush racecourse. It contrasted this healthy open-air sporting lifestyle with 'a notorious Collingwood gambling institution' to which the unsuccessful gambler descends, the symbolically opposed geography of virtue and vice being emphasised by the claustrophobic corridors, secret doors and passages and the generally seedy surroundings in which John Wren's real-life tote operated. However, Holt's production was cynically indifferent to the play's morality, for the *Age* noted:

a striking contrast . . . between the high moral purpose of the dramatist and the business instincts of the printer of the programme—on the one page are the details of this highly moral play, a notification of Tattersall's latest consultations, and, suggestively enough, the advertisement of a money-lending institution.

For Holt, Dyson wrote a new final scene and some additional dialogue to allow the steeplechase scene to be lengthened,[91] but otherwise the substitution of local scenes and characters was predictable, with a 'breezy mannered generous hearted young squatter' providing a wholesome counterbalance to the moral failings of the gambling, city-seeking man.

It should not be thought that Holt's patently token transpositions, which made no concession whatsoever to any concept of *difference* between eighteenth-century English and early twentieth-century Australian social organisation, were a special or unusual case. Most of the locally written popular Australian dramas between the 1880s and the First World War were no more original than his. George Darrell's version of *The Double Event* (1893) concerned the fortunes of a 'present plunger and a possible baronet' Richard Marston, played by the author. This character's story is indistinguishable from that of dissolute English heroes of this and earlier decades, and from less 'original' localisations. Darrell's character has lost disastrously at gambling and his only chance of retrieving his fortunes 'is by winning the double with his horse Caloola'. The villain is a corrupt horse trainer and the 'double' is two horse-races, the Derby (the Victoria Derby, but the English analogy is clear) and the Melbourne Cup. As usual the hero's horse is the favourite and the villain tries to nobble first the horse and then the jockey; at least two

'Under the elms at Flemington': William Anderson's and Temple Harrison's *The Winning Ticket*, 1910 (Eric Irvin, *Australian Melodrama*).

characters were even recognised as being imitations of Nat Gosling and Mo Davis from *Flying Scud*; and the play ends in the aristocratic surroundings of Lord and Lady Mayfield's Melbourne mansion.[92]

Seventeen years later, in 1910, Anderson's and Harrison's Melbourne Cup play *The Winning Ticket* offered some minor variations, but the structure was essentially unaltered. It included the visiting English actor Roy Redgrave as a member of the 'French decadent aristocracy', the Count de Cartel. His role in Australia is that of a 'spieler', one of a trio of 'racecourse rogues' who attempt to nobble the favourite for the Melbourne Cup, Kookaburra. By displacing the evils of the nobility geographically, the play enabled the *Argus* to distinguish one kind of aristocracy from another. It commented on the ease with which the Count caused havoc in the squatting household by remarking: 'it is to be hoped that all farmer's sons do not so easily give themselves up as beaten by the effete French aristocracy'.[93] Silly but well-connected young British men portrayed comically in their quest for colonial experience, like Charles Harold Cholmondeley Vane Somers Golightly in *Marvellous Melbourne* and Archie McPherson in *The Squatter's Daughter*, nevertheless display great courage when required; it was only by crossing the English channel that a less favourable representation could be made of an upper-class character.

The allegiance of the working class to the squatters and their racing interests was encapsulated in *The Winning Ticket* by the play's railway swinging-bridge sensation (III,iii) when the signalman Surly Briggs has to choose between saving the train transporting Kookaburra to Flemington or saving his small daughter Jenny whom the villain has thrown into the river below:

Biggs turns from lever, bridge ceases to revolve
Biggs: My child! My child. What can I do? (*Whistle and sound of approaching train*) Jenny or the train, which? Her life or theirs? (*Comes to steps, turns back*) No, I leave her to God. I must do my *Duty*! (*Falls across levers clutching them. Bridge revolves*)
Ruth: (*Off (R)*) Jenny. Jenny. (*Thunder of train. Double for Ruth appears (R) dives into tank. As child and she form picture in (C) of tank, bridge locks and train dashes across from (R)*)

    Quick Curtain

(III,iii,p.9)[94]

The working-class Biggs saves the squatter's horse, the squatter's daughter Ruth saves the working-class child, and Kookaburra goes on to win the Cup. The high-diving act introduced as a sporting spectacle in Holt's non-sporting *The Breaking of the Drought* is here reworked as a non-sporting sensation in a sporting play.

The characters in Australian sporting plays were also heavily indebted to English models. The most extreme example of this is the horse-riding heroine who has been seen by several commentators as a distinctively Australian development;[95] the currency lass/squatter's daughter who uses her athletic prowess to define her Australian individuality. Such characters were certainly given speeches which suggested this brash nationalistic quality. Violet Enderby, the squatter's daughter in Bailey and Duggan's play of that name, rebukes Dudley Harrington, a dissolute young suitor who complains 'A little encouragement from you would make me a better man', by responding:

That is only a mean excuse, to throw upon my shoulders the responsibility of your conduct . . . You forget Dudley, that I am an Australian girl. I've been accustomed to station life from childhood, and when I am thrown upon my own resources you will find me quite capable of managing my own affairs without your assistance. (I,ii,p.26)[96]

Nevertheless the character type was an English one. The most distinctive individual motif of these young women—apart from such claptrap utterances—was their delivery of a long race-call speech in which their love of horse-riding and horse-racing is expressed. The earliest known example is in Boucicault's *London Assurance* (1841), where Lady Gay Spanker, described in an aside as a 'she-Bucephalus tamer', is asked to describe a steeplechase in which she recently participated:

There were sixty horses in the field, all mettle to the bone: the start was a picture—away we went in a cloud—pell-mell—helter-skelter—the fools first, as usual, using themselves up—we soon passed them—first your Kitty, then my Blueskin, and Craven's colt last. Then came the tug—Kitty skimmed the walls—Blueskin flew o'er the fences—the Colt neck and neck, and half a mile to run—at last the Colt baulked a leap and went wild. Kitty and I had it all to ourselves—she was three lengths ahead as we breasted the last wall, six feet, if an inch, and a ditch on the other side. Now, for the first time, I gave Blueskin his head—Ha! Ha!—Away he flew like a thunderbolt—over went the filly—I over the same spot, leaving Kitty in the ditch—walked the steeple, eight miles in thirty minutes, and scarcely turned a hair.
All: Bravo! Bravo! (III,i,p.41)[97]

The American version of *Flying Scud* contained three such speeches; later Boucicault's *The Jilt* also had a race call, although the speech was divided amongst three characters.[98]

   The poor survival of texts makes it difficult to determine when this set scene with its character typology first entered Australian plays. The earliest noted example of a race call is a Melbourne Cup description in George Darrell's 1879 play *The Forlorn Hope*—though it is not clear who delivers the speech or why— and the first usage by a female character seems to be Dorothy Deane in *Marvellous Melbourne*. In reply to her earnest lover Frank Seymour's question: 'But are you as fond of racing as ever?' Dorothy replies:

Fond of it? I dote on it. Just fancy now the horses start. They look as beautiful as a rainbow bursting from a dark cloud. Quick as the lightning flash they fly over the turf cerise and blue leads then yellow and black cap, then green then brown, then crimson, then blue and white shoots ahead from the ruck, now yellow comes to the front and steals along side of cerise swift and sure as an arrow. Now they're neck and neck whip and spur dig deep into their foaming flanks their veins start out like whip cord. They're in the straight and now for home. The winning post is in sight— still neck and neck, but now, now, now within twenty yards of the Judge's box the jockey shakes up his reins, his horse answers to the call, and amidst the frantic cheers of thousands he wins by a neck. (I,i,p.16-17)

The speech is a poor one. The horses are anonymous and it is not clear which horse wins; nor does it matter, since the speech is simply a set piece and is unconnected to the plotting. Furthermore although she makes her first entrance on horseback, Dorothy describes the race from a spectator's point of view and, unlike Lady Gay Spanker in *London Assurance* and Phyllis Welter in *The Jilt*, she does not ride in horse races. Later Australian equestrian heroines were more competitive and directly informative about their own horse-riding ability than Dorothy, but not more so than these English models. Violet Enderby in *The Squatter's Daughter* also makes her first entrance on horseback after 'a glorious gallop' chasing a kangaroo, which she describes in a long speech ending:

> I was alone in the chase now. The kangaroo made for the stockyard
> fence, and I was close on him. 'Pull up Miss, said someone don't tackle
> that fence or you'll be killed.' Death was my last thought at that moment
> I felt brave enough to lead the Light Brigade. I raced Sweet Briar at it.
> One touch of the whip, she rose like a rocket, never struck a fetlock,
> landed me safe on the other side, and I captured the kangaroo in the
> stockyard. (*She laughs heartily*)
> *Omnes:*   Bravo, bravo . . . (I,i,p.11)

A few pages later (pp.14-16) Archie McPherson, the new chum, describes his comically inept contribution to the same chase, much as Bob Buckskin had echoed Nat Gosling's race call.

Ruth Willoughby in *The Winning Ticket* has a similar racing speech (III,ii,pp.11-13), and so has Kate Kelly in Mabel Mills's and Frank Shepard's *The Kelly Gang; or, Outlaw Kelly* (1911), showing that the race-call speech could be appropriated by outlawed lower-class Irish heroines just as easily as by Australian squatter's daughters, Yorkshire men and women, or the English nobility. The convict heroine, Margaret Catchpole, the subject of both Alfred Dampier's and C. H. Krieger's play *An English Lass*[99] and Raymond Longford's 1911 film *The Romantic Story of Margaret Catchpole*[100]was an earlier horse-riding outlaw, famous for the ride she made through the Suffolk countryside to join her smuggler-lover.[101] Kate Kelly's ride to warn her brothers of the troopers' whereabouts was also a long-standing legend. The 1906 film *The Story of the Kelly Gang* had a version which revealed that the actress playing Kate Kelly was not a very good rider; consequently a better version was made and cut into the prints of the film some months after its first release.[102]

In Mills's and Shepard's stage version of the Kelly legend, first performed in Adelaide in 1911, Kate's entrance is anticipated by Ned Kelly's description of her offstage ride as she approaches their hideout:

Kate: [*Off*] Cooee!
Ned: Why, here she comes now. There's a picture for you boys, did you ever see anything to beat that, look now, she takes to the big fence—over like a bird —hurrah!
Omnes: Hurrah! Hurrah! (*Enter Kate Kelly*)
Ned: Bravo, Kate, Bravo. You've had a long ride of it, Kate, and you must be tired out.
Kate: Yes, Ned. I've just left a party of troopers on their way here. They have made a warrant out for your arrest, so I made the old mare go for all I knew—They saw me, and tried to follow, I gave them a good gallop across Murphy's five-mile paddock, at the first big fence Steele came to grief, but the others still kept going. One of them tried to bring old Possum down with his shotee, but I spurred her on and soon got out of his reach. Then we came to the big stone wall near the old log hut.
Omnes: Yes, Yes.
Kate: Kennedy parted from his comrades there.
Ned: Parted, why?
Kate: To keep an engagement he had in the ditch. The last I saw of them was the new-chum Trooper O'Toole hanging on to his horse's tail. Then I took the bush track and arrived here unobserved.[103]

Yet this apparently strongly 'Australian' female set-piece was also one of the most hackneyed and overworked of English sporting play motifs. Like other character types and narrative sequences, the love of horse-riding expressed by vigorous heroines in locally written plays remained firmly in the centre of orthodox English dramatic material, and was simply appropriated and localised as required. Specific national and class meanings were inscribed by the narrative and production contexts; the essential reference was to gender behaviour, through the representation of active working or sportswomen. Although somewhat more insistent in 'pioneering' societies like the United States and Australia than in England, this type was one of the major responses of all nineteenth-century English-speaking stages to the position of women in their societies.

Rewritings: revising the ideology

Neil: The trickery of business is condoned if it fails and applauded if successful. Our civilisation has made us parasites, and wise men accumulate fortunes at the expense of fools.
Alma: Certainly. In the big race for Wealth the mugs get the outside running, whilst the cunning ones hug the rails. Why should we care how many we bump, jostle or bring to grief in the struggle, so long as we get a place in the world's Great Handicap?[104]

There were a few texts, distinct from such local exploitations of racing drama, which were linked not simply by the desire to localise the genre but by their authors' belief that the narrative paradigm of such plays was an unsatisfactory model for Australian society. These dramatists were not themselves opposed to the dominant ideals of sport; like the majority they set out to celebrate it, but rather than localise the known formula they attempted to revise its structure and subject matter. In particular they saw the idea that life is a horse-race run according to bloodlines, influenced by luck but ultimately rewarding the well-bred English gambler, as inappropriate to the emerging Australian national identity. Consequently they sought sporting subjects with a different symbolic iconography or plotlines with different moral conclusions.

The first major text of this kind was Garnet Walch's 1873 Christmas panto-mime *Australia Felix; or, Harlequin Laughing Jackass and the Magic Bat*. This play has been the subject of several commentaries,[105] but what has not been explicated is the play's immediate colonial context, and its relationship to the emerging tradition of sporting drama which, at the time Walch wrote his 'Original Extravaganza',[106] was chiefly represented by *Flying Scud*.

Australia Felix was written and performed during one of the short periods in colonial history when the majority of Anglo-Australians were forced to recognise that their attitudes towards the 'mother country' were complex, and when the colonial stage could reflect and exploit this ambivalence. One reason for this unease was the claim in 1866 of a Wagga Wagga butcher, 'Thomas Castro' (Arthur Orton) that he was heir to the Tichbourne baronetcy and estates in England, the rejection of his claim in 1872, and his trial for perjury which was in its last days when *Australia Felix* was performed.[107] The defendant was widely viewed in England and Australia as the victim of snobbishness and bigotry on the part of the British upperclasses (represented by the Tichbourne family and the law lords), and on 3 September 1873 the trial judge was forced to move to suppress the many popular demonstrations of support for the defendant by forbidding him from attending public meetings.[108] Two later texts which we will examine shortly, George Darrell's *The Sunny South* and Edmund Duggan's *The Democrat/The Southern Cross*, exploited the sense of outrage felt by many Australians at Orton's conviction and sentencing to fourteen years' jail with hard labour. Garnet Walch, writing during the trial, tended to the other view, that Orton was an impostor and that the trial—the longest and most widely reported in England to that time—was a slur on Australia's good name. Kantankeros, the 'Demon of Dullness' in *Australia Felix*, mentions in a list of his misdeeds that he has 'Forged Orton-Tichbourne twenty brand-new lies'(p.10).

However, the principal cause of disharmony in 1873 between London and the colonies was the English novelist Anthony Trollope, who visited Australia in 1871–72. His impressions were collected and published in London in 1873 as *Australia and New Zealand*,[109] although most Australians would have known of them through their serial publication in *The Australasian* the previous year.[110] Trollope's Australian novel, *Harry Heathcote of Gangoil*, based on his son and dealing with the squatter/settler conflict in New South Wales from the squatters' point of view, was also being serialised in the *Age* that same Christmas of 1873.[111]

Forty years earlier Fanny Trollope had saved her family from poverty, and outraged readers in the United States, by publishing *Domestic Manners of the Americans*, a caustic and highly successful account of her experiences in North America.[112] Her son no doubt remembered this profitable approach when penning his impressions of Australia, one notorious comment being:

I suppose that a young people falls naturally into the fault of self-adulation . . . for which the colonial phrase of 'blowing' has been created . . . They blow a good deal in Queensland;—a good deal in South Australia. They blow even in poor Tasmania. They blow loudly in New South Wales, and very loudly in New Zealand. But the blast of the trumpet as heard in Victoria is louder than all the blasts—and the Melbourne blast beats all the other blowing of that proud colony.[113]

Walch was only one of a number of Australian authors who were quick to defend their homeland during the furore over Trollope's travel book and novel, and from this time the character of a famous English writer, travelling and making a record of Australian life for London publication, appeared frequently in Australian plays. Another consequence of the controversy was that several subsequent ambulatory authors felt it necessary to reject Trollope's point of view to appease Australian sentiment.[114]

The one factor working to improve England-Australia relationships in 1873–74 was the visit to Victoria and New South Wales of an English cricket team led by W. G. Grace, which commenced its tour with a match in Melbourne on the same day that *Australia Felix* had its premiere.[115] Walch set out to rebut Trollope by portraying England as a society divided between a dull, pompous, tax-grabbing, respectable officialdom and ruling class, represented by Kantankeros and his minions; and a mirth-loving, decent sporting middleclass, represented by the English cricket team. In a dream sequence Kantankeros is distressed to see a 'Great Local Panorama' of Victoria, including a picture of 'a *good-humoured* face,/The lion of the day— bold Captain Grace!' The squatters are the representatives of the Trollope/ Tory section of English society in Australia; Katankeros objects to a painting of a 'Wimmera Free Land Selector' because 'certain friends of mine don't like the theme' (p.12).

By establishing as a basic structural component of his plot that there were both admirable and reprehensible sides to English society, Walch, in the climate of the Trollope and Tichbourne controversies, was able to suggest in *Australia Felix* that white Australian society could and should select and reject from its Anglo-Celtic heritage and create in Australia a *better* English society than the original. The story Walch devised concerns a magic cricket bat which the 'etherial genius' Mirth gives to the young country lass Victoria, who in turn gives it to her betrothed Felix ('Young Australia') to use in the cricket match at the Melbourne Cricket Ground. Felix, like the dissolute young men of English racing drama, begins a career of gambling in the immoral world of sport and fashion, represented by 'Miss Collyns Treeter', and loses both the bat and the cricket match. (In real life the Victorian XVIII won handsomely, though aided by handicap odds, against the English XI.)

It was not just topical opportunism which caused Garnet Walch to select cricket as the game to be used in his sporting story. Cricket was becoming strongly identified with Australian nationalism,[116] and was mythically a less tainted sport than racing; Mirth in *Australia Felix* specifically refers to the magic cricket bat as:

> . . . the symbol of the manliest game
> To which I've ever lent my royal name,
> Type of true British sport, without alloy
> Where you, friend Mischief, are *de trop*, old boy,
> No swindling blacklegs soil the turf I prize,
> Them and their filthy lucre I despise,
> The cricket field's the modern tournament.(p.17)

Racing is the sport associated with English 'Mischief'; cricket therefore becomes the allegory of Walch's improved Anglo-Australian society, though it is a middle-class ideal of cricket rather than real cricket which Walch invokes. Real cricket in Australia in the 1870s was characterised by heavy gambling and what the Sydney *Punch* called 'battering and bawling' instead of batting and bowling.[117] The Victoria-New South Wales match at the Melbourne Cricket Ground immediately prior to the All-England game, at which Grace and some of his team were present as spectators, ended with a full-scale riot in which 'roughs . . . pelted the visiting team with road metal' as they left the ground;[118] and the crowd at the All-England match were said to have openly hooted as the English wickets fell, causing 'bitter feeling'.[119] Mythically cricket was a civilised game bringing classes and nations together in social harmony and in the spirit of fair play; a game which promoted not dissipation or corruption but physical agility, manliness, citizenship and military valour. *Australia Felix*'s cricket match was an allegory of a society built upon 'healthy and animating field sports'[120] which were threatened both by high-Tory reactionaries and by the kind of 'refined' and corrupting amusements which Miss Collyns Treeter had to offer.

Garnet Walch's belief that Australia could excel over England as a nation by carefully selecting and encouraging certain English social values and suppressing others is also found in the only text of any of George Darrell's plays which is extant, *The Sunny South* (1883). Set in the gold-rush 1850s, but with the technology of the 1880s freely used to suggest the contemporary world, *The Sunny South* inverts the story of the Tichbourne inheritance and revises the plotting of English sporting drama by showing in the first Act an English gentleman, Worthy Chester, and the usual dissolute younger gambler,

Ivo Carne, both heavily in debt and about to lose their English country estate to Eli Grup, a moneylender and an *English* 'descendant of a butcher' (p.19).[121] The situation is similar to that in the first act of *Flying Scud*, but is resolved not by an unexpected bequest or a horse-race but by the arrival from Australia of Matt Morley, 'the rightful owner of this estate'(p.19). Chester has frittered away Morley's inheritance, but Matt cheerfully forgives him and persuades the whole household to accompany him back to Australia where he has been working as a miner, and where he has learnt 'the truth of the old claptrap proverb that the crust earned by labour was sweeter than the meal eaten in idleness'(p.24). The paralysis which affects the landowning classes in England and leaves them financially prey to middle-class opportunism and the vices of gambling is broken not by victory in a horse race but by a more practical and virtuous option—hard work in the colonies.

The Sunny South's first image of Australia—the opening of Act III—is one of simple, innocent sporting pleasures. The scene is the Queen's Birthday sports carnival on the gold diggings, with dancing, singing, a sack race, a wrestling match, and a sequence taken directly from the pantomime opening to the Derby scene in *Flying Scud* where two cockneys are duped by thimble-riggers. The only difference is that Darrell has written dialogue to accompany the stage business, emphasising the comic aspects of the deception and finishing with the trickster being arrested (pp.31-4). In *Flying Scud* the thimble-riggers escape, and in some later English sporting plays the villains walk out of the play entirely unpunished, but in *The Sunny South* Darrell rejects the construction of the Australian bush as the lawless frontier, and insists that Australia (unlike England) is a country where laws are generally obeyed and effectively enforced.

This return to innocence is followed by an image of prosperity—Matt Morley and his partner Ben Brewer strike it rich when Ben discovers a huge gold nugget in their claim. Although bushrangers and Eli Grup's scheming delay the victory, at the end of the play Matt Morley and his friends are able to return to England prosperous and triumphant, thus marking a new solution to the drama of the declining fortunes of the English landed gentry. *The Sunny South* was Darrell's most popular play both in Australia and in England, where he played it in 1885 and again, more successfully, at the Surrey Theatre in 1898.[122] Although *The Sunny South* cannot be classified as a sporting play, its opening situation—the English gentry in financial decline—derives from plays like *Flying Scud*, and its central allegorical image of Australia—old English sports on a village green—is of a new Britannia: a Merrie England reborn in a law-abiding land of equal opportunity for individuals from all classes of society who are willing to work hard: 'There's a chance out there for everybody with pluck and determination, and there's scope for brains as well as muscle'(p.23).

A play very similar in theme and narrative structure to *The Sunny South* was Edmund Duggan's *The Democrat; or, Under the Southern Cross*. It was performed unsuccessfully for one night in Sydney in 1891 and more hopefully for seven nights as *The Eureka Stockade; or, The Fight for the Standard* in Adelaide in 1897, and was further revised by Duggan in 1907 as *The Southern Cross* and staged in Newcastle, Sydney and Melbourne in that and the following year.[123] Scripts for the later two versions have survived;[124] they appear to differ significantly from the first version only in the second Act which in the original *The Democrat* showed the running of the English Derby but which in *The Eureka Stockade* and *The Southern Cross* staged the wreck of the *Dunbar* off Sydney's South Heads in 1857.

Unfortunately the text of Duggan's final and most successful version, *The Southern Cross*, shows it to be a dull and puritanical piece that progresses in a sequence of contrived situations which allow Duggan to preach, principally through his humourless and impossibly upright hero and heroine, the virtues of charity, thrift, aristocratic benevolence and honest labour. The *Dunbar* scene enables Duggan to show the evils of naval discipline and stage a shipwreck sensation, but even without the Derby scene from the earlier *The Democrat* the storyline of *The Southern Cross* is primarily an attempt to confront head-on the ideology of the English aristocratic sporting play. Its more successful revival may be partly attributed to the outcries against gambling in England and Australia in the early years of the twentieth century which, as noted earlier, influenced Sutton Vane's *The Betting Book*, and which may have made Duggan's austere and high-minded sermon more palatable to contemporary taste.

In the first Act of *The Southern Cross* Duggan deceives his audience into thinking that they are watching an orthodox English racing drama of the kind staged by Bland Holt. The setting is the drawing room of Lisle Manor in Kent, the first sound that of a bugle call, and the first image, seen through the open windows at the rear of the room, that of a crowd of ladies and gentlemen in hunting costume and mounted on horseback leaving for a morning's sport. The opening dialogue concerns the profligate ways of the young Lord George Lisle, Earl of Eldermere, who is being rapidly stripped of his fortune by the usual dissembling rogue, aided and abetted by a corrupt bookmaker. In turn, George, sole executor of his father's estate, is financing his journey down the road to ruin by drawing on his younger brother Walter's inheritance as well as his own. Predictably, his only chance of restoring his family's fortunes is by winning the Derby.

However, later in the Act the stock formula abruptly changes direction. The heroine Linda Lovelace—also the child of an Earl, and the heir to a substantial fortune of her own—knows that George hopes to solve his financial problems by marrying her, but, unlike the heroine of Meritt's and Rowe's *New Babylon* and other English sporting plays, Linda has no intention of aiding in the young Earl's 'redemption' and is totally unsympathetic towards his advances. She preaches to George and his mother Lady Lisle the democratic philosophy which the younger brother Walter has introduced to her:

Linda: An empty title and a few acres of land does not constitute a nobleman, an honest man is the noblest work of God.

Lady L: You've obviously been taking a leaf out of Walter's book. How you can tolerate his horrible democratic ideas is more than I can understand. I consider him a disgrace to my family. (I,i,p.12)

Linda also refuses to take part in the fox hunt, stating that she prefers her charity work, and declines to join their forthcoming 'nice, sociable Derby Party' because she is 'not an advocate of cruelty to animals', adding 'I can derive no pleasure in seeing a noble animal cut and torn by whip and spur to gratify a gambling mania' (I,i,p.14). To complete her rejection of the world of racing and fashion, Linda refuses to go up to London for 'the season', despising the custom in which young ladies of fashion exhibit themselves in Hyde Park. Linda, and Walter himself when he appears later in the scene, are mouthpieces for Duggan's swingeing attack on the morality of the aristocratic sporting play. Together they lament the bad effect which the sporting world is having on Linda's brother Julian: 'horseracing, cardplaying and drink will bring the best man to ruin'(I,i,p.19). Yet Duggan's democrats are in fact condescending philanthropists, forever indulging in good deeds and believing that 'a few charitable millionaires' could solve most of society's problems.

The play proceeds in a series of short sequences, each of which attacks perceived social evils caused by the behaviour of the English ruling class. The tenant farmers on the estate come to complain about the way George is treating them, making this the only play in which the traditional English aristocracy is shown as being other than wholly in sympathy with the modest demands of a grateful peasantry. Walter supports the peasants, is banished from the house, and announces his intention to leave for Australia to 'realise the dream of my life, be dependent on my own exertions' (I,i,p.26).

The play, again like *The Sunny South*, then moves away from the English sporting setting to the Victorian goldfields, where Walter becomes involved with the struggle of the miners at Ballarat, and argues against taxation without representation:

Walter: . . . we cannot call ourselves free men. We have no voice in the framing of the laws by which we are governed and are expected to bear the burden of unjust taxation without a murmur. (III,ii,p.11)

This is reinforced by the presence of an American miner, Yank, who taunts the others to stand up for their rights as his country once did. The mining community is shown in racial terms, but as one in which the Irish, Americans, English and even Chinese diggers share the bond of mateship. Yet Walter is chosen by this community to be its leader primarily because of his lineage:

Yank: Say Lawson, that Lisle's a noble fellow. He's been well brought up I guess.
Lawson: Rather. He's an English aristocrat by birth.
Yank: I like to hear him talking politics.
Lawson: He can give most politicians a long start. His proper place is in Parliament. (III,ii,p.10)

In the Bakery Hill scene at the end of Act IV, Linda arrives from England to join Walter just minutes before the military storm the Eureka Stockade:

> (. . . *Linda who is behind Walter fires three shots and shoots three soldiers who attempt to cut Walter down. Walter kills his man and is shot in the left arm. Falls L.C. Diggers are defeated. Captain Lorimer hauls down the Southern Cross from flagpole comes down to Walter with it.*)
>
> *Cap.L:* Thus so I trample your insurgent flag in the dust.
> *Walter:* (*Draws pistol, Shoots Lorimer. Staggers to his feet, seizes flag.*) Never. This flag is destined to wave over free and united Australia. (*Folds flag round him, sinks down C., Linda holding his head. Stockade is set on fire. Picture. Curtain.*)

The last Act returns to England and to the sporting story. George's horse has failed to win the Derby (the scene enacted in Act II of the earlier version *The Democrat*). Lisle Manor is about to be auctioned, and there is a falling out between George and Linda's brother Julian, over the fact that George has squandered Walter's share of the estate as well as his own:

Julian: . . . You and your thieving companions gambled it away at Epsom.
George: If he received it he would only give it away to all the filthy paupers in the country.
Julian: It might afford him quite as much pleasure to distribute his money among the poor as it afforded you, to squander yours in champagne, cards and horseracing. (V,i,p.2)

Walter and Linda arrive back in England just in time to bid successfully to become the new owners of Lisle Manor. Unlike Matt Morley in *The Sunny South* however, Walter cannot forgive any of his relatives, except his mother, for their behaviour. He orders his brother off the estate with the words 'Go and work for your living as I have done':

George: But I can't work.
Walter: Then you deserve to starve, the estate is mine and I won't tolerate you here in idleness. (V,i,p.9)

Although more a moral tract than a play, *The Southern Cross* makes explicit many of the values of racing drama and in mounting a savage attack on them articulates many of the alternative values which at least a minority of native Australians must have shared. Duggan does not break the image of the aristocratic social structure; his supposed democrat simply restores himself as a generous paternalistic landlord in place of an exploitative one. Walter tells the tenant farmers they can have a year's relief from rent payment, and he throws a handful of silver coins to these workers, who depart in grateful delight. Walter and Linda leave Julian in charge of the estate and return to Australia where Walter is to represent Ballarat in the Victorian parliament. In this respect Duggan expresses later social attitudes than did Darrell, who thought it right and proper that Matt Morley should spend his fortune in England. Walter comments: 'I accumulated a large fortune in Australia and I wouldn't be doing justice to that country, by becoming an absentee'(V,i,p.9).

Rejections: *An Englishman's Home* (1909) and Australian chauvinist war plays

Walch and Darrell each sought to substitute other sports for horse-racing, and thereby change the connotations which sport in an Australian setting might invoke. Duggan's attack was on that part of the English aristocracy which had abandoned its sense of *noblesse oblige* in a welter of selfishness and self-indulgence; the racetrack was only the appropriate scene and symbol for that social evil, and the English racing play the stock dramatic framework in which those values could be exposed. But in 1909, with dramatic suddenness, anti-sport attitudes of a savageness until then restricted to minority groups suddenly entered the commercial drama through a remarkably successful English play, *An Englishman's Home*. Although some earlier stories and novels had been written on similar themes,[125] the controversy and publicity surrounding this play give it major significance in the history of popular sporting narratives and, to the extent that its alternative paradigm contributed to cultural attitudes, in the construction of sport as a value-system in British and Australian social ideology.

Originally advertised in London as by 'A Patriot', *An Englishman's Home* was later revealed to be the first (and only) play of a dramatic novice: an army officer, Major Guy Du Maurier. His only connection with the professional stage was through his brother, the actor-manager Gerald Du Maurier, already famous as 'Raffles' and the original Captain Hook in *Peter Pan*.[126] The play was produced at Wyndham's Theatre in London on 27 January 1909 and caused widespread public and press comment over its bitter attack on the incompetence of the average British army officer, its satire on the obsession with sport and the music hall of a representative English middle-class family 'the Browns', its representation of the invasion of England by 'Nearlanders' (at a time when the military and naval rearmament of Germany was causing comment and concern), and its depiction of old Mr Brown (a typical 'John Bull' figure) as unable to even recognise that his house has been invaded, mistakenly interfering with and hampering the defence effort, and feebly resisting when he finally does discover who the intruders are.

The male Browns do not know how to use a rifle, the females do not know how to render first-aid to the wounded; the volunteers do not know how to find ranges, how to fortify a house, or how to scout; the doctor has no supplies . . . and so on.[127]

Du Maurier ended his play, after Mr Brown has been shot for resisting the enemy, with the invaders firmly in control, but the London production tacked on a short and unconvincing happy ending in which the Nearlanders are suddenly and inexplicably repulsed by more competent English 'bluejackets' including the daughter Maggie Brown's boyfriend, a private in the Volunteers. What *The Times* called 'the great National Defence question' was given a major impetus during the following highly successful season, and an officer from the Territorial Army was stationed at the theatre every night to sign up new recruits after the performance.[128]

Under the advertising slogan 'The Play That Has Roused the Empire' J. C. Williamson quickly organised no fewer than three simultaneous productions in Australia—an extraordinary and commented-on exposure of a single text.[129] The Sydney premiere, with the cockney actor, Eardley Turner, as Mr Brown and an American, Ola Humphrey, as Maggie Brown, opened on 10 April while a separate production starring Julius Knight and Beatrice Day played in other major cities. The provincial rights were leased to another entrepreneur, Edwin Geach, whose production began touring New South Wales country towns in June. As Mr Brown, Geach cast a minor actor with several years' stage experience, Raymond Longford, and a young newcomer to the profession, Lottie Lyell—later the most famous names in Australian silent film.[130]

Although the staging of the invasion and battle in the third Act required complex technical effects, *An Englishman's Home* was otherwise a simple story set in a single 'Playroom' of Mr Brown's house in Essex, where the entire cast, Maggie Brown partly excepted, indulge in endless chatter about football and cricket matches, complete limerick competitions from the newspapers, and sing 'amazingly commonplace' music hall tunes. At the back of the stage Mr Brown alternately mouths empty platitudes about the state of the nation and the failings of the government (which he blames for everything from a strike at the post office to the state of the weather), and practises his skills at a stick-and-cone children's game called Diabolo.[131]

Sport is relentlessly satirised throughout the play, and Du Maurier takes pains to contrast the fact that while a heavy fog has prevented the army volunteers' rifle practice, it hasn't stopped the football matches. The first Act begins with a stock sporting 'bounder', Geoffrey Smith, reading out a long and extravagantly-phrased newspaper account of one such match:

Geoff: 'Little Teddy took the pass on the wind and, jinking closely, raced along hugging the cushion at lightning speed, steadied at the distance and centred full in front of the E.F.F. goal.'

Amy & Ada:	Yes, yes—go on!
Geoff:	'George took it on the hop, and shooting hard and high netted the mud orange within ten seconds of time.'
Syd:	Hurrah! (p.3)

Geoffrey is impatient of Mr Brown's complaint that the strike has cut off news of the money market, trade, foreign affairs, and 'our great Over Sea Dependencies', commenting 'We get most of the football news anyway'(p.7). It is not surprising therefore that when the battle begins at the end of Act II—Du Maurier's moment of moral reckoning—Geoffrey stands on a table 'as he would be [if] looking on at a football match' and is the first to die, shot through the heart(p.35). Crude as his allegory of English society was, it seems highly probable that Du Maurier was familiar with Chekhov's *The Cherry Orchard* (which was not, however, staged in England until 1911), and his characters' inability to recognise the *physical* danger they are in is one of several elements which suggest that George Bernard Shaw's later 'Fantasia in the Russian Manner on English Themes' *Heartbreak House* may have borrowed some of its incidents and allegorical structure from Du Maurier's stage success as well as from Chekhov's original. In its anti-climactic final scene, when the Zeppelin attack misses Heartbreak House (even though the characters have turned on all the lights and stand unprotected in the garden), Shaw is possibly commenting from a post-First World War perspective on the failure of Du Maurier's prophecy of doom and destruction.

In 1871 General Sir George Tomkyns Chesney had published in the May issue of *Blackwood's Magazine* a story 'The Battle of Dorking', in which an old soldier looks back from fifty years in the future and, as a warning to his listeners, describes how an unprepared Britain was overrun during the Franco-Prussian War.[132] The 'Battle of Dorking Controversy' was remembered by a number of reviewers of *An Englishman's Home*, and a relative of Chesney's, Francis Rawdon Chesney Hopkins, was a major Australian playwright of the 1870s and 1880s. In 1909 Hopkins was still actively writing and publishing short stories and poetry, and was one of several Australian dramatists who noted Du Maurier's success and rushed to offer their own alarmist prognostications for Australia's future history.

Hopkins's play *Reaping the Whirlwind. An Australian Patriotic Drama* was published (like Du Maurier's, anonymously) within months of *An Englishman's Home*'s Australian premiere, but was not performed. A much more successful play was Randolph Bedford's *White Australia; or, The Empty North* which received a major commercial production by William Anderson's company commencing on 26 June 1909 at the King's Theatre in Melbourne. *Australia Calls* by J. Clarence Lee and S. Mackay was another play on a similar theme which had a copyright reading in Sydney five weeks earlier; its subsequent performance history is unknown, although an *Australia Calls* film was made in 1913. All three plays and the film took as their principal subject the fear of military conquest of Australia by an Asian nation, and endorsed and embellished Du Maurier's anti-sport attitudes, arguing that young Australian men were being diverted by sport from their social responsibilities and so seriously weakening Australia's ability to defend itself against invasion.

The film begins with scenes of Australians at play—at the beach, at the race-track, and at the football,—and over each scene is superimposed a looming vision of a menacing Asiatic invader.[133]

Of the stage plays Bedford's and Hopkins's texts are extant, and both see the Asian hordes in unpleasant racial terms, but neither underestimates their strength of character or their intelligence. Hopkins refers to the people of an unspecified Asian country—the costumes are 'hybrid . . . half Japanese, half Chinese' (I,p.7) - as 'industrious, law-abiding' people (I,p.5);[134] Bedford's Japanese villain Yamamoto has been educated in England (I,i,p.16);[135] echoing the *Bulletin*'s long-running campaign against Britain's military alliance with Japan.[136]

Randolph Bedford's story concerns an Australian engineer, Jack Macquarie, who has invented an airship which alone might protect Australia from the Japanese naval fleet that is expected to attempt to invade Australia at any moment. He gains assistance and financial backing from a public-spirited squatter, Geoffrey Pearse, and his daughter Victoria; but is frustrated in his attempts to get the airship assembled and ready for battle by Pearse's nephew, an English-educated traitor and would-be quisling ruler of a Japanese-controlled Australia; and Pearse's son, a useless drunk. This character layout, clearly allegorical of Australian society as Bedford saw it, reflects his perception of the scientist as the military hero of the future; his acceptance of the ideals of the noble squatter and his daughter (the young woman who is here, as always, a symbol of the spirit of the nation); his argument that the younger Australian male generation had neglected to preserve rural/ aristocratic ideals by failing to shoulder the reponsibilities of leadership and by perverting or abandoning their duty to the nation; and his contempt for English Imperialism and English meddling in Asian and Pacific affairs. Yet even this apparently intensely chauvinistic, republican, anti-British piece was based on a clever amalgamation of elements from the paradigms of both English aristocratic drama and *An Englishman's Home*.

Predictably Bedford's symbol of Australia's lack of concern for the threat from the north is sport. Yamamoto, plotting the capture of the airship and exulting in the success of his plans so far, declares:

Yamamoto:　At any moment we may hear that the Mikado's fleet has reached Australia. Those fools who think but of racing—pulling the horse you say, I think—who keep with much money the bookmakers—who are lower than the coolie—who spend their lives to cheer players of cricket and football, amateurs who play for love of the game, [not] cash. These Australians who see not the peril at the gate. Our fleet will explode

> Sydney to pieces, will take the money of the banks. They are stubborn
> these enthusiasts of the horse race and the football—they shall have
> their lesson. (I,i,p.16)

In the third scene, set at an Overland Telegraph station in the Northern
Territory, the operator ('Mat Flinders') is relaying to the south messages about
the imminent war, but a young stockman only wants to hear the news coming
the other way about 'who's been picked for the Australian eleven' (I,iii,p.31).
While the operator continues to relay political news, the stockman and a
drunken swagman argue about which year a particular horse won the Oakleigh
Plate. At the end of the scene their indifference to the national emergency
allows the enemy to murder the operator before he can pass to the south the
message that Japan has declared war on Australia.

Eventually Jack Macquarie gets the airship aloft and flies towards Sydney.
The journey was shown using a variation on the *County Fair* staging
mechanism, with either a biograph backscene or a revolving backcloth, and
ascending and descending sky borders and ground rows as the airship rises
and descends (IV,i,p.1). It arrives over Sydney Harbour as the Japanese fleet
begins its bombardment, and successfully sinks all the ships before landing
in Macquarie Street, where the Eureka Flag flies 'from almost every building'
and where Jack addresses the cheering crowds:

Jack: Our rich and empty land is a permanent temptation to the poor and
overcrowded world and if we would hold Australia we must be strong.
No more unpreparedness. No more mad devotion to vicarious sport—arm
yourselves and think, get guns and resolution. (IV,v,p.5)

Hopkins's *Reaping the Whirlwind* is by contrast a simple narrative without
visual sensations of any kind. He expresses similar anti-sport attitudes, but
endorses the efforts of Australian sporting champions to promote military
training and social harmony. The first speaker at a public meeting in a Sydney
suburban town hall is Mr Wallace Hammerton 'the well-known athlete' who
argues in favour of conscription and a 'National Patriotic Tax'(II,p.22). He
is heckled by the crowd who shout sporting phrases such as 'Leg before wicket'
and 'Bowled out' (II,p.23); a scene imitated three years later by Louis Esson
in *The Time Is Not Yet Ripe*.[137] Unlike Bedford, Hopkins was not anti-British,
but in *Reaping the Whirlwind* Britain is preoccupied with a war of its own,
and an Asiatic army is coming to invade Australia which is in the grip of
a general strike. Fletcher, a guest at the Hammerton household, is forced to
admit: 'Wally Hammerton was right . . . He's preached defence since the first
day I knew him, but the stronger crowd preached football, cricket, golf, the
Federal Capital, Free Trade, the other sort of Protection, land scandals and
the Lord knows what besides' (III,p.38). Hopkins and Bedford were not original
prophets—they were drawing on the stock political rhetoric of the time[138]
as well as localising parts of *An Englishman's Home*—but *White Australia*

seems to have been the only play of its time to achieve commercial production which openly articulated this rhetoric and directly attacked the Australian passion for sport.

No place for sport: the Australian bush comedies

The major breakthrough in Australian dramatic narrative came in 1912 when Steele Rudd, Beaumont Smith, Bert Bailey and Edmund Duggan contributed to the successful dramatisation of Rudd's *On Our Selection* stories. For the first time the life of the small-selection farmer became the central subject of Australian dramatic narratives, more than fifty years after the squatter-selector struggles had begun. It is probably not coincidental that sport, always associated on stage with the aristocratic model of society and with urban life, largely disappears from this new genre of bush comedy. As Dad observes in *On Our Selection*: 'Oh, sometimes we have a wedding or a funeral, but it ain't much of a place for sport' (I,p.84).[139] However, even this play does not break with the sporting drama entirely, since Dad delivers a comic race-call speech in the third Act (III,i,p.119).

In the bush comedies squatter-selector confrontations are seen from the selector's point of view, as in Dad's struggles with his creditor and rival landowner John Carey. But geography is still employed as a non-controversial displacement of class conflict, with the opposition of bush and city being foregrounded in the plotting. The sinful city remains the usual habitat of, or a major influence on, the corrupt character, as it had been in the English sporting drama from the 1821 *Tom and Jerry* onwards. Young villains who do have rural squatter origins, such as Dudley Harrington in *The Squatter's Daughter* and Jim Carey in *On Our Selection*, have been tainted by city life; in most respects they are versions of the same character who earlier appeared as the hero in English sporting drama, but without redeeming features and therefore unredeemed. By replacing the moral complexity of sporting drama with a cruder country *vs* city morality, the bush comedies were a significant shift away from English dramatic stereotypes, and there was a proliferation of this new genre after the success of *On Our Selection*, with Waybacks, Hayseeds, Dawsons and others following the Rudds on to Australian stages.

Some of these, such as Philip Lytton's 1915 dramatised version of Henry Fletcher's short stories *The Waybacks in Town and At Home*, looked back on the pseudo-Australian drama of a decade earlier with obvious derision, and openly satirised the differences between their view of Australian society and earlier stage representations. This was the same Henry Fletcher who localised plays for Bland Holt, and in one scene of Lytton's play an old Shakespearean actor, Dickens Thackeray Scott Brown, comes to Dingo Flat outside Barjo where the Wayback family live, in order to find 'local colouring' for his 'great Australian play':

Dads: I don' know what yer means Mister, does yer mean yous going to make a play out of animals—native bears and opossums?
Mums: Kangaroos and wallabies!
Brown: No, I use the friskin' animal for local colouring for the bush scene only. The plot will be my great play 'The Worst Woman in Woolloomooloo.' What a success it will be. The 'Worst Woman in London' may be very bad, but she cannot be so horribly fascinating to us as 'The Worst Woman in Sydney.'
Mums: No indeed!
Brown: I believe we can be quite as bad and worse here than anywhere else. I stand up for Australia I do. (I,i,p.19)[140]

The Worst Woman in London, a play loosely based on Boucicault's *Formosa*, had been in William Anderson's repertoire when Fletcher wrote his *Wayback* stories, and when he was also doing for Bland Holt exactly the kind of token play-localising satirised here.

This sudden shift in popular Australian drama, the death or retirement of most of the actor-managers associated with the earlier genres, the questioning and restructuring of society both in England and Australia which followed the First World War, the arrival of film as a major narrative medium, and the continuing splitting of Australian live entertainment into gender and class-specific forms, all signalled the effective end of the kind of spectacle sporting melodrama in which Bland Holt had excelled, and which Australian writers as various as the Anglophilic George Darrell and the Anglophobic Randolph Bedford had attempted to appropriate for Australian national propaganda. The form had always attempted to reconcile oppositions within a society which it conceived as a single, unified (or unifiable) whole. The breakdown in patterns of social organisation, dramatic styles and performance conventions led to a rapid shift away from past ideologies and their consequent narrative constructs. Although the Land Selection Acts were passed in the same decade that produced *Flying Scud*, it took forty-five years for the play of *On Our Selection* to appear, challenging the paradigm of rural aristocratic drama with a more democratic yeomanry drama. However, as we shall see in examining Australian films up to the time of the Second World War, the squattocracy would take another thirty years to be displaced from the centre of the sporting narrative.

The sporting utopia

Entertainment offers the image of 'something better' to escape into, or something we want deeply that our day-to-day lives don't provide. Alternatives, hopes, wishes—these are the stuff of utopia, the sense that things could be better, that something other than what is can be imagined and maybe realised.[141]

Although in nineteenth- and early twentieth-century Australian society the phrase 'sport and drama' was interpreted differently by different individuals and groups, it retained a core of common understanding which made it comprehensible within any particular context. Such contexts might include the unifying idea of commercial mass entertainment in general, or any or several of a large number of rich connotative patterns of oppositions: male/female; popular/elite; vigorous/refined; participation/observation; physical/intellectual; lowerclass/upperclass; spontaneous/rehearsed; day/evening; open field/enclosed stage. Closer consideration of the dramatic treatment of particular sports and games reveals other connotative clusters: aristocratic activities (fox-hunting/grouse shooting); cross-class pursuits (horse-racing); embodiments of middle-class morality (cricket); working-class sports (football/boxing); courting games (croquet, tennis); innocent village-green pastimes (sack races/gymkhanas/skating/children's games); corrupt gambling activities (club card games); and so forth. Theatre in its treatment of such subjects and imagery reflected and developed these connotations, and also selected sports for narrative treatment based on its own technical limitations and inventions and its own audience base, which was shifting and fragmenting throughout the period.

Within this diversity of manifestations of sport and drama and sport in drama, a dominant and extremely popular narrative paradigm emerged. The precision of its structure and the relatively little variation which occurred throughout the period suggest that it met very real needs of hundreds of thousands of white Australian citizens, but those needs were not necessarily the same for each and every individual. An outstandingly popular narrative like *Flying Scud* was able to offer a number of contradictory messages which could be read simultaneously by different groups within the audience; indeed we might speculate that the ability of a text to be decoded according to several different dominant interpretations is one essential criterion of mass appeal. Horse-racing, overwhelmingly singled out for dramatic treatment, had this quality in its own connotative system. It was a sport in which kings, aristocrats and the gentry traditionally participated and was organised to reflect their elevated social status; it provided different, complementary activities for women, and invited the subservient participation of the lower orders as workers in the industry and as spectators and fellow gamblers.

All the sporting plays conformed to what the film critic, Richard Dyer, has classified as an unusual 'classic' form of utopian narrative: one which actually presents a model of a utopian world.[142] As well as offering audiences the chance to feel a heightened sense of pleasure through idealised and vivid sporting characters, panoramic spectacles and exciting sensations, and simplified and more easily soluble life situations, the sporting plays suggested that the utopian world did actually exist—in the English or Australian countryside. Dyer observes that in order to make a utopian world credible it has to be removed 'in time and space . . . to places, that is, where it can be believed.'[143] For the predominantly urban audiences of English popular drama this credibility was achieved by romanticising the English countryside as a place essentially untouched by social change and where close personal relationships and a mutual interest in sport created a bond between master and man and ensured just dealings on both sides. For Australian urban audiences the English utopia was geographically doubly removed and consequently more impervious to doubt or ridicule, and this was surely a major problem with which the Australian play had to contend. It is pertinent to note that many of the most successful Australian dramas (*The Sunny South, Robbery Under Arms, The Squatter's Daughter*) were also removed in time by being set in the mythical past of the early gold-rushes and of bushrangers like the Ben Hall gang. By combining the frontier genre and the sporting narrative the basis of an Australian utopia was seen being established in the past rather than being directly asserted to exist in the present. Contemporary anachronisms were freely allowed and as the bush came increasingly to represent a modified alternative Australian utopia, the contemporary world slid back into the paradigm.

However we read the sporting narratives, it is clear that a powerful process of ideological entrapment took place. A problem of English society, the transition from agrarian to industrial forms of social organisation, was resolved through narrative fantasy and narrated to and accepted by Anglo-Australians whose history had for a century and more forced them to confront and cope with different life experiences, and who had not experienced directly an industrial revolution. In order to imitate and localise these enormously successful stories, Australian authors were obliged to distort Australian society in order to make it fit a pre-existing narrative pattern. The image of the bush as a harsh, hostile environment of fire, flood and famine, in which a number of opportunistic squatters had seized large quantities of the best land and were holding on to it in spite of the efforts of the selectors and the parliamentary land reforms, had to be reconciled with the image of the idyllic and ordered pastoral, in which exciting sporting occasions were organised to re-establish an accepted social hierarchy.

On another level the sporting dramas addressed not particular problems of English or Australian culture, but problems of western industrialism which remained valid across national boundaries. In particular, the utopian world offered compensation for deeper social insecurities which might be summed up as a perceived lack of stability in modern society and a sense that this sprang from a lack of any correspondence between power and morality. The image of the ideal suggests by its reverse that in reality people felt themselves to be in the power of entirely unprincipled economic and political leaders, who would behave without scruple or compassion in their dealings with people of moderate or little wealth who found themselves in their paths or in their employment, and who would themselves be controlled only by their own venal inadequacies. Equality, which George Kateb in *Utopia and Its Enemies* includes in a list of the qualities of 'perfection' which ordinary people seek,[144] was in this context so irrelevant a concept as to lack any force in their visualisation of an ideal world. The struggle was not against hierarchical authority, but against its arbitrariness and its excesses; those with limited or non-existent power saw authority as inevitable and were primarily concerned that a system be instituted by which rulers most favourable to their interests might be found. The sporting narratives suggested that a combination of traditional authority and sporting codes of behaviour could provide such an ideal.

Interestingly one of the few significant shifts within the paradigm during the fifty-year period from 1866 onwards suggests that individuals within society felt themselves to be less powerful in the face of wealth and established authority at the end of the period than they were at the beginning. This shift involved the replacement of working-class heroes and motivators of action (Nat Gosling in *Flying Scud*) by firstly middle-class professionals (the detective Flotsam in *New Babylon*) and then by aristocrats (Lord Deerwood in *The Great Millionaire*) and equivalent squatters (Geoffrey Pearse in *White Australia*). The shift as it expressed itself through working-class characters moved unmistakeably away from centrally important, autonomous, self-directed behaviour, towards that of minor supportive oppressed menials like Surly Briggs in *The Winning Ticket*. To some extent this shift may be explained by the gradual disappearance of the working classes themselves from the 'popular' playhouses as entertainment forms and venues diversified, but it also seems to suggest that Western industrial society was becoming less secure about its social relationships and its ability to control its own destiny. As the decades passed, and as this compensating vision of aristocrats making society perfect for themselves and for everyone else as well, became increasingly remote from any recognisable world in any time or place, it was the details of contemporary life—particularly, in the genre we are considering, sport—which had the most direct connection to known social behaviour and which were therefore powerfully motivated with meanings inherited from utopian fantasy. While Australian sport was developing strong nationalistic connotations, sporting drama provided a complementary dominant reading of sports, games and leisure pursuits as activities conducted according to behavioural codes which might bring some form of stability, order, and fair and just dealings amongst individuals and groups within Western industrial society.

Sport in
Australian Film

Bricolage/montage: from theatre to film

The study of sport in Australian film deserves separate, book-length analysis, and indeed one such project has been mooted.[1] We are concerned here only with the appropriations which film has made of the genre(s), the iconography, and the themes of the sporting live drama: with the bricolage of inherited texts, ideologies and discourses, and with the technical and artistic reconstruction of the sporting genre through the mise en scene and montage possibilities of the new medium. No attempt has been made to ascertain the extent to which there existed a sport and film industry in the same sense as the sport and theatre industry, although a cursory examination of the published research to date would suggest an initial tendency in this direction, fading away as in the theatre during the 1929–30s depression.[2] We have already seen some links through early sportsmen and/or sports promoters who became film entrepreneurs: W. J. Howe, Snowy Baker, E. J. Carroll; and there do seem to have been occasional attempts to publicise films through sporting events: from *How McDougall Topped the Score* in 1924 which opened in Adelaide during a tour by an English cricket team, to *The Great MacArthy* which premiered 'at the height of the 1975 football season'.[3] A more substantial and recent example was *The Coolangatta Gold* (1984) which initiated, with co-sponsorship from a breakfast cereal company, an 'ironman' surf competition on Queensland's Gold Coast which was incorporated into the film's climax.[4] The latter two examples are occasional, opportunistic couplings; not evidence of any systematic interpenetration of capital or organisational infrastructure. John Tulloch has noted during the 1930s depression a 'tendency [of cinema organisations] to diversification into broader aspects of the leisure and media industries', citing Union Theatres' use of closed-down cinemas as mini-golf courses and skating rinks.[5] In fact, the tendencies were in the other direction, and such examples were returns to earlier cross-leisure practices motivated by the short-term desperation of near-bankruptcy rather than evidence of a growing conglomerate grouping of linked entertainment investments.

The willingness of sporting champions to exploit their popularity by appearing in films, either as themselves or as characters in narrative, is perhaps the area of closest resemblance between earlier theatre and later film practices, but again the evidence is strongest in the pre-depression silent film era and fragmentary after that time. The coming of film made it easier for athletes to move from sport into narrative drama: the silent film actor did not require the vocal strength and agility, the powers of memory or stage presence of the stage performer, and was free to ride, shoot, swim, dive and fight unencumbered by the restrictions imposed by stage and proscenium arch. Hard riding action (particularly by women) was commended from the first. We have already noted its importance for Kate Kelly's ride in *The Story of the Kelly Gang* film early in 1907, and a year later the MacMahon Bros' *Robbery Under Arms* was able to attract comments such as:

The camera has several advantages over the ordinary stage setting, where, owing to the exigencies of space many events have to be presented in narrative instead of in reality. . . . one of the finest views of the lot was that where the rugged old veteran was chased by the police. . . . Another . . . was . . . the wife's magnificent ride to the bank . . . The foaming horse, fording a river with its fair rider's hair streaming in the wind, formed an impressive picture.[6]

The first Australian to exploit for sporting action the possibilities of what the same reviewer called 'the wonderful silent machine' was the heavyweight boxing champion in 1913, Dave Smith, who made two films for the producer, John Stephen McCullagh, in that year. The second, which is known only through a surviving scenario and may not have been completed, was a city/ bush melodrama *An Australian Hero and the Red Spider*. In it Smith begins as the school cricket captain who hits a six to win the championship, marries his sweetheart in spite of her parents' objections, becomes a boxer in order to support their family, and then turns to farming in association with one of his former ring opponents.[7] In 1916 after he retired from the ring Smith returned to the screen in a full-blooded sporting melodrama *In the Last Stride*, based on a racing novel by Arthur Wright which had been serialised in the *Referee*. As well as owning and training the Sydney Cup winner, his role required him to take part in the obligatory three-round boxing contest as well as play in a rugby league match and pilot a speedboat in a chase across Sydney Harbour.[8]

Smith was followed on to stage and screen by the boxer he trained and seconded, Les Darcy, and by Darcy's manager, Snowy Baker. An American director working in Australia in 1915–16, J. E. Matthews, made a number of films including a comedy *The Unknown* which used two minor boxers, and a semi-documentary starring Darcy, *The Heart of A Champion*.[9] Darcy's Australian manager, Reginald Leslie 'Snowy' Baker, was a remarkable all-round athlete who won a boxing silver medal in the middleweight division at the 1908 Olympics, was a state swimming champion and an international

'Snowy' Baker doing his morning exercises in *The Enemy Within*, 1918, watched by
the boxer Sandy Mc\`Vea (National Film and Sound Archive).

rugby player, amongst other sporting achievements. Baker was the leader of
the business syndicate which bought Hugh D. McIntosh's Sydney Stadium in
1912, and was active as a sports promoter and boxing and athletics coach
before making his own screen debut in 1918 in *The Enemy Within*, the first
of several films he made before going to live in Hollywood.[10] His films, like
those of Dave Smith, gave him ample opportunity to display his sporting skills
in heroic fashion, and Baker often interrupted the narrative to insert covert
advertisements asserting that his physical prowess was directly linked to
sporting training. Baker's commercial interests included fitness gyms, and a
title early in *The Enemy Within* announces that his character 'never neglects
his morning exercises' and then shows Baker using a rowing machine and
a punching bag.[11] In *The Man from Kangaroo* (1920) Baker's parson character
teaches young men boxing to make them 'manly and self-reliant' (as Baker

did when not making films), and the film includes a long non-narrative sequence in which Baker demonstrates different kinds of high dives into a rock pool.[12] Several other Australian boxers have played roles on screen, including Sandy McVea and Colin Bell in Baker's films, and in sound film Tommy Burns, Ron (Grant) Taylor and Michael Karpaney.[13] Jockeys Darby Munro, Jack Purtell, George Moore and Roy Higgins, footballer Lou Richards and surf ironman Grant Kenny have appeared more or less as themselves in fictional stories,[14] but the sporting champion cast as the central character in a feature length film is unknown in Australian cinema since Snowy Baker's departure for Hollywood in 1920. Subsequent production assumptions have privileged physical similarities over representations of performance capabilities: look-alike (or simply goodlooking) actors to play athletes, even a failed racehorse as Phar Lap instead of a real champion, though in every case audiences are consequently alerted to the manipulation of the contest required to get the desired result.

Although the discourse of 'reality' as promulgated through film posters, press publicity and reviews suggested that all sporting and adventure sequences were filmed on location, in fact many of the 'realistic' effects of the Hollywood (and later the Australian) cinema were filmed in the studio using the mechanisms devised for races and chases on the live stage. (A major source of evidence is Mack Sennett's 1924 comedy *The Laugh Factory*, which exposes and parodies the artifice.)[15] The most obvious example is the use of moving backscenes, and an examination of this shows some ways in which new technology could influence narrative elements as well as mise en scene possibilities.

One story motif, first introduced in the sub-genre of boxing dramas, involves foul play during the contest itself; the analogous situation in many racing films is the sequence in which the corrupt jockey attempts to interfere with the hero's horse or jockey during the race. This was not technically feasible in the theatre until ways were found to hold centrestage for a significant length of time the foregrounded image of the two competitors and their horses (or cars or chariots). The discourse of 'realism' eliminated any possibility of a stylised mime or slow motion form of representation for such a scene, but the treadmill and moving backscene mechanisms were acceptably realistic, and an unexpected narrative development during a race (rather than spectacle and the unimpeded victory of the favourite) first appears on the live stage in *Ben Hur* in the early years of the century, when 'The wheel rolls from Messala's chariot and Messala falls as Ben Hur draws past him'.[16]

Filming close detail shots for such a sequence was no easier in cinema than staging it had been, since it required fast tracking by a camera parallel to the galloping horses, with consequent problems with framing, camera stability and focus, not to mention the danger to the riders. The solution used for many years was to imitate the stage illusion, but without real horses: the riders sat on saddles mounted on a see-saw mechanism (to give an up and down

Back projection in cinema: filming *Come Up Smiling*, 1939 (National Film and
Sound Archive, courtesy Greater Union).

'galloping' motion) and were positioned in front of either a moving panorama
painted with a landscape, or a back-projected film tracking shot. The camera
was set up as the ideally positioned spectator in the theatre would have been,
and the image was framed to exclude everything below the saddle, allowing
hard focus on the riders and a fast moving and blurred background of trees,
grass etc. For chases on foot or in cars a large circular revolving stage was
used. The edge provided a treadmill-like moving platform on which the
combatants ran or drove 'on the spot' while being filmed from a fixed camera
position, while the painted surface of a large drum in the centre of the circle
revolved to give the moving background. The camera became a one-eyed
credulous observer of a theatrical illusion, and the resulting footage was cut
into a location race or chase sequence.[17]

This technical solution enabled film makers to extend into the last moments
of the narrative the alternating stable/unstable episodic pattern of conflict in
the sporting success story, but the result did not just add new excitement to
the formula; it transformed it. Previously the race had been a spectacle of
triumph following the drama; genre expectations were that once the race
began, breeding held good. Now the anxiety of uncertain victory had entered
the competition itself, the sanctity of sport in action was violated, and its
allegorical resonances of society in action suggested new constructions of the
race of life in which individual skill and effort, science, luck and evil had

new purpose and power. This may well have contributed, as we shall see shortly, to the fragmenting of the ideology of racing drama between 1930 and 1950.

The impact of the commercial sporting drama on popular narrative film can hardly be overestimated. Sporting events were in any case a favoured subject in documentary film from the Lumiere's December 1895 screening in Paris onwards (one of their thirty-second shorts was of a game of bowls); by 1906 Richards' Entertainers were touring Eastern Australia with a film programme including 'a very real [fictional] racing episode' *Nobbling the Derby Favourite*.[18] The racecourse story quickly became by far the most common genre of Australian feature film narrative between 1911 and 1949. *Keane of Kalgoorlie* (1908 play, 1911 film) and *The Double Event* (1893 play, 1911 film) are very early examples of direct stage-to-screen adaptations of horse-racing stories, both originally from novels—examples also of the extent to which stage and screen now exploited sporting stories and themes originating in popular literature. *The Cup Winner* (1911) was a particularly successful (though certainly not the first) example of the intercutting of documentary and fictional story material:

The main distinction of the film was the inclusion of actual footage of the Melbourne Cup race for 1911 . . . presenting the newsreel footage in a dramatic context. The narrative scenes were shot in Sydney well before the race, and six cameramen were hired to shoot scenes of the Cup Day crowds and the main racing events. The film was immediately processed and printed, and the completed drama was shown that night, 7 November 1911, at five Melbourne theatres . . . The gimmick was effective, for hundreds were reportedly turned away from the crowded theatres on the opening night, and even months later, in February 1912, when the film ran in Hobart, it could still attract 'immense audiences'.[19]

Beaumont Smith's *Desert Gold*, named after and starring a champion mare, was a similar success in 1919, and another highly successful racehorse, Kinnequhair, appeared in John K. Wells' *Silks and Saddles* in 1921. Horse-racing stories can also be found in *A Ticket in Tatts* and *Gambler's Gold* (both 1911), *Won on the Post* (1912), *The Hayseed's Melbourne Cup* (1918), *A Rough Passage* (1922), and *Odds On* (1928), to name only some of the major productions in the silent period. Even Raymond Longford's social problem drama *The Woman Suffers* (1918) proved, when a nearly complete print was discovered in 1983, to be in part a bush/city racing story using documentary footage of the 1917 Melbourne Cup—a fact not previously noted, probably because it was the most predictable (and least controversial) element in the narrative.[20] Both Frank Thring (*A Ticket in Tatts* 1934) and Ken G. Hall (*Thoroughbred* 1936) introduced the racecourse drama into early sound film and Hall's Cinesound team continued with other sports in *Gone to the Dogs* and *Come Up Smiling* (both 1939). Other producers contributed *Racing Luck* (1941) and *Into the Straight* (1949), after which the sporting feature lapsed for a time with the exception of children's movies (*Bungala Boys* 1961 and *Blue Fire Lady* 1977) and *The Great MacArthy* (1975). It had a brief revival in the early 1980s notably in *The Club* (1980), *Gallipoli* (1981), *Phar Lap* (1982), and *The Coolangatta Gold* (1984), while *Archer* (1985) appeared on television where several mini-series, notably *Bodyline* (1985) and *The Four Minute Mile* (1989), also addressed sporting subjects.

Little has been written about the early Australian sporting films, probably because, with few exceptions, they are amongst the least nationalistic and innovative of story subjects. Their appearance and the few surviving films support points made elsewhere: that the feature film was initially directed at principally working-class audiences, with elements supposedly attractive to wealthier patrons being progressively introduced, and with the genre being further modified in sound films to include the vaudeville routines which earlier had appeared live on the same programme. This shifting target audience, exploitation of technology, and appropriation of stage entertainments affected both the choice of and insistence on particular spectacle and narrative elements regardless of genre, but sporting stories were distinctive in that they were considered amongst the most internationally marketable of genres. Australian commercial live theatre had little international success; plays were nearly always constructed primarily for domestic consumption. As we have seen, it was a process of colonial mirroring of the 'parent' culture that made these plays so similar to the imported originals, and in fact this hegemony had been broken on the stage at about the time the Australian film industry was establishing itself. In film, however, there were good commercial reasons for minimising the differences between Australian and British or American society, since the film itself might well be exported to both countries; this gave a new incentive for film makers to exploit the old aristocratic sporting drama. One of the Australian-made international successes of the early 1920s, *Silks and Saddles*, was directed by an American and starred another, though a London reviewer noted 'how very English' many of the locations were.[21] Its Australian release print inscribed nationalism on to the story through an opening title which superimposed lines from the last two stanzas of Dorothea Mackellar's 'My Country' ('Core of my heart, my country' . . . 'I know to what brown country/My homing thoughts will fly') over a fluttering Australian flag; for its American screenings this was omitted and the intertitles changed to suggest that the bush locations were in Virginia.[22] It was, of course, a simple matter to re-edit silent film to include and/or exclude titles, intertitles and distinctively national or geographical mise en scene elements and so reframe and to some extent reconstruct the narrative for English or American consumption. What was required was that the central storyline should reflect accepted overseas generic expectations and representational race, gender and class stereotypes. The cultural mirroring of England by Australia had been given a new industrial impetus by the transatlantic marketplace.

First World War recruiting poster (B. Carroll, *The Australian Poster Album*).

Sport, war and the bush

In films which did address a primarily Australian audience, the first challenge which had to be resisted was the sudden eruption of anti-sport plays and films, which occurred in 1909–13. This new discourse was enthusiastically embraced by the non-commercial Australian literary theatre, as we shall see in the next chapter, but was quickly contained and redefined by the commercial cinema—as it was in government propaganda where recruiting advertisements for the First World War included one, 'Enlist in the Sportsmen's Thousand', which showed men who had been playing hockey, football, tennis, cricket, rowing, golf, and duck hunting and motoring, all turning to look at the dominant

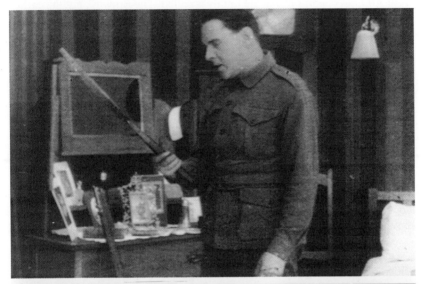

Men and sport: a) goodbye to tennis, b) off to war; from *The Hero of the Dardanelles*, 1915 (National Film and Sound Archive).

figure of 'Lieut. Jacka V.C.', accompanied by the exhortation 'Show the enemy what Australian sporting men can do'.[23] Alfred Rolfe's 1915 war propaganda film *The Hero of the Dardanelles* opens with a very similar image: the young Australian male hero looks lovingly at his tennis racquet and cricket bat before putting them away and determinedly picking up a rifle. As he does so the film cuts to a closer shot from a different angle, bringing into prominence a photograph of his fiancee who is smiling as though approving of his action.[24] As in *An Englishman's Home* the family is called 'The Browns', but the earlier attack on sport is redefined by a direct appeal to sporting men to use their agility and skill for a 'higher' purpose. War hysteria and the search for recruits required the assertion of a new national consensus, based on the old idea of sport as training for war and work.

However, it is only *manly* sports which are so redefined. In the later *Spirit of Gallipoli* (1928) a 'wild' young man is shown being moulded into an upright citizen by military training, which includes swimming for practical purposes (saving a drowning mate) and winning the 'Brigade Boxing Championship Final'.[25] His fiancee's picnic games of tennis and quoits are represented negatively, and he forces her to abandon this lifestyle when they marry, take a sheep farm and become a prosperous family. In the same year Scott Dunlap's *The Romance of Runnibede* (from Steele Rudd's novel) employed the same iconography: Dorothy is playing tennis at school in Sydney when she is summoned home to her family's cattle station. She is obliged to put away city/

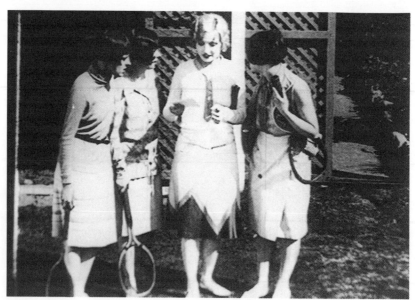

Women and sport: goodbye to tennis, off to the bush; from *The Romance of Runnibede*, 1927 (National Film and Sound Archive, courtesy Greater Union).

childish things, and her sporting skills, unlike Snowy Baker's, are not shown as being of benefit to her in her subsequent adult adventures.[26] In another Steele Rudd-derived film, *Dad and Dave Come to Town* (1938), sport is displaced entirely from the paradigm. The storyline is clearly appropriated from the 1935 Radio Pictures' musical *Roberta*, in which an American football star inherits a Parisian fashion store, allowing for the usual reconciliation of high class/ low class, female/male interests. In the Australian film it is Dad Rudd who inherits a Sydney fashion shop. The role of Jill Rudd, often acclaimed as being an example of the representation of independent-minded and high-spirited young 'Australian' women (the 1985 documentary *Don't Call Me Girlie* is titled from one of her lines) is, in fact, closely modelled on that played by Irene Dunn in *Roberta*: in both stories this character takes over the fashion store, endures the taunts of doubting men, and manages the business successfully, allowing the mise en scene to indulge in extensive fashion parade sequences which undercut her challenge to objectified femininity.[27] The major difference between the two films is that in *Dad and Dave Come to Town* the reconcilia- tion of bush and city is foregrounded over that of class or gender differences by erasing the world of sport from the paradigm. Sport always carried strong connotations of a class-divided society, perhaps because it could not be represented except by specific sports, which themselves had in this era strong class- and/or gender-based associations. Replacing sporting society with the 'classless' world of the small farmer/businessperson allowed Cinesound to continue promulgating Rudd's antipodean version of the Genesis myth, where effort and good-heartedness were sufficient to ensure success anywhere, from selection farming to *haute couture*. Such an assertion was restricted in Australian narrative to non-sporting genres; the paradox therefore in 'sporting' Australia during the time of Bradman and Phar Lap was that the most assertively 'Australian' of feature films eschewed sporting subjects, while those aimed at the international marketplace embraced them.

More than forty years later the intersecting mythologies of sport, war and the bush, and the competing target strategies for Australian and for English and American audiences, resurfaced largely unchanged in the 1981 feature *Gallipoli*, directed by Peter Weir.[28] David Williamson's script gives us two young sprinters, one country-bred and heroic, the other from the city and more self-centred, who meet at a country sports carnival. As in 'Dad and Dave' and other bush narratives, the country world is relatively classless compared to the city; as in the old sporting drama reaching back to *Tom and Jerry* it is relatively untainted by vices such as gambling. (The city boy bets on his own success, and loses to the non-gambling 'pure' country lad.) This textual evocation of overtly national mythologies was contradicted industrially by the strong impetus in the Australian cinema at this time towards overseas sales, leading to the curious advertising slogan devised for North America: 'From a place you've never heard of comes a story you'll never forget'.[29] *Gallipoli*'s positive reception overseas indicates certain commonalities of sporting, country/city and war myths across Western cultural boundaries; it also reactivated very similar generic constructions of those myths which had occurred in the sport and war stage melodramas of the Boer War period and the First World War propaganda films, suggesting a degree of transhistorical common ground as well: a sportsground exposition followed by the sport of war; superiority of country over city; sport as a male bonding ritual and as a symbol of 'manliness' and military prowess. As in the Drury Lane sport and war dramas and the Snowy Baker films, athletic training is directly related to military valour, although with a late-twentieth century interrogation of militarism. In *Gallipoli* both young men answer the call to arms and both eventually arrive at Gallipoli where the city lad fails to run fast enough as a messenger with a counter-order cancelling a particularly suicidal attack, condemning the country lad to run to his death with the pep-talk indoctrination of his old athletic coach uncle echoing in his ears. The minor character of a third young man who prefers boxing and horse-riding to athletics provides token conflict within the otherwise undifferentiated male sporting society, but this theme is not pursued, with all the soldiers in Egypt playing Australian Rules football near the Gaza pyramids; the emblems of the singular nation are stronger than those of class. Although *Gallipoli* succeeded in questioning its own mythic reappropriation and reconstruction of national sporting heroism, largely through the counter-mythic strategy of satirising and blaming the British commanders of the Gallipoli campaign, its determined exclusion of any significant female characters, subsuming of race and class antagonisms beneath the myth of the bush and the nation, racist parody of Egyptian traders, and its insistent inclusion of all the young male character types in the ranks of the volunteers, effectively restricted the range of voices in the text. Not surprisingly given the ideological origins of the sport and war melodrama in British Imperialism, *Gallipoli*'s national projection proves to be exclusively male and Anglo-Australian.

Victory: breeding, science and luck, or skill and effort?

Although the first horse racing films (mostly lost and known only through trade publicity and newspaper reviews) suggest that their appropriations of the stage storylines were within the normal parameters of the genre as it then existed, this uniformity did not last long. The racing play had for so long resisted the changing social context in which it was consumed that the built up transgressive pressures finally caused the explosion of the underlying ideology into competing forms and fragments during the 1930s. The iconography could remain the same, but could be sequenced into very different narrative styles. An example is *Silks and Saddles* and *A Ticket in Tatts*, both of which make a fetish of detail shots of Australian racecourses in operation (turnstiles, starting mechanisms, stop clocks, winning and correct weight signals, boards and announcements), as well as offering the usual social class divisions, racing location scenes, thoroughbred horses and their trainers, jockeys, stable-hands, bookmakers etc.; but which have fundamentally divergent storylines. The first continues the drama of good breeding, a decade later the second celebrates luck and working class ingenuity.[30] Instead of having an unexamined eugenic answer, 'Who wins and why?' became the major question of the plotline.

At least three films attempted to continue the racing drama of good blood; to assert, as did the title of Arthur Wright's 1919 racing and war novel, that *The Breed Holds Good*.[31] The three films are *Silks and Saddles* (1921), *Thoroughbred* (1936), and *Into the Straight* (1949), but in each case the old discourse is blurred by uncertainty. In *Silks and Saddles* all the usual plot and character motifs are used (for example, bribing the jockey, the heroine's dash to the course to take his place, interference during the race) and the only novelty is that the opposing horses dead heat for first. This impasse is resolved when the villains' horse is declared short of weight and disqualified; the audience already knows of this probability since the squatter's Aboriginal stablehand, overhearing the villains' plans, decides to respond in kind and has cut a hole in the bottom of their horse's saddlebag. Although this honest roguery is in the tradition started by Nat Gosling in *Flying Scud* fifty-five years earlier, its introduction into the race marginalises the triumph of breeding within the race as social symbol; we are denied an unbiased test as to which is the 'better' horse. Nevertheless, it is still the squatter class whose celebrations we share after the race, not those of the workers whose actions have determined its outcome. While genre traditions still determine the dominant paradigm, the individual plot novelties and incidents have become a confused pattern of contradictory ideological statements.

In the 1930s and 1940s *Thoroughbred* and *Into the Straight* consciously attempt to reactivate the genre by reworking its elements into new forms; both only serve to demonstrate the collapse of the discursive certainties on which it was based. *Thoroughbred*'s American scriptwriter, Edmond Seward, reveals throughout this 1936 Cinesound drama his uneasy awareness of the closeness of the racing genre's ideology to that being promulgated in Europe at the time by Adolf Hitler.[32] Seward also attempts unsuccessfully to intro-duce Hollywood-style class mobility into the formula. Unlike American films of the time, class and gender mobility in the Australian feature film is almost never foregrounded,[33] and all sports are appropriated into a hierarchical social structure. In the 1939 Cinesound comedy *Gone to the Dogs* even dog racing, in most representations of Australian society a distinctive working-class pursuit, is socio-centralised and universalised: the middle-class hero and heroine are seen mixing freely with both the Rolls Royce set and with George and Henry, keepers at Taronga Park Zoo. All share the dog-racing passion, but no-one is shown changing status as a result.[34]

In *Thoroughbred* the racing story is used to raise eugenic arguments at every opportunity, and is introduced early in the film by a long-running argument between a rich squatter, Russell Peel, and his neighbour, the poor selector and horsetrainer Ma Dawson:

Some day I'll convince Ma that blood tells in humans as well as in equines. Inferior sires and dams are responsible for inferior horses *and people*. Now, if we could only eliminate love and breed a scientific race of humans . . . I've no use for a crock, human or otherwise.

Peel's Nazi ideology is rendered unobjectionable by the bland and ineffectual persona the actor Harold Meade adopted for the role, and by the mutual affection and good humour with which Peel and Ma Dawson conduct their disagreement, which has still not been resolved at the end of the story:

Peel: So you'll admit that blood tells in people as well as in horses?
Ma: What? In horses, yes, but in humans? Oh me eye!

As well as this surface exposition, the eugenics theme is structured into the story by the preference of the middle-class Canadian heroine, Joan, for Ma's gauche Australian son, Tommy, over the sophisticated and English-educated Bill, Peel's son. She tells Bill, 'I know you don't think he [Tommy] has all the qualities your father looks for in a champion . . . at heart he's a little boy.' Nothing in the film corrects this evaluation: Tommy is dim-witted, stubborn, unaware of Joan's abilities and indifferent to her requests, and obsessed with becoming 'a big man with a pearl grey top hat'. Even at the end of the film when he has the chance to prevent a Squizzy Taylor-like gangster from shooting their horse, he pauses in his dash to the racecourse to get such a top hat, undercutting the seriousness of this test of his 'big'-ness.

Nevertheless, the screenplay attempts to impose on the genre and on Tommy's character in particular the American social mythology of the working-class man who achieves upward mobility by marrying a better-bred woman. (Frank Capra's 1934 Academy Award and popular triumph *It Happened One Night* would have been one example screening in Australian picture palaces at the time Seward wrote the screenplay for *Thoroughbred*.) However, the Australian plotline lacks both compositional and realistic motivation: even at the end of the film the heroine spends most of her time in the company and on the arm of the rejected Bill, whose behaviour is at all times intelligent, sincere, amusing and, when he intervenes in plot episodes, brave and effectual. Joan's declared preference for Tommy is at odds with both the mise en scene and narrative causality, and her support for Tommy in another argument with Peel throws expectations on to Tommy's character which the narrative fails to deliver:

Tommy: Ma used to be crazy about family trees, until she found Uncle Willy hanging from the first bough for horse stealing.

Peel:	That wasn't your uncle Willy, that was your grandfather. Yes, Tommy, you come from a long line of crocks.
Joan:	According to Mr Peel's standpoint Shakespeare, Napoleon, Beethoven, Lincoln and Nelson were all crocks.
Peel:	My dear, there are exceptions.

While Tommy proves himself no exception, the unknown and apparently unpedigreed horse he buys in New Zealand is. (As we shall see shortly, *Thoroughbred* is in many respects a covert response to the anti-breeding myth contained within the legend of Phar Lap.) 'Stormalong' wins both the AJC Derby in Sydney and the Melbourne Cup (as did Phar Lap in 1929-30), but this apparent victory for 'crocks' is reversed when it becomes known that the horse is the lost son of the famous English racehorse Merlin, 'the finest blood on earth', as Peel declares. Although Stormalong is clearly intended as a racial symbol of Anglo-Australian society ('lost son'/ 'finest blood on earth'), the concept fails to transfer itself to humans. Even the Australian Tommy's attempts to feed and train the horse are inept, unlike the Canadian heroine's interventions, and the English Bill Peel's decision to let Stormalong mate with his father's prize mare Lady Windsor, thus ensuring a continuation of the bloodline after Stormalong is killed by the gangster as he crosses the finishing line to win the Melbourne Cup. In *Thoroughbred* the attempt to parallel the Australian man (for which read nation) with a thoroughbred horse is never plausible enough to be persuasively foregrounded, unlike other stock metaphors such as the comparison between beautiful women and prize horses, and between breaking in horses and domesticating men through marriage, which here, as in most racing films in any period, continue to be activated. *Thoroughbred* is an uneasy compromise on every level: its ineffectual questioning and revision of the expectations of the racing genre are repeatedly subverted by its own deference to such conventions, and its weak surface questioning of Nazi ideology through disagreements with Peel's blandly delivered comments is undercut by its more explicit contextual paralleling of the arch-villain with the real-life Czech anti-fascist journalist, Egon Kisch. The thickly accented mastermind behind the plot to kill Stormalong is prevented from entering Australia by a language test and confined on board ship, as Kisch had been in 1934.

An odd and historically isolated survival screened in 1949, *Into the Straight*, reveals its desire to reactivate myths of good breeding without inciting anti-democratic controversy by fusing binary opposites: it is an Australian squatter who despairs that Australian horses (and again by implication people) 'don't win' and hopes 'a strain of English blood may give stamina and horsepower', while a young English gentleman proves him wrong by purchasing his rejected Australian colt 'Revolt' which wins the Melbourne Cup.[35] The film picks up the theme of the racial reconstruction of Australian society caused by the post-Second World War migrant programme. However, it limits its awareness of new breeding possibilities to *British* immigrants, who are mistakenly considered 'terrible types' by an Australian character. One English migrant-gentleman later marries the Australian heroine, and the 'stamina and horsepower'—and sophistication and status—he will bring to Australian society and its future generations are deliberately inferred. *Into the Straight* also recognises that racing has become a predominantly male obsession and offers a parallel romance melodrama plotline involving the squatter's daughter's struggle to become a successful classical composer, though here too the story hedges its potentially socio-political statements by making the bar to her achievement physical (a riding accident) rather than gender or post-colonial inhibitors. The construction of *Into the Straight* recognises the need for diversity within the worlds of horses and music in trying to offer something for all classes, while as usual suggesting a universal acceptance of both by all the characters: the upper-middleclass watch buckjumping and bull-riding at a rodeo with the same enthusiasm as the workers follow the success of the squatter's horses; in music the mise en scene and soundtrack give equal emphasis to a country and western song, a jazz number at a nightclub, and a classical piano concerto. Unchanging class divisions without social mobility, endemic to the genre, are still assumed and neutralised by mise en scene assertions about 'universal' tastes and interests.

As with dramas of breeding, the 1930s were a crucial decade for other kinds of sporting films, which began to replace good blood with other qualities: acquired skill and effort in democratic narratives and, in parody dramas, science and luck. *Thoroughbred* hints at these developments: in one comic sequence Tommy attempts to feed Stormalong his own salad recipe, only to have the horse refuse to eat it and lose his first race; in a later linked sequence Joan takes over the horse's training and by hard exercise makes him a winner: 'He needed work'. The parody texts which use science and luck will be examined shortly but first, as with *Gallipoli* and sport and war dramas, it is necessary to arch over several decades of Australian cultural history to find a significant racing drama which raises the question of breeding and nationhood yet again, and which in doing so also considers the free-enterprise 'democratic' ideology of success through effort. *Phar Lap* (1983), like *Thoroughbred*, celebrates the story of the unknown and ugly horse, apparently from poor bloodlines and bought for a paltry 'One Hundred and Sixty Eight Pounds' (as the dialogue reminds us several times), whose track career and mysterious death during the depression became one of Australia's most enduring sporting legends.[36] *Phar Lap*'s historically distanced subject matter allows it to represent less evasively than *Thoroughbred* the popular construction in 1929–32 of Phar Lap's victories as triumphs for the masses over a discredited establishment: rather than asserting a cross-class construction of the nation, its juxtapositions of rich and poor invite a reading of social oppositions, as sweeping pans past excited working-class punters celebrating another race victory are intercut with static shots of equally static and gloomy upper-class racing club members.[37] However, like other 'end-of-the-genre' texts *Phar Lap* ultimately fails to deal adequately with the ideology of a form of sport which, within its own terms of reference, insistently demonstrates the validity of selective interbreeding, precisely because the film cannot resist (as Ma Dawson does in *Thoroughbred*) the allegorical construction of such an animal sporting contest as a discourse of nationalism. The class oppositions are allowed to slide out of focus and be replaced by 'natural' talent in a 'national' quest for fame and fortune.

The narrative offers four points of view on breeding, the Australian nation, and the reasons why Phar Lap was 'the best', beginning with the horse's American part-owner Dave Davis, who represents the upfront, quick profit making approach to racing: 'Some guy told me his sire and dam were hopeless. Didn't win a single race between them . . . *Did not win a single race, either one of them.*' Davis has no conception of the slow-maturing process which is shown to lead ultimately to more substantial and enduring success. The Chairman of the Victoria Racing Club, Lachlan McKinnon, occupies the opposite polarity as a figure of the Australian pseudo-aristocracy and the neo-colonial establishment, talking about the good of racing and the country while determinedly clinging to traditional wealth and power by controlling the membership of his exclusive club. (In one iconoclastic moment, the van hurrying Phar Lap to Flemington for the 1930 Melbourne Cup races illegally down the Members' Drive.) Both McKinnon's snobbish 'You can't buy real quality for 160 Guineas', and Davis's sudden enthusiasm for the horse once its money-earning capacity has been demonstrated, are freely and explicitly satirised, although neither man's power is subverted. McKinnon's dislike of the 'freak' and his influence with the handicapper make it impossible for Phar Lap to continue racing in Australia, and Davis's gambling plans are the major actants in an otherwise elegiac and episodic plotline. As always the allegoric reifications (here of 'colonial English', 'American', and 'Australian' social attitudes) are clear, as Phar Lap's victories are put together in a montage with images of the upperclasses holding their champagne breakfasts in the members' carpark, news of the New York stock market crash, and the cheers of the masses.

Greater weight is given in the text to the argument between Phar Lap's other part-owner and trainer, Harry Telford, and the young strapper Tom Woodcock. Telford shares with *Thoroughbred*'s Tommy Dawson traits of stubborness, social climbing and indifference to his wife/fiancee's concerns; his assertion that Phar Lap has 'Good blood further back' and his belief in relentless hard training are set against Woodcock's gentleness and motivational conditioning: 'He's got to learn to be a winner.' Both positions again have overtones of national achievement, but Telford is ultimately forced to share McKinnon's belief that the horse is 'a freak', since his other purchases have proved worthless:

Telford: For years I've kidded myself that I made that horse. The truth is he would
            have been a champion no matter who trained him. I've got twenty colts
            out there with bloodlines as good or better than his, and I've trained them
            all exactly the same. Every one's a dud. He's a freak.

The narrative ultimately rejects this attitude too; when an injured and unfit Phar Lap splits his hoof and almost breaks down during the 'world's richest horse race', then struggles on to a narrow victory against the 'finest racehorses in the world', Woodcock's belief in Phar Lap's great courage ('heart') are finally confirmed as the key factor in his success. *Phar Lap*'s ideological position on achievement is reminiscent of the belief, common from the 1950s to the 1970s but then laid to rest by poor international performances, that innate 'Australian' sporting talent and 'democratic' individual attitudes would more than offset the lack of investment capital and ignorance of 'totalitarian' training techniques which supposedly characterised the preparation of other national sporting teams for events like the Olympic Games. While recognising the contributions to the legend made by Telford's utilitarianism and Davis's assertiveness, *Phar Lap* ultimately foregrounds innocent, allegedly non-ideological 'natural, national' qualities over breeding, class struggle, physical effort, and social aggression.

Parody dramas

One possible grouping of many Australian film texts is that of comedies of naive mise en scene starring theatre, vaudeville or revue stars: W. S. Percy, Fred Niblo, Claude Dampier and others in the silent period; Pat Hanna, Bert Bailey, George Wallace, Dorothy Brunton, Roy Rene, Will Mahoney, Evie Hayes, and Joe Valli in sound film 1931–41; Walter Chiari, Graeme Blundell, Barry Humphries, Bruce Spence, Barry Crocker, Max Gillies and Reg Livermore during the early revival period 1966–76. In each case substantial sequences if not most of the film follow theatrical conventions of representation rather than exploring filmic possibilities; often too, as in the (in)famous case of the 'Mo' film *Strike Me Lucky* (1935),[38] the failure to solve the problems of transcoding stage acts into cinematic form has resulted in uneven and unsuccessful films.

Within this loose grouping of films by star type and style, four early sound films (*A Ticket in Tatts* 1934, *Gone to the Dogs* and *Come Up Smiling* both 1939, and *Racing Luck* 1941) exploit sporting subjects as vehicles for comic inversion, parody, and in the case of *Come Up Smiling*, joyously anarchic carnivalesque, systematically destroying the ideologies of caste, stability, work and selfless duty. Frank Thring's *A Ticket in Tatts*, starring George Wallace, is the earliest and least adventurous, offering a working-class perspective (rather than conscious parody) on a plot close in incident and sequence to *Flying Scud*. A somewhat token love triangle involving two squatting families is backgrounded, and the horse 'Hotspur' wins not because of innate superiority but because George, who has trained him to respond to his whistle by rewarding him with sugar, rushes to the rails when it is clear that the substitute jockey is corrupt and 'pulling' his mount. Hotspur responds to George's command and wins in spite of his jockey's efforts; but in the quick wind-up of romance elements class relationships remain stable.

Both Wallace's *Gone to the Dogs* and *Racing Luck*, starring Joe Valli, develop this idea of performance-modifying stimulants into mock-scientific fantasy. In the former, zoo workers George and Henry accidentally combine chemicals in the veterinary laboratory, producing a huge carrot-shaped compound which when eaten gives extra speed to both animals and humans; in the latter a medicine used on camels during the First World War is tried on a rejected racehorse by two down-and-out war veterans, with predictable and profitable results.[39] A more interesting and substantial text is *Come Up Smiling*, the only Cinesound feature not directed by Ken G. Hall.[40] Since supporting cast and crew remained largely unchanged during the life of this company, some combination of the English scriptwriter-director, William Freshman,[41] and the American husband and wife vaudeville stars, Will Mahoney and Evie Hayes, must be credited with the lightness in style, rich inventiveness, and carefully plotted narrative causality which are unique in Cinesound's output and unusual in Australian screen narrative in any genre or period.

Come Up Smiling is also the only feature-length Australian-made boxing movie since sound on film was introduced (several proposals for Les Darcy films having failed to appear), and it offers a unique and significant example

Male sport *vs* male theatre, while the woman plays on; from *Come Up Smiling*, 1939 (National Film and Sound Archive, courtesy Greater Union).

of an upwardly mobile female character, Pat Howard. Played by the young singer-actress Jean Hatton (who to her annoyance was advertised by Cinesound as 'Australia's Deanna Durbin')[42] Pat is a gifted but penniless young soprano, performing with her father in a down-and-out tent theatre. When her voice fails her, requiring an expensive throat operation, the third member and leader of their company, Barney O'Hara, reluctantly agrees to try to win £500 by lasting five rounds with 'The Killer'. The other block to Pat's career is her lack of social status which prevents her gaining entrance to the world of high society where the contacts necessary for an operatic singing career can be made. This problem is solved by the intervention of a friendly squatter's daughter, and the film ends with Pat's departure to study in Italy. This plotline shows the different constructions of Europe for women as against men in post-colonial Anglo-Australian society: for Pat it represents an opportunity for a satisfying career with status-enhancing possibilities. But since the nineteenth-century 'equal but different' assertions of national achievement—men in sport, women in drama—are no longer active, Pat's success is personal, not cultural. She is outside the male Australian construction of nationality, and questions of inferiority/superiority *vis-a-vis* Europe do not arise.

Appropriately for this most carnivalesque of Australian films, *Come Up Smiling* opens in sideshow alley, with an affectionate parody of the old tent melodramas of the 1900s–1920s. Barney O'Hara's tent theatre offers a singer (Pat), a tap-dancing Irish tenor (Barney), and Pat's father, a grandly heavy actor of the old school. The three are performing, as the tent hoarding announces:

THE WOMAN WHO ERRED
EVERY HOUR FROM 10 TO 10

Audiences, however, are shown turning from theatre to sport, represented in the diegesis by the sideshow opposite Barney's, a Jimmy Sharman-like boxing tent where volunteers can win £5 fighting 'The Killer'. The one surviving link between theatre and sport is the interest in both by a squatter, Colonel Cameron, a character clearly based on Hugh D. McIntosh. The Colonel suggests to the Killer's promoters that more money could be made by presenting him at Cameron's 'old Stadium'; he and his daughter also act as hosts to international opera stars and the cream of Sydney's artistic and social community, and it is singing at this party which gives Pat her opportunity for stage stardom. As noted earlier in discussing *Into the Straight*, bringing together into one film text the world of sport and the arts (particularly opera, ballet and classical music) was a common response to the industry's perceptions of the bifurcation of men's and women's interests, as well as subverting the counter attractions of live sporting contests and theatrical performances.

The narrative carefully structures incidents and character traits and types, all of which are brought together into the burlesque boxing contest between Barney and the Killer. Stock sporting and heroic values are parodied: Barney is a most reluctant hero who when kidnapped and then found yells 'Save me. I'm being rescued.' He is also entirely uninterested in being fit for the fight: told to practise on a punching bag, he first sleeps and then tap dances a punching rhythm to deceive the listening instructor. The ethics of sport are travestied: before the contest Pat's father dips Barney's right hand in cement before putting the boxing glove on and later sprinkles the glove with pepper, not to mention putting first slippery powder and later glue on the Killer's shoes. Barney does a tightrope walk along the ropes, Pat enters singing, the Killer loses all interest in fighting at the sound of her voice (a previously established character trait), a Bagpipe Band follows which enrages Barney (another trait), a small boy puts ants in Barney's boxing shorts to further torment him to greater effort, and Barney's girlfriend hits the fallen Killer with a bottle, to which he replies 'Thank you'.

Come Up Smiling is ignored by even specialised books on Australian film history and Cinesound's contribution to it,[43] but is virtually unique within this grouping of Australian films starring stage comedians in successfully transposing the codes of stage performance into those of film narrative. Although there are several semi-detached stage-based routines, the plotline is central to most of the comic situations, rather than principally being a way of avoiding episodic discontinuity, and the rhythms of narrative flow and montage are allowed to control or replace comic dialogue and business. It is also unique in consciously inverting the culturally inscribed values of sport and sporting champions (courage, fair play, fitness), although as an allowed parody text it is doubtful whether it could be said to be implying, in the sense of carnivalesque used by Bakhtin,[44] any political critique of them. What does emerge more strongly from the narrative is a sense of release from the inhibiting insistence on male nationalism, flowing from the focus on an Australian woman's career. Other contributing factors might well include the recently arrived American stars, Mahoney and Hayes, whose presence placed the text outside national discourses, and perhaps the imported screenwriter's indifference to them. *Come Up Smiling* lacks most of the geographical or national icons so beloved of local film makers of the time, but treats women as individuals and protagonists. Romance coupling is almost entirely absent from the plot: Pat has no boyfriend/lover figure in the text; an engagement between the squatter's daughter and a soldier is picked up just after his proposal and remains static thereafter, and Barney's engagement to the female gym instructor is an entirely whimsical addition to the final scene. By mocking the sporting males and treating the opera story seriously (yet within an overtly popular narrative style) *Come Up Smiling* presents female characters more successfully than any other Australian film of the thirties.

Gender representation/representations: better a horse than a woman

The ability of the camera to record action on location increased the variety of sports which could be used as dramatic subjects, though this too had narrative and generic consequences. The theatrical presentation of young women diving and swimming, which had begun in a Bland Holt melodrama

The sportswoman as hero: Annette Kellerman in *Queen of the Sea* c.1918 (*Fairy Tales of the South Seas*).

in 1903, was internationalised in London and New York vaudeville by that production's sporting star, Annette Kellerman, who also introduced it into Hollywood after 1916, when her second film *The Daughter of the Gods* 'staggered America'.[45] The genre reached its apotheosis in the career of Esther Williams who played Kellerman in the 1952 Hollywood aquatic colour spectacular *Million Dollar Mermaid*, with Kellerman herself co-writing the screenplay story of her life and working as a consultant during the filming.[46] However, the struggle over the ways in which women could be represented as stars and as active protagonists in drama caused this genre to develop without the central structuring element of competitive sport. Kellerman's films were action adventures involving diving and swimming; in later features romance melodrama was used for the storylines and water sports (for example, precision swimming in *Million Dollar Mermaid*) were located not in competition but within the mise en scene motif of the female body as spectacle. Amongst Australian examples *Come Up Smiling* contains a scene set in a women's gym, the 'Beauty Through Health Charm School', where the female chorus do a mock fitness dance routine while their teacher 'Kitty Katkin' sings 'That's the Way to Handle Your Man'. Achievement through marriage rather than for oneself is inscribed on to the physically fit female body, and the hard-riding and/or sporting female character—developed on the popular stage in England, America, and Australia throughout the nineteenth century and in some early silent films—disappeared.

The decline and eclipse of active female sportswomen characters in Australian film is allied to the changing mythology of women and work in twentieth century Australian society, and within the film industry by the different uses which both Hollywood and local film makers made of the same images. The nineteenth-century active Australian woman character was represented as the product of a puritan, pioneering tradition; she lived in a society in which, mythically at least, no-one could assume a merely biological or decorative role. This myth is captured in a defiantly antiquated way in Raymond Longford's 1920 film *On Our Selection*, at the same time as Hollywood's representations of women were beginning to dominate Australian screens. One of the most distinctive images in *On Our Selection* is of the whole family, male and female, young and old, hoeing the paddock, with an accompanying title which emphasises the equality of men's and women's labour. In American film such an image would connote either black slavery or poor white tenant farming; to use it to indicate the origins of prosperity shows a different Australian inflection to the pioneering myth. Female manual work signifies comradeship rather than sexuality, shared hardship, and an equal right to the economic benefits of labour. This rural puritan discourse suggested that the images of horse-riding and swimming which most commonly expressed female activity should be decoded in a practical, non-sexual way. In romance the active woman of Australian stage melodrama was sometimes no more assertive than her traditional ingenue sister, but where this occurs

No place for sport: *On Our Selection*, 1920 (National Film and Sound Archive).

her romantic function was clearly distinguished from her heroic one, the integrity of which remains intact. This tradition was challenged by the later reworking of these same images of riding and swimming to offer different connotations which subverted the egalitarianism of the outback images and suggested instead voyeuristic readings.

In the Hollywood film and its Australian imitations the subversion acted principally by the suppression of work as the basis of riding and swimming, in favour of sexual metaphor and the display of the female body. The open-thighed pounding pelvic pleasure of horse-riding had always invited a potential sexual interpretation; if the purpose of horse-riding were changed from the economic (mustering/farm life generally) to the purely recreational, then this sexual reading of the image might predominate. Where a patently decorative-passive actor was cast as an economically active heroine, one might get both readings simultaneously and so satisfy the mythic expectations of Australian audiences exposed to both Hollywood and the bush ethos. John Tulloch's discussion of Franklyn Barrett's *A Girl of the Bush* (1921) amplifies this exactly:

As leading lady Barrett chose Vera James, who was later to have a minor Hollywood career. Although advertised by Barrett as perfect for the station-running heroine of the film because she was 'a good horse-woman and swimmer', James later said that far from being the classical country type, she could neither ride nor swim, took her first riding lessons in a city suit, turbaned hat with a quill and very high heeled shoes, and that her only screen parts had been in 'society' roles.

She evidently convinced the critic of *Picture Show*, who described her as 'a living, human creature, who is expert at branding, at mustering, at doing a thousand other station jobs . . . She is Fairbanksian in her athletic skill, and her personality simply radiates good-fellowship'.[47]

Swimming, a less obviously necessary pioneering skill which exposed the female body, was even easier to subvert. In the same film a city 'cad' walks into the foreground of an idyllic innocent bush scene of two girls bathing naked in the distance, enabling the audience, who see the girls over his shoulder, to both enjoy the voyeuristic spectacle and condemn the viewer. The leisure of beach and lagoon and the sexuality of nakedness and 'rational' bathing costumes promoted the myth of woman as object. As with horse-riding, two readings were for a time simultaneously possible, but when the bush pioneering image became too distant to be recognised, the Australian sportswoman-type lost its distinctive meaning, and began to be written out of the narrative, and later the mise en scene.

This eclipse was completed by the mid 1930s. As mentioned earlier, the 1921 *Silks and Saddles* repeated a stock motif dating back at least to Boucicault's 1885 *The Jilt* by having the heroine ride her own horse to victory, and several other films of the period include as a stock sequence shots of a woman character breaking in horses. The 1920 film of *The Breaking of the Drought* is one; the woman character involved has no function in the plot, though the images are partly intended to encode utilitarian horse-riding as a moral opposition to the son's obsession with gambling on horses at Randwick.[48] The heroine in *Thoroughbred* is also shown conquering an untamed horse; again the sequence has no causal narrative function and it also defies narrative realism by occurring the morning after we have seen her knocked unconscious in a motor car accident. As with the other aspects of *Thoroughbred* analysed earlier, the use of this stock generic motif has become dislodged from plausibly motivated diegesis. It is the only known example in Australian sound feature film and the last of its kind.

The marginalisation and exclusion of women from sporting films has been tacitly acknowledged or challenged in three recent Australian features: *Dawn* (1978), the previously discussed *Phar Lap* (1983), and *The Coolangatta Gold* (1984). Each however ultimately demonstrates the difficulty of working outside known generic boundaries and dominant constructs in movies intended for mainstream cinemas and commercial television. *Dawn* was an attempt to present a pseudo-documentary biography of the swimmer Dawn Fraser; its almost total disappearance even from television repeats within a few years of its first screening is perhaps the most objective testimony to its failure to find a way to arouse viewer interest in some remarkable source material.[49] Reviewers found it fragmentary, lacking any interest in explaining the central character's dedication to her goal, and noted in particular the complete omission of the generically expected scenes of preparation for events: 'Gruelling and endless training sessions, the lot of any swimming hopeful, are omitted. But then suddenly, it seems, here's Dawn winning championships and breaking world records.'[50] By contrast both *The Coolangatta Gold* and *Phar Lap* through lyrical slow motion make a fetish of the dedication of male athletes and horse trainers to performance-enhancing fitness training, and whereas *Dawn* minimises the working relationship between Fraser and her trainer Harry Gallagher, both *The Coolangatta Gold* and *Gallipoli* contain long sequences of intense psychological brainwashing of athletes by coaches. There are clearly significant areas of representation of female athletes yet to be colonised by feminist writers and directors.

The Coolangatta Gold alone attempted to include a high-achieving woman as a central character.[51] Like *Come Up Smiling* and *Into the Straight* before it, the script offers parallel stories of a young male sportsman and a female artist, in this case a ballet dancer. (No tradition of Australian film-making should be implied here; dozens of Hollywood movies offer gender-divided sport and drama scenarios and have been the primary carriers of the ideology in twentieth-century Western popular culture.) *The Coolangatta Gold*'s opening sequence offers images of two young physically active bodies in adjacent classrooms, as Steve studies martial arts and Kerri rehearses for a ballet performance.[52] Both have strong platonic(?) relationships with their respective instructors, although this attempt at male/female parallelism is undercut by stylistic differences encoding self and other, complete and incomplete: Steve is shown predominantly in facial close up, with closed-off, onanistic self-absorption, while Kerri's upper body is revealed in mid shot, as she smiles and rehearses for an audience. Later as their relationship develops each watches the other in performance, though she is unaware of Steve's secret presence in the darkened auditorium while she dances, but is obliged to make a public statement of her interest in his participation in the surf triathlon which gives the film its title.

In *The Coolangatta Gold*'s narrative development the film's generic and thematic uncertainty is revealed. It was initially intended as a teen-market text for both sexes (a sub-plot concerns Steve's own artistic interests—his involvement in a rock group). As the story progresses it increasingly marginalises both characters' artistic quests and, in particular, Kerri's individual ambitions. Initially she rejects Steve's advances because of her single-minded dedication to her career; as she does so the framing offers us behind Steve's head a poster of the 1980–81 'Women and Arts' festival in Sydney, at that time viciously attacked as a separatist (and implicitly lesbian) movement.[53] Nevertheless, as the film progresses Kerri's career is forgotten as Steve and the storyline become obsessed by his bizarre and unpleasant identity struggle with his father and elder brother over the outcome of the surf race; she fulfils the displaced and therefore legitimated Oedipal role of mother/lover/comforter.[54] A generically alien and gratuitous sex scene (though possibly analogous to the gratuitous woman-rides-horse scene in earlier films), shot using a body double after the actress who played Kerri refused to participate, was cut into the print just before the premiere screening, further rewriting her role as marginal love interest and voyeuristic object rather than co-protagonist.[55] Ultimately female achievement remains a threat to heterosexual role orthodoxy and the singular happy ending.

Phar Lap addresses the same problem and seeks to defuse it by comically acknowledging its male characters' primary allegiance to horses rather than women. In the most explicit instance, two of Tom Woodcock's fellow stablehands arrive at his wedding to announce that Phar Lap is 'fretting' at his absence and 'won't eat', and demanding that he come immediately:

Tom: But what about Emma? What about the honeymoon?
Cashy: There's no time mate. Bobbie's real bad.

It is only when Tom turns away to tell his wife that they break down in laughter, revealing the joke. Several times the same point is made more subtly in incongruous images of man and horse while women are being discussed; again the most explicit is where Mrs Davis advises Tom to go and propose to Emma. Her line 'Sometimes I wonder how Australian men ever manage to find themselves wives' is followed by a big close up of Phar Lap's and Tom's heads close together, considering the problem. Scenes of men saying goodbye to women fill the episodic interstices, and Tom's habit of sleeping in Phar Lap's stable during his American trip causes a reporter to demand, 'What is he, some kind of pervert?' Both *Phar Lap* and *The Coolangatta Gold* have stock complaining wife characters (Telford's wife, Steve's mother) whose plausible objections to the absurdity of their spouses' obsessions are swept away by the narrowing visual and narrative focus on the ultimate male national or psycho-climactic sporting contest. Although not explicitly onanistic or homoerotic, recent films about competitive sport certainly allow such readings; it is only the extreme and therefore laughable perversion of bestiality that enables *Phar Lap* to make jokes about the problem of gender and sport which it, like all the recent films discussed here, then seeks to erase from the text. The echoes of nineteenth-century educational ideology are unmistakeable: sport as a substitute for and sublimation of sex. If earlier films included women riding horses partly as sexual innuendo, more recent works were predicated on the world of Thomas Arnold and William Acton: better a horse than a woman. It is perhaps significant that after this flurry of late 1970s and early 1980s films sporting subjects dropped out of the Australian feature film again. As we shall see in the next chapter, the usefulness of sports as codified story material offering the possibility for popular celebrations and/or significant social analysis is now in question in both film and stage representations. By becoming so closely associated with particular and partial social ideologies of Anglo-maleness and nation, it seems that narratively constructed sport has been displaced from both industrial and social constructions of Australian audiences and their central concerns and interests.

Sport in the
Literary Drama
1909–89

While sport has continued to function as a major subject in twentieth-century Australian stage plays, such dramatic storytelling, unlike the practices of the film industry, has been outside the tradition of—and generally not influenced by—the popular sporting plays analysed in chapters 3, 4, and 5. Except for a small number of early literary playwrights, such as Louis Esson and William Moore who were writing at the end of the high years of stage sporting melodrama and reacting against it, twentieth-century dramatists using sport as subject matter have worked within the European literary-intellectual construction of sport *versus* drama with which this study began.

Their texts were also produced in very different economic circumstances. Until the 1960s the financial base of the amateur theatres for which most of these authors wrote was virtually non-existent; certainly they had neither the capital nor the technical resources to stage sporting spectacles, even if they had wished to do so. Without acknowledging or examining closely the popular tradition, literary playwrights nevertheless borrowed the language of sport with its by then codified connotations; resonances which audiences recognised from the passing into general Western culture of the usages we have seen in the popular sporting dramas of the commercial stage and the feature film.

The conditions in which the twentieth-century Australian stage playwright worked can be divided broadly into four periods: those in non-commercial theatre up to the mid-1950s; those of the next fifteen years during which low-scale government support and interference in that activity commenced; those in the government-subsidised theatre industry in the 1970s; and in the more diverse and many-voiced theatre of the 1980s. For present purposes the first two periods can be combined; the significant changes in dramatists' interest in and approach to sport in theatre can be dated approximately to 1909, 1968, and 1980.

As early as the colonial period a number of important writers observed the sports-mad Australian male and expressed reservations about him. Marin

La Meslee's comment made in the late 1870s: 'Australian men often desert their girls for the superior attractions of athletic games, horses, races and *cricket*'[1] would, as we shall see shortly, resonate a hundred years later in the nationalistic sporting plays of the 1970s. But while first the live stage and later the film industry were commercial enterprises they shut out fundamentally negative or questioning utterances about sport—*An Englishman's Home* and its immediately pre-First World War imitations being the only exceptions, and for particular jingoistic reasons. In the non-commercial environment, however, a very different view of sporting Australia predominated. Without implying the existence of an indigenous tradition in so fragmented, socially marginal and eurocentric an activity as Australian literary theatre before 1968, one central and common factor in successive stage utterances can still be observed: an expression of uneasiness, and at times revulsion, at the sports-loving Australian, seeing him—and occasionally her—as the quintessential product of a society devoted to mindless philistinism, childishness, self-indulgence, and short-sighted hedonism. Often expressed in coded forms identical to those used in the plays of Edwardian military chauvinists such as Guy Du Maurier and Randolph Bedford, the attitudes of such writers emerged from very different political attitudes, predominantly liberal-humanist intellectual concepts, and strong cultural-elitist beliefs about these writers' own place in Australian society. Their bewilderment at living in a society which admired sports heroes and not 'people of culture and intellect' gave rise to a general rejection of those aspects of that society and even, as early as the character Sydney Barrett in Esson's *The Time Is Not Yet Ripe* (1912), to a self-inflicted martyrdom. Their revulsion expressed itself most urgently in what they wrote about sporting Australia.

The one play from the colonial period which hints at some of these alternative constructs is Marcus Clarke's unfinished and until recently unperformed farce, *Reverse* of 1876. Here sport, possibly for the first time in locally written drama, becomes evidence of the neglect of intellect in Australian society. From this perspective *Reverse* is best examined in the light of two of Clarke's non-dramatic writings from the same time. In his famous preface to the second edition of Adam Lindsay Gordon's *Sea Spray and Smoke Drift* (1876), Clarke portrays Gordon as a famous Australian sportsman who concealed his literary ability because of his society's anti-intellectual bias. Clarke describes him as 'Intensely nervous, and feeling much of that shame at the exercise of the higher intelligence which besets those who are known to be renowned in field sports'.[2] He argues that Gordon worked through this cultural insecurity and emerged as both an *un*ashamed poet and a champion steeplechase jockey, able to shine on the racecourse and also gain 'welcome entrance to the houses of all who had pretensions to literary taste'.

Although Clarke is only half-serious in his delineation of an opposition between sport and poetry (he was himself an experienced horse rider and the author of the racing novel *Long Odds* mentioned in chapter 3) he took up the theme again a year later, also in a comic way, in his essay 'The Future Australian Race'. His approving and often quoted comment on his own time:

Look at the schools, libraries and botanic gardens of Australia. Read the accounts of the boat race, the cricket matches, and say if our youth are not manly. Listen to the plaudits which greet a finished actor, or a finely-gifted singer, and confess also that we have some taste and culture.[3]

needs to be considered alongside his prognosis for the future: 'we cannot expect men of genius unless we beget them by frequent intermarriage . . . the Australasian will be freed from the highest burden of intellectual development'.[4] It is difficult to know how seriously Clarke intended the mock-eugenic argument he pursues in this essay, but the repetition of the idea in both prose works and the play *Reverses* during the two-year period 1876–77 shows that it was a matter which intrigued him at the time, and which must have been current in contemporary debate.

In *Reverses* Clarke uses a stock farce situation: two young men who decide to exchange names in order to amuse themselves at the expense of the other persons of the drama.[5] (The play is closely based on the 1875 London success *Our Boys*.) Their characters are exact opposites, though, improbably, they are Oxford college chums. Lord Henry Gauntlet is a hearty British aristocrat, a manly sportsman and captain of the Oxford rowing eight, but uninterested in intellectual matters; Bob Mundic is a romantic, world-weary young Australian aesthete who was sent to England as a small child to be educated, who has achieved great intellectual distinction and won the Oxford Vice-Chancellor's poetry prize, but who despises all physical exertion. Both travel to Australia when Bob's father summons him home, and find themselves amongst the Melbourne *nouveau riche*, a world indicated in part by the playing on stage of croquet and ecarte. Before they meet their Australian hosts a servant mistakes the English Harry for the Australian Bob, and the two consequently decide to exchange identities; a deception which works perfectly because it is exactly what colonial society expects: that a representative of the English aristocracy will be pale, cultured, effete, and indifferent to sport; and that the Australian youth will be an athletic horse-lover. It is the dual identity which Clarke argued Adam Lindsay Gordon was forced to adopt, expressed in the play as two farcically simplified characters, and is also the comic reversal of Clarke's predictions for the future Australian race. Unfortunately the play does not build on the theme, possibly because Clarke left it unfinished and did not write the scene in which the deception is revealed; nevertheless, read in conjunction with his other writings at the time, *Reverses* shows Clarke's uncomfortable awareness of the poet and scholar's exclusion from the emerging myth of sporting, anti-intellectual Australian society.

Countertexts: 1909–68

The attitudes of the literary intellectuals to sport and to sporting drama were not taken up again in Australian drama until thirty-three years later, in the work of William Moore and Louis Esson. In literature the objections were frequent, as G. A. Wilkes has noted in *The Stockyard and the Croquet Lawn*,[6] but possibly the first overt attack, in a performed play, on the commercial stage in Australia and its obsession with the sporting genre, was Moore's short 'satirical burlesque' *Acting a la Mode*. Performed for one night only in 1909 at the first of Moore's annual drama nights in Melbourne, *Acting a la Mode* satirises the sensational English drama which Bland Holt in particular had offered Australian audiences. Set on the stage of a commercial theatre, this twenty-minute sketch begins with a stage manager/theatre producer rewriting a script by adding a totally gratuitous sensation to a 'tea and talk' scene at a bishop's garden party:

> *Stage M:* We'll have a parachutist drop down while the bishop is addressing them
> on the first fruits of the Pan-Anglican Congress. (*Leaves speaking tube
> and writes on pad*) 'The parachutist cannons off the left shoulder of the
> Bishop of Dullham, who collapses with a thud. Crowd rushes to assist
> bishop and gets hopelessly entangled in the ropes of the parachute—wild
> consternation—tableau—curtain'. (p.2)[7]

He then rehearses a wealthy young man who he hopes to induce to join the company (bringing his money with him), and shows him how to make a melodramatic exit in a military and sporting play as he leaves 'To fight for home and country—for football and cricket grounds—for this sea-washed isle—for God save the King and Rule Brittania!!!'(p.9) Finally the stage manager also auditions a young amateur actress who has been given a race-call scene to learn for her audition:

> *Stage M:* Now I'll just tell you the story of the first scene. The hero is a minor poet.
> He published a volume of verse and it was genuinely slated by the
> London press. This drove him to drink. Before rushing headlong on the
> downward path tenders were called for a new National Ode, and he sent
> in his sample. You bring him news that the ode has been accepted. You
> also remind him that he has a horse entered for the Derby. Cheered by
> the news that the ode has been accepted he rouses himself and
> determines to depart with the heroine at once for Epsom—curtain. (p.13)

The stage manager and the actress then play out this ridiculous scenario and the following scene at Epsom on Derby Day, where she calls out the names of the horses in great excitement. The name of the poet's victorious horse, 'New Broom', is shouted repeatedly at the end of the sequence (p.18) and is obviously Moore's comment on the staleness of the sporting drama, its plotting and cliched motifs.

In later years William Moore was given to claiming that his series of drama nights were the first attempt to establish an Australian literary theatre.[8] This claim is factually incorrect,[9] but more importantly (from a modern perspective) it implies a nationalism which, since Moore's own plays were set in England, were comments on English drama, and were intended for eventual production in England, is misleading. Moore did stage the first one-act plays of Katharine Susannah Prichard and Louis Esson, but most of the plays given were his own slight efforts such as *Acting a la Mode*, *The Only Game*, *The Mysterious Moonlight*, *The Tea Shop Girl*, and *Killed By Laughter*.[10] Plays by Australians about Australia were just as rare in the minority repertory theatres after the First World War as they had been in the commercial theatre before it, and Moore's objections to English commercial drama were not national but culturally elitist.

However, the same cannot be said for Louis Esson, whose plays were also among the first written for the new non-commercial and to some extent anti-popular theatre. Esson's response to the sport *versus* drama binary was a complex one; he was himself both a self-proclaimed dramatic nationalist intellectual and a keen member of the Melbourne Cricket Club. Nevertheless Esson also perceived as a dilemma the situation where Australian sportsmen were being mythically constructed as non-intellectual alternatives to Australian writers, as is revealed in the letter which he wrote from England to Vance Palmer after he [Esson] had witnessed the triumphant 1921 Australian cricket tour of England:

There is such energy in the . . . cricketers who are infinitely superior in character and temperament to our writers . . . they really do represent Australia. They are not pleasant players. A good English journalist described them as 'hard-bitten', 'grim' and 'pitiless'. We shouldn't be a soft, mushy, maudlin race . . . In politics we're a shingle-short, a nation of grinning village idiots. The cricketers fill me with great enthusiasm. They can lose, for there is luck in the game, but they'll never crack up like the English.[11]

In this same year Esson was writing plays in collaboration with his half-brother Frank Brown, a former international athlete and boxing and athletic editor of the Melbourne *Sporting Globe*.[12] Brown contributed ideas and some drafts or revisions to at least two of Esson's one-act plays: the bush tragedy *The Drovers* (1919), and the farce *Mates* (1923). Read in conjunction with the earlier *The Woman Tamer* (1910),[13] and *The Time is Not Yet Ripe* (1912),[14] these plays show Esson moving to resolve the conflict between sport and intellect, since all four take as their central concern the relative merits of a 'sportsman' and a 'philosopher'.

In the early slum comedy, *The Woman Tamer*, Esson downgrades his poet and intellectual to the character of Chopsey Ryan 'an unsuccessful thief, . . . a street musician and a pessimist philosopher'(p. 63). His poetry is in his street ballads and his philosophy extends no further than a conviction that he knows how to handle a woman. Not surprisingly he is given his marching orders by his *de facto*, Katie, when a better lover, Bongo, gets out of jail. Bongo is a professional boxer who knocked out 'Bunny Thompson in five rounds at the Stadium'(p. 74) and a rough thug into the bargain, but he is infinitely preferable in Katie's eyes to the unimpressive Chopsey. In the city slums the ideals of poetry are no match for those of sport, and the same is true in Melbourne high society. Esson's more substantial political comedy *The Time is Not Yet Ripe*, given a successful amateur production by Gregan McMahon in 1912, moves up the social scale, and the contest is not for the affections of the heroine but for the hearts and minds of voting Australians. The sporting figure is Bertie Wainwright, 'an athletic young man'; the philosopher is Sydney Barrett, a left-wing intellectual. The two are compared in a conversation between Bertie and a woman lawyer, Violet:

Bertie:　He [Barrett] was eccentric then, always reading and studying. He won all
　　　　　the prizes. . . . The pater wanted me to do law. He said it was a training
　　　　　for the mind. But I never had much time for study. . . . Cricket is the only
　　　　　subject I can talk intelligently about. They say I have the makings of a
　　　　　good left-hand bowler. I can swerve two and a half inches from the leg.
Violet:　After all, physical culture was the Greek ideal.
Bertie:　I don't know, Miss Faulkner, I didn't do Greek. I did Latin instead. Latin
　　　　　was compulsory.(p. 28)

For Sydney Barrett Melbourne society and Australian politics are a world of sporting platitudes, the ideology of middle-class games, and muscular mindlessness. A coming election is several times referred to as if it were a cricket match; Bertie urges the crowd to be 'sports'(p.40); the working-class crowd resents the fact that the Prime Minister has attempted to ban gambling at Tattersall's (p. 42); and find Sydney Barrett's plan to ban working-class sporting pleasures and all other popular amusement even more insane. Esson, who some years earlier had contributed warnings about an imminent Asian invasion to the *Bulletin*, is clearly working in the genre established by *An Englishman's Home*, although paradoxically the theme of military unpreparedness is omitted. The play is full of sporting dialogue, and its links to the theme of national neglect are set out very early, when Barrett says:

We prate of progress, and what is Australia's chief contribution to civilization? Frozen mutton and the losing hazard. [A modification of the rules of billiards] . . . Every country must have a national ideal. We have nothing, absolutely nothing. Australia is an empty country. We produce wool and cricketers and factory butter and legislative councillors, but we do not produce ideas. (p.12)

The electorate, however, does not wish to hear Barrett's complaints; there is no place for the sensitive soul or the radical intellectual in Esson's city. In the slums Chopsy is sexually inadequate; in the halls of realpolitik Sydney Barrett is driven to a despairing retreat and an overseas honeymoon.

By turning to the myth of the bush Esson resolves this impasse and puts the poet/philosopher back on top of the sportsman. By 1921 when he wrote the letter to Vance Palmer quoted earlier, Esson had come to appreciate that the Australian cricketers could embody the 'national ideal' he seeks. They are 'hard-bitten', 'grim', and 'pitiless'. The words he selected from an English news report are those which we associate with the bush rather than with cricket, and in at least two plays, *Mates* and *The Drovers*, the action, set in the bush, has as one pivot point a character who is a city-bred sportsman out of his element. *Mates*:

is about two mates, of contrasting personalities, who are on their way to opal fields in New South Wales. The slightly-built Joe, a disqualified jockey, is a man of the city, sharp, self-confident and cheeky. Big Bill Ross is a shearer, a man of the bush for whom even Bourke is too near Sydney . . . A great believer in mateship, he has done what he considers he was obliged to do in carrying the exhausted Joe, with his swag, for the last ten miles of their journey to the bush shanty where the action of the play takes place.[15]

The two mates fall out over the barmaid, who turns out to be the shanty-owner's wife, and the bush-wise Bill learns not to trust the city-slicker sportsman Joe. They are 'mates' no longer.

In *The Drovers*[16] a similar situation occurs. The Jackeroo is 'an athletic young man' (the same description that Esson gave to Bertie Wainwright in *The Time Is Not Yet Ripe*) 'city-bred, out for experience'(p. 5). He has shot at a dingo and accidentally stampeded the cattle, who have trampled the old drover Brigalow Bill, causing fatal internal injuries. The Jackeroo is naive rather than untrustworthy, but again the sportsman is shown to be lacking in mature life-values; values based on bush experience rather than the 'play' experience of city-based sporting contests. For Esson, the poet and philosopher fails in the cities before the sportsman, who in turn fails before the mythic supermen of the bush. The true philosophers are the bush stoics, the Boss and Brigalow Bill; the true poet is the Aboriginal boy Pidgeon, who provides an elegiac chant for the dying man as the play ends. Esson, excited by cricket and disappointed by Australian literary nationalism, reached for the bush myth and grasped an explanation for his observation that sportsmen embodied an Australian national ideal. It was not their sporting values which made them unique but, like C. E. W. Bean's Anzacs, the philosophic profundities of their mythic bush origins.

It is in the inter-war period that Australian women playwrights began to find and use distinctive dramatic voices. The female actor-managers of the late nineteenth and early twentieth centuries—May Holt, Kate Howarde, Nellie Bramley, Yvonne Banvard, to mention but a few—were not interested in challenging social ideas which they could exploit for financial gain; like their male counterparts they actively promoted the idea of a sports-loving gender-harmonious Australia. The women who were prominent in the early non-commercial theatres came from different social and intellectual backgrounds and came to a very different kind of theatre with other intent. However, their discourse, like Esson's, was only faintly heard, since their plays were written for the socially-marginal Repertory, New, Little, and other amateur theatre groups. Such groups were characterised by the involvement of a large number of women directors, writers, and actors; testament to the way in which the presence or absence of capital speculation and large-scale financial management determined the extent to which men were involved in theatrical organisations, and suggestive too of the degree to which notions of 'high' or 'artistic' culture were at this time placed within the domain of the female. While it would be wrong to imply any consistency or unity of utterance across these groups—which varied from radical communist and nationalist organisations to uncritical reproducers of English bourgeois culture—their isolation from and often contempt for the cultural marketplace gave them a commonality in which sport, represented as a popular obsession, was a stock symbol.

Plays by two of the major women playwrights of the period, Betty Roland and Katharine Susannah Prichard, can serve as examples. As authors they were fundamentally different in their attitudes to bush and city. While Roland expressed the city-dweller's dislike of the bush's harshness, aridity and loneliness, Prichard was one of the few Australian authors who genuinely researched her outback novels and sympathised with that environment beyond the orthodox mythic representations of a Louis Esson. Roland and Prichard nevertheless used sport for similar dramatic purposes. Both Roland's drama *The Touch of Silk* (1928)[17] and Prichard's comedy *Bid Me to Love* (c.1927)[18] open in the world of the country-town tennis club; and in both the heroes and heroines are defined by an 'otherness' measured by their distance from a world of sport which, interestingly, is heterosexually equal instead of male-dominated. One feature of this world, as both writers see it, is that it is one in which silly athletic young women attempt to entice interesting men:

Miss Patterson: Playing tennis this afternoon, Mr. Osborne?
Osborne: No, not this afternoon. I'm going down to the river to have a bit of a fish. (p. 5)

These are the opening lines of *The Touch of Silk*, and demonstrate admirably the wide range of connotative meanings which discussions of sport in Australian stage dialogue can offer to writer and audience. The setting is a shop; the reference to tennis reinforces the visual clues that it is in a country town, for the game has strong rural and squattocratic associations. The half-day of work and half of leisure indicates that the time is Saturday morning. In most theatrical usages tennis is a heterosexual game, played not so much for itself but for its social and sexual possibilities, and it defines a class status to which the characters adhere or aspire. It also circumscribes the possible genres, subject matter and approaches which the play will offer. The woman proposes a game, the man defines his quality of 'uniqueness' by rejecting the offer; he prefers a solo sporting pastime. This immediately indicates that Miss Patterson is a vapid minor character, and that Osborne will be more central to the play's development (and more interesting to its heroine), and that the action of the play will locate itself outside—but not too far outside—a world in which sexual behaviour is governed by the rules of mixed doubles and the social committee. In English light comedies this is the world of 'Anyone for tennis?'; in Australian scripts it can also carry suggestions of an uncomfortable pseudo-civilisation. As the play progresses, 'Having a bit of a fish', becomes a euphemism for quiet, wise thought, and for Osborne's knowledge of and sensitivity to a larger world which touches that of the main character, a French war bride. Jeanne is stranded in an intolerant community with a husband increasingly unable to cope with the strain of running a farm and beginning to lapse back into the shell shock she nursed him through a decade earlier. Osborne too has been to the war and then travelled the world as a seaman, and his interests cannot be contained by Miss Patterson's small world. Later we find that he has not only joined the tennis club, but is on the committee and is organising the dance. This of course does not negate his 'otherness', but rather shows his adaptability and complexity. It is the familiarity of audiences with the resonances of Australian sporting life which enables such meanings to be extracted from simple, even slight dialogue.

The Touch of Silk links this understanding of the centrality of sport in structuring Australian social life with another major theme of Australian drama from the end of First World War to the 1970s—the dislocation of heterosexual relationships by the intrusions of the state. Men and women are divided by war (Sumner Locke Elliott's *Rusty Bugles* 1948)[19], by work (Ray Lawler's *The Summer of the Seventeenth Doll* 1955)[20], by the educational system (Dymphna Cusack's *Morning Sacrifice* 1948).[21] These major plays share with many others a view of this dislocation as an unwilling separation forced on people by state responses to the bigotries and catastrophes of the twentieth century and as a major determinant of both male and female behaviour in this country; as we shall see later, plays of the 1970s add sport to the causes of this divided culture.

Rusty Bugles contains an extremely resonant scene in which some of its all-male cast are grouped around a faulty one-line telephone, and are forced to shout intimacies to their faraway wives and girlfriends, as their relationships break up and new ones are formed. Central to *The Summer of the Seventeenth Doll* is the pattern of seasonal work which divides Roo and Barney from Olive and Nance, and the play explores the ultimately unsatisfactory nature of that division. Ray Lawler has described the theme of *The Doll* as being 'alternatives to marriage';[22] *The Touch of Silk* works out in an earlier decade and a less tolerant environment the consequences of even an innocent deviation (a platonic heterosexual friendship) from a puritan morality which cannot accept that the dislocation of war, which has brought Jeanne to the community, and the dislocation of work, which puts strains on her marriage relationship, require a redefinition of what is permissible and possible. If life is a game, then the conditions of play require new rules.

Prichard's *Bid Me To Love* opens even more squarely in the world of the social tennis match, with the husband Greg in his white flannels being called away by the flirtatious Molly to play a game on the court nearby. The central character's 'otherness' is defined quickly and deftly:

Woodbridge: You don't play, Louise?
Louise: I'm not a sport of any sort.
Molly: Oh I say. (p. 9)

The tempting other man, Don, has his uniqueness defined by both work and sport: Molly wants him to join the game but he is too busy picking apples and ploughing. The symbols of the sporting world are made explicit in this light comedy: conducting one's life by the rules and the rituals of sport is a denial of the necessity of labour and the consequences of sexuality. Life is too serious and the results too real for it to be played with a tennis racquet in hand. This thought carries through into Prichard's major drama *Brumby Innes* (1927),[23] which like Roland's play brings together the themes of gender separation and sporting Australia. Unlike Roland, however, Prichard endorses bush values, represented in part by the brutal, animalistic horse breaker 'Brumby' Innes. May, a 'pretty, shallow, city-bred girl' (p.84), flirts with Brumby but finds her assumptions about the proprieties of sexual negotiation quickly brushed aside. When the curtain goes up on Brumby's kitchen in Act III, the fact that May has moved in with him is shown by the presence in the room of a few selected items of feminine civilisation, including a tennis racquet— useless, of course, in the raw outback. That this is the only sporting reference in the play does not deny the importance of the theme as a frame of reference; it rather shows how far from 'play' Katharine Prichard saw the bush world of *Brumby Innes* as being. For her the city-bred sporting female is inadequate in the bush, as the sporting male had been for Louis Esson.

In the inter-war period and through to the late 1960s sport in plays which comment on the 'state of the nation' is at best neutral and more usually the cliche symbol of Australian philistinism and idleness. The writers were often conscious intellectuals and aesthetes; they were sometimes known principally for work in other literary forms or else wrote for radio and for the Australian Broadcasting Commission in particular. A thoroughly ABC-oriented writer like Max Afford could (in *Lazy in the Sun* 1951)[24] use sport and gambling as images of a childish, self-indulgent nation which had failed to heed the lessons of the Second World War; a less critical author like George Landen Dann represented the same behaviour as an inevitable comic foible of man (and woman) which could be reconciled with other values. His radio comedy

Ring Out Wild Bells! (1958)[25] gives us a gambling vicar's wife, and a conflict between the Saturday afternoon church wedding bells which prevent the patrons at the adjoining racetrack from hearing the race descriptions, and those same loudspeaker descriptions which have a habit of intruding at inappropriate moments in the church wedding ceremonies. The resolution (after much moral huffing and puffing) is a simple matter of cooperation between God and Mammon in working out a compatible timetable. In serious drama sport is on the side of the devil, in comedy it is tolerated by a benevolent God.

In the 1950s some writers began to use sport in plays as a motif which is used not to define the 'otherness' of characters of special interest, or to deplore popular values, but to link to Anglo-Australian society, albeit in a limited way, characters whose 'otherness' is seen as a problem rather than a desirable condition. (It is not surprising to note that this is also the period of the doctrine of assimilation for Aborigines and migrants.) One such play is David Ireland's 1958 study of Aboriginal fringe-dwellers, *Image in the Clay.*[26] The play is structured around the separate homecomings of two brothers, Billy and Gordon. Each tells in his own long set scene what he did while 'on walkabout'. Gordon has tried to make it in white society, going to high school and taking an office job in Sydney. Billy has more literally gone walkabout, 'jumping the rattler' (p. 45) and working his way around Australia. Billy's story is one of success: winning 'a coupla quid' (p. 47) in a buckjump, a night in bed with a white female station worker; 'And then I got a game of football with a team . . . and I scored'(p. 48). This comes near the climax of the speech, which drives his father Gunner to an impassioned reminder to Billy that he's not white, but black: 'And it's too early for trying to dress up like your brother and mix with the whites. You're not one of them. You're something to gape at'(p. 49).

Gordon's story occurs later in the play and is an embodiment of Gunner's warning. He has been denied responsibility in his job, failed to be accepted by the white city, been reduced to drinking alone in his room, and can't even walk down a street without inviting comment and alarm. But like Billy, he has found his only point of acceptance by white Australia in the world of sport: through boxing and martial arts. Unable to accept the black world either, he leaves at the end of the play with a white friend Sonny whom he met at school; 'we played football together'(p. 98). They intend to take a franchise on a service station, and Gordon's dream is: 'Brand new car and a brick house. With that I'll soon get a wife. My kids'll be whiter than I am, and their kids won't be any different from whites'(p. 100). He knows his skin colour isn't dirt, but in a pre-'black is beautiful' age it is his only way of fighting for acceptance. The possibility of autonomous cultural independence isn't suggested, and for both brothers the only positive steps they have been able to take towards being tolerated by white Australia is by playing well the kinds of games which white Australia values.

A similar though more complex comment on the symbolism of the same situation can be found in two plays by the prolific Queensland writer, George Landen Dann, a major figure (albeit in a minor artform) in Australian playwriting between 1931 and the 1960s. The first play, *Fountains Beyond*, was first produced in 1942 and published in 1944;[27] it was much admired and frequently produced by little theatre groups over the next twenty years, though with white actors 'blacked up' for the Aboriginal roles.[28] The second, *Rainbows Die at Sunset*, was never performed and exists only in a late manuscript dating from the mid-1960s, but offers an interesting development of Dann's thoughts on sport and Aboriginal assimilation twenty years later.[29]

The central character in *Fountains Beyond*, Vic Filmer, is a half-caste Aborigine who lives with his wife Peggy on an Aboriginal settlement near a coastal town. The action of the play concerns two intrusions into Aboriginal life made by sport-loving white society, both of which are resisted by Vic to his great disadvantage and personal distress. The first is an attempt by a local alderman to get Vic to organise a corroboree for a visiting English travel writer. The alderman sees the exercise as a civic and commercial exercise; it will take place on the sportsground, the council will charge admission and raise money for a children's playground as well as impressing the distinguished visitor. Vic refuses to assist in this blasphemous farce; he also knows that the site for the future playground is to be the Aboriginal settlement itself, and cannot be persuaded that assisting in his own eviction is a worthy thing to do. However another younger Aborigine, Wally, agrees to stage the corroboree. A sacred ritual becomes a sporting spectacle.

Next the alderman tries to get Vic to leave town by offering him money. Vic refuses; he intends to stay and lead the fight against the eviction order. Sport is central to the development proposals; it is the surfing craze which has caused the town to grow towards the seafront where the Aboriginal camp is located, and the playground replacing it will contain a cricket pitch. The idea of the cricket ground as the white 'sacred' site replacing an Aboriginal one is a motif taken up by Louis Nowra in *Inside the Island* nearly forty years later; he too sees it as the imposition of an alien and absurd spiritual ceremony in place of an authentic one.[30]

Fountains Beyond ends with unresolved tragedy. Peggy, Vic's wife, resents the poverty which Vic's principles have inflicted on them. Wally, flush with financial success after staging the corroboree, is able to buy her presents and show her a good time. He gives her earrings (here and elsewhere there are echoes of Buchner's *Woyzeck*) which cause Vic to discover the affair, and in an argument he shoots Peggy dead. The play ends with an old tribal elder leading Vic away with him to their ancestral home, an offshore island. Vic exits carrying Peggy's body; his friend carries the incriminating gun.

Rainbows Die at Sunset uses a similar character layout. Alfie and Pearlie Raymond are living in a shack on an Aboriginal settlement four miles from a coastal town frequented by tourists. Alfie has left a steady job on a tin dredge to try to make big money as a professional boxer (he admires Lionel Rose and Hector Thompson). Pearlie is most unhappy at this; she has had to take a cleaning job to support them both and has given up her ambition to buy an old house in the town. She is desperate to escape from the settlement, and her lack of faith in Alfie's boxing career leads them to quarrel. They patch up their differences, and Alfie, who has been promised a big fight by the local promoter, sets off to ask for an advance of $200 so that he can put down a deposit on the house.

Sport, it seems, is to be Alfie's entrance into 'mainstream' Australian society, but Dann develops his story to suggest the false equality, exploitation and betrayal that lie behind the myth of assimilation. The second Act begins with a scene at the auction sale of the house, and is based on a newspaper report of an infamous 1958 Nambucca Heads incident which partly inspired the play.[31] Alfie successfully bids for the house, but the white neighbours at the auction riot in opposition to the idea of a black family moving in and Pearlie, in fright, persuades Alfie to withdraw before the auctioneer closes the bidding.

The resolution of this play, like that of *Fountains Beyond*, is a savage comment on the impossibility of Aboriginal people escaping through assimilation and sporting success from the tyranny of racism and exploitation. A rich old lady, one of those who employs Pearlie, has died of shock after discovering her money has been stolen. Pearlie hadn't cleaned for her on that day because she'd been at the auction, but she had sent Alfie to let the old lady know she wasn't coming. Pearlie thinks Alfie got the deposit for the house from the fight promoter, and offers this explanation to an inquiring police sergeant, who goes off temporarily satisfied. Alfie breaks down and admits to Pearlie that he has in fact stolen the money, been surprised by the old woman, and run off as she collapsed. Alfie leaves and goes to a secret Aboriginal sacred meeting and initiation site where Billy Boil, an older man who remembers something of tribal custom, joins him. The two re-enact fragments of traditional ceremonies. While they are doing this the sergeant enters; Billy Boil has betrayed Alfie to the police.

In the last scene Alfie is allowed to visit Pearlie back at the settlement before being taken to jail. He enters in handcuffs, his face still smeared with the ochre Billy had painted on it during the ceremony. As the play ends the actor playing Alfie turns to the audience, drops the character, and delivers a short poem which sums up the betrayal of the ideals of assimilation into sporting Australia by the brutal and shabby dealings of an ignoble society:

> This is the way you fight a bout . . .
> Yer hands chained up—yer shirt hangin' out!
> You paint yer dial like a bloody myall!
> You claw the air like a trapped old hare,
> And you wait for the score that'll count yer.

The play is a much richer study of boxing and Aboriginal society than Harry Martin's *Come Out Fighting*, a Pram Factory production from the early 1970s which was also filmed and became a small but significant early step in the Australian film revival.[32] That Dann's play should have remained unknown and unperformed is a comment on the fact that in this period it was not just the quality of Australian scripts which determined success or failure as the contemporary opportunities for performance.

Almost without exception a major reason for the presence of sport in modern Australian drama has been its ability to define and locate 'the nation' as a construct within which, or against which, individual destinies are worked out. It is noteworthy therefore that during the Menzies years, in the few major Australian stage successes, sport is either absent or has been reduced to background noise, like the offstage two-up game in *Rusty Bugles*. These are the years when decisions about which stories were to be staged or filmed were almost exclusively in the hands of British arts mandarins. Historical subjects were favoured in 'national' stories, while the quest for 'international standards' and 'universal' themes directed attention away from contemporary national concerns towards 'guided tours' of the exotic and marginal.[33] There had never been a place for sport in the historical myths of convictism (since it would deny the totality of suffering) or of pioneering (since it would dilute the work ethic), and even in the colonial era it had required a fanciful distortion of the legends of the bushrangers in order to include an occasional horse race in their activities. It is in contemporary society, as we have seen throughout the present study, that sporting subjects were favoured; but in the years when Australian sporting champions were making perhaps their strongest contribution to the dominant national self-image (in athletics and swimming at the 1956 Olympics and afterwards, and in tennis, motor racing, cricket, rugby league *et al*), the national stage offered not a single extended narrative which represented, let alone interrogated, this period of intense sporting mythmaking.

National mediations: 1968–80

In the decade following the sudden expansion in subsidised theatre and Australian playwriting in the late 1960s, sport returned triumphant to the Australian stage in dialogue, narrative and onstage action for the first time since the First World War. This renewed interest did not mean necessarily that modern Australian sporting plays embraced the popular discourses of the old commercial stage, but there was a significant weakening of the condemnation and doubts of the intelligentsia, resulting in both celebrations of and satires on sporting Australia. Government subsidisation of professional theatre broke the rules of the market place, but also encouraged coterie theatres to try to address wider audiences. Consequently, the relative consistency of utterance for or against sport in the earlier periods broke down into the widely differing attitudes of individual authors. At one extreme is Alexander Buzo's *The Front Room Boys* (1969), which in several sections reads like a rewriting of *An Englishman's Home* or *White Australia*, with sport again the mindless obsession of trivial people:

Jacko: Ay Robbo, what'd you get up to over the weekend?
Robbo: Ar, nothing much. Played bowls on Saturday and had a round of golf with Owen Peters on Sunday.
Jacko: . . . Who won the bowls on Saturday?
Robbo: The singles championship was won by G. Davies and the runner up was B. Townsend. The pairs went to P. Wallace and H. Macdonald, who defeated C. Hamilton and J. Simpson.[34]

At the other extreme are celebrations of sport and sporting champions (real and fictitious) such as Alan Hopgood's *And the Big Men Fly* (1963) and *And Here Comes . . . Bucknuckle* (1980), Jack Hibberd's *The Les Darcy Show* (1974), John Timlin's and Hibberd's *Goodbye Ted* (1975), Albert Hunt's *The Grand Grand Final Show* (1978), and William Henderson's *The Reverend's Powerful Backhand* (1979, later revised, performed and published as *Courting Disaster*).[35] Of these *The Grand Grand Final Show* was perhaps the most overtly popular and pro-sport, being written with the cooperation of Melbourne's Collingwood Australian Rules Club and performed for their supporters and others 'because we liked football and enjoyed working with footballers' as the director described it;[36] while others such as *Goodbye Ted* (again a Melbourne product about Australian Rules) were also primarily celebratory, consciously setting out to celebrate extravagant sporting language:

Ted: . . . I'll take the punt, son,' I said, 'throw us the Denzil Don'.[37]

Some of these 'celebratory' plays were not entirely uncritical of sport, and the dominant note of 1970's discourse was one of national mediation: a style of address which celebrated the energy, physical freedom and egalitarian possibilities of sport within an asserted national ideology, while continuing to express doubt about (often through satire of) its conformist and anti-intellectual tendencies.

For some authors Australian nationalism was endorsed principally as part of the anti-Imperial struggle against the United States (in military politics) and England (in theatrical culture); for others it was a direct weapon for asserting a national vision for Australian society. This latter goal can be illustrated by a speech from Jack Hibberd's play *A Stretch of the Imagination* (1972), in which the central character, Monk O'Neill, remembers what the great boxing champion Les Darcy supposedly said to him after they had both climbed Mt Kosciusko:

Monk, he said, one day Australia, that great nation out there of soldiers and sports and athletes, cereals and wool, will one day rule the Pacific. . . . England will one day lick the elastic of our boots. America will extend to us an equal hand. The Indon and Kanaka we will civilize.[38]

This is a conscious, but not necessarily mocking, rewrite of part of the Prologue to E. W. O'Sullivan's *Coo-ee; or, Wild Days in the Bush* (1906), in which Jack the stockman declaims in similar phrases on Australia's future greatness; also from the top of Mt Kosciusko:

Our country is full of rich resources, that someday will maintain a population of tens of millions. Our Island continent stands between the Pacific and the Indian Oceans, around the shores of which more than half of the human race are living. When we get a sea and land power, as we will some day, we'll hold supremacy on these oceans, and in doing so we will control more than half mankind . . . Given us a century of peace and progress, with a powerful army and navy, and our descendants will show the world quite as powerful a nation as the United States.[39]

The two speeches differ only in their varying approach to colloquial Australian dialect (as John Romeril has noted in relation to early 1970s playwrights, they were 'trying to save Sidney Baker's Australian language')[40] and in Hibberd's addition of 'sports and athletes' to the national attributes which would lead the imagined future Australian society to the heights of greatness.

Les Darcy's vision also illustrates by its absences and intolerances the elements which the emphasis on a unified Australian nation displaced or marginalised: women, Asians, other non Anglo-Australians, and non-sporting intellectuals. Instead, sport was used overwhelmingly to analyse male relationships within this asserted national ideology; most obviously in the situation where two antagonists are reconciled, or where two men with nothing in common find a mutual bond by talking about or playing sport together. The nationalistic function of sport was internalised to the extent that it could be used as a symbol of the fundamental union of all Australian men and, through the absence or easy assimilation of other groups, of an Australian nation. In this communion of mates, where conflicts of class, race and politics were thought to be transcended, sport by chauvinist self-projection became the basis for a universal brotherhood of men.

The theme is baldly expressed in novice playwriting like V. J. Moran's one-act *Find Me at the Federal*, where a North Queenslander violently objects to his daughter marrying an Italian migrant, only to find out that the youth is a champion boxer. In less than half a page a swift reversal of attitude is wrought, and they exit together with the father's arm around his future son-in-law's shoulder as he takes him off to look at a photo of *his* past boxing career.[41] The idea appears almost as baldly in more significant writers. It was a recurring scene in David Williamson's early stage work, particularly in the linked trilogy *The Coming of Stork, Jugglers Three* and *What If You Died Tomorrow*, where talking about sport or playing a game is a way for men to ease potentially explosive tensions. *What if You Died Tomorrow* links this to another Anglo-Australian myth, that of the home handyman. The father not only plays billiards on his son's table while they talk; it's a table the son has made himself, and they talk about that too.[42] A refusal by an Australian male to take part in sporting activity indicates a major personal or interpersonal crisis:

Paddy: We going to the races this arvo?
Alex: No.
Paddy: (Amazed) Eh?
Alex: No.
Paddy: Why not? (Pause. Silence.)
          You all right?

There is an element of satire here, but the cathartic function of sporting discussions amongst Australian males is not limited to comedy. It is also part of the future Australia imagined by the radical intellectual playwright Stephen Sewell. When the political activist Dan and his worker brother Mikey meet again in *The Father We Loved on a Beach by the Sea*, their conversation is halting, awkward, marked by the author with the stage direction 'pause' in no fewer than eleven places, until:

Dan: (Pause. Suddenly) Yeah well it's gone now. You still play footy?
Mikey: Yeah, oh geez, we had a good game last week. Against Cronulla, you know. Nearly got sent off but.
Dan: (Bemused) What'd you do?
Mikey: Oh, this bloke hit me in the scrum, you know. Right on the nose. Boy, did it hurt. Yeah, so I stiff armed him. Musta nearly broke his neck I reckon. (They both laugh.)[44]

The relief is evident. Dan may be a communist ratbag, but he is willing to endorse basic 'Australian' values. Alex Buzo's *Norm and Ahmed* uses the same motif for more substantial questioning of those values:

Norm: Anyway, Ahmed, what do you do in your spare time? Got any hobbies, play any sport?
Ahmed: No I don't really have time for that sort of thing.
Norm: No time for sport??[45]

This was a rare consideration of the plight of the non-sporting non Anglo-Australian during the 1970s, with the Pakistani student Ahmed being abused, cajoled and finally beaten up by the sports-loving Norm. The non-sporting character, who pre-1969 was usually autobiographical, is here sympathetically portrayed in a play of national and foreign stereotype.

The most obviously 'popular' use of sport during this decade of Australian drama was the playing of sport on stage. There is a cricket match in both

Boddy and Ellis's *The Legend of King O'Malley* (1970) and Romeril's *I Don't Know Who to Feel Sorry For* (1971); a wrestling match in Barry Oakley's *The Feet of Daniel Mannix* (1971); squash in the same author's *Politics* (1981); boxing in Hibberd's *The Les Darcy Show* (1974); karate in John Powers' *The Last of the Knucklemen* (1974); and, in David Williamson's plays, football in *The Coming of Stork* (1970), table tennis in *Jugglers Three* (1973), and billiards in *What If You Died Tomorrow?* (1974).[46] The actions of sporting contests (especially cricket, football, and boxing) were also widely used in Brechtian demonstration scenes staged by a number of small political and theatre in education companies, although here the populist tendencies were evident; often they were using the images of what they assumed to be a sports-loving nation for other purposes.

Although sporting plays (and the 'larrikin'[47] theatre in general) claimed to be returning Australian culture to the 'popular' tradition, this claim was not, except for David Williamson's work, reflected at the box office.[48] Various reasons for this suggest themselves. One is the token nature of some modern sporting plays, which exploit what was assumed to be a popular subject but use a discourse (stylistic or ideological) very different from that of popular celebration, and which are unlikely therefore to attract new sports-loving but theatre-wary audiences. (Real sporting champions, for example, were never invited to participate, except in *The Grand Grand Final Show*.) Another difficulty is the dominant sport *versus* drama binary of later twentieth-century Western culture, which makes existing audiences and critics unlikely to respond positively to sporting celebrations. Many writers of sporting plays chose to equate what they asserted were 'working-class' and 'nationalist' values with 'popular' theatre, and placed this imagined art form in opposition to 'bourgeois' theatre. Something of the divisive and intolerant (rather than inclusively cross-class and cross-gender and therefore genuinely popular) nature of much of this larrikin drama can be seen in the Introduction to a sporting play consciously written for non-theatre-going male audiences, John Timlin's and Jack Hibberd's *Goodbye Ted*:

Goodbye Ted is likely, and was probably calculated, to offend . . . vegetarians, toffs, loud-mouthed anti-footballers, people who think their own generation or the Sydney Opera House constitutes an Australian cultural renaissance, and others too hazardous to mention. But they may be safely ignored; they won't come anyway.[49]

Performed throughout Eastern Australia in theatre restaurants during 1975, *Goodbye Ted* uses a testimonial to a retiring Australian Rules footballer as an excuse for a series of sexist and racist jokes and sequences by and about stereotype characters (an Italian butcher is the butt of much humour, as are several nymphomaniac women); it was evidently assembled in great haste for its alcohol-primed audiences, whom it assumes are mostly Anglo-Australian men.

The most obvious limitation to the nationalistic Australian sporting play is this gender-biased assumption made about the appeal of sport in popular culture, particularly since much Australian theatre continued to be patronised disproportionately by women. Sport insistently emerged in the Australian theatre of the 1970s as the one sure ground on which the greatest number of people could make some contact, but the consensus was not inclusive enough, any more than the various ideological projections of Australian nationalism have been, and hence the included characters and persons usually turned out to be male, with both the sports-loving heroines of the colonial melodramas and the silly sportswomen of Betty Roland and Katharine Susannah Prichard's plays having disappeared from the cast lists. Even in those works where sport is overtly or coincidentally exposed as a limited and limiting bond between men, the insistence with which it was treated could not but tacitly marginalise or exclude those areas of Australian experience where, for various reasons, sport or 'manliness' loomed less large.

In the all-male environment of these sporting plays, the language of sport is frequently used for sexual innuendo designed to objectify the female body as a game or sporting object. There are some earlier examples of this: successful flirting in Louis Esson's *The Woman Tamer* is 'being on a good wicket'(p.70). But sport's many appearances in 1970s drama to refer to casual sexual activity made it probably a more widely used metaphor than the car/ woman analogy identified by Peter Fitzpatrick in *After 'The Doll'*.[50] Stork, wanting to hear about West's involvement in a gang bang, asks 'what position did you go in to bat?'(p.13). Stud's sexual potency in Romeril's *I Don't Know Who to Feel Sorry For* involves keeping your 'end up longer than Bradman'(p.45). All three examples—and many others in Romeril's play— are from cricket, the major Freudian bat and ball game still carrying traditional connotations of 'manly' behaviour. Sexual sublimation is several times associated with football—most extensively in *The Club* but also in *The Coming of Stork* where Stork works off his sexual frustrations by kicking a football made out of his socks—but Mike Giles's *Scoring* makes the obvious pun for the sexual attitudes of the football-playing male. Giles's play concerns a group of soccer coaches in a leagues club bar, with the central character finally coming to a personal realisation that he wants a long lasting heterosexual relationship instead of dehumanised sex.[51]

In almost all references to sport in recent Australian drama, the accompanying connotations of manliness exclude women, and those of sex objectify them. There are no female characters in *The Club* (though women and sex are incessantly discussed),[52] and the cricket match in Romeril's *I Don't Know* . . . drives the girlfriends into the kitchen and out of the scene(p.51-2). *The Club* goes further in its retreat from heterosexuality, concluding with an ultimately soft-centred acceptance of the *voluntary* woman-excluding world of Australian Rules football. But Williamson's play also renews and develops that major theme of the playwrights of the 1909–69 era: the desperate attempts by men and women to form orthodox heterosexual relationships in a society which in war, work, and education make the sexes strangers to one another, and it adds sport to this list of influential and primarily monosexual institutions.

Williamson's earlier linked trilogy begins this reconsideration of the divided society in the modern period, with *Jugglers Three* in particular looking at the return of two Vietnam veterans and their discovery that their wives have moved on to new lovers. The theme is often reversed: Stork and West—the best men at a double wedding—flush the rings down the toilet and lock the flat as the phone rings frantically. Heterosexuality is resisted by a pessimistic refusal to grow up, to let wedding bells break up the gang. *Jugglers Three* reverts to desperate optimism, ending with an unusual image of heterosexual sport where the lights fade on Graham and Keren playing table tennis; an attempt to apply to a man and a woman the psychological bonding mechanism of mateship. By *What If You Died Tomorrow?* the optimism has died, and in *The Club* sport itself is added to the dividing forces within Australian society.

An all-male play about Australian Rules (the story borrows from the events surrounding the appointment of Tom Hafey as coach of Collingwood in 1976), *The Club* is on other levels not about football or even man-to-man relationships. Structurally it is close to Williamson's earlier *The Department* (committee meeting politics and personalities)[53] and one of its major themes is men without women. The failure to achieve a satisfactory relationship with a woman is an obsession for most of the characters, and mateship and all-male sporting clubs are presented not as positive manifestations of a pleasurable lifestyle, nor as expressions of platonic male friendships or sublimated homosexuality, but as the negative reaction to a need for female companionship which society's institutions and the social conditioning of men has made not just difficult (as in earlier playwrights) but impossible.

At the heart of this theme in the play is the Club President's misdemeanour with a stripper at a social evening. His drunken, pawing attack on a (to him) dehumanised female body is only told to us in retrospect, but it is still a potent symbol of the perversion of heterosexual needs in an unnatural sport-saturated world. The progression of this theme of heterosexual failure is in the direction of its acceptance as a permanent feature of Australian society, and behind much of the affirmation of sport can be discerned the tortured attempt by men to shore up something out of the wreck of their heterosexual experiences. Sport is presented satirically as an escape from adulthood back to adolescent male bonding, and the major commercial success which *The Club* became in 1978-79 need not indicate necessarily that its audiences were either sports lovers, predominantly male, or concerned with Australian nationalism. Sport is no longer simply a game, but an institution, and it is the satire on the manipulation of institutional power within an all-male environment which is foregrounded. *The Club*'s limitation is that without a woman character to sharpen its satire on the partial, self-obsessed and homoerotic nature of this world (as the figure of Moira does so effectively in Greg McGee's 1981

New Zealand rugby play *Foreskin's Lament*[54]); without any representative of the non Anglo-Australian community to enlarge its concept of the nation; and without a narrative climax which could provoke the characters to make choices about their behaviour; the play slides away from confronting the questions it begins to ask about the way sport has been constructed and positioned in the organisation of modern Australian society.

Exit sport: feminist, black, and multicultural Australia 1980–1989

The late 1970s and early 1980s saw the collapse of theatre companies such as the Pram Factory and Nimrod which, at least in their earliest years, had done most to promulgate an Australian dramatic nationalism in which sport loomed large; the emergence of a new generation of playwrights and directors from more diverse gender and cultural backgrounds who wished to address other subjects and other concerns; and other kinds of subsidised companies whose charter was to give voice to other traditions of Australian living than the Anglo-male hegemony.[55] It is perhaps indicative of the extent to which that dominant voice in the 1970s had appropriated the metaphoric resonances of sport that little attempt was made to dramatise the lives of great Australian sportswomen, or black Australian sports of both sexes, or to consider the subject in the context of the NESBIAN (Non-English Speaking Background)[56] community's own interest in games. While a form of semi-spontaneous improvised drama, 'Theatresports' enjoyed a period of popularity by exploiting the unpredictability of its story sequences (the most obvious quality which it shared with competitive games and which explains its nomenclature), sporting stories themselves largely disappeared.

In the 'mainstream' subsidised theatres as well, where English and Anglo-Australian men continued to dominate at all levels (and where the aggressively national and anti-British larrikin theatre had made only a limited impact), sport is absent from nearly all the major plays of the decade; the occasional fragmentary reference simply defines a part—and not a dominant part—of the world outside the play. Janis Balodis's *Heart for the Future* (1989, Melbourne Theatre Company) had as the central character a long-distance woman runner, but its partial concern with media images could have been applied to many different kinds of public figures, and the sporting symbols are conventional and undeveloped.[57]

A late, rare and mawkishly nostalgic exception which attempted to cling to sport as a celebration of something central and potentially vital in Australian cultural life was the Melbourne writer Barry Dickens's *Royboys*, staged at the Playbox in 1987.[58] Yet another Australian Rules play, this time celebrating the Fitzroy club, it charted the game's progression from 'traditional' tribal to transnational business values, and ended in unconvincing fantasy as 'Gail Noble' the daughter of a football family dedicated to the old ways, changes from 'loathing footy' (p.5) to being the first 'Roygirl' (p.42) and kicking the winning goal in the 1987 grand final. Its old-fashioned racist satire on an equally fantasised 'Tokyo-Oz footy match' (p.37) and its attempt to incorporate a woman into the pantheon of male sporting heroes exposes what had been evident if unwritten throughout the decade: the uses of sport in Australian theatre had reached an impasse.

In 1983 the playwright Alison Lyssa gave a talk at a writers' workshop in Adelaide, later published as 'Feminist theatre: a monologue to start discussion', which began:

Not long ago at the end of the winter in Sydney where I come from, it was presentation night at my eleven-year-old's Aussie Rules Club. . . . I'm going to make a presentation too, an award to the first person to put their hand up with the correct answer, 'What sex is my child?'[59]

Her analysis of the marginalisation of female culture by male sporting events occupies the first five pages of the published version and was a resurfacing of the pre-1968 use of theatre as one of the few public forums in which anti-sport attitudes could be expressed. The difference between the pre- and post-1970s playwrights was that the latter now had a significant and diversified government-subsidised Australian theatre industry willing to give more than token attention to such voices, although at least one Sydney critic suggested the 1981 production of Lyssa's play *Pinball* still would appeal primarily to 'the feminist sub-culture'.[60] Its offstage child character, the centre of a custody dispute, is used to define sport both as male and as the past: he wants a space invader machine instead of a cricket bat.[61] Pinball, a game of aggression and the male youth sub-culture, becomes as well a symbol of chance and destiny through winning a free game, though by the conclusion he has outgrown this obsession.

Elsewhere women writers gave scant attention to sport. In Gunzburg, Black and Fischer's *A Touchy Subject* (1987)—a community theatre script about sexual harassment in schools and in the workplace—the male physical education teacher uses sport to humiliate the girl students and trivialise their own sporting successes: 'with legs like those you could be in show business',[62] and in Suzanne Spunner's *Running Up a Dress* (1986), about mother-daughter relationships, the daughter's insecurity with her shape is once blamed on swimming: 'My shoulders are enormous'.[63] This concern with the body and sport reflects the male fetish of the sportswoman as sex object which dates back at least to Annette Kellerman, and has been internalised even within female culture where the woman is subject:

I can hear my mother now saying, '. . . None of my women friends will come to enjoy my spa pool, they say they're too fat—it's a terrible thing to get old.' (*Running Up a Dress*, p.44)

Nevertheless such references are minor in the themes and concerns of women's theatre; displacement is the dominant strategy for asserting the subject status of the sport-defined other.

Black and multicultural writers have also chosen to ignore sport. Jack Davis's *No Sugar* begins with the children playing cricket: '*Woolah!* Don Bradman'.[64] This defines the period of the 1930s but does not build on the interesting contradictions suggested by black emulation of the white sporting hero; in his children's play *Honeyspot* the meeting ground for Aboriginal and Anglo-Australian culture is in the combining of Aboriginal dance drama and ballet.[65] Soccer, the 'ethnic' game in Australian narrative, is so used by the European Jewish author David Martin in the novel (1962), play (1966), and television drama (1985, adapted by Linda Aronson) versions of *The Young Wife*; the stock 'sport for men and theatre for women' binary is employed to suggest an unchanging gender-divided culture, with the wife acting in a classic Greek play while the husband, a Greek Cypriot, incites inter-migrant tension by playing for an Italian team.[66] Soccer also provides a remarkable image of cultural dislocation in Louis Nowra's television play *Displaced Persons* (1985) where an imprisoned European refugee tries to practise soccer with an oval rugby ball.[67] Richard Barrett's *The Heartbreak Kid* (1987) builds on this idea by having a group of Euro-Australian schoolboys demanding to be allowed to play soccer in a school where the sports master insists they play rugby; eventually separatism rather than reconciliation or multi-skilling is allowed when the headmaster announces 'There may be funds for a proper soccer field next year' in addition to the rugby oval.[68]

The only text known to attempt a serious examination of the ideology of sport from a feminist and multicultural perspective is Zeny Giles's *Zorica*, a theatre-in-education play about a champion school runner, devised in collaboration with Newcastle's Freewheels Company and performed by them in 1984–85. Sport is represented in this play as even more gender-dividing amongst migrant communities than it is in Anglo-Australian society, as the accompanying 'Notes for Teachers' argues:

Amongst non-English speaking groups, and in particular those from southern
Europe, sport is generally a male-dominated part of life. Zorica cuts across this by
being a female athlete, despite her Macedonian background.[69]

Sport is constructed positively as an opportunity for escape both from her own culture's gender-typing, and from cultural ghettoism. The latter makes this text consistent with Tom Shapcott's observation on multicultural writing in Australia:

The problem of the second generation is universal. In non-English language
cultures, the children usually deny their own language and culture and seek to be
sometimes more stridently identified with the apparent local culture than even
their neighbours.[70]

However, the play, consistent with its overt pedagogical context and intent, is left open-ended: 'In the end . . . it is Zorica who must decide what matters more: her ethnic heritage or her sporting ability' (p.13). Zorica's parents give her both running shoes and a Macedonian national costume to wear at a party; she wins two races at the Newcastle city zone carnival, but also reluctantly wears the costume in the traditional dance which concludes the play. From a non Anglo-Australian perspective, sport within the Anglo community is not the male-dominated phenomenon which Lyssa and others have suggested, and one of the attractions of the Anglo community for Euro-Australian women is its relative lack of sexism; playing and excelling at sport is part of that freedom.

It is the school setting of *The Heartbreak Kid, Zorica*, and several other theatre-in-education plays which selects sport as a suitable subject for debates about gender and cultural roles. Sport when used as a major dramatic symbol, as we have seen incessantly across two centuries, suggests a cultural totality, an allegorical representation of units of society organised as a functioning system through their pattern of similarities and oppositions and placements. The school is one of the few institutions within Australian society which itself symbolises a cultural meeting place rather than being class, gender, or ethnically specific; it is also one principal area where sporting achievement is still highly valued across such boundaries. The collapse of the singular vision of Australian society suggests that while dominant myths could well be interrogated by sporting stories which themselves challenge those constructions (as, for example, in biographical accounts of Aboriginal, female, and NESBIAN sporting champions), sporting narratives beyond the schoolgates have ceased to function as adequate or believable studies of Australian society.

Notes

1 Sport and Drama: the Uneasy Playmates

1 Ric Sissons, 'Thommo and the punk', *Sydney Morning Herald*, 8 November 1986, p.49.
2 Lawrie Kavanagh, 'Ice dancing not Olympic', *Courier Mail*, 18 February 1984.
3 Adrian McGregor, *National Times*, 18 August 1979, p.13.
4 Keith Dunstan, 'Day of heroes, chants, and sobriety—without Lillee', *Courier Mail*, 9 January 1984.
5 *Australian*, 8 August 1984, p.9.
6 H. C. J. Lingham, *Juvenal in Melbourne* (Melbourne: Lingham, 1892), p.39.
7 G. A. Wilkes, *The Stockyard and the Croquet Lawn: Literary Evidence for Australia's Cultural Development* (Melbourne: Edward Arnold, 1981).
8 *Sydney Morning Herald*, 29 November 1986, p.43.
9 *Weekend Australian*, 1–2 April 1989, Weekend 8; 26–27 August 1989, Weekend 12.
10 John Cargher, *Opera and Ballet in Australia* (Stanmore: Cassell Australia, 1977), p.xi.
11 Roger Covell, *Australia's Music: Themes of a New Society* (Melbourne: Sun Books, 1967), p.237.
12 John Willett, ed. & trans., *Brecht on Theatre: The Development of an Aesthetic* (New York: Hill and Wang, 1964), pp. 6–9.
13 Willett, pp.16–17.
14 Antonin Artaud, 'An affective athleticism', in his *Collected Works*, trans. V. Corti (London: Calder & Boyars, 1974), IV, 100–6. See also John Lahr, 'Athletes of the heart',*New Society*, 29 July 1982, pp.188–89.
15 C. L. R. James, *Beyond A Boundary* (London: Hutchinson, 1969), p.202.
16 B. Lowe, *The Beauty of Sport: A Cross-Disciplinary Inquiry* (Englewood Cliffs: Prentice Hall, 1977).
17 V. A. Kolve, 'The drama as play and game', reprinted in *Medieval English Drama*, ed. Peter Happé (London: Macmillan, 1984), pp.54–68.
18 Glynne Wickham, *The Medieval Theatre* (London: Weidenfeld & Nicholson, 1974), p.3.
19 Wickham, p.21; *The 'Revels' History of Drama in English*, II (London: Methuen, 1980), p.25.
20 Mary McElroy, 'Organised sporting contests in the early English professional theatre', *Canadian Journal of Sports History* 21, No.1 (May 1990), p.33.
21 David Wiles, *Shakespeare's Clown: Actor and text in the Elizabethan playhouse* (Cambridge: Cambridge University Press, 1987), p.169.
22 Don Morrow, 'Sport as metaphor: Shakespeare's use of falconry in the early plays', *Aethlon*, 5, No.2 (Spring 1988), 119–129.
23 Kolve, p.55.
24 George Speaight, *A History of the Circus* (London: Tantivy, 1980), p.24.
25 George Rowell, *The Victorian Theatre 1792–1914* (1956, rev. edn. Cambridge: Cambridge University Press, 1978), p.9.

26 A. H. Saxon, *Enter Foot and Horse* (New Haven: Yale University Press), p.6ff.
27 Saxon, p.10–11.
28 Saxon, pp.91–2; 103; 110.
29 Edward Geoghegan, *The Currency Lass; or, My Native Girl* (Sydney: Currency, 1976), p.31.
30 Eric Irvin, *Theatre Comes to Australia* (St Lucia: University of Queensland Press, 1971), p.246.
31 *Hobart Town Courier*, 4 August 1837, facs. in W. D. Hudspeth, *The Theatre Royal, Hobart 1837–1948* (Hobart: n.p., 1948), p.23.
32 Alec Bagot, *Coppin the Great* (Melbourne: Melbourne University Press), p.106.
33 Mark St Leon, *Spangles and Sawdust: the circus in Australia* (Richmond: Greenhouse, 1983), p.14; Harold Love, ed., *The Australian Stage: A Documentary History* (Kensington: NSW University Press, 1984), p.48.
34 St Leon, pp.16–20.
35 William Acton, *The Functions and Disorders of the Reproductive Organs in Childhood, Youth, Adult Age, and Advanced Life Considered in their Physiological, Social, and Moral Relations.* 4th edn. (London: Churchill, 1865).
36 See Margaret Drabble, ed., *The Oxford Companion to English Literature* (Oxford: Oxford University Press, 1985), p.481.
37 See Acton, *Functions*, p.103.
38 William Acton, *Prostitution Considered in its Moral, Social, and Sanitary Aspects in London and Other Large Cities and Garrison Towns with Proposals for the Control and Prevention of its Attendant Evils* (1857: republ. London: Cass, 1972).
39 *We* (Hobart), No.1 (February 1867), pp.8–10.
40 Wayland Young, *Eros Denied*, rev. edn. (London: Corgi, 1968), p.190.
41 *Argus* (Melbourne), 29 August 1854, p.5.
42 P. C. McIntosh, *Sport in Society* (London: Watts, 1963).
43 *Argus*, 6 November 1854.
44 *Argus* (Melbourne), 29 August 1854, p.8.
45 *Argus* (Melbourne), 2 October 1854, p.8.
46 *Argus* (Melbourne), 29 May 1866, p.8.
47 Saxon, pp.205–6.
48 *Sydney Morning Herald*, 21 October 1854, p.2.
49 *Sydney Morning Herald*, 26 May 1862, p.2.
50 *Le Entr'Acte* (Melbourne), 28 March 1863.
51 *Sydney Morning Herald*, 9 April 1894, p.6; 18 April, p.2.
52 See E. I. Cole Collection, Picture Acquisitions 5497, Mitchell Library, Sydney.
53 Nat Phillips, 'Cinderella', t.s. (1920), CRS A1336/2, item 8910, Australian Archives, ACT.
54 *Argus* (Melbourne), 28 June 1862, p.8; *Illustrated Melbourne Post*, 5 July 1862, p.10; *Argus* (Melbourne), 30 June 1862, p.14.
55 *Argus* (Melbourne), 28 July 1862, p.8.
56 *Illustrated Melbourne Post*, 2 August 1862, p.14.
57 *Argus* (Melbourne), 17 September 1866, p.8.
58 *As It Is* (Melbourne), No.232 (June 1887).
59 See J. C. Reid, *Bucks and Bruisers: Pierce Egan and Regency England* (London: Routledge, 1971), pp.50–1, and Margaret Drabble, ed., *The Oxford Companion to English Literature* (London: Oxford University Press, 1985), pp.762–3.

60   Pierce Egan, *Tom and Jerry: Life in London; or, the Day and Night Scenes of Jerry Hawthorn Esq., and his elegant friend Corinthian Tom, in their Rambles and Sprees through the Metropolis* (London: Chatto & Windus, 1869).

61   W. T. Moncrieff, *Tom and Jerry; or, Life in London*, in *Nineteenth-Century Popular British Drama Acting Editions*, Part 3, Comic Plays, series ed. Richard L. Lorenzen (London & Seattle: University of Washington Press, 1977).

62   Reid, pp.81–2.

63   Saxon, p.234.

64   Reid, p.85.

65   Richard Waterhouse, *From Minstrel Show to Vaudeville: the Australian Popular Stage 1788–1914* (Kensington: NSW University Press, 1990), pp.24–5.

66   W. Wilde, J. Hooton & B. Andrews, *The Oxford Companion to Australian Literature* (Melbourne: Oxford University Press, 1985), pp.370–1.

2   The Sport and Drama Industry 1788–1930

1   Hugh Cunningham, *Leisure in the Industrial Revolution c.1780–c.1880* (London: Croom Helm, 1980), p.35.

2   For a brief comment on English provincial theatre at this time, see Allardyce Nicoll, *A History of Late Eighteenth Century Drama 1750–1800* (Cambridge: Cambridge University Press, 1927), p.3. Nicoll argues that the strolling players were on the decline as provincial cities built major theatre buildings; however one of his sources is Tate Wilkinson's company, analysed more closely by Arthur W. McDonald, 'The Social Life of the Performer on the Yorkshire Circuit, 1766–1785', *Theatre Survey*, 25, No.2 (November 1984), pp.167–76. As discussed later in this chapter, McDonald's research shows clearly that a circuit system was still the basis of Wilkinson's operations. For provincial management in nineteenth-century England, see Clarance Holt, 'Twice Round the World; or, Fifty Five Years of an Actor's Life', ed. Charles Osborn, unpublished m.s., Bland Holt Papers, MS 2244, series 2, items 240–625, National Library, Canberra.

3   Wray Vamplew, 'The Sport of Kings and Commoners: the Commercialisation of British Horse-Racing in the Nineteenth Century', *Sport in History* (St Lucia: University of Queensland Press, 1981), pp.307–8.

4   William J. Baker, *Sport in the Western World* (Totowa, N.J.: Rowman and Littlefield, 1982), pp.89–90; Cunningham, pp.3–11.

5   McDonald, pp.167–76.

6   McDonald, p.169.

7   Frank Hance, *Stamford Theatre and Racecourse* (Stamford: 1970), n.p.

8   Oliver Goldsmith, 'Adventures of a Strolling Player', in his *Selected Essays*, ed. J. H. Lobran (Cambridge: Cambridge University Press, 1929), p.119.

9   Douglas Pike, gen. ed., *Australian Dictionary of Biography I* (Melbourne: Melbourne University Press, 1966), pp.62–3.

10 McDonald, p.173.

11 Alec Bagot, *Coppin the Great* (Melbourne: Melbourne University Press, 1965), p.32; p.35.

12 See, for example, *Bell's Life in London and Sporting Chronicle*, 23 August 1863, Supplement, p.1.

13   Edward Geoghegan, *The Currency Lass; or, My Native Girl*, ed. Roger Covell
     (Sydney: Currency Methuen, 1976), p.5.
14   See, for example, the relevant entries in the *Australian Dictionary of Biography*
     and in Eric Irvin, *Dictionary of the Australian Theatre 1788-1914* (Sydney:
     Hale & Iremonger, 1985).
15   For an account of the change in English provincial theatre see Kathleen
     Barker, 'Bristol at Play 1801-53', in *Western Popular Theatre*, ed. David Mayer
     and Kenneth Richards (London: Methuen, 1977).
16   Alfred Dampier & Garnet Walch, *Robbery Under Arms*, ed. Richard
     Fotheringham (Sydney & Brisbane: Currency/ADS, 1985), pp.xiii, xv, lxxv.
17   John West, *Theatre in Australia* (Stanmore: Cassell, 1978), p.26.
18   West, p.29.
19   Bagot, p.336. The programme for the opening night performance on
     Wednesday 6 November 1872 is preserved in Victorian Copyright Exhibits,
     CRS A1188, p.47, Australian Archives, ACT.
20   *Lorgnette* (Melbourne), No.95 (December 1892).
21   Irvin, pp.249-50; see in particular Rowe's sporting melodrama *New Babylon*,
     discussed in Chapter 3.
22   *Sydney Morning Herald*, 10 April 1862, p.1.
23   *Argus* (Melbourne), 27 December 1861, p.5; *Illustrated Melbourne Post*, 1,
     No.1 (January 1862).
24   Edmond Marin La Meslee, *The New Australia*, trans. Russel Ward (1883;
     trans. & rpt. Melbourne: Heinemann Educational, 1979), p.22.
25   Harold Love, *The Golden Age of Australian Opera* (Sydney: Currency, 1981),
     p.137.
26   Harold Love, 'A Lesson from Lyster; or, How to Run an Economical Opera
     Company', *Meanjin*, 36, No.2 (July 1977), p.214.
27   Love, *The Golden Age of Australian Opera*, p.139.
28   W. F. Mandle, 'Sports History', in *New History: Studying Australia Today*,
     ed. G. Osborne & W. F. Mandle (Sydney: George Allen & Unwin, 1982),
     p.85.
29   *Lorgnette* (Melbourne), No.256 (July 1896).
30   *Flag* (Melbourne), 19 July 1895, p.5.
31   *Lorgnette* (Melbourne), No.224 (July 1895).
32   Lisa Whitcher, 'Bland Holt', four books of press clippings 1898-1903,
     uncatalogued, Fryer Library, University of Queensland.
33   *Bendigo Advertiser*, 10 May 1860, p.1.
34   *Bendigo Advertiser*, 30 November 1880, p.1; 6 December 1880, p.1.
35   *Maitland Mercury*, 10 March 1855, p.3.
36   *Maitland Mercury*, 10 February 1855, p.2.
37   *Maitland Mercury*, 14 October 1865, p.1.
38   *Bendigo Advertiser*, 13 October 1890, p.1.
39   *Bendigo Advertiser*, 25 November 1890, p.1.
40   *Maitland Mercury*, 19 January 1885, p.1.
41   *Maitland Mercury*, 16 April 1885, p.1.
42   *Maitland Mercury*, 21 January 1905, p.1.
43   *Maitland Mercury*, 1 April 1905, p.3.
44   *Bendigo Advertiser*, 2 January 1860, p.1.
45   Randolph Bedford, *Naught to Thirty Three* (1944; rpt. Melbourne: Melbourne
     University Press, 1976), p.78.

46 W. F. Mandle, 'Cricket and Australian Nationalism in the Nineteenth Century', *Journal of the Royal Australian Historical Society*, 54, 4 (December 1973), pp.233–5.

47 J. A. Mangan, *Athleticism in the Victorian and Edwardian Public School: The Emergence and Consolidation of an Educational Ideology* (Cambridge: Cambridge University Press, 1981); Keith Dunstan, 'The Passion at School', in his *Sports* (South Melbourne: Sun, 1981), pp.26–40.

48 Watts Phillips, 'Lost in London' (1867) in *Hiss the Villain: Six English and American Melodramas*, ed. Michael Booth (New York: Arno Press, 1964).

49 Mandle, 'Cricket and Australian Nationalism', p.233.

50 Mandle, 'Sports History', p.84.

51 Michael Baker, *The Rise of the Victorian Actor* (London: Croom Helm, 1978), pp.9–12.

52 Irvin, p.12.

53 *Argus* (Melbourne), 22 December 1880, p.7.

54 *Bell's Life in Victoria and Sporting Chronicle* (Melbourne), 30 May 1857, p.2.

55 *Brisbane Courier*, 13 July 1908, p.2; 6 December 1909, p.2.

56 *Sydney Morning Herald*, 2 November 1869, p.2.

57 *Illustrated Melbourne Post*, 25 April 1863, p.10; Bagot, p.334.

58 *Maitland Mercury*, 17 January 1885, p.1.

59 *Australasian Sketcher*, 17 September 1881.

60 *Today: Society, Drama, Sports and Politics* (Melbourne), 12 July 1894, p.5.

61 *Triad* (Sydney), 1 January 1925, p.4.

62 *Illustrated Melbourne Post*, 24 March 1864, p.3; Bagot, p.190.

63 See letter from Bland Holt to 'Edwards', 27 October 1897, MS 11606, Box 1827/5, Coppin-Holt Collection, La Trobe Library, State Library of Victoria, Melbourne; *Lorgnette*, No.201 (December 1894).

64 Claude Kingston, *It Don't Seem A Day Too Much* (Adelaide: Rigby, 1971), p.16.

65 *Argus*, 18 October 1909, p.15.

66 Margaret Williams, ' "The Barnum of Australia": William Anderson', *Australasian Drama Studies*, 2, No.2 (April 1984), p.59.

67 *Lorgnette* (Melbourne), No.268 (April 1897).

68 *Argus* (Melbourne), 3 October 1859, p.5.

69 *Sydney Morning Herald*, 7 May 1862, p.2.

70 *Sydney Morning Herald*, 5 September 1868, p.6; 7 September 1868, p.5.

71 *Argus* (Melbourne), 7 November 1893, p.8.

72 *Argus* (Melbourne), 18 October 1909, p.9.

73 *N.S.W. Sporting Magazine* (Sydney), No.1 (October 1848), p.43.

74 *Argus* (Melbourne), 6 February 1860, p.5.

75 *Illustrated Melbourne News*, 16 January 1858, p.34.

76 *Argus* (Melbourne), 4 March 1861, p.5; 14 June 1861, p.5.

77 *Argus* (Melbourne), 30 December 1861, p.5.

78 *Argus* (Melbourne), 26 December 1861, p.8.

79 *Argus* (Melbourne), 27 December 1861, p.5.

80 *Illustrated Melbourne Post*, January 1862, p.3.

81 *Sydney Morning Herald*, 1 February 1862, p.5.

82 Mandle, 'Cricket and Australian Nationalism', p.228; Dunstan, p.72.

83 William J. Baker, pp.150–1; Mandle, 'Cricket and Australian Nationalism', p.227.

84 *Bell's Life in London and Sporting Chronicle*, 21 June 1863, p.6.

85 *Bell's Life in Sydney and Sporting Reviewer*, 23 January 1858, p.4.

86 See H. H. Stephenson's comments at Green's benefit performance, *Bell's Life in London and Sporting Chronicle*, 23 August 1863, Supplement, p.1.

87 *Bell's Life in London and Sporting Chronicle*, 23 August 1863, Supplement, p.1.

88 For details of the race see *Bell's Life in London and Sporting Chronicle*, 21 June 1863, p.6; *Bell's Life in Sydney and Sporting Reviewer*, 15 August 1863, p.2; *Sporting Gazette* (London), 20 June 1863; *Bell's Life in Sydney and Sporting Reviewer*, 22 August 1863, p.4.

89 Ken Goswell, 'Richard Augustus Willoughby Green', t.s. 4pp., in possession of the present author. Goswell is Green's grandson and is writing his biography.

90 *Bell's Life in Sydney and Sporting Reviewer*, 26 September 1863, p.3.

91 *Bell's Life in London and Sporting Chronicle*, 26 July 1863, p.6; *The Times* (London), 22 July 1863, p.5.

92 *Bell's Life in Sydney and Sporting Reviewer*, 12 September 1863, p.2; 19 September 1863, p.2. The second is a reprint of an article first published in *Bell's Life in London*.

93 *Bell's Life in London and Sporting Chronicle*, 23 August 1863, Supplement, p.1.

94 *Sydney Morning Herald*, 16 March 1864, p.1.

95 *Sydney Morning Herald*, 17 March 1864, p.5.

96 See, e.g., *Bell's Life in Sydney and Sporting Reviewer*, 14 January 1862, p.2.

97 *Sydney Morning Herald*, 11 March 1864, p.1.

98 *Argus* (Melbourne), 28 December 1866, p.1; 31 December 1866, p.1; 2 January 1867, p.5.

99 *Sydney Morning Herald*, 15 November 1876, p.2; 16 November 1876, p.5.

100 *Sydney Morning Herald*, 25 November 1878, p.2; 30 November 1882, p.2.

101 *Sydney Morning Herald*, 19 August 1884, p.2; 20 August 1884, p.10.

102 *Sydney Morning Herald*, 16 December 1902, p.3.

103 *Sydney Morning Herald*, 10 December 1902, p.2.

104 Michael McKernan, ' "Muddied Oafs" and "Flannelled Fools": Sport and War in Australia', in his *The Australian People and the Great War* (Melbourne: Nelson, 1980), pp. 105–112.

105 *Sydney Morning Herald*, 28 August 1880, p.2; 31 August 1880, p.5.

106 *Argus* (Melbourne), 23 August 1887, p.8.

107 *Australian Dictionary of Biography* III, 1851–1890 A–C, 1970, p.253.

108 *Argus* (Melbourne), 9 November 1859, p.8.

109 *Argus* (Melbourne), 10 November 1859, p.8.

110 *Argus* (Melbourne), 26 June 1860, p.8.

111 Peter Corris, *Lords of the Ring* (North Ryde: Cassell, 1980), p.45.

112 Corris, p.50.

113 *Maitland Mercury*, 1 September 1885, p.4.

114 *Argus* (Melbourne), 9 July 1892, p.16.

115 Corris, pp.91–2.

116 Corris, p.98.

117 *Magpie* (Melbourne), 1 December 1865.

118 *Australasian Sketcher* (Melbourne), 29 November 1873, p.158

119 *Brisbane Courier*, 20 March 1907, p.2, p.6.

120 Corris, p.22, p.25.

121 *Empire* (Sydney), 27 April 1857, p.1.

122 Odell, XV, 223.

123 Odell, XV, 624; 632.

124 For details of Sullivan's tour, see Dunstan, pp.158–60.

125   *Lorgnette* (Melbourne), No.30 (August 1891).
126   *Lorgnette* (Melbourne), No.30 (August 1891).
127   *Lorgnette* (Melbourne), No.24 (July 1891); No.27 (July 1891); No.28 (August 1891).
128   *Referee* (Sydney), 5 August 1891, p.6; 30 September 1891, p.6.
129   *Referee* (Sydney), 7 October 1891, p.6.
130   *Referee* (Sydney), 30 September 1891, p.6.
131   *Lorgnette* (Melbourne), No.44 (November 1891).
132   *Referee* (Sydney), 30 September 1891, p.6.
133   *Referee* (Sydney), 30 September 1891, p.6.
134   Odell, XV, 362.
135   Bland Holt Papers, series 1, item 229.
136   Bland Holt Papers, series 1, item 267.
137   Dunstan, pp.161–3.
138   *Referee* (Sydney), 25 November 1896, p.6.
139   Bland Holt Papers, series 1, item 427.
140   *Referee* (Sydney), 22 September 1897, p.6.
141   *Referee* (Sydney), 22 September 1897, p.6.
142   Bland Holt Papers, series 1, item 520.
143   *Referee* (Sydney), 22 September 1897, p.6; *Brisbane Courier*, 4 November 1897, p.4.
144   West, p.11.
145   Irvin, *Dictionary of the Australian Theatre 1788–1914*, pp.273–4.
146   Hudspeth, p.5.
147   Thorne, I, 84ff (See II, 135, for an index listing).
148   Thorne, I, 222–3.
149   Edmund Duggan Coll., MS 6304, folder 4, item 3, National Library, Canbera.
150   Arnold, p.133.
151   Pat Finn, *Australian Theatrical, Football, Cricketing and General Sporting Songbook* (Melbourne: McKinley, n.d. [1891]).
152   *Bulletin* (Sydney), 3 September 1887.
153   *Australasian Stage Annual* (Melbourne), No.5 (January 1904).
154   Bland Holt Papers, series 1, item 553.
155   *Argus* (Melbourne), 8 June 1886, p.5.
156   Bagot, p.134.
157   Dunstan, pp.228–9.
158   Dunstan, p.230.
159   *Everyones*, 14 September 1921, p.3; quoted in John Tulloch, *Legends on the Screen: The Australian Narrative Cinema 1919–1929* (Sydney: Currency/AFI, 1981), p.184.
160   West, p.110.
161   Pike and Cooper, p.102; Dunstan, pp.235–6.
162   Pike and Cooper, pp.126–8.
163   Williams, p.44.
164   Corris, p.98.
165   See Adams's obituary in *Steele Rudd's Magazine* (May 1905).
166   West, p.135.
167   Nathaniel Gould, *On and Off the Turf in Australia* (London: Routledge, n.d. [1895]), p.233.
168   Viola Tait, *A Family of Brothers* (Melbourne: Heinemann, 1971), p.19.

169 John Hetherington, 'Hugh D. McIntosh: The Unrepentant Buccaneer',
    in his *Australians: Nine Profiles* (Melbourne: Cheshire, 1960), p.52. See also
    Charles Cochran, *The Secrets of a Showman* (London: Heinemann, 1925),
    pp.vii-ix.
170 Hetherington, pp.43-62; Hugh D. McIntosh, 'Beginnings', *Triad* (Sydney), 2
    February 1925, p.10, p.48.
171 Frank Van Straten, 'The Tivoli: A Chronology of Melbourne's Home of
    Vaudeville', *The Passing Show 3*, (Melbourne: Victorian Arts Centre, 1981),
    p.2.
172 Kingston, p.56.
173 Hetherington, p.55.
174 Hetherington, p.56; McIntosh, p.48.
175 Hetherington, p.60.
176 Corris, p.94.
177 Hetherington, pp.60-2.
178 *Argus* (Melbourne), 16 October 1909, p.24.
179 Lurline Stuart, *Nineteenth Century Australian Periodicals* (Sydney: Hale and
    Iremonger, 1979).
180 *Flag* (Melbourne), 6 July 1895, p.2.
181 Sylvia Lawson, *The Archibald Paradox* (Ringwood: Allen Lane, 1983), p.83
182 *Australasian Stage Annual* (Melbourne), No.2 (January 1901), p.50.
183 Chris Cuneen, 'Elevating and Recording The People's Pastimes: Sydney
    Sporting Journalism 1886-1939', *Sport: Money, Morality and the Media*, ed.
    Richard Cashman & Michael McKernan (Kensington: NSW University Press,
    n.d. [1981?]), pp.162-76.
184 *Referee* (Sydney), 2 January 1907.
185 *Dead Bird* (Sydney), 27 July 1889.
186 *Arrow* (Sydney), 7 January 1911.
187 *Dead Bird* (Sydney), 27 July 1889, p.5.
188 *Dead Bird* (Sydney), 30 August 1889, p.5.
189 For example, *Dead Bird* (Sydney), 30 November 1889, p.4.
190 *Arrow* (Sydney), 14 January 1911, p.1.
191 *Arrow* (Sydney), 21 January 1899, p.6.
192 *Arrow* (Sydney), 7 January 1911, p.1.
193 *Criterion* (Melbourne), 15 September 1892, p.7.
194 *Australian Sporting and Dramatic News* (Sydney), 1 September 1928,
    pp.13-14.
195 *Flag* (Melbourne), 6 July 1895, p.1.
196 *Flag* (Melbourne), 13 July 1895, p.13; 19 July 1895, p.5.
197 *Today* (Melbourne), 2 August 1894, p.4.
198 *Today* (Melbourne), 28 June 1894.
199 *Australian Sporting and Dramatic News* (Sydney), 9 November 1929, p.7.
200 *Theatre of Australasia* (Melbourne), August 1889, p.5.
201 *Australasian Gazette*, [1929], NA1577, National Film and Sound Archive,
    Canberra.
202 *Today* (Melbourne), 28 June 1894.
203 *Arrow* (Sydney), 17 August 1907, p.10.
204 Helen King, 'The Sexual Politics of Sport: An Australian Perspective', *Sport in
    History*, pp.68-85.
205 *Age*, 8 June 1903, p.7.

206   Compare, for example, the publicity photographs of Annette Kellerman published in the *Theatre* (Sydney), 1 March 1909, p.5, and 1 December 1910 (Supplement), with the illustrated programme of 'Poses Plastiques' for the variety artist, Juliette Lotty, sold during her Australian tour in 1902. CRS A1723, item 107, Australian Archives, ACT.

207   Programme, (2 April 1892), f.79, J. C. Williamson scrapbook, uncatalogued m.s., Dennis Wolanski Library, Sydney.

208   Arnold, pp.164–5.

209   *Australasian Stage Annual* (Melbourne), January 1905.

210   For example, the different approach taken to actors as against that taken for actresses in the many biographical sketches in the *Theatre of Australasia* (Melbourne, 1889–90), and *Melbourne Mirror* (1888–89).

211   Finn, frontispiece.

212   CRS A1716, item 262, Australian Archives, ACT.

3   The First Sporting Dramas 1866–80

1   R. Mander & J. Mitchenson, *The Lost Theatres of London* (London: Rupert Hart-Davis,1968), p.187.

2   *Bell's Life in London and Sporting Chronicle*, 20 October 1866, p.11.

3   *Era* (London), 19 January 1868, p.10; see also 20 January 1867, p.11; 16 June 1867, p.15.

4   For example, *The Times* (London), 19 September 1892, p.8; *Sydney Morning Herald*, 15 January 1906, p.4. The critic for the latter paper referred to a later racing drama as differing 'very little from similar dramatic ventures that have been presented here since the production over a generation ago of a sterling "horsey" piece called the "Flying Scud" '.

5   John McCormick, *Dion Boucicault* (Cambridge: Chadwyck-Healey, 1987), p.44.

6   *Sydney Morning Herald*, 18 January 1906, p.2.

7   George Darrell, *The Sunny South*, ed. Margaret Williams (Sydney: Currency Methuen, 1975), pp.31–4.

8   Albert Bailey & Edmund Duggan, *The Squatter's Daughter*, Australian Archives (Canberra) TS, CRS A1336/1, item 22, pp.10–14.

9   Rolf Boldrewood, *Robbery Under Arms* (Sydney 1882–83, rpt. London: Macmillan, 1966), pp.381–414.

10   Alfred Dampier & Garnet Walch, *Robbery Under Arms*, ed. Richard Fotheringham (Sydney & Brisbane: Currency/ADS,1985). pp.67–76.

11   Modern stage historians and Boucicault's biographers have, with two recent exceptions, dismissed *Flying Scud* in a few (often disparaging) sentences. G. C. D. Odell, referring to its 1867 New York season, stated that it was 'certainly one of the first plays to center in a horse race', and added with considerable understatement that 'it caught popular fancy'. [*Annals of the New York Stage* VIII (New York: AMS, 1970), p.134.] Townsend Walsh noted in 1915 that *Flying Scud* was 'one of the first of that interminable series of plays called "racing dramas", full of claptrap appeals which the gallery never fails to answer'. [*The Career of Dion Boucicault* (New York: Benjamin Blom, 1967), p.12.] Later biographers have also dismissed the play in passing, sometimes repeating the inaccurate claim made by Walsh that it was a critical failure. [Robert Hogan, *Dion Boucicault* (New York: Twayne, 1969), pp.70–1;

Richard Fawkes, *Dion Boucicault* (London: Quartet, 1979), pp.164–5.]
Among recent critics only Michael Booth in his *English Melodrama* (London:
Herbert Jenkins, 1965) has commented on *Flying Scud*, and his brief plot
description does not explain either the play's uniqueness or its success,
although he agrees with earlier critics that it is 'the first of many melodramas
of the turf'(p.168). Booth classifies it as an 'ordinary domestic' melodrama
'featuring one physically elaborate and thrilling scene dependent for success
largely on stage mechanism' which is 'preceded by a spectacle crowd
scene'(p.170). Elsewhere Booth has noted the play's debt to William Powell
Frith's celebrated painting 'Derby Day' (1858); and also discusses the ways in
which horse races were staged in the later racing dramas of the 1880s.
[*Victorian Spectacular Theatre 1850–1910* (London: Routledge, 1981), p.13,
p.68.] A. H. Saxon notes that in *Flying Scud* the race scene was not staged
with real horses; he therefore excludes it from *Enter Foot and Horses*, his
history of the hippodrama in England and France. However, he does provide a
small amount of information about the play in a footnote. [(New Haven: Yale
University Press, 1968), p.223–4]

12   James Rice, *History of the British Turf* (London: Low,1879), II, 18–23.
13   Wolf Mankowicz, *Mazeppa: The Loves, Lives, and Legends of Adah Isaacs
     Menken* (London: Blond & Briggs, 1982), pp.123–33.
14   *Australasian*, 23 March 1867, p.369.
15   Walsh, p.112.
16   The 1866 script is held at Add. MS 53053.L, Lord Chamberlain's Collection,
     British Library, London. The later version is published in Dion Boucicault,
     Flying Scud in *America's Lost Plays I*, ed. A. Nicoll & F. T. Cloak
     (Bloomington: Indiana University Press, 1964), pp.151–227. A 'side' of Julia
     Latimer's role in an Australian production c.1900 survives in the Bert Bailey
     Papers, series 1, folder 12, MS 6141, National Library, Canberra.
17   I have used the Lord Chamberlain's copy for this reconstruction.
18   'The Druid' [Henry Hall Dixon], *The Post and the Paddock* (London:
     Frederick Warne, 1856), p.4.
19   Cloak, p.154.
20   *The Times* (London), 8 October 1866, p.7.
21   *Bulletin* (Sydney), 2 October 1886, p.7.
22   Dion Boucicault, *London Assurance*, adapt. & ed. Ronald Eyre (London:
     Methuen, 1971), p.40.
23   For example, see the advertisement for Richard Stewart's benefit performance
     in the *Age* (Melbourne), 11 December 1868, p.4, where the Jockey Hornpipe
     from *Flying Scud* was to be performed by 'eight young ladies and Mr. R.
     Stewart'.
24   For example, see the *Argus* (Melbourne), 30 November 1867, p.8. The
     advertisement states 'Magnificent racehorse from McKenzie & Riggs
     Repository'.
25   In the American script only.
26   Quoted in Christopher Wood, *Victorian Panorama: Paintings of Victorian Life*
     (London: Faber, 1976), p.173.
27   *Era* (London), 7 October 1866, p.11.
28   *Era* (London), 20 January 1867, p.11.
29   Erroll Sherson, *London's Lost Theatres of the Nineteenth Century* (London:
     John Lane, 1925), p.191.
30   *Bell's Life in London and Sporting Chronicle*, 13 October1866, p.3.
31   *The Times* (London), 8 October 1866, p.7.
32   *Argus* (Melbourne), 17 December 1864, pp.4–5.

33   *Argus* (Melbourne), 15 March 1867, p.5.
34   *Argus* (Melbourne), 18 March 1867, p.5.
35   *Argus* (Melbourne), 5 June 1867, p.8; 14 June 1867, p.8.
36   *Argus* (Melbourne), 30 May 1867, p.8.
37   J. H. Heaton, *Australian Dictionary of Dates and Men of the Times* (Sydney: George Robertson, 1879), p.210.
38   *Australasian* (Melbourne), 7 December 1867, p.722.
39   *Argus* (Melbourne), 24 December 1867, p.8; see also *Age* (Melbourne), 26 December 1867, p.4.
40   Rice, p.374.
41   *Argus* (Melbourne), 3 October 1859, p.5; 24 May 1861, p.4.
42   *Daily Southern Cross* (Auckland), 29 July 1868, n.p.; *New Zealand Herald* (Auckland), 29 July 1868, n.p.
43   *Empire* (Sydney), 5 September 1868, p.1.
44   *Lorgnette* (Melbourne), No.214 (April 1895).
45   *Argus* (Melbourne), 3 October 1859, p.5.
46   *Bell's Life in Sydney and Sporting Reviewer* 'Edition Extraordinary', 1 October 1859, p.1.
47   *Argus* (Melbourne), 7 November 1878, p.8.
48   *Lorgnette* (Melbourne), 14 June 1890, p.6.
49   *Age* (Melbourne), 11 December 1868, p.4.
50   *Sydney Morning Herald*, 13 May 1871, p.1.
51   *Age* (Melbourne), 26 July 1880, p.5.
52   *Age* (Melbourne), 24 July 1880, p.8.
53   *Age* (Melbourne), 31 October 1887, p.8.
54   *Leader* (Melbourne), 28 June 1890, p.27; see also J. C. Williamson Scrapbook, fol.43.
55   *Lorgnette* (Melbourne), 77 (July 1892), n.p.
56   *Age* (Melbourne), 15 October 1898, p.24.
57   *Referee* (Sydney), 13 November 1889, p.7.
58   *Town and Country Journal* (Sydney), 16 November 1889, p.31.
59   *Referee* (Sydney), 13 November 1889, p.31.
60   *Sydney Morning Herald*, 4 June 1894, p.2; p.6.
61   Howard McNaughton, comp., *New Zealand Annals: Christchurch 1900–1919* (Wellington: Playmarket, 1983), p.57.
62   *Lorgnette* (Melbourne), 28 June 1890, p.5.
63   William Paul Steele, *The Character of Melodrama* (Orono: University of Maine Studies, 1968).
64   *The Times* (London), 19 September 1892, p.8.
65   For a discussion of the issues here see David Mayer, 'Towards a Definition of Popular Theatre', *Western Popular Theatre*, ed. D. Mayer & K. Richards (London: Methuen, 1977), pp.272–3.
66   William J. Baker, *Sports in the Western World* (Totowa: Rowman & Littlefield, 1982), pp.103–7.
67   Rice, I, 242–6; 263–5.
68   Rice, II, 351.
69   For example, see The Druid, *The Post and the Paddock*, pp.17–18; *Silk and Scarlet* (London: Frederick Warne, 1859), p.155, p.219.
70   For a discussion of these writers see Virginian Blain, 'Editor's Introduction,' R. S. Surtees, *Mr Sponge's Sporting Tour* (1853, new edn. St Lucia: University of Queensland Press, 1981), pp.ix–xvi.
71   Blain, p.xi.

72   Blain, p.xi.
73   E. W. Bovill, *The England of Nimrod and Surtees 1815–1854* (London: Oxford University Press, 1959), p.21.
74   Bovill, pp.10–11.
75   Bovill, pp.4–6.
76   Bovill, p.8.
77   Blain, p.xi.
78   See Laurence Senelick, ' "Dead! And Never Called Me Mother!" The Legacy of Oral Tradition from the Nineteenth-Century Stage,' *Theatre Studies*, 26–27 (1979–80/80–81), pp.14–15. However Senelick is not aware that the phrase was a later addition.
79   Peter Corris, in his *Lords of the Ring* (North Ryde: Cassell Australia, 1980), p.37, points out that cricket was for a time in the 1860s heavily associated with gambling, as were boxing, cockfighting, ratting and other blood sports. Horse-racing, however, was still by far the most important gambling sport across the century as a whole.
80   *Illustrated London News*, 13 October 1866, p.370.
81   William F. Mandle, 'Sports History', in *New History: Studying Australia Today* ed. G. Osborne & W. F. Mandle (Sydney: Allen & Unwin, 1982), p.85.
82   Mandle, p.84.
83   William F. Mandle, 'Cricket and Australian Nationalism in the Nineteenth Century,' *Journal of the Royal Australian Historical Society* 59, No.4 (December 1973). pp.233–6.
84   Martha Vicinus, ' "Helpless and Unfriended," Nineteenth-Century Domestic Melodrama,' *New Literary History* 13, No.1 (Autumn 1981), pp.128–9.
85   Vicinus, p.138.
86   *Argus* (Melbourne), 17 December 1864, p.4.
87   *Era* (London), 16 June 1867, p.6.
88   *Era*, 16 June 1867, p.6.
89   For example, *Sydney Morning Herald*, 3 November 1871, p.2.
90   Dion Boucicault, *Formosa "The Most Beautiful"; or, The Railroad to Ruin*, in *Popular Nineteenth Century Drama on Microfilm*. All page references are to this edition.
91   John Russell Stephens, *The Censorship of English Drama 1824–1901* (Cambridge: Cambridge University Press, 1980), p.86.
92   John Russell Stephens, pp.86–7.
93   *Argus* (Melbourne), 31 October 1870, p.5; 25 August 1884, p.6; 28 July 1890, p.7.
94   *Argus*, 11 November 1870, p.8.
95   *Argus*, 31 October 1870, p.5.
96   *Argus*, 29 October 1870, p.5; 25 August 1884, p.6.
97   For example, the *Age* (Melbourne), 31 October 1870, p.5.
98   Keith Dunstan, *Sports* (Melbourne: Sun, 1981), pp.136–9. The date is incorrectly given as 29 March instead of 29 August.
99   *Argus*, 26 July 1890, p.16.
100 *Argus*, 9 August 1890, p.7; *Lorgnette*, 9 August 1890, p.7; 16 August 1890, p.5.
101 *Bell's Life in London and Sporting Chronicle*, 1 October 1870, p.2.
102 *The Times* (London), 4 October 1870, p.9.
103 *Australasian* (Melbourne), 6 April 1872, p.434.
104 Samuel R. Simmons, *A Problem and A Solution: Marcus Clarke and the Writing of "Long Odds" His First Novel* (Melbourne: Simmons, 1946).

105   Marcus Clarke, *Long Odds*, 2nd edn. (Melbourne: Clarson, Messina, 1869),
      pp.11–13.
106   *Bell's Life in London*, 3 October 1870, p.4.
107   *Long Odds*, p.211.
108   *Bell's Life in London*, 3 October 1870, p.4.
109   *Australasian*, 6 April 1872, p.434.
110   In addition to Marcus Clarke's comments in the *Australasian* (note 109
      above), see George Rowell, *The Victorian Theatre 1792–1914* (1956; rev. edn.
      Cambridge: Cambridge University Press, 1978), p.164; and the copyright case
      Weekes v. Williamson (1886) 12 V.L.R. 483.
111   Raymond Mander & Joe Mitcheson, *The Lost Theatres of London* (London:
      Rupert Hart-Davis, 1968), p.199.
112   Richard Fotheringham, 'Sport and Nationalism on Australian stage and
      screen: from *Australia Felix* to *Gallipoli*', *Australasian Drama Studies*, 1, No.1
      (October 1982), pp.65–8.
113   George C. D. Odell, *Annals of the New York Stage*, IX (New York: AMS,
      1970), p.328, p.598, p.632.

4   The Golden Age of Sporting Melodrama 1880–1910

1   A. H. Saxon, *Enter Foot and Horse* (London: Yale University Press, 1968),
     p.94.
2   *Lorgnette* (Melbourne), 21 June 1890, p.5.
3   For clippings of reviews of these and other Bland Holt productions between
     31 December 1898 and 3 April 1903, see Lisa Whitcher, 'Bland Holt', four
     books of press cuttings, Fryer Library, University of Queensland.
4   *Argus*, 24 December 1900, p.6.
5   William Young, 'Ben Hur', t.s. in J. C. Williamson Papers, MS 5783, Box 23,
     National Library, Canberra.
6   Cecil Raleigh & Henry Hamilton, 'The Whip', t.s. in CRS A 1336/2,
     item 18753, Australian Archives (ACT). Nat Gould, 'The Chance of A
     Lifetime', Coppin-Holt Coll., La Trobe Library, State Library of Victoria,
     Melbourne.
7   *Age*, 29 October 1898, p.12.
8   *Age*, 30 October 1905, p.8; 27 July 1903, p.9; *Referee* (Sydney), 2 January
     1907, p.12.
9   *Argus*, 28 January 1901, p.9.
10   *Argus*, 28 October 1901, p.7.
11   *Sydney Morning Herald*, 27 December 1902, p.8; 11 June 1904, p.2; *Age*, 31
     October 1903, p.18; 30 October 1905, p.8; *Table Talk* (Melbourne), 14
     October 1907, p.23.
12   John Russell Stephens, *The Censorship of English Drama 1824–1901*
     (Cambridge: Cambridge University Press, 1980), pp.86–7.
13   Bland Holt Papers, MS 2244, series 1, item 1, p.41, National Library,
     Canberra.
14   Clarance Holt, 'Twice Round the World; or, Fifty Five Years of an Actor's
     Life', ed. Charles Osborn. Unpublished m.s., Bland Holt Papers, series 2,
     item 585.

15   Roger Allan Hall, 'Frontier Drama Classification', *Nineteenth Century Theatre Research*, 7, No.1 (Spring 1979), pp.27–38.
16   Dion Boucicault, *The Jilt*, in *Popular Nineteenth Century Drama on Microfilm* (Canterbury: University of Kent at Canterbury Library, n.d.[1983]). All page references are to this edition.
17   See, for example, the negotiations between Bland Holt and his English agents: Bland Holt Papers, series 1, items 48, 63, 133, 315.
18   Bland Holt Papers, series 1, items 1138, 1163, 1177, 1189, 1504.
19   *Bulletin* (Sydney), 6 June 1896, p.8.
20   For previous writing in this area see Michael Booth, *Victorian Spectacular Theatre 1850–1910* (London: Routledge, 1981), pp.68–73; Donald F. Recklies, 'Treadmills, Panoramas and Horses in Neil Burgess's *The County Fair*', *Theatre Studies*, Nos. 24–5 (1977–78 & 78–79), pp.9–18; and A. H. Saxon, *Enter Foot and Horse*.
21   Clarance Holt, 'Twice Round the World'. For a short abstract of his career, see 'Clarance Holt: Actor, Author, Manager, Traveller; 1899', Bland Holt Papers, series 2, items 626–33.
22   Erroll Sherson, *London's Lost Theatres of the Nineteenth Century, With Notes on Plays and Players Seen There* (London: John Lane, 1925), p.194.
23   *Sydney Morning Herald*, 26 April 1880, p.6.
24   No script of *New Babylon* has been sighted, and the British Library has been unable to locate the script which according to Nicoll was held in the Lord Chamberlain's collection. The plot description here is based on those given in the *Sydney Morning Herald*, 26 April 1880, p.6, and *Bulletin* (Sydney), 24 April 1880, p.3, and 1 May 1880, pp.3–4.
25   Clarance Holt, 'Twice Round the World', items 580–1.
26   Mander & Mitcheson, pp.201–3.
27   Sherson, pp.195–6.
28   Clarance Holt, 'Twice Round the World', items 593, 598.
29   'Clarance Holt, Actor', item 631.
30   *The Call: The Journal of Theatrical Managers* (Melbourne), 20 April 1889.
31   See Bland Holt Papers, series 1. This series largely comprises letters from these authors and managers.
32   *Bulletin* (Sydney), 24 April 1880, p.3.
33   Bland Holt Papers, series 1, item 1, f.40.
34   Arthur Shirley, Letter to Bland Holt, 25 January 1901; Bland Holt Papers, series 1, item 59. The date has been misread as 1891 and the letter filed with correspondence for that year.
35   Arthur Shirley, Letter to Bland Holt, 29 March 1906; Bland Holt Papers, series 1, items 1415–16.
36   Bland Holt Papers, series 5, item 44.
37   *Bulletin*, 1 May 1880, pp.3–4.
38   Townsend Walsh, *The Career of Dion Boucicault* (1915; re-issued New York: Benjamin Blom, 1967), p.165.
39   Richard Fawkes, *Dion Boucicault* (London: Quartet, 1979), p.225.
40   Walsh, p.166; *Leader* (Melbourne), 1 August 1885, p.26.
41   For example, Bert Bailey & Edmund Duggan, *The Squatter's Daughter; or, The Land of the Wattle*, CRS A 1336/1, item 22, Australian Archives (ACT). In Act 4, p.17, the 'fallen woman' Sarah assists the hero and heroine, and is told 'Don't go. You have brought us happiness and we'll endeavour to make your future life as happy as our own.'

42   *Age*, 27 July 1885, p.5.
43   *Leader*, 1 August 1885, p.26.
44   Walsh, p.166.
45   *Age*, 1 December 1890, p.6.
46   See note 24 above. Presumably the Lord Chamberlain's collection holds MS
     of other sporting plays of the 1880s, but no texts are known to be available
     in Australia.
47   Sheila Rowbotham, *Hidden From History* (Ringwood: Penguin, 1975), p.50.
48   The exact agreement between Williamson and Holt is not known. The poster
     for *A Run of Luck* states that Williamson, Garner and Musgrove 'beg to
     announce the Return to Australia . . . of Mr Bland Holt'. (Bland Holt Playbills
     3/2, Coppin-Holt Coll., La Trobe Library, State Library of Victoria,
     Melbourne.) However the press advertisements state 'Bland Holt's Own
     Specially Organised Company', (*Argus*, 9 April 1887, p.16), and only mention
     the Triumvirate as the managers of the Theatre Royal. The Sydney Theatre
     Royal season in June and July 1888 was also 'announced' by Williamson,
     Garner and Musgrove (*Sydney Morning Herald*, 14 July 1888, p.2).
49   Charles Taylor, Letter to Bland Holt, 24 January 1908; Bland Holt Papers,
     series 1, item 1556.
50   Harold Love, ed., *The Australian Stage: A Documentary History* (Kensington:
     NSW University Press, 1984), p.116.
51   Richard Hughes, 'Bland Holt—Idol of "The Gods" ', *Sporting Globe*
     (Melbourne), 5 February 1949, p.11; plus eight further articles in subsequent
     issues.
52   *Argus*, 11 April 1887, p.6.
53   Booth, p.68.
54   *Daily Telegraph* (Melbourne), 11 April 1887.
55   For example, Isadore Brodsky, *Sydney Takes the Stage* (Sydney: Old Sydney
     Free Press, 1963), p.23.
56   *Argus*, 11 April 1887, p.6.
57   Henry Pettitt and Augustus Harris, 'A Million of Money', t.s. in
     J. C. Williamson Papers, MS 5783, Box 113, National Library, Canberra.
     Pencil sketch on reverse folio facing II,ii.
58   Nat Gould, 'The Chance of A Lifetime', Coppin-Holt Coll. Pencil sketch on
     reverse folio facing III,ii.
59   'A Million of Money', II,iv, f.17.
60   *Argus*, 11 April 1887, p.8.
61   Arthur Shirley, Letter to Bland Holt, 25 September 1895; Bland Holt Papers,
     series 1, item 246.
62   George Musgrove, Letter to J. C. Williamson, quoted in J. C. Williamson,
     Letter to Bland Holt, 25 October 1895; Bland Holt Papers, series 1,
     item 252.
63   *Flag* (Melbourne), 19 July 1895, p.5.
64   Booth, pp.12–13.
65   *Bulletin*, 23 April 1887, p.7.
66   *The Times* (London), 19 September 1892, p.8.
67   *Lorgnette*, No.201, December 1894.
68   *Argus*, 13 May 1901, p.9.
69   *Sydney Morning Herald*, 29 September 1871, p.4.
70   *Lorgnette*, No.172, May 1894.
71   Arthur Shirley, Letter to Bland Holt, 15 September 1894; Bland Holt Papers,
     series 1, item 149.

72   For example, the scene plot for I,iii of Alfred Dampier and J. H. Wrangham, 'Marvellous Melbourne', MS B753, Mitchell Library, Sydney, which states 'Matting under stage cloth . . . for horse'.

73   Arthur Shirley, Letter to Bland Holt, 6 December 1898; Bland Holt Papers, series 1, item 677.

74   *Sydney Morning Herald*, 9 July 1894, p.3.

75   Arthur Shirley, Letter to Bland Holt, 27 December 1895. Bland Holt Papers, series 1, item 266.

76   For example, the advertisement for George Darrell's *The Lucky Lot* in the *Argus*, 11 August 1890, p.8, which claimed the Theatre Royal had 'The Deepest Stage in the World'.

77   Recklies, pp.13-14.

78   Booth, p.64; Recklies, p.9, p.17.

79   Recklies, p.18.

80   *Index to New South Wales Letters Patent 1887-1891* (Sydney: Government Printer, 1894), p.671. CRS A 1084/4, Australian Archives, ACT.

81   *Argus*, 31 August 1901, p.20.

82   Recklies, p.9.

83   Arthur Shirley, Letter to Bland Holt, 20 September 1901; Bland Holt Papers, series 1, item 1051.

84   Recklies, p.14, p.16.

85   For example, *Australian Cyclist and Motor Car World* (Melbourne), 5 September 1901, p.5. The review of the bicycle race in *Riding to Win* stated that 'The effect made the public think that the theatre was moving'.

86   Arthur Shirley, Letter to Bland Holt, 16 April 1902; Bland Holt Papers, series 1, item 1121.

87   Arthur Shirley, Letter to Bland Holt, 20 September 1901; Bland Holt Papers, series 1, item 1051. For the difficulties experienced in staging *The Great Millionaire*, see Bland Holt Papers, series 1, items 1051, 1053, 1061, 1074, 1084-5, 1100. For *The Whip*, see J. C. Williamson scrapbook, f.292, uncatalogued, Dennis Wolanski Library, Sydney.

88   Recklies, p.16. See also the *New York Times*, 13 November 1892, p.13. There is contradictory information about the number of horses used in Sydney and Melbourne. The playbill in the *Lorgnette*, No.25, 11 July 1891, credits four horses with their jockeys; an earlier notice of the Sydney season (No.19, June 1891) mentions three horses.

89   Booth, pp.72-3. See also Arthur Shirley, Letter to Bland Holt, 16 April 1902. Bland Holt Papers, series 1, 1121.

90   Arthur Shirley, Letter to Bland Holt, 10 June 1897; Bland Holt Papers, series 1, item 439.

91   *Manchester Guardian*, 4 April 1902, p.6.

92   *Australian Cyclist and Motor Car World*, 12 September 1901, p.29.

93   Recklies, pp.9-10.

94   *Lorgnette*, No.25, 11 July 1891.

95   Recklies, p.10.

96   *Lorgnette*, No.25, 11 July 1891.

97   *Lorgnette*, No.19, June 1891.

98   *Lorgnette*, No.21, June 1891; No.25, July 1891.

99   For the problems encountered in America, see Recklies p.14; for the method of transportation, see Recklies, p.15; for the difficulties experienced in Australia, see the *Lorgnette*, No.21, June 1891.

100 *Australian Cyclist and Motor Car World*, 5 September 1901, p.7.
101 *Australian Cyclist and Motor Car World*, 12 September 1901, p.29.
102 *Australian Cyclist and Motor Car World*, 10 October 1901, p.27.
103 *Australian Cyclist and Motor Car World*, 10 October 1901, p.27; 17 October 1901, p.18.
104 *Sydney Morning Herald*, 27 December 1902, p.8.
105 *Age*, 8 June 1903, p.7.
106 Marcelle Wooster, 'Annette Kellerman', unpublished biography, t.s., Annette Kellerman Papers, A2 58/2, Dennis Wolanski Library, Sydney.
107 Wooster, p.8.
108 Wooster, p.9.
109 Arthur Shirley, Letter to Bland Holt, 29 March 1906; Bland Holt Papers, series 1, items 1414–15.
110 Wooster, p.17.
111 *Argus*, 26 October 1901, p.16.
112 Howard McNaughton, *New Zealand Stage Annals: Christchurch 1900–1919* (Wellington: Playmarket, 1983), p.16.
113 *Sydney Morning Herald*, 14 April 1906, p.7.
114 Arthur Shirley, Letter to Bland Holt, 20 September 1901; Bland Holt Papers, series 1, item 1051.
115 Arthur Shirley, Letter to Bland Holt, n.d.; Bland Holt Papers, series 1, item 1100.
116 Sidney Cook, Letter to Bland Holt, 18 May 1906; Bland Holt papers, series 1, item 1434.
117 *Sydney Mail*, 3 January 1907, p.48.
118 'The Great Rescue', t.s. in CRS A 1336/2, item 257, Australian Archives (ACT). See also Williams, p.215.
119 *Age*, 2 November 1903, p.6.
120 'A Million of Money', IV,ii,p.14.
121 *Age*, 2 November 1903, p.10.
122 *Bulletin* (Sydney), 5 November 1903, p.10
123 *Bulletin* (Sydney), 5 November 1903, p.10.
124 *Table Talk*, 5 November 1903, p.16.
125 *Age*, 30 September 1905, p.16.
126 Harry McClelland, Letter to Bland Holt, 19 April 1900; Bland Holt Papers, series 1, item 885.
127 *Argus*, 2 September 1901. The t.s. of *Riding to Win* is held in the Coppin-Holt Coll., MF 223, La Trobe Library. The barbecue scene is III,iii.
128 George Musgrove, Letter to J. C. Williamson, quoted in J. C. Williamson, Letter to Bland Holt, 25 October 1895; Bland Holt Papers, series 1, item 252.
129 J. C. Williamson [Producer], 'The Whip', by Cecil Raleigh and Henry Hamilton, t.s., CRS A1336/2, item 18753, Australian Archives, ACT. This was a new copyright application for a new season, but the times and places of those performances have not been checked.
130 I am grateful for this information to Mr Alan Edwards, who acted in the production.
131 Max Goldberg, *Won By A Neck*, t.s., CRS A 1336/2, item 9405, Australian Archives, ACT.
132 *Bulletin* (Sydney), 10 February 1921, p.34.

5   The Australian Sporting Play on the Commercial Stage

1   See in particular Eric Irvin, *Australian Melodrama* (Sydney: Hale & Iremonger, 1981); Margaret Williams, *Australia on the Popular Stage 1829–1929* (Melbourne: Oxford University Press, 1983).
2   Williams, pp.190ff; see also Irvin, pp.60ff.
3   Irvin, p.87.
4   Eric Irvin, *Dictionary of the Australian Theatre 1788–1914* (Sydney: Hale & Iremonger, 1985), p.253, and the individual entries for the named artists in the same volume.
5   See, for example, *Argus*, 9 April 1887, p.12, where Gordon and Brunton are given separate credits for different settings for *A Run of Luck*.
6   Daniel Thomas, 'Australian Art', in *Australian National Gallery: An Introduction*, ed. James Mollison & Laura Murray (Canberra: Australian National Gallery, 1982), p.215.
7   *Argus*, 26 December 1861, p.8.
8   Garnet Walch, *Australia Felix; or, Harlequin Laughing Jackass and the Magic Bat, An Original Extravaganza* (Melbourne: Azzopardi, Hildreth, 1873), p.25. All references are to this edition.
9   *Argus*, 25 December 1873, p.8.
10 *Lorgnette* (Melbourne), No.114 (April 1893).
11 *Argus*, 25 December 1879, p.8.
12 Alfred Dampier & J. H. Wrangham, 'Marvellous Melbourne', MS B753, Mitchell Library, Sydney. All references are to this typescript.
13 Entry on 13 July 1906, Register of Inward Letters, Colonial Copyright Office NSW, SP1006/6, Australian Archives, Sydney.
14 *Ballarat Courier*, 25 December 1906, p.8; *Brisbane Courier*, 18 September 1909, p.2.
15 *Nothern Star* (Lismore), 14 August 1909.
16 *Sydney Morning Herald*, 20 April 1908, p.3.
17 *Argus*, 10 September 1910, p.22.
18 *Argus*, 17 September 1910, p.22.
19 *Argus*, 12 September 1910, p.9; 19 September 1910, p.9.
20 *Argus*, 25 November 1910, p.16.
21 According to *As It Is* (Melbourne), No.93 (January 1887), *The New Rush* had a race scene, but other reviews do not mention this; nor does Eric Irvin in his *Gentleman George: King of Melodrama* (St Lucia: University of Queensland Press, 1980).
22 Alfred Dampier & Garnet Walch, *Robbery Under Arms*, ed. R. Fotheringham (Sydney & St Lucia: Currency/ADS, 1985), p.67.
23 Williams, p.197; Entry on 4 June 1902, Registrar of Inward Letters SP1006/6, Australian Archives, Sydney. For a racecourse scene in a Ned Kelly play, see *Brisbane Courier*, 23 August 1909, p.6.
24 Philip Lytton & W. E. Vincent, 'The Girl from Outback', t.s., CRS A1336/2, item 2339, Australian Archives, ACT. All references are to this typescript.
25 Irvin, *Dictionary of the Australian Theatre*, pp.76–7.
26 Irvin, *Dictionary of the Australian Theatre*, p.260.
27 *Sydney Morning Herald*, 26 December 1902, p.2.
28 *The Times*(London), 8 September 1905, p.5.
29 Williams, pp.223–4.

30   E. W. O'Sullivan, 'Coo-ee; or, Wild Days in the Bush', t.s., Hanger Coll., Fryer Library, University of Queensland; copied from ML A2694, Mitchell Library, Sydney.
31   *Age*, 22 September 1894, p.10.
32   Wilton Welch, 'The Wool King', t.s., CRS A1336/1, item 2026, Australian Archives, ACT.
33   See E. I. Cole Coll., Pic Acq 5497, Mitchell Library, Sydney.
34   *Brisbane Courier*, 31 May 1907, p.2; 1 June, p.2; 4 June, p.2.
35   There is no known research on Kehoe's career, but see the forthcoming *Encyclopaedia of Australian Music, Radio and Recorded Sound*, ed. Jane O'Brien.
36   *Lorgnette*, No.114, April 1893.
37   Williams, p.272.
38   See note 24 above.
39   *Bohemia* (Melbourne), 26 November 1891, p.4.
40   *Bulletin* (Sydney), 14 February 1907.
41   Claude McKay, illust. Harry Julius, *Theatrical Caricatures* (Sydney: NSW Bookstall Co., 1912), pp.120-1, pp.125-6.
42   Bert Bailey Papers, Folder 12.
43   Williams, p.224.
44   *Argus* (Melbourne), 12 September 1910, p.9.
45   W. Wilde, J. Hooton, & B. Andrews, *The Oxford Companion to Australian Literature* (Melbourne: Oxford University Press, 1985), p.212.
46   *Argus*, 27 December 1854, p.4.
47   *Argus*, 28 January 1899, p.16; 2 March 1901; *Sydney Morning Herald*, 14 July 1900, p.2; 21 July 1900, p.2.
48   Bland Holt, Copy of letter to Ambrose Pratt, 26 March 1903; Bland Holt Papers, series 1, item 1193.
49   Ambrose Pratt, Letter to Bland Holt, 27 March 1903; Bland Holt Papers, series 1, item 1194.
50   Bland Holt, Copy of letter to Ambrose Pratt, 30 March 1903; Bland Holt Papers, series 1, item 1195.
51   Ambrose Pratt, Letter to Bland Holt, 16 November 1905; Bland Holt Papers, series 1, item 1374.
52   See Bland Holt Papers, series 1, items 773, 850, 1106, 1185, 1190, 1681; series 5, item 64. See also the letters by Lawson and Paterson to Holt in the Coppin-Holt Coll., La Trobe Library, State Library of Victoria.
53   For an analysis of pictorialism in late-nineteenth-century drama, see Booth, esp. pp.12-13; 64-5; 70-1.
54   *Argus*, 29 July 1899, p.12.
55   *Sydney Morning Herald*, 26 October 1900, p.6.
56   *Sydney Morning Herald*, 24 October 1900, p.10.
57   For example, Henry Fletcher, Letters to Bland Holt, 4 February 1903, 26 April 1903; Bland Holt Papers, series 1, items 1177, 1196.
58   Arthur Shirley, Letter to Bland Holt, 29 May 1901; Bland Holt Papers, series 1, item 1010.
59   *Era* (London), 28 July 1900. A cutting of this review is held in the Coppin-Holt Coll., La Trobe Library, State Library of Victoria.
60   Henry Lawson, Letter to Bland Holt, n.d. (*c.*1900); Coppin-Holt Coll., La Trobe Library

61   See note 52 above.
62   See the playbill for *Riding to Win*, which is attached to the cover of the script. Coppin-Holt Coll., MF 223, La Trobe Library, State Library of Victoria.
63   Hal Porter, *Stars of Australian Stage and Screen* (Adelaide: Rigby, 1965), p.59.
64   Williams, p.204.
65   Williams, pp.204-5.
66   The licence for *Riding to Win* issued by the Lord Chamberlain was to Ernest Leicester and Walter Howard (Williams, p.297). However all other sources state that Frank Herbert and Walter Howard wrote the original English provincial play, so Herbert may have been Leicester's stage name.
67   *Argus*, 31 August 1901, p.20.
68   Arthur Shirley, Letter to Bland Holt, n.d. (1901, filed incorrectly as 1891); Bland Holt Papers, series 1, item 64.
69   Arthur Shirley, Letter to Bland Holt, 29 May 1901; Bland Holt Papers, series 1, item 1010.
70   Edward Dyson, Letter to Bland Holt, n.d.; Bland Holt Papers, series 2, item 24.
71   Norman Lindsay, 'Edward Dyson', in *Bohemians of the Bulletin* (Sydney: Angus & Robertson, 1973), pp.153-60.
72   Edward Dyson, *Fact'ry 'Ands* (Sydney: NSW Bookstall Co., 1906).
73   Porter, pp.60-1.
74   Williams, pp.204-5.
75   For example, *Daily Telegraph* (Sydney), 6 September 1902; *Sydney Morning Herald*, 8 September 1902; *Australian Star* (Sydney), 8 September 1902; *Evening News* (Sydney), 8 September 1902.
76   Edward Dyson, Letter to Bland Holt, 7 June 1902; Bland Holt Papers, series 1, item 1138.
77   Arthur Collins, Letter to Bland Holt, 16 October 1901; Bland Holt Papers, series 1, item 1068.
78   *Argus*, 2 September 1901, p.6.
79   *Australian Star*, 8 September 1902.
80   Edward Dyson, Letter to Bland Holt, 7 June 1902; Bland Holt Papers, series 1, item 1138.
81   *Sydney Morning Herald*, 26 December 1902, p.2.
82   *Bulletin* (Sydney), 10 January 1903, p.10.
83   *Oxford Companion to Australian Literature*, pp.264-5.
84   'A Desperate Game; or, Jim of the Sage Brush', t.s. in Coppin-Holt Coll., La Trobe Library, State Library of Victoria. See also Henry Fletcher, Letter to Bland Holt, 4 December 1902; Bland Holt Papers, series 1, item 1163.
85   Bland Holt Papers, series 1, items 1138, 1163, 1174-5, 1180, 1196, 1203, 1216, 1225, 1229, 1297, 1321, 1338, 1383, 1393, 1404, 1408, 1412, 1422, 1455, 1511; series 2, item 24. See also Bland Holt correspondence, Coppin-Holt Coll., La Trobe Library, State Library of Victoria.
86   Henry Fletcher, Letter to Bland Holt, 3 July 1903; Bland Holt Papers, series 1, item 1203.
87   Sutton Vane, Letter to Bland Holt, 1 August 1901; Bland Holt Papers, series 1, item 1033.
88   Sutton Vane, Letter to Bland Holt, 3 January 1901; Bland Holt Papers, series 1, item 984.
89   *Age*, 30 October 1905, p.7.

90   *Age*, 30 October 1905, p.8.
91   Edward Dyson, Letter to Bland Holt, 12 December 1904; Bland Holt papers, series 1, item 1297.
92   *Argus*, 3 April 1893, p.9.
93   *Argus*, 12 September 1910, p.9.
94   William Anderson & Temple Harrison, 'The Winning Ticket', m.s., CRS A1336/2, item 1656, Australian Archives, ACT.
95   For example, Roger Covell, 'Introduction' to Edward Geoghegan, *The Currency Lass; or, My Native Girl* (Sydney: Currency Methuen, 1976), p.xiii.
96   Bert Bailey & Edmund Duggan, 'The Squatter's Daughter; or, The Land of the Wattle', t.s., CRS A1336/1, item 22, Australian Archives, ACT. References are to this typescript.
97   Dion Boucicault, *London Assurance*, adapt. & ed. Ronald Eyre (London: Methuen, 1971), p.41.
98   Dion Boucicault, *The Jilt*, in *Popular Nineteenth Century Drama on Microfilm* (Canterbury: University of Kent at Canterbury Library, n.d. [1983?]), pp.39-40.
99   *Sydney Morning Herald*, 21 February 1887, p.7.
100 Andrew Pike and Ross Cooper, *Australian Film 1900-1977* (Melbourne: Oxford University Press, 1981), pp.31-2.
101 *The Oxford Companion to Australian Literature*, p.148.
102 *Ballarat Courier*, 28 February 1907, p.6.
103 Mabel Eliza Mills & Frank Edwin Shepard, 'The Kelly Gang; or, Outlaw Kelly', t.s., CRS A1336/1, item 1662, Australian Archives, ACT.
104 Bert Bailey & Edmund Duggan, 'The Native Born', t.s. in CRS A 1336/1, item 2749, Australian Archives (ACT), III,i,p.1.
105 See Harold Love, *The Golden Age of Australian Opera* (Sydney: Currency, 1981), pp.240-2; Paul Richardson, 'Garnet Walch's *Australia Felix*: a reconstruction', *Australasian Drama Studies*, 1, No.2 (April 1983), pp.63-81.
106 See note 8 above.
107 J. H. Heaton, *Australian Dictionary of Dates and Men of the Time: Containing the History of Australasia from 1542 to May 1879* (Sydney: George Robertson, 1879), pp.271-4; pp.280-1.
108 Heaton, p.281.
109 Anthony Trollope, *Australia and New Zealand* (London: Dawsons, 1968).
110 G. F. James, 'Anthony Trollope's *Australia*', *Meanjin Quarterly*, 28, No.116 (Autumn 1969), p.127.
111 For a comment on this controversy see *'Possum* (Melbourne), 3 January 1874, p.39.
112 Fanny Trollope, *Domestic Manners of the Americans* (1832; Oxford: Oxford University Press, 1984). For a brief account of the reaction to this work, see Margaret Drabble, ed., *The Oxford Companion to English Literature* (Oxford: Oxford University Press, 1985), p.1002-03.
113 Trollope, I, 386-7.
114 For example, Edmond Marin La Meslee, *The New Australia 1883*, trans. & ed. Russel Ward (1883; Richmond: Heinemann Educational, 1979), p.147; Nathaniel Gould, *On and Off the Turf in Australia* (London: Routledge, n.d. [1895]), p.2.
115 For the correspondences between play and cricket match, see Richard Fotheringham, 'Sport and Nationalism on Australian Stage and Screen, from *Australia Felix* to *Gallipoli*', *Australasian Drama Studies* 1, No. 1 (October 1982), 65-70.

116   W. F. Mandle, 'Cricket and Australian Nationalism in the Nineteenth
      Century', *Journal of the Royal Australian Historical Society*, 59, Part 4
      (December 1973), 225–46.
117   *Punch* (Sydney), 12 February 1870, p.71.
118   Thos. Hayden, *Sporting Reminiscences* (London: Bliss, Sands & Co., 1898), p.219.
119   *'Possum*, 3 January 1874, p.35.
120   *We* (Hobart), No.1 (February 1867), pp.8–10.
121   George Darrell, *The Sunny South*, ed. Margaret Williams (Sydney: Currency
      Methuen, 1975). All references are to this edition.
122   Arthur Shirley, Letter to Bland Holt 30 September 1898; George Darrell,
      Letter to Bland Holt 11 November 1898; Bland Holt Papers, MS 2244, series
      1, items 649, 666, National Library, Canberra.
123   *Australian Melodrama*, pp.90–1.
124   Edmund Duggan, 'The Eureka Stockade; or, The Fight for the Standard',
      t.s., Hanger Collection, Fryer Library, University of Queensland;
      'The Southern Cross', CRS A1336/2, item 158, Australian Archives, ACT.
125   See, for example, Erskine Childers, *The Riddle of the Sands: A Record of Secret
      Service* (London, 1903; reprinted Harmondsworth: Penguin, 1979).
126   Phyllis Hartnoll, ed., *The Oxford Companion to the Theatre* (Oxford: Oxford
      University Press, 1953), p.210.
127   *Clarion* (London), 5 February 1909, p.3.
128   *The Times* (London), 28 January 1909, p.10.
129   See *Evening Post* (Wellington), 19 June 1909, p.11.
130   See *Sydney Morning Herald*, 10 April 1909, p.2; 12 April 1909, p.7; *Brisbane
      Courier*, 16 August 1909, p.2; *Dubbo Liberal*, 3 July 1909, p.5; 10 July 1909,
      p.3. For Lottie Lyell's role see *Theatre Magazine*, July 1913, p.34.
131   A script for *An Englishman's Home* is held in the J. C. Williamson papers, MS
      5783, National Library, Canberra. Plot summaries are based on this script and
      on contemporary press accounts.
132   See Ada Briggs, intr., *The Battle of Dorking Controversy* (London: Cornwall
      Reprints, 1972); includes a reprinting of General Sir George Tomkyns
      Chesney's *The Battle of Dorking* (1871). For F. R. C. Hopkins' relationship to
      this author, see *Sydney Morning Herald*, 22 July 1916, p.9.
133   Pike & Cooper, p.50.
134   Anon. [F. R. C. Hopkins], *Reaping the Whirlwind* (Sydney: Websdale,
      Shoosmith, 1909). References are to this edition.
135   Randolph Bedford, 'For Australia; or, White Australia; or, The White Man's
      Land', t.s., CRS A1336/2, item 931, Australian Archives, ACT. References
      are to this typescript.
136   See John Barrett, *Falling In: Australian 'Boy Conscription' 1911–1915* (Sydney:
      Hale & Iremonger, 1979), p.16.
137   Louis Esson, *The Time Is Not Yet Ripe*, ed. Philip Parsons (Sydney: Currency
      Press, 1973), pp.39–52.
138   Michael McKernan, ' "Muddied Oafs" and "Flannelled Fools", Sport and War
      in Australia', in his *The Australian People and the Great War* (Melbourne:
      Nelson, 1980), pp.94–115.
139   Bert Bailey, *On Our Selection*, ed. Helen Musa (Sydney: Currency, 1984).
140   'Philip Lytton' [Charles E. Phillips], 'The Waybacks in Town and At Home',
      t.s., CRS A1336/2, item 4405, Australian Archives, ACT. References are to
      this typescript.
141   Richard Dyer, 'Entertainment and Utopia', in *Genre: The Musical*, ed. Rick
      Altman (London: Routledge & Kegan Paul, 1981), p.177.

142 Dyer, pp.187–8.
143 Dyer, p.188.
144 Quoted in Dyer, p.182.

6 Sport in Australian Film

1 Toby Miller, 'Imagined Communities in Australian Sport on Film', unpublished paper for the Fourth Australian History and Film Conference, University of Queensland, 3–6 December 1987.
2 See in particular John Tulloch, *Australian Cinema: Industry, Narrative, Meaning* (Sydney: Allen & Unwin, 1982).
3 Andrew Pike and Ross Cooper, *Australian Film 1900–1977* (Melbourne: Oxford University Press/ Australian Film Institute, 1980), p.161, p.366.
4 Stephen Crofts, 'The Coolangatta Gold: Men and Boys on the Gold Coast', *Queensland Images in Film and Television*, ed. Jonathan Dawson & Bruce Molloy (St Lucia: University of Queensland Press, 1990), pp.112–131.
5 Tulloch, p.64; see also Ken G. Hall, *Directed by Ken G. Hall* (Melbourne: Lansdowne, 1977), p.51.
6 *Brisbane Courier*, 17 February 1908, p.6.
7 The scenario for this film may be found in CRS A1336/1, item 3195, Australian Archives, ACT.
8 Pike & Cooper, pp.82–3.
9 Pike & Cooper, pp.69–70.
10 Pike & Cooper, pp.101–2.
11 Roland Stavely dir., *The Enemy Within* (n.p., 1918), print in National Film and Sound Archive (NFSA).
12 John K. Wells dir., *The Man from Kangaroo* (Snowy Baker Films, 1920), print in National Library, Canberra.
13 Pike & Cooper, p.275; Hall, p.157; Pike & Cooper, p.348.
14 Pike & Cooper, p.255, pp.272–3; pp.402–3; p.365; for Kenny see Crofts, p.115.
15 Excerpts from this comedy can be viewed in Robert Youngson dir., *The Golden Age of Comedy* (1957; CFL Video Re-release, n.d.)
16 Gen. Lew Wallace, 'Ben Hur', as staged by Klaw & Erlanger; script in Box 23, J. C. Williamson Papers, MS 5783, National Library, Canberra; Stage direction to Act V scene 2. See also John West, *Theatre in Australia* (Stanmore: Cassell, 1978), p.94.
17 See note 15.
18 *Albury Daily News and Wodonga Chronicle*, 19 September 1906, p.2; 21 September, p.3.
19 Pike & Cooper, p.38.
20 Raymond Longford dir., *The Woman Suffers* (Southern Cross Feature Film Co., 1918). A print of this film was found during 'The Last Film Search' undertaken by the NFSA in 1982–83. Print held by the NFSA, Canberra.
21 Quoted in Graham Shirley and Brian Adams, *Australian Cinema: The First Eighty Years*, rev. ed. (Sydney: Currency, 1989), p.68.
22 John K. Wells dir., *Silks and Saddles* (Commonwealth Pictures, 1921), print in NFSA, Canberra. See also Pike & Cooper, p.139, although Shirley & Adams, p.68, quote a *Bulletin* claim that it was screened in the USA as a 'South American' film.

23   Reproduced in B. Carroll, *The Australian Poster Album* (Melbourne: Macmillan, 1974), p.97.

24   Alfred Rolfe dir., *The Hero of the Dardanelles* (Australasian Films, 1915). Print in NFSA, Canberra.

25   Keith Gategood & William Green dirs., *Spirit of Gallipoli* (Federal Films, 1928). Print in NFSA, Canberra.

26   Scott R. Dunlap dir., *The Romance of Runnibede* (Phillips Film Productions, 1928). Print in National Library, Canberra.

27   Ken G. Hall dir., *Dad and Dave Come to Town* (Cinesound, 1938); William D. Seiter dir., *Roberta* (Radio Pictures, 1935).

28   Peter Weir dir., *Gallipoli* (Associated R & R Films, 1981).

29   For a discussion of *Gallipoli*'s reception overseas, see David White, *Australian Movies to the World* (Sydney & Melbourne: Fontana Australia & Cinema Papers, 1984).

30   Frank Thring dir., *A Ticket in Tatts* (Efftee, 1934). Print in National Library, Canberra.

31   Arthur Wright, *The Breed Holds Good* (Sydney: NSW Bookstall Co., 1919).

32   Ken G. Hall dir., *Thoroughbred* (Cinesound, 1936); print in the National Library, Canberra.

33   For a discussion of this see Bruce Molloy, *Before the Interval: Australian mythology and feature films, 1930-1960.* (St Lucia: University of Queensland Press, 1990), pp.86-100; for his analysis of *Thoroughbred*, which covers some of the same points made by the present author, see pp.78-9, 92-4.

34   Ken G. Hall, *Gone to the Dogs* (Cinesound, 1939); print in National Library, Canberra.

35   T. O. McCreadie, *Into the Straight* (Embassy Pictures, 1949); print in National Library, Canberra.

36   Simon Wincer dir., *Phar Lap* (John Sexton/Michael Edgley International, 1983).

37   Michael Wilkinson, *The Phar Lap Story* (Melbourne: Schwartz, 1980).

38   Hall, *Directed by Ken G. Hall*, p.92.

39   Rupert Kathner dir., *Racing Luck* (Fanfare Films, 1941); print in National Library, Canberra.

40   William Freshman dir., *Come Up Smiling* (Cinesound, 1939); the viewing print from the National Library lending collection is slightly incomplete, but does not affect the above analysis, except that it is not clear how the three actors become friends of the squatting family.

41   Hall (p.154) credits Freshman's wife Lydia Hayward with being co-screenwriter for the film.

42   See Stewart Young & Andree Wright dirs., *Don't Call Me Girlie* (Double L Films, 1985), and Bill Rout's review of this film in *Cinema Papers* 53 (September 1985), 65-6.

43   *Come Up Smiling* is not mentioned by either Molloy or Tulloch, or by *Cinema in Australia: A Documentary History*, ed. Ina Bertrand (Kensington: NSW University Press, 1989), but receives an entry in Pike & Cooper pp.243-4, and brief mention from Shirley & Adams, p.160. Hall pp.154-5 seems determined to belittle Freshman's contribution beside his own, but agrees that the boxing match was 'one of the funniest things' ever filmed at Cinesound.

44   See Mikhail Bakhtin, *Rabelais and His World* (Cambridge, Mass.: MIT Press, 1968).

45   Paul Rotha, *The Film Till Now: A Survey of World Cinema* (1930, rev. edns. 1949, 1960; London: Spring Books, 1967), p.209; see also Annette Kellerman, *Fairy Tales of the South Seas* (London: Sampson Low, n.d.).

46   Mervyn Le Roy dir., *Million Dollar Mermaid* (MGM, 1952); see also Marcelle
     Wooster, 'Annette Kellerman', unpublished biography TS, Annette Kellerman
     Papers, A2 58/2, Dennis Wolanski Library, Sydney.
47   Franklyn Barrett dir., *The Breaking of the Drought* (Golden Wattle Film
     Syndicate, 1920). Composite print (constructed from two incomplete prints) in
     NFSA; it is possible that the character of 'Molly Henderson, a champion
     horserider' has some narrative function which has been lost from the extant text.
48   John Tulloch, *Legends on the Screen: the narrative film in Australia 1919-1929*
     (Sydney & Carlton: Currency/AFI, 1981), pp.140-1.
49   Ken Hannan dir., *Dawn* (Production Company not known, 1978); the most
     recent TV screening noted was in 1982.
50   Peter Dean, 'A timely tribute to Dawn . . . and Bronwyn', *Courier Mail*
     (Brisbane), 14 October 1982.
51   Igor Auzins dir., *The Coolangatta Gold* (Angoloro, 1984).
52   This parallelism is discussed by Brian McFarlane, 'The Coolangatta Gold',
     Cinema Papers 50 (February-March 1985), 68-9.
53   See Chris Westwood, 'The Women and Theatre Project 1980-81',
     Australasian Drama Studies 1, No.1 (October 1982), 47-8.
54   For a fuller discussion of this aspect of the film, see Stephen Crofts, 'The
     Coolangatta Gold: Men and Boys on the Gold Coast'.
55   I am grateful for this information to Professor Graeme Turner, based on an
     unpublished interview with members of the production team.

7   Sport in the Literary Theatre 1909-89

1   Edmond Marin La Meslee, *The New Australia 1883*, trans. Russel Ward
     (London: Heinemann, 1979), p.147.
2   Marcus Clarke, 'Preface to Gordon's *Poems*', in *The Writer in Australia: A
     Collection of Literary Documents 1856-1964*, ed. John Barnes (Melbourne:
     Oxford University Press, 1969), p.33.
3   Marcus Clarke, *The Future Australian Race* (Melbourne: Massina, 1877),
     pp.15-16.
4   Clarke, *The Future Australian Race*, p.23.
5   Marcus Clarke, *Reverses*, ed. Dennis Douglas (Clayton: Monash University
     English Department, 1981).
6   G. A. Wilkes, *The Stockyard and the Croquet Lawn: Literary Evidence for
     Australian Cultural Development* (Port Melbourne: Edward Arnold, 1981).
7   William Moore, 'Acting a la Mode', t.s., CRS A1336/1, item 1027, Australian
     Archives, ACT. All references are to this typescript.
8   William Moore, 'A Manager for a Night', *The Community Magazine* (Sydney),
     1, No.1 (November 1930), p.2.
9   See Harold Love, *The Australian Stage: A Documentary History* (Kensington:
     NSW University Press, 1984), pp.153-6, where the more substantial work of
     the Adelaide Repertory Society at the same time is documented.
10   William Moore, 'The Only Game', t.s., CRS A1336/1, item 1026; 'The
     Mysterious Moonlight', t.s., CRS A1336/1, item 2471; 'Killed By Laughter',
     t.s., CRS A1336/1, item 6862; Australian Archives, ACT.
11   Esson's letter to Palmer is reproduced in W. F. Mandle, *Going It Alone:
     Australia's national identity in the Twentieth Century* (Ringwood: Allen Lane,
     1978), p. 32.

12   John Hainsworth, 'Some Louis Esson manuscripts', *Southerly* (September 1983), pp. 347–57.

13   Louis Esson, *The Woman Tamer* (Sydney: Currency, 1976).

14   Louis Esson, *The Time Is Not Yet Ripe* (Sydney: Currency, 1973).

15   'Some Louis Esson manuscripts', p. 352.

16   Louis Esson, *The Drovers*, in *Five Plays for Stage, Radio and Television*, ed. A. Sykes (Brisbane: University of Queensland Press, 1977).

17   Betty Roland, *The Touch of Silk* (Sydney: Currency, 1974).

18   Katharine Susannah Prichard, *'Brumby Innes'* and *'Bid Me to Love'* (Sydney: Currency, 1974).

19   Sumner Locke Elliot, *Rusty Bugles* (Sydney: Currency, 1980).

20   Ray Lawler, *The Summer of the Seventeenth Doll* (London: Fontana, 1959).

21   Dymphna Cusack, *Morning Sacrifice* (Sydney: Currency, 1986).

22   'Interview: Ray Lawler talks to Alrene Sykes', *Australasian Drama Studies* 3, No.2 (April 1985), p.22.

23   See note 18.

24   Max Afford, *Mischief in the Air: Radio and Stage Plays* (Brisbane: University of Queensland Press, 1974).

25   George Landen Dann, 'Ring Out, Wild Bells!', unpublished ts., Hanger Coll., Fryer Library, University of Queensland.

26   David Ireland, *Image in the Clay* (Brisbane: University of Queensland Press, 1964).

27   George Landen Dann, *Fountains Beyond* (Sydney: Australasian Publishing Co., 1944).

28   Alrene Sykes, ed. in chief, *Australian Drama Productions 1950–1969* (St Lucia: University of Queensland Library, 1984).

29   George Landen Dann, 'Rainbows Die at Sunset', unpublished t.s., Hanger Coll., Fryer Library, University of Queensland.

30   Louis Nowra, *Inside the Island* (Sydne Currency, 1981), pp.59–60.

31   *Courier Mail* (Brisbane), 21 August 1⅁ ⅁, p. 2. A cutting is held in the Dann papers in the Hanger Coll., Fryer Library; it makes brief reference to *Fountains Beyond*. Dann has made marginal annotations; he kept a collection of references to his work. Consequently the year (1958) is useful only as a guide to the earliest possible date he could have considered writing 'Rainbows Die at Sunset'; he may have had no sur ' plan when he clipped the cutting.

32   For details of this play and the subsequent film see Andrew Pike & Ross Cooper, *Australian Film 1900–1977* (Melbourne: Oxford University Press, 1981), p.348.

33   See Alrene Sykes, 'Theatrical Events 1950–1965 and the Rise of Subsidised Theatre', in *The Australian Stage: A Documentary History*, ed. Harold Love (Kensington: NSW University Press, 1984), p.208.

34   Alexander Buzo, *The Front Room Boys* in Buzo, Hibberd, Romeril, *Plays* (Ringwood: Penguin, 1970), pp.22–3.

35   Alan Hopgood, *And the Big Men Fly* (Richmond: Heinemann Educational, 1969); *And Here Comes . . . Bucknuckle* (Richmond: Heinemann Educational, 1980); Jack Hibberd *Three Popular Plays* (Melbourne: Outback Press, 1976); John Timlin & Jack Hibberd, *Goodbye Ted* (Montmorency: Yackandandah, 1983); Albert Hunt, 'The Grand Grand Final Show', unpublished t.s. in possession of the present author; William Henderson, *Courting Disaster* (Richmond: Heinemann Educational, 1987).

36   Albert Hunt, letter to Roberta Bonnin, 13 November 1981. Copy in possession of the present author.

37 *Goodbye Ted*, p.37.
38 Jack Hibberd, *A Stretch of the Imagination* (Sydney: Currency, 1973), p.37.
39 E. W. O'Sullivan, 'Cooee; or, Wild Days in the Bush', unpublished t.s., Fryer Library, University of Queensland, f.9.
40 Leah Mercer, 'A fairly hybrid talent: an interview with John Romeril', *Australasian Drama Studies* 17 (October 1990), p.54.
41 V. J. Moran, 'Find Me at the Federal', unpublished t.s., Hanger Collection, Fryer Library, University of Queensland.
42 David Williamson, *Three Plays* (Sydney: Currency Methuen, 1974).
43 Jack Hibberd, *Who*, in *Four Australian Plays* (Ringwood: Penguin, 1970), p.135.
44 Stephen Sewell, *The Father We Loved on a Beach by the Sea* in *Three Political Plays*, ed. Alrene Sykes (St Lucia: University of Queensland Press, 1980), p.83.
45 Alex Buzo, *Norm and Ahmed* (Sydney: Currency Methuen, 1976), p.21.
46 Michael Boddy & Bob Ellis, *The Legend of King O'Malley* (Sydney: Angus & Robertson, 1974); John Romeril, *I Don't Know Who to Feel Sorry For* (Sydney: Currency Methuen, 1973); Barry Oakley, *The Feet of Daniel Mannix* (Sydney: Angus & Robertson, 1975); *'Marsupials' and 'Politics'* (St Lucia: University of Queensland Press, 1981); John Powers, *The Last of the Knucklemen* in *Penguin Australia Drama 1* (Ringwood: Penguin, 1974).
47 See in particular Dorothy Hewett, 'Shirts, prams, and tomato sauce: the all-Australian theatre', *Meanjin Quarterly*, 35, No.3 (September 1976), pp.316–23; and Katharine Brisbane, 'From Williamson to Williamson: Australia's larrikin theatre', *Theatre Quarterly* VII, 26 (Summer 1977).
48 See James McCaughey, 'Jack Hibberd and Popular Theatre', *Meanjin Quarterly*, 35, No.4 (December 1976), pp.412–5.
49 Don Watson, 'The Play' (Introduction to *Goodbye Ted*), p.iii.
50 Peter Fitzpatrick, *After 'The Doll': Australian Drama since 1955* (Melbourne: Edward Arnold, 1979), pp.134–5.
51 Mike Giles, 'Scoring', unpublished t.s., Hanger Coll., Fryer Library, University of Queensland.
52 David Williamson, *The Club* (Sydney: Currency, 1978).
53 David Williamson, *The Department* (Sydney: Currency, 1975).
54 Greg McGee, *Foreskin's Lament* (Wellington: Price Milburn with Victoria University Press, 1981).
55 For a fuller account of this change, see Richard Fotheringham, 'Introduction' to *Community Theatre in Australia* (Sydney: Methuen, 1987), pp.11–29.
56 See Veronica Kelly, 'Projecting the inner world onto an existing landscape: an interview with Janis Balodis', *Australasian Drama Studies* 17 (October 1990), p.8.
57 Janis Balodis, 'Heart for the Future', unpublished t.s., in possession of the present author.
58 Barry Dickens, *Royboys* (Sydney: Currency, 1987).
59 Alison Lyssa, 'Feminist theatre: a monologue to start discussion', *Australasian Drama Studies* 2, No.2 (April 1984), p.27.
60 Colin Menzies, 'On-stage', *Sun Herald* (Sydney), 13 September 1981, p.103.
61 Alison Lyssa, 'Pinball', unpublished t.s., Hanger Coll., Fryer Library, University of Queensland, f.6.
62 Darrelyn Gunzburg, Ollie Black, & Margaret Fischer, *A Touchy Subject*, in *Australasian Drama Studies* 14 (April 1989), pp.69–71.
63 Suzanne Spunner, *Running Up a Dress* (Melbourne: McPhee Gribble, 1988), p.30.

64 Jack Davis, *No Sugar* (Sydney: Currency, 1986), p.15.
65 Jack Davis, *Honeyspot* (Sydney: Currency, 1987).
66 David Martin, *The Young Wife* (London: Macmillan, 1962); unpublished t.s. play version, Hanger Coll., Fryer Library, University of Queensland; adapt. Linda Aronson, dir. Oscar Whitbread (ABC TV, 1985).
67 Louis Nowra, *Displaced Persons*, dir. Geoffrey Nottage (ABC TV, 29 September 1985).
68 Richard Barrett, *The Heartbreak Kid* (Sydney: Currency, 1988).
69 Zeny Giles and Freewheels, 'Zorica', unpublished t.s., in possession of the present author; 'Notes for Teachers', ibid. The quotation is from p.13 of the latter document.
70 Tom Shapcott, 'Multicultural Literature and Writing in Australia', *Writing in Multicultural Australia 1984: an Overview* (North Sydney: Australia Council, 1985), p.6.

Bibliography

Unpublished Sources

Plays (Unperformed plays appear in quotation marks)

Adair, Frank. *The Favourite; or, The Sport of Kings*, ts. Anderson Collection. La Trobe Library, Melbourne.

Anderson, William & Harrison, Temple. *The Winning Ticket*, ms. Australian Archives (ACT): Series CRS A1336/2, item 1656.

Bailey, Albert and Duggan, Edmund. *The Man from Outback; or, Stockwhip and Saddle*, ts. Australian Archives (ACT): Series CRS A1336/2, item 1002.

—— and Smith, Frank Beaumont. *On Our Selection*, ts. Australian Archives (ACT): Series CRS A1336/2, item 2391.

—— and Duggan, Edmund. *The Native Born*, ts. Australian Archives (ACT): Series CRS A1336/1, item 2749.

—— and Duggan, Edmund. *The Squatter's Daughter; or, The Land of the Wattle*, ts. Australian Archives (ACT): Series CRS A1336/2, item 22. Bedford, Randolph. *For Australia; or, White Australia—The White Man's Land* (Perf. as *White Australia; or, The Empty North*), ts. Australian Archives (ACT): Series CRS A1336/2, item 931.

Balodis, Janis. *Heart for the Future*, ts. In possession of Dr V.E. Kelly.

Boucicault, Dion. *Flying Scud*. Add. ms. 53053.L, Lord Chamberlain's Coll., British Library, London.

Carter, Lincoln J. (Adapt. Dyson, Edward and Holt, Bland and Fletcher, Henry.) *The Great Rescue*, ts. Australian Archives (ACT): Series CRS A1336/2, item 257.

Dampier, Alfred and Mackay, Kenneth. *To The West*, ts. ML ms B751. Mitchell Library, Sydney.

—— and Wrangham, J. H. *Marvellous Melbourne*, ts. ML ms B753. Mitchell Library, Sydney.

—— and Walch, Garnet. *The Scout*, ts. ML ms B752. Mitchell Library, Sydney.

Dann, George Landen. *Ring Out Wild Bells*, ts. Hanger Coll., Fryer Library, University of Queensland.

—— 'Rainbows Die at Sunset', ts. Hanger Coll. Fryer Library, University of Queensland.

Davis, Arthur Hoey ('Steele Rudd'). *Duncan McClure and the Poor Parson*, ts. Bert and Tim Bailey Manuscript Collection (ms 6141). Series 1, Folder 11. National Library of Australia, Canberra.

—— *Gran'dad Rudd*, ts. Australian Archives (ACT): Series CRS A1336/2, item 5698.

—— *In Australia; or, The Old Selection*, ts. Australian Archives (ACT): Series CRS A1336/2, item 5174.

—— *On Budgee Creek*, ts. Australian Archives (ACT): Series CRS A1336/1, item 4985.

Drew, Con and Anderson, Oswald. *Jinker, The Grafter's Mate*, ts. Australian Archives (ACT): Series CRS A1336/2, item 5712.

Duggan, Edmund. *The Eureka Stockade; or, The Fight For The Standard*, ts. Hanger
    Coll., Fryer Library, University of Queensland.
────── *My Mate*, ms. Australian Archives (ACT): Series CRS A1336/2, item 1869.
────── *The Southern Cross*, ts. Australian Archives (ACT): Series CRS A1336/2,
    item 158.
Du Maurier, Guy. *An Englishman's Home*, ts. J. C. Williamson Collection (ms 5783,
    Box 48), National Library, Canberra.
Giles, Mike. *Scoring*, ts. Hanger Coll, Fryer Library, University of Queensland.
Giles, Zeny. *Zorica*, ts. In possession of author.
Goldberg, Max. *Won By A Neck*, ts. Australian Archives (ACT): Series CRS A1336/
    2, item 9405.
Gould, Nathaniel. *The Chance Of A Lifetime*, ts. Anderson Collection. La Trobe
    Library, Melbourne.
Herbert, Frank and Howard, Walter. (Adapt. Arthur Shirley.) *Riding to Win*, ts. (MF
    222 223). La Trobe Library, Melbourne.
Hunt, Albert. *The Grand Grand Final Show*, ts. In possession of author.
Lyssa, Alison. *Pinball*, ts. Hanger Coll., Fryer Library, University of Queensland.
Lytton, Philip and Vincent, William Edward. *The Girl From Outback*, ts. Australian
    Archives (ACT), Series CRS A1336/2, item 2339.
────── *The Waybacks in Town and At Home*, ts. Australian Archives (ACT): Series
    CRS A1336/2. item 4405.
McCullagh, J. S. *An Australian Hero and the Red Spider*, ts. Film scenario. Australian
    Archives (ACT): Series CRS A1336/1, item 3195.
Moore, William George. *Acting A La Mode*, ts. Australian Archives (ACT): Series
    CRS A1336/1, item 1027.
Moran, V. J. *Find Me at the Federal*, ts. Hanger Coll., Fryer Library, University of
    Queensland.
O'Sullivan, Edward William. *Coo-ee; or, Wild Days in the Bush*, ts. Hanger Coll.,
    Fryer Library, University of Queensland.
Pettitt, Henry and Harris, Augustus. *A Million of Money*, ts. J. C. Williamson
    Collection (ms 5783, Box 113). National Library of Australia, Canberra.
Phillips, Nat. *Cinderella*, ts. Australian Archives (ACT): Series CRS A1336/2, item
    8910.
Raleigh, Cecil and Hamilton, Henry. *The Whip*, ts. Australian Archives (ACT): Series
    CRS A1336/2, item 18753.
Shepard, Frank Edwin and Mills, Mabel Eliza. *The Kelly Gang; or, Outlaw Kelly*, ts.
    Australian Archives (ACT): Series CRS A1336/1, item 1662.
────── *The Waybacks in Town*, ts. Australian Archives (ACT): Series CRS A1336/1,
    item 3974.
Welch, Wilton. *The Wool King*, ts. Australian Archives (ACT): Series CRS A1336/1,
    item 2026.
Young, William. *Ben Hur*, ts. J. C. Williamson Collection (ms 5783, Box 23).
    National Library of Australia, Canberra.

Manuscript Collections, Items, and Theses

Anderson, William. Papers (ms 1412). Mitchell Library, Sydney.
────── Papers. La Trobe Library, Melbourne.
Arnold, Trevor C. 'Sport in Colonial Australia, 1788-1850'. Doctoral Diss.,
    Queensland, 1979.
Australian Drama Bibliography. Files, 1850-1869. Department of English,
    University of Queensland.

Bailey, Bert and Tim. Manuscript Collection (ms 6141). Australian National Library, Canberra.

Cole, Edward Irham. Collection. Picture Acquisitions 5497, Mitchell Library, Sydney.

Conway, John. 'Memoirs of A Sporting Voyager 1878'. Introduction by Ronald Conway. Unpublished Article in author's possession.

Conway, Ronald. 'John Conway and the First Australian Eleven of 1878'. Unpublished article in author's possession.

Coppin-Holt Collection. La Trobe Library, Melbourne.

Copyright Office, Commonwealth. Records 1907-1969 (CRS A1336/1-3; A1187; A1957-62). Australian Archives (ACT).

Copyright Office, New Zealand. Records Relating to Copyright, 1886-1963 (PC Series 13). National Archives, Wellington.

Copyright Office, New South Wales. Records, 1879-1907 (SP1006/3-7). Australian Archives, Sydney.

Copyright Office, Queensland. Records 1887-1907 (BP 5/10-12). Australian Archives, Queensland.

―――― Records 1887-1907 (CRS A1716). Australian Archives (ACT).

Copyright Office, Victoria. Records 1869-1907 (CRS A1720; A1786; A2389). Australian Archives (ACT).

Copyright Office, Western Australia. Records 1889-1907 (A1722-23). Australian Archives (ACT).

Corrick Family Scrapbook. National Film and Sound Archive, Canberra.

Dann, George Landen. Papers. Fryer Library, University of Queensland.

Duggan, Edmund. Papers (ms 6304). Australian National Library, Canberra.

Goswell, Ken. 'Richard Augustus Willoughby Green', ts. In possession of the author.

Hergenhan, L.T., ed. *An Index to Selected Melbourne Magazines and Newspapers, 1880-1900*. St Lucia: Fryer Library Card Index.

Holt, Joseph Bland. Papers (ms 2244). Australian National Library, Canberra.

Holt, Clarance. 'Actor, Author, Manager, Traveller', ts. Bland Holt Papers (ms 2244 series 2). Australian National Library, Canberra.

―――― Diary. Microfilm CY Reel 576 from A1981. Mitchell Library, Sydney.

―――― 'Twice Round the World; or, Fifty-Five Years of an Actor's Life', ms. ed. Charles Osborne. Bland Holt Papers (ms 2244, series 2). Australian National Library, Canberra.

Ives, Bert. Scrapbook. National Film and Sound Archive, Canberra.

Kellerman, Annette. Papers. Dennis Wolanski Library, Sydney.

Longford, Raymond. Papers (not yet accessed). Australian National Library, Canberra.

Maslen, Joan. 'Melbourne Cup Entertainments 1880-1909'. Library Bibliography File. La Trobe Library, Melbourne.

Miller, Toby. 'Imagined communities of Australian sport on film'. Paper for the Fourth Australian History and Film Conference, University of Queensland, 3-6 December 1987.

Patents Office, New South Wales. Records 1855-1905 (CRS A1084). Australian Archives (ACT).

Power, Leo. 'The Alfred Dampier Sydney Season Oct. 1885—May 1888'. Typescript in author's possession.

Registrar of Probates. File re John Ringrose Atkins (Dan Barry). Melbourne.

Seymour, T. 'Motoring in Australia, from its Inception to 1925'. Unpublished paper in author's possession.

Tait, Charles. Index to Actors, Plays, Musicians, Concerts 1885–1932, ts. National Film and Sound Archive, Canberra.
——— Papers (ms 2434). National Library, Canberra.
Tauchert, Arthur. Scrapbook. National Film and Sound Archive, Canberra.
Whitcher, Lisa. Bland Holt Press Cuttings 1898–1903. Fryer Library, University of Queensland.
Williamson, J. C. Papers (ms 5783). Australian National Library, Canberra.
——— Papers. Performing Arts Museum, Melbourne.
——— Scrapbook. Dennis Wolanski Library, Sydney.
Wooster, Marcelle. Biography of Annette Kellerman, ts. Dennis Wolanski Library, Sydney.

Published Works

Plays

Afford, Max. *Mischief in the Air: Radio and Stage Plays.* Brisbane: University of Queensland Press, 1974.
Akhurst, William Mower. *Gulliver on His Travels.* Melbourne: n.p., n.d. [1866].
Bailey, Bert. *On Our Selection.* Ed. Helen Musa. Sydney: Currency, 1984.
Barrett, Richard. *The Heartbreak Kid.* Sydney: Currency, 1988.
Boddy, Michael and Bob Ellis. *The Legend of King O'Malley.* Sydney: Angus & Robertson, 1974.
Boucicault, Dion. *Flying Scud; or, A Four-Legged Fortune.* In *America's Lost Plays 1.* Ed. A. Nicoll and F. T. Cloak. Bloomington: Indiana University Press, 1964, pp.151–227.
——— *London Assurance.* Adapt. and Ed. Ronald Eyre. London: Methuen, 1971.
——— *Formosa* and *The Jilt*, in *Popular Nineteenth Century Drama on Microfilm.* Canterbury: University of Kent at Canterbury Library, n.d. [1982].
Buzo, Alex. *The Front Room Boys.* In Buzo, Hibberd, Romeril. *Plays.* Ringwood: Penguin, 1970.
——— *Norm and Ahmed.* Sydney: Currency Methuen, 1976.
Clarke, Marcus. *Reverses.* ed. Dennis Davison. Melbourne: Monash Nineteenth-Century Drama Series No.5, 1981.
Cooper, Walter. *Colonial Experience.* Rev. R. Roberts. ed. Eric Irvin. Sydney: Currency, 1979.
Cusack, Dymphna. *Morning Sacrifice.* Sydney: Currency, 1986.
Dampier, Alfred and Walch, Garnet. *Robbery Under Arms.* ed. R. Fotheringham. Sydney and Brisbane: Currency/ ADS, 1985.
Dann, George Landen. *Fountains Beyond.* Sydney: Australasian Publishing Co., 1944.
Darrell, George. *The Sunny South.* ed. Margaret Williams. Sydney: Currency, 1975.
Davis, Jack. *Honeyspot.* Sydney: Currency, 1987.
——— *No Sugar.* Sydney: Currency, 1986.
Dickins, Barry. *Royboys.* Sydney: Currency, 1987.
Dutruc, P.A. *A Desirable Quarantine.* Sydney: F. White, 1878.
Esson, Louis. *The Drovers.* In *Five Plays for Stage, Radio and Television*, ed. A. Sykes. Brisbane: University of Queensland Press, 1977.
——— *The Time Is Not Yet Ripe.* ed. Philip Parsons. Sydney: Currency, 1973.
——— *The Woman Tamer.* Sydney: Currency, 1976.

Geoghegan, Edward. *The Currency Lass; or, My Native Girl.* ed. Roger Covell. Sydney: Currency, 1976.

Gunzburg, Darrelyn, Ollie Black & Margaret Fischer. *A Touchy Subject.* In *Australasian Drama Studies* 14 (April 1989), 69–71.

Henderson, William. *Courting Disaster.* Richmond: Heinemann Educational, 1987.

Hibberd, Jack. *A Stretch of the Imagination.* Sydney: Currency, 1973.

——— *Three Popular Plays.* Melbourne: Outback Press, 1976.

——— *Who.* In Buzo, Hibberd, Romeril. *Plays.* Ringwood: Penguin, 1970.

Hopgood, Alan. *And the Big Men Fly.* Richmond: Heinemann Educational, 1969.

——— *And Here Comes . . . Bucknuckle.* Richmond: Heinemann Educational, 1980.

Hopkins, Francis Rawdon Chesney. *Reaping the Whirlwind.* Sydney: Websdale, Shoosmith, 1909.

Ireland, David. *Image in the Clay.* Brisbane: University of Queensland Press, 1964.

Lawler, Ray. *The Summer of the Seventeenth Doll* London: Fontana, 1959.

Leigh, Euston and Clare, Cyril. *The Duchess of Coolgardie.* London: Henry J. Drane, n.d. [1896?].

Locke Elliot, Sumner. *Rusty Bugles.* Sydney: Currency, 1980.

McGee, Greg. *Foreskin's Lament.* Wellington: Price Millburn with Victoria University Press, 1981.

Moncrieff, W. T. *Tom and Jerry: or, Life in London.* New York: Samuel French, n.d. In *Nineteenth Century Popular British Drama: Acting Editions.* ed. Richard L. Lorezan. London & Seattle: University of Washington Press, 1977.

Nowra, Louis. *Inside the Island.* Sydney: Currency, 1981.

Oakley, Barry. *The Feet of Daniel Mannix.* Sydney: Angus & Robertson, 1975.

——— *'Marsupials' and 'Politics'.* St Lucia: University of Queensland Press, 1981.

Phillips, Watts. *Lost in London* in *Hiss the Villain: Six English and American Melodramas.* ed. Michael Booth. New York: Arno Press, 1964.

Powers, John. *The Last of the Knucklemen.* In *Penguin Australian Drama 1.* Ringwood: Penguin, 1974.

Prichard, Katharine Susannah. *'Brumby Innes' and 'Bid Me to Love'.* Sydney: Currency, 1974.

Romeril, John. *I Don't Know Who to Feel Sorry For.* Sydney: Currency Methuen, 1973.

Rowell, George, ed. *Nineteenth Century Plays.* London: Oxford University Press, 1953.

Sewell, Stephen. *The Father We Loved on a Beach by the Sea.* In *Three Political Plays,* ed. A. Sykes. St Lucia: University of Queensland Press, 1980.

Spunner, Suzanne. *Running Up a Dress.* Melbourne: McPhee Gribble, 1988.

Timlin, John and Jack Hibberd. *Goodbye Ted.* Montmorency: Yackandandah, 1983.

Walch, Garnet. *Australia Felix; or, Harlequin Laughing Jackass and the Magic Bat.* Melbourne: Azzopardi, Hildreth, 1873.

Williamson, David. *The Club.* Sydney: Currency, 1978.

——— *The Department.* Sydney: Currency, 1975.

——— *Three Plays.* Sydney: Currency Methuen, 1974.

Films and TV Plays

Auzins, Igor. *The Coolangatta Gold.* Angoloro, 1984.

Barrett, Franklyn. *The Breaking of the Drought.* Golden Wattle Film Syndicate, 1920.

——— *A Girl of the Bush.* Barrett's Australian Productions, 1921.

Dunlap, Scott R. *The Romance of Runnibede.* Phillips Film Productions, 1928.

Freshman, William. *Come Up Smiling.* Cinesound, 1939.

Gategood, Keith & William Green. *The Spirit of Gallipoli*. Federal Films, 1928.
Hall, Ken G. *Dad and Dave Come to Town*. Cinesound, 1938.
—— *Gone to the Dogs*. Cinesound, 1939.
—— *Thoroughbred*. Cinesound, 1935.
Hannan, Ken. *Dawn*. 1978.
Kathner, Rupert. *Racing Luck*. Fanfare Films, 1941.
Le Roy, Mervyn. *Million Dollar Mermaid*. M.G.M., 1952.
Longford, Raymond. *The Woman Suffers*. Southern Cross Feature Films, 1918.
—— *On Our Selection*. E .J. Carroll, 1920.
McCreadie, T. O. *Into the Straight*. Embassy Pictures, 1949.
Rolfe, Alfred. *The Hero of the Dardanelles*. Australasian Films, 1915.
Seiter, Willian D. *Roberta*. Radio Pictures, 1935.
Stavely, Roland. *The Enemy Within*. 1918.
Thring, Francis W. *A Ticket in Tatts*. Efftee, 1934.
Weir, Peter. *Gallipoli*. Associated R & R Films, 1981.
Wells, John K. *The Man from Kangaroo*. Snowy Baker Films, 1920.
—— *Silks and Saddles*. Commonwealth Pictures, 1921.
Whitbread, Oscar. *The Young Wife*. Adapt. from novel by David Martin. ABC Television, 1985.
Wincer, Simon. *Phar Lap*. John Sexton/Michael Edgley International, 1983.
Young, Stewart & Andree Wright. *Don't Call Me Girlie*. Double L Films, 1985.
Youngson, Robert. *The Golden Age of Comedy*. Youngson, 1957.

General Reference Works, Checklists, Annals Etc.

Adamson, Judith. *Australian Film Posters 1906-1960*. Sydney & Carlton: Currency/A.F.I., 1978.
Borchardt, D. H. *Australian Bibliography. A Guide to Printed Sources of Information*. Rushcutters Bay: Pergamon, 1976.
Checklist of Plays in the Hanger Collection and Manuscript Collection, Fryer Library To August 1985, A. St Lucia: Fryer Library, 1985.
Drabble, Margaret, ed. *The Oxford Companion to English Literature*. 5th edn. Oxford: Oxford University Press, 1985.
Feely, J. A. *Index to 'The Argus' 1846-1854*. Melbourne: Library Council of Victoria, 1976.
Genealogical Sources. Melbourne: Public Records Office, 1976.
Hartnoll, Phyllis. *The Oxford Companion to the Theatre*. London: Oxford University Press, 1951.
Heaton, J. H. *Australian Dictionary of Dates and Men of the Time: Containing the History of Australasia from 1542 to May, 1879*. Sydney: George Robertson, 1879.
Humphreys, Capt. H. Comp. *Men of the Time in Australia*. Victorian Series. 2nd edn. Melbourne: McCarron, 1882.
Irvin, Eric. *Dictionary of the Australian Theatre 1788-1914*. Sydney: Hale & Iremonger, 1985.
Johnston, Grahame. *Annals of Australian Literature*. Melbourne: Oxford University Press, 1970.
Lock, Fred and Lawson, Alan. *Australian Literature—A Reference Guide*. 2nd edn. Melbourne: Oxford University Press, 1980.
Love, Harold, ed. *The Australian Stage: A Documentary History*. Kensington: New South Wales University Press, 1984.
—— 'W. S. Lyster's 1861-68 Opera Company: Seasons and Repertoire'. *Australasian Drama Studies*, 2, No.1 (October 1983), 113-24.

McNaughton, Howard. *New Zealand Theatre Annals: Christchurch 1900-1919*. Wellington: Playmarket, 1983.

Morley, Sheridan. *The Great Stage Stars: Distinguished Theatrical Careers of the Past and Present*. North Ryde & London, Angus & Robertson, 1986.

Nicoll, Allardyce. *A History of English Drama 1660-1900*. Cambridge: Cambridge University Press, 1952-9.

Odell, George C.D. *Annals of the New York Stage*. 1927-46; rpt. New York: AMS, 1970.

Pike, Andrew and Cooper, Ross. *Australian Film 1900-1977*. Melbourne: Oxford University Press, 1980.

—— *Reference Guide to Australian Films 1906-1969*. Canberra: National Library of Australia National Film Archive, 1981.

Pike, Douglas, gen. ed. *Australian Dictionary of Biography 1-12*. Carlton: Melbourne University Press, 1966-1990.

Russell, W. Clark. *Representative Actors*. London: Frederick Warne and Co., n.d.[1868?].

Smith, James. *The Cyclopedia of Victoria I*. Melbourne: Cyclopedia Co., 1903.

Spearritt, Peter and Walker, David. 'Popular Culture 1900-1960: A Bibliography'. In *Australian Popular Culture*. ed. P. Spearritt & D.Walker. Sydney: George Allen & Unwin, 1979, pp.222-48.

Stuart, Lurline. *Nineteenth Century Australian Periodicals*. Sydney: Hale & Iremonger, 1979.

Wearing, J. P. *The London Stage 1890-1899: A Calendar of Plays and Players*. London: Metuchen, 1976.

Wilde, William H., Hooton, Joy and Andrews, Barry. *The Oxford Companion to Australian Literature*. Melbourne: Oxford University Press, 1985.

Selected Books and Articles

Acton, W. *The Functions and Disorders of the Reproductive Organs in Childhood, Youth, Adult Age, and Advanced Life Considered in their Physiological, Social, and Moral Relations*. 4th edn. London: Churchill, 1865.

—— *Prostitution Considered in its Moral, Social, and Sanitary Aspects in London and Other Large Cities and Garrison Towns with Proposals for the Control and Prevention of its Attendant Evils*. rpt. London: Cass, 1972.

Altick, Richard D. 'Dion Boucicault Stages *Mary Barton*'. *Nineteenth-Century Fiction*, 14 (1959), 129-41.

—— *The Shows of London*. Cambridge, Massachusetts: Harvard University Press, 1978.

Altman, Rick, ed. *Genre: The Musical*. London: Routledge & Kegan Paul/British Film Institute, 1981.

Andrews, Barry. 'The Willow Tree and the Laurel: Australian Sport and Australian Literature'. In *Sport in History*. ed. Richard Cashman and Michael McKernan. Brisbane: University of Queensland Press, 1979, pp.43-67.

—— 'Tugging Four Bits off the Deck at the WACA: Australian Sport and Australian English'. In *Sport: Money, Morality and the Media*. Ed. Richard Cashman & Michael McKernan. Kensington: NSW University Press, n.d. [1982?].

Appelbaum, S., ed. *Scenes from the Nineteenth Century Stage in Advertising Woodcuts*. New York: Dover, 1977.

Arnold, Trevor C. 'Sport in Colonial Australia: The Military Influence'. *Interaction*, 7, No.1 (1976), 19-23.

Artaud, Antonin. 'An affective athleticism'. In his *Collected Works*. Trans. V. Corti. London: Calder & Boyars, 1974.

Asche, Oscar. *Oscar Asche. His Life*. London: Hurst & Blackett, 1929.

Ashbolt, Alan. 'Courage, Contradiction and Compromise: Gregan McMahon 1874–1941'. *Meanjin*, 37, No.3 (October 1978), 343–4.

Australian Etiquette. 1885, Facs.Rpt. Knoxfield: J. M. Dent, 1980.

Bagot, Alec. *Coppin the Great*. Melbourne: Melbourne University Press, 1965.

Bailey, Peter. *Leisure and Class in Victorian England*. London: Routledge, 1978.

Baker, Michael. *The Rise of the Victorian Actor*. London: Croom Helm, 1978.

Baker, William J. *Sports in the Western World*. Totowa, N. J.: Rowman and Littlefield, 1982.

Bank, Rosmarie K. 'Melodrama as Social Document: Social Factors in the American Frontier Play'. *Theatre Studies*, No.22 (1975–76), pp.42–9.

Barnard, H. *Military Schools and Courses of Instruction in the Science and Art of War*. 1872, rpt. New York: Greenwood, 1969.

Barnes, John, ed. *The Writer in Australia: A Collection of Literary Documents 1856–1964*. Melbourne: Oxford University Press, 1969.

Barrett, J. *Falling In. Australians and 'Boy Conscription' 1911–1915*. Sydney: Hale & Iremonger, 1979.

Bedford, Randolph. *Naught to Thirty-Three*. 1944, rpt. Melbourne: Melbourne University Press, 1976.

Bergan, Ronald. *Sports in the Movies*. London & New York: Proteus, 1982.

Bertie, C. H. *The Story of the Royal Hotel and the Theatre Royal, Sydney*. Sydney: Simmons, 1927.

Bertrand, Ina. ed. *Cinema in Australia: A Documentary History*. Kensington: NSW University Press, 1989.

—— *Film Censorship in Australia*. Brisbane: University of Queensland Press, 1978.

Boldrewood, Rolf. *Robbery Under Arms*. London: Macmillan, 1966.

Booth, Michael. *English Melodrama*. London: Herbert Jenkins, 1965.

—— ed. *Hiss The Villain. Six English and American Melodramas*. London: Eyre & Spottiswood, 1964.

—— *Victorian Spectacular Theatre 1850–1910*. London: Routledge & Kegan Paul, 1981.

Boucicault, Dion. 'Leaves from A Dramatist's Diary'. *North American Review*, 149 (1889), pp.228–36.

Bovill, E. W. *The England of Nimrod and Surtees 1815–1854*. London: Oxford University Press, 1959.

Brasmer, William. 'The Wild West Exhibition and the Drama of Civilisation'. In *Western Popular Theatre*. Ed. D. Mayer & K. Richards. London: Methuen, 1977, pp.133–56.

Bodsky, Isidore. *Sydney Takes the Stage*. Sydney: Old Sydney Free Press, 1963.

Brecht, Bertolt. *Brecht on Theatre: The Development of an Aesthetic*. Trans. & ed. John Willett. New York: Hill & Wang, 1964.

Burn, David. *Vindication of Van Diemen's Land; In a Cursory Glance at Her Colonies As They Are, Not As They Have Been Represented to Be*. London: Southgate, 1840.

Cargher, John. *Opera and Ballet in Australia*. Stanmore: Cassell, 1977.

Carlyle, Billie. *Claude Dampier, Mrs Gibson and Me*. N.p.: privately printed, 1978.

Carroll, Brian. *Australian Poster Album*. Melbourne: Macmillan, 1974.

—— *Australian Stage Album*. Melbourne: MacMillan, 1976.

Cashman, Richard and McKernan, Michael. *Sport in History*. St Lucia: University of Queensland Press, 1979.

—— *Sport: Money, Morality and the Media.* Kensington: New South Wales University Press, n.d. [1982?].

Castle, Dennis. *Sensation Smith of Drury Lane.* London: Charles Skilton, 1984.

Chuck, Thomas. *"One Story Is Good Until Another Is Told," or, A Reply to Mr. Anthony Trollope, On That Part of his Work, Entitled "Australia and New Zealand," Relating to the Colony of Victoria.* Melbourne: The author, n.d. [1873?]

Clarke, Marcus. *The Future Australian Race.* Melbourne: Massina, 1877.

—— *Long Odds.* 2nd edn. Melbourne: Clarson, Massina, 1869.

Cochran, Charles. *The Secrets of a Showman.* London: Heinemann, 1929.

Corris, Peter. *Lords of the Ring. A History of Prize Fighting in Australia.* Sydney: Cassell, 1980.

Covell, Roger. *Australia's Music: Themes of a New Society.* Melbourne: Sun, 1967.

Crawley, W. A. *Favourites of the Footlights . . . photographs and autographs.* Sydney: NSW Bookstall Co., 1902.

Crofts, Stephen. 'The Coolangatta Gold: Men and Boys on the Gold Coast'. In *Queensland Images in Film and Television.* Ed. Jonathan Dawson & Bruce Molloy. St Lucia: University of Queensland Press, 1990.

Csida, J. & J. B. *American Entertainment.* New York: Billboard, 1978.

Cumes, J. W. C. *Their Chastity Was Not Too Rigid: Leisure Times in Early Australia.* Melbourne: Longman Cheshire, 1979.

Cunneen, Chris. 'Elevating and Recording "The People's Pastimes": Sydney Sporting Journalism 1886-1939'. In *Sport: Money, Morality and the Media.* Ed. Richard Cashman and Michael McKernan. Sydney: N.S.W. University Press, n.d. [1982?], pp.162-76.

Cunningham, Hugh. *Leisure in the Industrial Revolution, c.1780-c1880.* London: Croom Helm, 1980.

Dicker, I. G. *J. C. W. A Short Biography of James Cassius Williamson.* Sydney: Elizabeth Tudor, 1974.

Dixon, Henry Hall ['The Druid']. *The Post and the Paddock.* London: Frederick Warne, 1856.

—— *Scott and Sebright.* London: Frederick Warne, 1862.

—— *Silk and Scarlet.* London: Frederick Warne, 1859.

Dunstan, Keith. *The Paddock That Grew.* Melbourne: Cassell, 1975.

—— *Sports.* Melbourne: Sun, 1981.

Dutton, Geoffrey. *Snow on the Saltbush: The Australian Literary Experience.* Ringwood: Viking, 1984.

Dyer, Richard. 'Entertainment and Utopia'. In *Genre: The Musical.* Ed. Rick Altman. London: Routledge, 1981.

Egan, Pierce. *Tom and Jerry: Life in London; or, The Day and Night Scenes of Jerry Hawthorn Esq., and his elegant friend Corinthian Tom, in their Rambles and Sprees through the Metropolis.* London: Chatto & Windus, 1869.

Elliot, Brian. *Marcus Clarke.* Oxford: Clarendon, 1958.

Esslin, Martin. 'The critic in the theatre No.2: Plumbing the Lower Depths'. *Theatre Quarterly,* 3, No.9 (January–March 1973), p.11.

Fawkes, Richard. *Dion Boucicault.* London: Quartet, 1979.

Finkelstein, Phil, ed. *Australian Play Pictorials 1911-?.* [1914?]. Melbourne: n.p., 1911-?.

Finn, Pat. *The Australian Theatrical, Football, Cricketers and General Sporting Songbook.* Melbourne: McKinley, n.d. [1891].

Fotheringham, Richard. 'Copyright Sources for Australian Drama and Film'. *Archives and Manuscripts,* 14, (November 1986), 144-53.

——— 'Sport and Nationalism on Australian Stage and Screen; from *Australia Felix* to *Gallipoli*'. *Australasian Drama Studies*, 1, No. 1 (October 1982), 65–88.

——— 'Sports Lovers and Sports Haters: Attitudes to Sport in Some Australian Plays'. In *Australian Drama 1920–1955*. Armidale: Department of Continuing Education, 1986.

Gerald, Frank. *A Millionaire in Memories*. London: Routledge, 1936.

Goldsmith, Oliver. *Selected Essays*. Ed. J. H. Lobran. Cambridge: Cambridge University Press, 1929.

Gover, A. T. 'The Pattern of Population Change in Australia'. *Royal Australian Historical Society Journal and Proceedings*. Vol. XXXIII, Pt.V (1946), 295–340.

Gould, Nathaniel. *On and Off the Turf in Australia*. London: Routledge, n.d. [1895].

——— *Town and Bush. Stray Notes on Australia*. 1896, Facs. rpt. Ringwood: Penguin, 1974.

Greene, Graham and Greene, Hugh, select. *Victorian Villainies*. Ringwood: Penguin, 1985.

Hadensmith, C. W. *A History of Physical Education*. New York: Harpur and Rowe, 1966.

Hainsworth, John D. 'Some Louis Esson Manuscripts'. *Southerly*, No.3 (1978), pp.347–57.

Hall, Ken G. *Directed by Ken G. Hall*. Melbourne: Lansdowne, 1977.

Hall, Roger Allan. 'Frontier Drama Classification'. *Nineteenth Century Theatre Research*, 7, No.1 (Spring 1979), 27–38.

Hance, Frank. *Stamford Theatre and Racecourse*. Stamford: n.p., 1970.

Haydon, Thomas. *Sporting Reminiscences*. London: Bliss, Sands & Co., 1898.

Hergenhan, L. T., ed. *A Colonial City: High and Low Life; Selected Journalism of Marcus Clarke*. St Lucia: University of Queensland Press, 1972.

Hetherington, J. *Australians: Nine Profiles*. Melbourne: Cheshire, 1960.

Hibberd, Jack, ed. *Performing Arts in Australia*. Melbourne: Meanjin, 1984.

Hobsbaum, E. J. *The Age of Capital 1848–1875*. London: Weidenfeld & Nicholson, 1975.

Hogan, Robert. *Dion Boucicault*. New York: Twayne, 1969.

Holloway, David. *Playing the Empire*. London: Harrap, 1979.

Houlding, J. A. *Fit for Service*. Oxford: Clarendon, 1981.

Howell, Maxwell L. and McKay, James, eds. *Proceedings of the VII Commonwealth and International Conference on Sport, Physical Education, Recreation and Dance*. [Conference '82]. Vol.9. 'Socio-Historical Perspectives'. University of Queensland: Dept. of Human Movement Studies, 1983.

Hudspeth, W.D. *The Theatre Royal, Hobart, 1837–1948*. Hobart, privately printed, 1948.

Hughes, Alan. 'A Melbourne Theatrical Newspaper'. *Nineteenth Century Theatre Research*, 3, No.1 (Spring 1975), 23–8.

Hutchinson, Garrie. 'The Howls of the Gallery Boys: Alfred Dampier and an Australian Popular Theatre'. *Meanjin*, 43, No.1 (March 1984), 49–55.

Ingleton, G. C., ed. *True Patriots All*. Sydney: Angus and Robertson, 1952.

Inglis, K. S. *The Australian Colonists: An Exploration of Social History 1788–1870*. Melbourne: Melbourne University Press, 1974.

Irvin, Eric. *Australian Melodrama*. Sydney: Hale & Iremonger, 1981.

——— *Dictionary of the Australian Theatre 1788–1914*. Sydney: Hale & Iremonger, 1985.

——— *Gentleman George, King of Melodrama*. Brisbane: University of Queensland Press, 1980.

———— 'Marcus Clarke and the Theatre'. *Australian Literary Studies*, 7, No.1 (May 1975), 3–14.

———— *Theatre Comes to Australia*. St Lucia: University of Queensland Press, 1971.

James, C. L. R. *Beyond A Boundary*. London: Hutchinson, 1963.

James, G. F. 'Anthony Trollope's *Australia*'. *Meanjin*, 28, No.116 (Autumn 1969), 124–9.

Jenkins, C. and Green, M., eds. *Sporting Fictions: Proceedings of a Workshop Held at the University of Birmingham, September 1981*. Birmingham: Centre for Contemporary Cultural Studies, 1982.

Kellerman, Annette. *Fairy Tales of the South Seas*. London, 1927.

Kelly, Veronica. 'Garnet Walch in Sydney'. *Australasian Drama Studies*, No.9 (October 1986), pp.93–109.

Kingston, Claude. *It Don't Seem A Day Too Much*. Adelaide: Rigby, 1971.

Kolve, V. A. 'The Drama as Play and Game'. *Medieval English Drama*. Ed. Peter Happe. London: Macmillan, 1984.

Lahr, John. 'Athletes of the Heart'. *New Society*, 29 July 1982, pp.188–9

La Meslee, Edmund Marin. *The New Australia 1883*. Trans. Russel Ward. Melbourne: Heinemann, 1979.

Laverty, Colin. *Australian Colonial Sporting Paintings*. Sydney: David Ell, 1980.

———— *Pastures and Pastimes: An Exhibition of Australian Racing, Sporting and Animal Pictures of the Nineteenth Century. Catalogue*. Melbourne: Victorian Ministry for the Arts, 1983.

Lawley, Francis Charles. *Life and Times of 'The Druid'*. London: Vintor, 1895.

Lawson, Sylvia. *The Archibald Paradox*. Ringwood: Allen Lane, 1983.

Lindsay, Norman. *Bohemians of the Bulletin*. Sydney: Angus and Robertson, 1973.

Lingham, H. J. C. *Juvenal in Melbourne*. Melbourne: Lingham, 1892.

Love, Harold. *The Golden Age of Australian Opera*. Sydney: Currency, 1981.

———— 'A Lesson from Lyster; or, How to Run an Economical Opera Company'. *Meanjin*, 36, No.2 (July 1977), 209–15.

———— 'More Melbourne Theatrical Newspapers'. *Nineteenth Century Theatre Research*, 4, No.1 (Spring 1976), 41–6.

Lowe, B. *The Beauty of Sport: A Cross Disciplinary Inquiry*. Englewood Cliffs: Prentice Hall, 1977.

McDonald, Arthur W. 'The Social Life of the Performer on the Yorkshire Circuit, 1766–1785'. *Theatre Survey*, 25, No.2 (November 1984), pp.167–76.

McElroy, Mary. 'Organised sporting contests in the early English professional theatre'. *Canadian Journal of Sports History*. 21, No.1 (May 1990), 30–48.

McGuire, Paul. *The Australian Theatre*. Melbourne: Oxford University Press, 1948.

McIntosh, P. C. *Sport in Society*. London: Watts, 1963.

———— *Physical Education in England Since 1800*. London: G.Bell, 1972.

McKay, Claude, illust. Julius, Harry. *Theatrical Caricatures*. Sydney: N.S.W. Bookstall Co., 1912.

McKernan, Michael. *The Australian People and the Great War*. Melbourne: Nelson, 1980.

MacKinnon, H. ed. *The Marcus Clarke Memorial Volume*. Melbourne: Cameron. Laing & Co., 1884.

Mahood, Marguerite. *The Loaded Line: Australian Political Caricatures 1788–1901*. Melbourne: Melbourne University Press, 1973.

Mander, Ray and Mitcheson, Joe. *The Lost Theatres of London*. London: Rupert Hart-Davis, 1968.

———— *Victorian and Edwardian Entertainment From Old Photographs*. London: B.T.Batsford, 1978.

Mandle, William F. 'Cricket and Australian Nationalism in the Nineteenth Century'. *Journal of the Royal Australian Historical Society*, 59, Part 4 (December 1973), 225-46.

—— 'Pommy Bastards and Damn' Yankees: Sport and Australian Nationalism'. In his *Going It Alone: Australia's National Identity in the Twentieth Century*. Ringwood: Allen Lane, 1978, pp.24-46.

—— 'Sports History'. In *New History: Studying Australia Today*. Ed. G. Osborne & W. F. Mandle. Sydney: Allen and Unwin, 1982.

Mangan, J. A. *Athleticism in the Victorian and Edwardian Public School: The Emergence and Consolidation of an Educational Ideology*. Cambridge: Cambridge University Press, 1981.

Mankowitz, Wolf. *Mazeppa: The Lives, Loves, and Legends of Adah Isaacs Menken*. London: Blond & Briggs, 1982.

Maslen, Joan. 'Victorian Pantomimes'. *La Trobe Library Journal*, 3, No.10 (October 1972), 42-7.

Maugham, W. Somerset. 'The Ant and the Grasshopper'. In *Collected Short Stories*, Vol.1. London: Pan/Heinemann, 1975, 109-12.

Mayer, David, ed. *Henry Irving and 'The Bells'*. Manchester: Manchester University Press, 1980.

—— and Richards, Kenneth, eds. *Western Popular Theatre*. London: Methuen, 1977.

Meudell, George. *The Pleasant Career of a Spendthrift*. London: Routledge, n.d. [1929].

Molloy, Bruce. *Before the Interval: Australian Mythology and Feature Films 1930-1960*. St Lucia: University of Queensland Press, 1990.

Moloney, W. *Memoirs of An Abominable Showman*. Adelaide: Rigby, 1968.

Morrow, Don. 'Sport as metaphor: Shakespeare's use of falconry in the early plays'. *Aethlon*, 5, No.2 (Spring 1988), 119-29.

Mulvaney, D. J. *Cricket Walkabout: The Australian Aboriginal Cricketers on Tour 1867-8*. Melbourne: Melbourne University Press, 1967.

Neild, J. E. (Cleofas). *A Bird in a Golden Cage*. Melbourne: Muskett, 1867.

Newbolt, Sir Henry. *Poems New and Old*. London: John Murray, 1912.

Palmer, Vance. *The Legend of the Nineties*. Melbourne: Melbourne University Press, 1954.

Pask, Edward H. *Enter the Colonies Dancing. A History of Dance in Australia 1835-1940*. Melbourne: Oxford University Press, 1979.

Pearson, Hesketh. *The Last Actor-Managers*. London: Methuen, 1950.

Porter, Hal. *Stars of Australian Stage and Screen*. Adelaide: Rigby, 1965.

Reade, Eric. *Australian Silent Films. A Pictorial History of Silent Films from 1896 to 1929*. Melbourne: Lansdowne, 1970.

Recklies, Donald F. 'Treadmills, Panoramas and Horses in Neil Burgess's *The County Fair*'. *Theatre Studies*, Nos. 24-5 (1977-78—1978-79), 9-18.

Rees, Leslie. *A History of Australian Drama. Vol.1. The Making of Australian Drama from the 1830s to the late 1960s*.
Rev. ed. Sydney: Angus and Robertson, 1978.

Rees, T. *Theatre Lighting in the Age of Gas*. London: Society for Theatre Research, 1978.

Reid, J. C. *Bucks and Bruisers: Pierce Egan and Regency England*. London: Routledge, 1971.

Rice, James. *History of the British Turf*. 2 vols. London: Sampson Low, 1879.

Richardson, Paul. 'Garnet Walch's *Australia Felix*: A Reconstruction'. *Australasian Drama Studies*, 1, No.2 (April 1983), 63-81.

——— 'Harlequin in the Antipodes'. *Southerly*, 42, No.2 (June 1982), 212–20.

Rotha, Paul. *The Film Till Now: A Survey of World Cinema*. 1930; rev. edns. 1949, 1960; London: Spring Books, 1967.

Rowell, George. *The Victorian Theatre 1792–1914*. 1956, rev. edn. Cambridge: Cambridge University Press, 1978.

Russell, Don. *The Lives and Legends of Buffalo Bill*. Norman: University of Oklahoma Press, 1960.

Ruston, Alan. 'Richard Nelson Lee and the Victorian Pantomime in Great Britain'. *Nineteenth Century Theatre Research*, 11, No.2 (Winter 1983), 105–17.

Saxon, A. H. *Enter Foot and Horse*. New Haven and London: Yale University Press, 1968.

——— *The Life and Art of Andrew Ducrow*. Hamden: Archon, 1978.

Schleppi, J. 'Sport, Theater and Literature'. *Journal of Physical Education and Recreation*, 47, No.9 (November–December 1976), 19.

Senelick, Laurence. ' "Dead! And Never Called Me Mother!"The Legacy of Oral Tradition from the Nineteenth-Century Stage'. *Theatre Studies*, Nos. 26–27 (1979–81), 7–20.

Sherson, Erroll. *London's Lost Theatres of the Nineteenth Century, With Notes on Plays and Players Seen There*. London: John Lane, 1925.

Shirley, Graham & Brian Adams. *Australian Cinema: The First Eighty Years*. Rev. edn. Sydney: Currency, 1989.

Simmons, Samuel R. *A Problem and a Solution: Marcus Clarke and the Writing of Long Odds, His First Novel*. Melbourne: Simmons, 1946.

Skill, Marjorie. *Sweet Nell of Old Sydney*. Sydney: Urania Publishing Co., 1973.

Smith, James. 'Reminiscences of the Melbourne Stage'. *The Australasian*, 18 September 1886, p.570.

——— 'The Year 1863'. Select. Lurline Stuart. *Meanjin*, 37, No.4 (December 1978), 411–33.

Southern, Richard. *The Victorian Theatre—A Pictorial Survey*. Newton Abbot: David and Charles, 1970.

Speaight, George. *A History of the Circus*. London: Tantivy, 1980.

Steele, William Paul. *The Character of Melodrama*. Orono: University of Maine Press, 1968.

Stephens, John Russell. *The Censorship of English Drama 1824–1901*. Cambridge: Cambridge University Press, 1980.

St. Leon, Mark. 'The Circus in the Context of Australia's Regional, Social and Cultural History'. *Journal of the Royal Australian Historical Society*, 72, Part 3 (December 1986), 204–25.

——— *Spangles and Sawdust: The Circus in Australia*. Richmond: Greenhouse, 1983.

Stoddart, Brian. *Saturday Afternoon Fever: Sport in the Australian Culture*. North Ryde: Angus & Robertson, 1986.

Straten, Frank Van. 'The Bijou: Theatre of Infinite Variety'. *The Passing Show: 4*. Melbourne: Victorian Arts Centre, 1981.

———'The Tivoli: A Chronology of Melbourne's Home of Vaudeville'. *The Passing Show 3*. Melbourne: Victorian Arts Centre, 1981.

Surtees, R. S. *Mr Sponge's Sporting Tour*. Ed. Virginia Blain. St Lucia: University of Queensland Press, 1981.

Tait, Viola. *A Family of Brothers*. Melbourne: Heinemann, 1971.

Thorne, Ross. *Theatre Buildings in Australia to 1905*. 2 vols. Sydney: Architectural Research Foundation, 1971.

Trollope, Anthony. *Australia and New Zealand*. 2 vols. 1872, rpt. London: Dawsons of Pall Mall, 1968.

Trollope, Fanny. *Domestic Manners of the Americans*. 1833, rpt. London: Oxford University Press, 1984.
Tulloch, John. *Australian Cinema: Industry, Narrative, Meaning*. Sydney: Allen & Unwin, 1982.
—— *Legends on the Screen: The Narrative Film in Australia 1919-1929*. Sydney and Melbourne: Currency/A.F.I., 1981.
Turner, Graeme. *National Fictions: Literature, Film and the Construction of Australian Narratives*. North Sydney: Allen & Unwin, 1986.
Van Der Merwe, Pieter. 'A Stage Panorama by Birkett Foster'. *Theatre Notebook*, 35, No.3 (1981), 131-2.
Vicinus, Martha. ' "Helpless and Unfriended": Nineteenth-Century Domestic Melodrama'. *New Literary History*, 13, No.1 (Autumn 1981), 127-43.
Walch, Garnet. *"Hash". A Mixed Dish For Christmas. With Ingredients By Various Australian Authors*. Melbourne & Sydney: Reynolds, 1877.
Walker, David. *Dream and Disillusion. A Search for Australian Cultural Identity*. Canberra: Australian National University Press, 1976.
Walker, Donald et. al. *Traps, Flaps and Transformations: The Vanishing Art of the Stage Mechanist*. London: Curtain Theatre, 1975.
Walsh, Townsend. *The Career of Dion Boucicault*. New York: Benjamin Blom, 1967.
Waterhouse, Richard. *From Minstrel Show to Vaudeville: the Australian popular stage 1788-1914*. Kensington: NSW University Press, 1990.
West, John. *Theatre in Australia*. Stanmore: Cassell, 1978.
White, Richard. *Inventing Australia*. Sydney: George Allen & Unwin, 1981.
Whitworth, Robert Percy. *Velvet and Rags*. Melbourne: Whitworth, n.d. [1886?].
—— and Windas, W. A. *Shimmer of Silk; A Volume of Melbourne Cup Stories*. Melbourne: W. M. Marshall, 1893.
Whyte, W. Farmer. 'The Australian Stage—A Glimpse of the Past'. *Royal Australian Historical Society Journal and Proceedings*, 4, No.1 (1917), 27-45.
Wickham, Glynne. *The Medieval Theatre*. London: Weidenfeld & Nicholson, 1974.
Wiles, David. *Shakespeare's Clown: Actor and Text in the Elizabethan Playhouse*. Cambridge: Cambridge University Press, 1987.
Wilkes, G. A. *The Stockyard and the Croquet Lawn. Literary Evidence for Australia's Cultural Development*. Sydney: Edward Arnold, 1981.
Wilkinson, Michael. *The Phar Lap Story*. Melbourne: Schwartz, 1980.
Williams, Margaret. *Australia on the Popular Stage 1829-1929*. Melbourne: Oxford University Press, 1983.
—— ' "The Barnum of Australia": William Anderson'. *Australasian Drama Studies*, 2, No.2 (April 1984), 43-64.
Wood, Christopher. *Victorian Panorama: Paintings of Victorian Life*. London: Faber, 1976.
Young, Wayland. *Eros Denied*. Rev. edn. London: Corgi, 1968.

Newpapers, Magazines, and Newsreels

Adelaide Mail
The Age (Melbourne)
Albury Daily News and Wodonga Chronicle
The Ant (Melbourne)
The Argus (Melbourne)
The Arrow (Sydney)
As It Is (Melbourne)
The Australasian (Melbourne)

Australasian Gazette (Sydney, newsreel)
Australasian Sketcher (Melbourne)
Australasian Stage Annual (Melbourne)
Australian (Sydney)
Australian Life (Melbourne)
Australian Cyclist and Motor Car World (Melbourne)
Australian Musical and Dramatic Review (Melbourne)
Australian Sporting and Dramatic News (Sydney)
Australian Women's Weekly (Sydney)
Bell's Life in London and Sporting Chronicle
Bell's Life in Sydney and Sporting Reviewer
Bell's Life in Victoria and Sporting Chronicle
Bendigo Advertiser
Bendigo Independent
Brisbane Courier
Bohemia (Melbourne)
Bohemian Girl (Melbourne)
The Bull Ant (Melbourne)
The Bulletin (Melbourne)
The Bulletin (Sydney)
The Call: The Journal of Theatrical Managers (Melbourne)
Champion (Melbourne)
Cinema Papers (Melbourne)
The Colonial Monthly (Melbourne)
The Community Magazine (Sydney)
Courier Mail (Brisbane)
Criterion (Melbourne)
Daily Southern Cross (Auckland)
Dead Bird (Sydney)
Electric Spark (Adelaide)
The Empire (Sydney)
Entr'Acte (London)
Le Entr'Acte and Playbill (Melbourne)
The Era (London)
Everyone's (Sydney)
The Flag (Melbourne)
Free Lance (Melbourne)
Gossip (Melbourne)
The Hawk
Hawklet: Sport and Stage
Hobart Town Courier
Hobart Mercury
Illustrated Australian Magazine
Illustrated Australian News for Home Readers
The Illustrated London News
Illustrated Melbourne News
Illustrated Melbourne Post
Illustrated Sporting and Dramatic News (London)
Leader (Melbourne)
Life Digest (Melbourne)
The Lorgnette (Melbourne)
Magpie (Melbourne)

Maitland Mercury
Melbourne Mirror
Melbourne Punch
My Note Book (Melbourne)
National Times
New South Wales Sporting Magazine
New Idea
The New York Times
New Zealand Herald (Auckland)
NSW Sporting Magazine (Sydney)
Pasquin (Melbourne)
The Playgoer
The 'Possum (Melbourne)
Red Funnel (Auckland)
The Referee (Sydney)
Sydney Morning Herald
Sydney Punch
Table Talk (Melbourne)
The Tatler (Melbourne)
Thalia (Melbourne)
The Theatre (Melbourne)
The Theatre of Australasia (Melbourne)
The Theatrical Courier (Melbourne)
The Times (London)
Today (Melbourne)
Touchstone (Melbourne)
Town and Country Journal (Sydney)
Town Talk (Melbourne)
The Triad (Melbourne)
Victorian Monthly Magazine
Victorian Review
We (Hobart)
Weekly Times (Melbourne)

Index